# Reader in Public Opinion and Mass Communication

Third Edition

# Reader in Public Opinion and Mass Communication

Third Edition

EDITED BY
**Morris Janowitz** and **Paul M. Hirsch**

**THE FREE PRESS**
*A Division of Macmillan Publishing Co., Inc.*
NEW YORK

Collier Macmillan Publishers
LONDON

The Free Press
A Division of Macmillan Publishing Co., Inc.
866 Third Avenue, New York, N.Y. 10022

Collier Macmillan Canada, Ltd.

Library of Congress Catalog Card Number: 80–2444

Printed in the United States of America

printing number

2 3 4 5 6 7 8 9 10

Library of Congress Cataloging in Publication Data
Main entry under title:

Reader in public opinion and mass communication.

Previous ed.: Reader in public opinion and communication. 1966.
Includes index.
1. Public opinion--Addresses, essays, lectures.
2. Communication--Addresses, essays, lectures.
3. Mass media--Addresses, essays, lectures.
I. Janowitz, Morris. II. Hirsch, Paul Morris.
III. Reader in public opinion and communication.
HM261.R38 1981    303.3'8    80-2444
ISBN 0-02-916020-0             AACR2

# Contents

# Contributors

*Kristi Andersen* received a Ph.D. in Political Science from the University of Chicago. She is currently a member of the Political Science Department at Ohio State University.

*Ben H. Bagdikian* is a well-known journalist, news editor, and critic of the press. He has also taught at some of the nation's major universities. In addition to *The Information Machines,* from which his contribution here is excerpted, he is also author of *The Effete Conspiracy.*

*Stephen E. Bennett* is Associate Professor of Political Science at the University of Cincinnati. His research interests include political psychology, public opinion, and belief systems among electoral masses.

*George F. Bishop* is Senior Research Associate at the Behavioral Sciences Laboratory, University of Cincinnati. He is interested in public opinion generally, mass belief systems, and attitude measurement.

*Jay Blumler* is Director of the Centre for Television Research, University of Leeds. He has written articles on audience uses and gratifications, the role of media in electoral campaigns, political socialization, political participation, and information transmission.

*James Bryce* (1838–1922) was a British politician, diplomat, and historian. At one time British Ambassador to the United States, his best-known book is *The American Commonwealth.*

*Steven H. Chaffee* is Director, School of Journalism and Mass Communication, University of Wisconsin at Madison. His major interests are in mass communications and political behavior.

*Alexis de Toqueville* was a nineteenth-century French historian and social scientist. He is best known for *Democracy in America,* from which his article here is taken, and for *The Old Regime and the French Revolution.*

*G. A. Donohue* is Professor of Sociology at the University of Minnesota. His areas of interest include social theory, socioeconomic development, and community organization.

*Aimee Dorr* is Associate Professor, Annenberg School of Communications at the University of Southern California. She has previously taught at Harvard University and has consulted for Children's Television Workshop and Massachusetts Educational Television. Her major research interests are in children's television and mass media usage and their effects on children.

*Beverly Duncan* is Professor of Sociology at the University of Arizona. She is interested in population studies and social change.

*Otis Dudley Duncan* is Professor of Sociology at the University of Arizona. He is coauthor (with Peter Blau) of *The American Occupational Structure,* and author of *Introduction to Structural Equation Models* as well as other books and articles on urban affairs and population.

*Andrew S. C. Ehrenberg* is on the faculty of the London School of Business. He is author of *Repeat Buying: Theory and Applications* and coauthor (with Gerald J. Goodhardt and M. A. Collins) of *The Television Audience: Patterns of Viewing.*

*George Gerbner* is Dean of the Annenberg School of Communications, University of Pennsylvania. He directs the Cultural Indicators research team there and conducts research on comparative national and international media content.

*Larry Gross* is Associate Professor at the Annenberg School of Communications at the University of Pennsylvania. He is coeditor of *Studies in the Anthropology of Visual Communication.*

*Paul M. Hirsch* is Associate Professor of Sociology in the Graduate School of Business of the University of Chicago. He is a coeditor of *New Strategies of Communication Research* and his articles on mass communications have appeared in *The American Journal of Sociology, American Behavioral Scientist, Social Research, The Wall Street Journal,* and *The Nation.*

*Ole Holsti* is George V. Allen Professor of Political Science at Duke University. His interests are in foreign policy decision-making, decision-making in crises, and political psychology. He is author of *Content Analysis for the Social Sciences and Humanities.*

*Peter Homans* is on the faculty of the School of Divinity of the University of Chicago. His books include *Jung in Context* and *Theology After Freud.*

*Morris Janowitz* is Lawrence A. Kimpton Distinguished Service Professor of Sociology at the University of Chicago. He has authored numerous books and articles on political sociology, military sociology, mass media, and political theory. His latest book is *The Last Half Century.*

*Daniel Katz* is Professor of Psychology at the University of Michigan. His principal research interests are in organizational and political psychology.

*Herbert C. Kelman* is Richard Clark Cabot Professor of Social Ethics at Harvard University. His interests are in social influence and attitude change, nationalism and political ideology, and conflict resolution.

*V. O. Key* was Professor of Government at Harvard. His best-known book is *Public Opinion and American Democracy.*

*Herbert Krugman* is Manager of Public Opinion Research for the General Electric Company. He holds a Ph.D. in Sociology from Columbia and has taught at Princeton University. His major research interests are in perception and learning.

*Gladys Engel Lang* is Professor of Sociology at the State University of New York at Stony Brook. She has authored articles and books on collective behavior, public opinion and mass communication, politics and television, and voting behavior.

*Kurt Lang* is Professor of Sociology at the State University of New York at Stony Brook. He has authored books and articles on collective behavior, mass communications, and military sociology.

*Harold D. Lasswell* was Ford Foundation Professor of Law and Social Science and Emeritus Fellow, Branford College of Yale University. He was known for his work in personality and politics, public opinion, and language and politics.

*Walter Lippmann* was a well-known American journalist, writer, and political philosopher. He wrote numerous books and articles on public opinion, news, the media, and politics.

*A. Lawrence Lowell* (1856–1943) was President of Harvard University from 1909 to 1933. He wrote *The Government of England, Public Opinion and Popular Government,* and *Essays on Government.*

*Robert D. McClure* is Associate Professor of Political Science at Syracuse University. He is interested in the responses of the electorate to media campaigns.

*Maxwell E. McCombs* is John Ben Snow Professor of Newspaper Research, Syracuse University, and Director of the Communication Research Center there. His research is in political behavior and mass communications, economics of the mass media, and information-seeking behavior.

*Denis McQuail* is Professor of Sociology at Massacommunicatie, Universiteit van Amsterdam, The Netherlands. He is author of *Towards a Sociology of Mass Communications,* coauthor of *Television in Politics* (with Jay Blumler), and editor of *The Sociology of Mass Communications.*

*John E. Mueller* is Professor of Political Science at the University of Rochester, where he has taught since 1965. He holds a Ph.D. from the University of California at Los Angeles and conducts research on public opinion.

*Horace Newcomb* is Associate Professor of English at the University of Texas, Austin. He is author of *TV: The Most Popular Art* and editor of *Television: The Critical View.*

*Norman H. Nie* is Professor of Political Science at the University of Chicago. He is author of *The Changing American Voter* (with Sidney Verba and John R. Petrocik). His research interests are in American and comparative political behavior, citizen participation, and mass belief systems.

*Robert W. Oldendick* is Research Associate, Behavioral Science Laboratory at the University of Cincinnati.

*Clarice N. Olien* is Associate Professor of Sociology at the University of Minnesota. Her research specialties include community organization, youth development, and mass communication.

*Thomas E. Patterson* is Associate Professor of Political Science at Syracuse University. He is interested in electoral responses to media campaigns.

*John R. Petrocik* received his Ph.D. in political science from the University of Chicago. He is currently Assistant Professor of Political Science at the University of California at Los Angeles. He is coauthor (with Norman H. Nie and Sidney Verba) of *The Changing American Voter.*

*John Robinson* is Professor of Sociology at the University of Maryland and Director of the Survey Research Center there. He has done extensive research on time budgeting, public opinion, and media use.

*Michael J. Robinson* is Associate Professor of Political Science at Catholic University. He has done research on politics, mass media, and news.

*Howard Schuman* is Professor of Sociology at the University of Michigan and is affiliated with the Survey Research Center there. He has written *Conversations at Random* and articles on public opinion and survey research methods, and has directed the University of Michigan's Detroit Area Study.

*Edward A. Shils* is Distinguished Service Professor Emeritus of Sociology and Social Thought at the University of Chicago. He has written extensively on culture, intellectuals, and social values. His recent writings include *The Intellectuals and the Powers*.

*Donald L. Shaw* is Professor of Journalism at the University of North Carolina at Chapel Hill. He is coauthor (with Maxwell E. McCombs) of *Handbook of Reporting Methods*.

*Philip J. Tichenor* is Professor of Journalism and Mass Communication at the University of Minnesota. His interests include mass communication theory and methodology, mass media and public opinion, and science journalism.

*Leonard P. Tipton* teaches in the Department of Journalism of the University of Kentucky, Lexington.

*Alfred J. Tuchfarber* is Director of the Behavioral Science Research Laboratory at the University of Cincinnati. His research interests are American political and electoral behavior, public opinion, and urban affairs.

*Gaye Tuchman* is Associate Professor of Sociology at Queens College and in the Graduate Center of the City University of New York. She is editor of *Hearth and Home: Images of Women in the Mass Media* (with Arlene Kaplan Daniels and James Benet), and *The TV Establishment: Programming for Power and Profit*, and author of *Making News: A Study in the Construction of Reality*.

*Jeremy Tunstall* is a sociologist who teaches at the City University of London. He is author of *The Media Are American* and editor of *Media Sociology*. He has written other books on media, advertising, and journalism.

*Sidney Verba* is Professor of Government at Harvard University. His research interests include comparative political behavior and public opinion. He is coauthor (with Norman H. Nie and John R. Petrocik) of *The Changing American Voter*.

*L. Scott Ward* is Associate Professor of Marketing at the Wharton School of Business at the University of Pennsylvania.

# Introduction

Public opinion and mass communication are such integral parts of modern industrial and postindustrial societies that one cannot afford to take them for granted. In the United States, for example, polling and mass media are now integral parts of virtually every election and advertising campaign clamoring for public attention. Neither politics nor the American economy would be recognizable without media coverage and access to voters and consumers. Popular culture today is almost synonymous with television exposure, radio air-play, newspaper columns, and magazine articles. Growing secularization has meant that more and more areas of life are open to opinion rather than divine law, to communication rather than revelation, though traditional sentiments do have a strong ability to endure. Advanced industrialization has not only extended literacy, it has also provided the technical facilities for mass communication. Urbanization has not only brought large audiences together, it has also created the need for communication within and between audiences, and among many diverse social groups. The development of democratic processes has increased the number of publics whose opinions count, and with it the social and political responsibilities of the communication media.

Public opinion and mass communication are so closely intertwined that one could barely exist without the other. Mass media simultaneously create and respond to public awareness, opinions, and taste. While this observation is widely accepted, it is the task of social science to study and specify the mechanisms by which tastes and opinions are formed and the conditions under which mass communication is most influential upon and responsive to its various publics. Each article we have selected for this volume addresses one or more of these important questions.

When the original edition of the *Reader in Public Opinion and Communication* was prepared in 1950, the formal study of this field was still in its infancy. College courses in which it was taught typically included it as a unit under such broader titles as political behavior, research methods, marketing, collective behavior, mass society, and mass culture. As research developed, the field expanded so dramatically that Schools of Communication have now been established whose curriculum is devoted to the numerous aspects and complexities of the communication process. Other schools and departments within universities now offer specialized courses in public opinion, mass communication, advertising, and popular culture, respectively. During this period we also have seen the rise of new concepts and paradigms (e.g., the "uses and gratifications" and "production of culture" perspectives); a revival of interest in the effects of mass media content (such as television violence and bias in news reporting); a surge of studies in England and the United States on how the mass media are organized to produce news and entertainment; the application of new statistical concepts and methods to long-standing issues in the study of public opinion and mass communication; an increased sophistication about how advertising works; and the appearance of longitudinal analyses and needed replications of earlier findings.

While no single volume can exhaustively sample all of these areas, the following selections include one or more recent articles on each of them (which, in turn, provide references to other relevant works on the same topic). We begin with five important "classics" which served to formulate the nature and role of public opinion in democratic societies. In Section 2, we explore how public opinion is formed, particularly in terms of how the mass media and personal influence interact within the larger social structures that provide the context for both. The institutional role of mass media in facilitating or impeding the political process in democracies is explored more explicitly in Section 3. This section also highlights some recent contributions and controversies about measurement issues and research methods, which in turn powerfully affect conceptual conclusions about the electorate.

Section 4 takes up the related question of how the mass media are organized and structured to produce the news and entertainment content, which both influences and responds to public opinion. These studies of the message senders address the first part of Harold Lasswell's classic definition of this field as the study of *who* says *what* to *whom* and with what *effect?* The second part of this formulation (the "what") is treated extensively in Section 5, which sets out the method of content analysis and provides recent examples of empirical work in this tradition. Sections 6 and 7 are concerned with the impact and effects of mass communication. In the first instance, our selections explore the impact of mass media content and coverage on other institutions in society. In Section 7 the question narrows to focus on the effects of mass media on individual members of society and groups (such as children, soldiers, and voters). Finally, the selections in Section 8 return us to the basic issues posed by the contributors at the beginning of the *Reader:* What is the relation of mass communication to the attitudes and behavior of its audiences toward political candidates and consumer products? Additionally, selections in this concluding section inform us about how closely mass media coverage is related to changes in public attitudes over time.

As in earlier editions, we have tried to select distinctive contributions by experts in the field and to represent fairly, within the constraints of one volume, the major schools of thought for each topic area. Our contributors, like the field, span a variety of disciplines and draw upon such diverse backgrounds and perspectives as political science, sociology, business administration, psychology, and journalism. Fewer than 25 percent of these selections appeared in the earlier editions. Many excellent articles had to be left out only with the greatest reluctance.

This book is designed primarily for the students in the field and in the various social science departments and professional schools where interest in this area continues to grow. We hope it will also be useful to practitioners, teachers, and researchers in public opinion and mass communication. The brief introductions to each section explain the significance of each article within the context of the issues addressed by the *Reader.*

In the selection and editing of articles for this volume, we have benefited greatly from helpful suggestions by Russell Newman, Thomas Pettigrew, John Robinson, and Howard Schuman. The yeoman assistance of Tom Panelas, Sally Kilgore, and Farag El-Kamel in the editing process also is gratefully acknowledged. We also wish to thank the authors of the selections included for granting permission to reprint them, and to gratefully acknowledge a grant from the John and Mary Markle Foundation, which enabled Paul Hirsch to co-edit this *Reader.*

University of Chicago
July, 1980

# Theories of Public Opinion

Contrary to popular notions and even to the ideas of some practitioners, the study of public opinion did not spring full-panoplied from the brow of George Gallup in the 1930s. Political theorists had long considered the problems of public opinion, though they did not always call it by that term. A series of their writings in the nineteenth and early twentieth centuries (represented here by Bryce and Lowell) began to give the field its modern definition.

The concept of public opinion was central to theories of democratic government. The vulnerability of popular government to despotic takeovers and infringements by private interests required a sphere outside the orbit of the state in which public goals could be formulated, issues discussed, and the exercise of power criticized. Democracy needed channels for the formation and expression of a public will, as well as mechanisms for translating that will into effective checks on leaders.

At the same time industrialization, urbanization, and the population increases that coincided with the rise of democracy aroused concern over the quality of public opinion. Political theorists fearing the perfidy of "the masses" wondered if a tractable public would submit easily to the exhortations of a demogogue. Consequently, many of the political theorists of the late nineteenth and twentieth centuries were less concerned with measuring public opinion than with studying the conditions under which it was formed.

This classical orientation is exemplified here in the selections by Bryce and Lowell. Although speculative in tone, they raise many of the issues taken up by contemporary researchers in empirical studies. Bryce discusses the stages of public opinion formation, stressing the importance of opinion leaders, news organs, and public debate. He also expresses the view that most individuals do not have a consistent and enduring ideology. This same issue is still debated by researchers today, as we shall see in Section 3 in the exchange between Nie and Andersen and Bishop et al. Lowell offers a set of still-contemporary requirements for the emergence of effective public opinion, maintaining that a high degree of social integration and political legitimation are necessary for the formation of a meaningful public consent.

The selections by Lasswell, Lippmann, and Katz are more concerned with social psychological aspects of public opinion. On several points, they are less optimistic than Bryce and Lowell in emphasizing individual patterns of affectivity and particularism, which impair the "rational" process of public discourse and opinion formation. For these theorists, impediments to the formation of intelligent public opinion should be analyzed at the level of individuals rather than that of social institutions. The problems they raise are inherent in the cognitive and affective limitations of human beings and therefore are less amenable to resolution through changes in social policy.

In his varied approaches, Lasswell emphasizes personality factors. He discusses symbols that inspire collective allegiances, grounding his discussion in Freudian psychoanalysis, which explains collective identifications as regressions to infantile affect. Here the meaning of Lasswell's famous "political personality" is clear: It entails the displacement of private affect onto public objects. The image is one in which politics becomes a ritual of obeisance to symbols "endowed with godlike attributes" in a "collective mission [which] is idealized."

Both Lippmann and Katz emphasize the positive functions of adaptive psychological mechanisms. Lippmann observes that while stereotypes distort, they also supply the cognitive information necessary for making a "hurried and multifarious" world intelligible. In Katz's treatment the components of values and the relationships among values are formalized in an effort to present a social psychology of attitudes. He offers a typology of the functions of attitudes for individuals that moves toward a model of the relationships among values, social integration, and the larger political process. This is the most contemporary of all the selections in this section. The reader may wish to compare Katz's maxim that "the raw material out of which public opinion develops is to be found in the attitudes of individuals" with Bryce's assertion that public opinion is neither "the aggregate of all that is thought and said on a subject" nor "merely the views of the majority" and decide whether or not Katz's view, tailored to the needs of present-day empirical research, represents a shift in the way public opinion is conceptualized. In the next section, Kelman offers a potential resolution of this issue.

# The Nature of Public Opinion

JAMES BRYCE

IN NO COUNTRY is public opinion so powerful as in the United States: in no country can it be so well studied. Before I proceed to describe how it works upon the government of the nation and the States, it may be proper to consider briefly how it is formed, and what is the nature of the influence which it everywhere exercises upon government.

What do we mean by public opinion? The difficulties which occur in discussing its action mostly arise from confounding opinion itself with the organs whence people try to gather it, and from using the term to denote, sometimes everybody's views,—that is, the aggregate of all that is thought and said on a subject,—sometimes merely the views of the majority, the particular type of thought and speech which prevails over other types.

The simplest form in which public opinion presents itself is when a sentiment spontaneously rises in the mind and flows from the lips of the average man upon his seeing or hearing something done or said. Homer presents this with his usual vivid directness in the line which frequently recurs in the Iliad when the effect produced by a speech or event is to be conveyed: "And thus any one was saying as he looked at his neighbour." This phrase describes what may be called the rudimentary stage of opinion. It is the prevalent impression of the moment. It is what any man (not every man) says, i.e. it is the natural and the general thought or wish which an occurrence evokes. But before opinion begins to tell upon government, it has to go through several other stages. These stages are various in different ages and countries. Let us try to note what they are in England or America at the present time, and how each stage grows out of the other.

A business man reads in his newspaper at breakfast the events of the

Reprinted from *The American Commonwealth*, Vol. II (1900), pp. 247–254 (New York: Macmillan, 1960).

preceding day. He reads that Prince Bismarck has announced a policy of protection for German industry, or that Mr. Henry George has been nominated for the mayoralty of New York. These statements arouse in his mind sentiments of approval or disapproval, which may be strong or weak according to his previous predilection for or against protection or Mr. Henry George, and of course according to his personal interest in the matter. They rouse also an expectation of certain consequences likely to follow. Neither the sentiment nor the expectation is based on processes of conscious reasoning—our business man has not time to reason at breakfast—they are merely impressions formed on the spur of the moment. He turns to the leading article in the newspaper, and his sentiments and expectations are confirmed or weakened according as he finds that they are or are not shared by the newspaper writer. He goes down to his office in the train, talks there to two or three acquaintances, and perceives that they agree or do not agree with his own still faint impressions. In his counting-house he finds his partner and a bundle of other newspapers which he glances at; their words further affect him, and thus by the afternoon his mind is beginning to settle down into a definite view, which approves or condemns Prince Bismarck's declaration or the nomination of Mr. George. Meanwhile a similar process has been going on in the minds of others, and particularly of the journalists, whose business it is to discover what people are thinking. The evening paper has collected the opinions of the morning papers, and is rather more positive in its forecast of results. Next day the leading journals have articles still more definite and positive in approval or condemnation and in prediction of consequences to follow; and the opinion of ordinary minds, hitherto fluid and undetermined, has begun to crystallize into a solid mass. This is the second stage. Then debate and controversy begin. The men and the newspapers who approve Mr. George's nomination argue with those who do not; they find out who are friends and who opponents. The effect of controversy is to drive the partisans on either side from some of their arguments, which are shown to be weak; to confirm them in others, which they think strong; and to make them take up a definite position on one side. This is the third stage. The fourth is reached when action becomes necessary. When a citizen has to give a vote, he votes as a member of a party; his party prepossessions and party allegiance lay hold on him, and generally stifle any doubts or repulsions he may feel. Bringing men up to the polls is like passing a steam roller over stones newly laid on a road; the angularities are pressed down, and an appearance of smooth and even uniformity is given which did not exist before. When a man has voted, he is committed: he has thereafter an interest in backing the view which he has sought to make prevail. Moreover, opinion, which may have been manifold till the polling, is thereafter generally twofold only. There is a view which has triumphed and a view which has been vanquished.

In examining the process by which opinion is formed, we cannot fail to note how small a part of the view which the average man entertains when he goes to vote is really of his own making. His original impression was faint and perhaps shapeless: its present definiteness and strength are mainly due to what he has heard and read. He has been told what to think, and why to think it. Arguments have been supplied to him from without, and controversy has imbedded them in his mind. Although he supposes his view to be his own, he holds it rather because his acquaintances, his newspapers, his party leaders all hold it. His acquaintances do the like. Each man believes and repeats certain phrases, because he thinks that everybody else on his own side believes them, and of what each believes only a small part is his own original impression, the far larger part being the result of the commingling and mutual action and reaction of the impressions of a multitude of individuals, in which the element of pure personal conviction, based on individual thinking, is but small.

Every one is of course predisposed to see things in some one particular light by his previous education, habits of mind, accepted dogmas, religious or social affinities, notions of his own personal interest. No event, no speech or article, ever falls upon a perfectly virgin soil: the reader or listener is always more or less biassed already. When some important event happens, which calls for the formation of a view, these pre-existing habits, dogmas, affinities, help to determine the impression which each man experiences, and so far are factors in the view he forms. But they operate chiefly in determining the first impression, and they operate over many minds at once. They do not produce variety and independence: they are soon overlaid by the influences which each man derives from his fellows, from his leaders, from the press.

Orthodox democratic theory assumes that every citizen has, or ought to have, thought out for himself certain opinions, i.e. ought to have a definite view, defensible by arguments, of what the country needs, of what principles ought to be applied in governing it, of the men to whose hands the government ought to be entrusted. There are persons who talk, though certainly very few who act, as if they believed this theory, which may be compared to the theory of some ultra-Protestants that every good Christian has or ought to have, by the strength of his own reason, worked out for himself from the Bible a system of theology. But one need only try the experiment of talking to that representative of public opinion whom the Americans call "the man in the cars," to realize how uniform opinion is among all classes of people, how little there is in the ideas of each individual of that individuality which they would have if he had formed them for himself, how little solidity and substance there is in the political or social beliefs of nineteen persons out of every twenty. These beliefs, when examined, mostly resolve themselves into two or three prejudices and aversions, two or three prepossessions for a particular leader or party or section of a party, two or three phases or catchwords suggesting or embodying arguments which the man who repeats them has not analyzed. It is not that these nineteen persons are incapable of appreciating good arguments, or are unwilling to receive them. On the contrary, and this is especially true of the working classes, an audience is pleased when solid arguments are addressed to it, and men read with most relish the articles or leaflets, supposing them to be smartly written, which contain the most carefully sifted facts and the most exact thought. But to the great mass of mankind in all places, public questions come in the third or fourth rank among the interests of life, and obtain less than a third or a fourth of the leisure available for thinking. It is therefore rather sentiment than thought that the mass can contribute, a sentiment grounded on a few broad considerations and simple trains of reasoning; and the soundness and elevation of their sentiment will have more to do with their taking their stand on the side of justice, honour, and peace, than any reasoning they can apply to the sifting of the multifarious facts thrown before them, and to the drawing of the legitimate inferences therefrom.

It may be suggested that this analysis, if true of the uneducated, is not true of the educated classes. It is less true of that small class which in Europe specially occupies itself with politics; which, whether it reasons well or ill, does no doubt reason. But it is substantially no less applicable to the commercial and professional classes than to the working classes; for in the former, as well in the latter, one finds few persons who take the pains, or have the leisure, or indeed possess the knowledge, to enable them to form an independent judgment. The chief difference between the so-called upper, or wealthier, and the humbler strata of society is, that the former are less influenced by sentiment and possibly more influenced by notions, often erroneous, of their own interest. Having something to lose, they imagine dangers to their property or their class ascendency. Moving in a more artificial society, their sympathies are less readily excited, and they more frequently indulge the tendency to cynicism natural to those who lead a life full of unreality and conventionalisms.

The apparent paradox that where the humbler classes have differed in opinion from the higher, they have often been proved by the event to have been right and their so-called betters wrong (a fact sufficiently illustrated by the experience of many European countries during the last half-century[1]), may perhaps be explained by considering that the historical and scientific data on which the solution of a difficult political problem depends are really just as little known to the wealthy as to the poor. Ordinary education, even the sort of education which is represented by a university degree, does not fit a man to handle these questions, and it sometimes fills him with a vain conceit of his own competence which closes his mind to argument and to the accumulating evidence of facts. Education ought, no doubt, to enlighten a man; but the educated classes, speaking generally, are the property-holding classes, and the possession of property does more to make a man timid than education does to make him hopeful. He is apt to underrate the power as well as the worth of sentiment; he overvalues the restraints which existing institutions impose, he has a faint appreciation of the curative power of freedom, and of the tendency which brings things right when men have been left to their own devices, and have learnt from failure how to attain success. In the less-educated man a certain simplicity and openness of mind go some way to compensate for the lack of knowledge. He is more apt to be influenced by the authority of leaders; but as, at least in England and America, he is generally shrewd enough to discern between a great man and a demagogue, this is more a gain than a loss.

While suggesting these as explanations of the paradox, I admit that it remains a paradox. The paradox is not in the statement, however, but in the facts themselves. Nearly all great political and social causes have made their way first among the middle or humbler classes. The original impulse which has set the cause in motion, the inspiring ideas that have drawn men to it, have come from lofty and piercing minds, and minds generally belonging to the cultivated class. But the principles and precepts these minds have delivered have waxed strong because the common people received them gladly, while the wealthy and educated classes have frowned on or persecuted them. The most striking instance of all is to be found in the early history of Christianity.

The analysis, however, which I have sought to give of opinion applies only to the nineteen men out of twenty, and not to the twentieth. It applies to what may be called passive opinion—the opinion of those who have no special interest in politics, or concern with them beyond that of voting, of those who receive or propagate, but do not originate, views on public matters. Or, to put the same thing in different words, we have been considering how public opinion grows and spreads, as it were, spontaneously and naturally. But opinion does not merely grow; it is also made. There is not merely the passive class of persons; there is the active class, who occupy themselves primarily with public affairs, who aspire to create and lead opinion. The processes which these guides follow are too well known to need description. There are, however, one or two points which must be noted, in order to appreciate the reflex action of the passive upon the active class.

The man who tries to lead public opinion, be he statesman, journalist, or lecturer, finds in himself, when he has to form a judgment upon any current event, a larger measure of individual prepossession, and of what may be called political theory and doctrine, than belongs to the average citizen. His view is therefore likely to have more individuality, as well as more intellectual value. On the other hand, he has also a stronger motive than the average citizen for keeping in agreement with his friends and his party, because if he stands aloof and advances a view of his own, he may lose his influence and his position. He has a past, and is prevented, by the fear of seeming inconsistent, from departing from what he has previously said. He has a future, and dreads to injure it by severing himself ever so little from his party. He is accordingly driven to make the same sort of compromise between his individual tendencies and the general tendency which the average citizen makes. But he makes it more consciously, realizing far more distinctly the difference between what he would think, say, and do, if left to himself, and what he says and does as a politician, who can be useful and prosperous only as a member of a body of persons acting together and professing to think alike.

Accordingly, though the largest part of the work of forming opinion is done by these men,—whom I do not call professional politicians, because in Europe many of them are not solely occupied with politics, while in America the name of professionals must be reserved for another class,—we must not forget the reaction constantly exercised upon them by the passive majority. Sometimes a leading statesman or journalist takes a line to which he finds that the mass of those who usually agree with him are not responsive. He perceives that they will not follow him, and that he must choose between isolation and a modification of his own views. A statesman may sometimes venture on the former course, and in very rare cases succeed in imposing his own will and judgment on his party. A journalist, however, is obliged to hark back if he has inadvertently taken up a position disagreeable to his *clientèle,* because the proprietors of the paper have their circulation to consider. To avoid so disagreeable a choice a statesman or a journalist is usually on the alert to sound the general opinion before he commits himself on a new issue. He tries to feel the pulse of the mass of average citizens; and as the mass, on the other hand, look to him for initiative, this is a delicate process. In European countries it is generally the view of the leaders which prevails, but it is modified by the reception which the mass give it; it becomes accentuated in the points which they appreciate; while those parts of it, or those ways of stating it, which have failed to find popular favour, fall back into the shade.

This mutual action and reaction of the makers or leaders of opinion upon the mass, and of the mass upon them, is the most curious part of the whole process by which opinion is produced. It is also that part in which there is the greatest difference between one free country and another. In some countries, the leaders count for, say, three-fourths of the product, and the mass for one-fourth only. In others these proportions are reversed. In some countries the mass of the voters are not only markedly inferior in education to the few who lead, but also diffident, more disposed to look up to their betters. In others the difference of intellectual level between those who busy themselves with politics and the average voter is far smaller. Perhaps the leader is not so well instructed a man as in the countries first referred to; perhaps the average voter is better instructed and more self-confident. Where both of these phenomena coincide, so that the difference of level is inconsiderable, public opinion will evidently be a different thing from what it is in countries where, though the Constitution has become democratic, the habits of the nation are still aristocratic. This is the difference between America and the countries of Western Europe.

# Notes

1. It may be said that this has been so because the movements of the last half-century have been mostly movements in a democratic direction, which obtained the sympathy of the humbler classes because tending to break down the power and privilege which the upper classes previously enjoyed. This observation, however, does not meet all the cases, among which may be mentioned the attitude of the English working classes towards Italy from 1848 onwards, as well as their attitude in the American Civil War from 1861 to 1865, and in the Eastern Question from 1876 onwards, for in none of these instances had they any personal interest.

# Public Opinion

## A. LAWRENCE LOWELL

"VOX POPULI MAY BE VOX DEI, but very little attention shows that there has never been any agreement as to what Vox means or as to what Populus means." In spite of endless discussions about democracy, this remark of Sir Henry Maine is still so far true that no other excuse is needed for studying the conceptions which lie at the very base of popular government. In doing so one must distinguish the form from the substance; for the world of politics is full of forms in which the spirit is dead—mere shams, but sometimes not recognized as such even by the chief actors, sometimes deceiving the outside multitude, sometimes no longer misleading anyone. Shams are, indeed, not without value. Political shams have done for English government what fictions have done for English law. They have promoted growth without revolutionary change. But while shams play an important part in political evolution, they are snares for the political philosopher who fails to see through them, who ascribes to the forms a meaning that they do not really possess. Popular government may in substance exist under the form of a monarchy, and an autocratic despotism can be set up without destroying the forms of democracy. If we look through the forms to observe the vital forces behind them; if we fix our attention, not on the procedure, the extent of the franchise, the machinery of elections, and such outward things, but on the essence of the matter, popular government, in one important aspect at least, may be said to consist of the control of political affairs by public opinion. In this book, therefore, an attempt is made to analyze public opinion in order to determine its nature, the conditions under which it can exist, the subjects to which it can apply, the methods by which it can be faithfully expressed, and the regulation under a popular government of affairs to which it is not directly applicable.

Each of the two words that make up the expression "public opinion" is

Reprinted from *Public Opinion and Popular Government,* 1913, pp. 3–15, by permission of the publisher, David McKay Co. Copyright 1913, by Longmans, Green and Co.

significant, and each of them may be examined by itself. To fulfil the requirement an opinion must be public, and it must be really an opinion. Let us begin with the first of these qualities.

If two highwaymen meet a belated traveller on a dark road and propose to relieve him of his watch and wallet, it would clearly be an abuse of terms to say that in the assemblage on that lonely spot there was a public opinion in favor of a redistribution of property. Nor would it make any difference, for this purpose, whether there were two highwaymen and one traveller, or one robber and two victims. The absurdity in such a case of speaking about the duty of the minority to submit to the verdict of public opinion is self-evident; and it is not due to the fact that the three men on the road form part of a larger community, or that they are subject to the jurisdiction of a common government. The expression would be quite as inappropriate if no organized state existed; on a savage island, for example, where two cannibals were greedy to devour one shipwrecked mariner. In short the three men in each of the cases supposed do not form a community that is capable of a public opinion on the question involved. May this not be equally true under an organized government, among people that are for certain purposes a community?

To take an illustration nearer home. At the time of the Reconstruction that followed the American Civil War the question whether public opinion in a southern state was, or was not, in favor of extending the suffrage to the negroes could not in any true sense be said to depend on which of the two races had a slight numerical majority. One opinion may have been public or general in regard to the whites, the other public or general in regard to the negroes, but neither opinion was public or general in regard to the whole population. Examples of this kind could be multiplied indefinitely. They can be found in Ireland, in Austria-Hungary, in Turkey, in India, in any country where the cleavage of race, religion, or politics is sharp and deep enough to cut the community into fragments too far apart for an accord on fundamental matters. When the Mohammedans spread the faith of Islam by the sword, could the question whether public opinion in a conquered country favored Christianity or Mohammedanism be said to depend on a small preponderance in numbers of the Christians or the followers of the Prophet; and were the minority under any obligation to surrender their creed? The government was entirely in the hands of the Mussulmans, but would it be rational to assert that if they numbered ninety-nine thousand against one hundred thousand Christians public opinion in the country was against them, whereas if they were to massacre two thousand of the Christians public opinion would then be on their side? Likewise in Bohemia at the present day, where the Germans and the Czechs are struggling for supremacy, would there not be an obvious fallacy in claiming that whichever race could show a bare majority would have the support of public opinion in requiring its own language to be taught to all the children in the schools.

In all these instances an opinion cannot be public or general with respect to both elements in the state. For that purpose they are as distinct as if they belonged to different commonwealths. You may count heads, you may break heads, you may impose uniformity by force; but on the matters at stake the two elements do not form a community capable of an opinion that is in any rational sense public or general. As Mr. Bryce points out, a great deal of confusion arises from using the term sometimes to mean everybody's views, that is, the aggregate of all that is thought, and sometimes the views of the majority. If we are to employ the term in a sense that is significant for government, that imports any obligation moral or political on the part of the minority, surely enough has been said to show that the opinion of a mere majority does not by itself always suffice. Something more is clearly needed.

But if the opinion of a majority does not of itself constitute a public opinion, it is equally certain that unanimity is not required. To confine the term to cases where there is no dissent would deprive it of all value and would be equivalent to saying that it rarely, if ever, exists. Moreover, unanimous opinion is of no importance for our purpose, because it is perfectly sure to be effective in any form of government, however despotic, and it is, therefore, of no particular interest in the study of democracy. Legislation by unanimity was actually tried in the kingdom of Poland, where each member of the assembly had the right of *liberum veto* on any measure, and it prevented progress, fostered violence, and spelled failure. The Polish system has been lauded as the acme of liberty, but in fact it was directly opposed to the fundamental principle of modern popular government; that is, the conduct of public affairs in accord with a public opinion which is general, although not universal, and which implies under certain conditions a duty on the part of the minority to submit.

If then unanimity is not necessary to public opinion and a majority is not enough, where shall we seek the essential elements of its existence? A suggestion much in point may be found in the speculations of the most ingenious political philosopher of the eighteenth century. In his *Contrat Social* Rousseau attempts to prove that in becoming a member of a state the natural man may remain perfectly free and continue to obey only his own will. He tells us that in forming a state men desire to enforce the common will of all the members; and he takes as the basis of all political action this common will, which is nearly akin to our idea of public opinion. Now, in order to reconcile the absolute freedom of every citizen to obey only his own volition, with the passing of laws in every civilized state against opposition, he says that when the assembled people are consulted on any measure, their votes express, not their personal wishes upon the subject, but their opinions in regard to the common will, and thus the defeated minority have not had their desires thwarted, but have simply been mistaken in their views about the common will. All men, he insists, want to give effect to this common will, which becomes, therefore, the universal will of everyone and is always carried out.

Though stated in a somewhat fanciful way, the theory contains a highly important truth, which may be clothed in a more modern dress. A body of men are politically capable of a public opinion only so far as they are agreed upon the ends and aims of government and upon the principles by which those ends shall be attained. They must be united, also, about the means whereby the action of the government is to be determined, in a conviction, for example, that the views of a majority—or it may be some other portion of their numbers—ought to prevail; and a political community as a whole is capable of public opinion only when this is true of the great bulk of the citizens. Such an assumption was implied, though usually not expressed in all theories of the Social Compact; and, indeed, it is involved in all theories that base rightful government upon the consent of the governed, for the consent required is not a universal approval by all the people of every measure enacted, but a consensus in regard to the legitimate character of the ruling authority and its right to decide the questions that arise.

The power of the courts in America to hold statutes unconstitutional furnishes an illustration of this doctrine. It rests upon a distinction between those things that may be done by ordinary legislative procedure and those that may not; the theory being that in the case of the former the people have consented to abide by the decision of the majority as expressed by their representatives, whereas in the case of matters not placed by the constitution within the competence of the legislature, the people as a whole have given no such consent. With regard to these they have agreed to abide only by a decree uttered in more solemn forms, or by the determination of something greater than a mere majority. The court, therefore, in holding a statute unconstitutional, is in effect deciding that it is not within the range of acts to which the whole people have given their consent; so that while the opinion in favor of the act may be an opinion of the majority of the voters, it is not a public opinion of the community, because it is not one where the people as a whole are united in a conviction that the views of the majority, at least as expressed through the ordinary channels, ought to prevail.

We have seen that in some countries the population has contained, and for that matter still contains, distinct elements which are sharply at odds upon the vital political questions of the day. In such a case the discordant forces may be violent enough to preclude a general consent that the opinion of the majority ought to prevail; but this is not always true. If they are not, the assumption which lies at the foundation of popular government remains unimpaired. If they are, the forms of democracy may still be in operation, although their meaning is essentially altered. It may be worth while to dwell on this contrast a moment because it makes clear the difference between true public opinion and the opinion of a majority.

Leaving out of account those doctrines whereby political authority is traced to a direct supernatural origin, government among men is commonly based in theory either on consent or on force, and in fact each of these factors plays a larger or smaller part in every civilized country. So far as the preponderating opinion is one which the minority does not share, but which it feels ought, as the opinion of the majority, to be carried out, the government is conducted by a true public opinion or by consent. So far as the preponderating opinion is one the execution of which the minority would resist by force if it could do so successfully, the government is based upon force. At times it may be necessary to give effect to an opinion of the majority against the violent resistance, or through the reluctant submission, of the minority. A violent resistance may involve the suppression of an armed insurrection or civil war. But even when there is no resort to actual force it remains true that in any case where the minority does not concede the right of the majority to decide, submission is yielded only to obviously superior strength; and obedience is the result of compulsion, not of public opinion. The power to carry out its will under such conditions must to some extent be inherent in every government. Habitual criminals are held in check by force everywhere. But in many nations at the present day there are great masses of well-intentioned citizens who do not admit the right of the majority to rule. These persons and the political parties in which they group themselves are termed irreconcilable, and when we speak of public opinion in that country we cannot include them. So far as they are concerned there can be no general or public opinion.

Let us be perfectly clear upon this point. The presence of irreconcilables does not mean that the government is illegitimate, or that it is not justified in enforcing its will upon the reluctant minority. That will depend upon other considerations. The use of force may be unavoidable if any settled government is to be upheld, if civic order is to be maintained. But it does mean that the fundamental assumption of popular government, the control of political affairs by an opinion which is truly public, is set aside. Florence may, or may not, have been justified in disfranchising her noble families, but Freeman was certainly right in his opinion that by so doing she lost her right to be called a democracy,—that is, a government by all the people,—and it makes little difference for this purpose whether a part of the body politic is formally excluded from any share in public affairs or overawed by force into submission.

One more remark must be made before quitting the subject of the relation of public opinion to the opinion of the majority. The late Gabriel Tarde, with his habitual keen insight, insisted on the importance of the intensity of belief as a factor in the spread of opinions. There is a common impression that public opinion depends upon and is measured by the mere number of persons to be found on each side of a question; but this is far from accurate. If forty-nine percent of a community feel very strongly on one side, and fifty-one percent are lukewarmly on the other, the former opinion has the greater public force behind it and is certain to prevail ultimately if it does not at once. The ideas of people who possess the greatest knowledge of a subject are also of more weight than those of an equal number of ignorant persons. If, for example, all the physicians, backed by all other educated men, are confident that an impure water supply causes typhoid fever, while the rest of the people are mildly incredulous, it can hardly be said that public opinion is opposed to that notion. One man who holds his belief tenaciously counts for as much as several men who hold theirs weakly, because he is more aggressive, and thereby compels and overawes others into apparent agreement with him, or at least into silence and inaction. This is, perhaps, especially true of moral questions. It is not improbable that a large part of the accepted moral code is maintained by the earnestness of a minority, while more than half of the community is indifferent or unconvinced. In short, public opinion is not strictly the opinion of the numerical majority, and no form of its expression measures the mere majority, for individual views are always to some extent weighed as well as counted. Without attempting to consider how the weight attaching to intensity and intelligence can be accurately gauged, it is enough for our purpose to point out that when we speak of the opinion of a majority we mean, not the numerical, but the effective majority.

No doubt differences in the intensity of belief explain some sudden transformations in politics and in ethical standards, many people holding their views with so little conviction that they are ready to follow in the wake of any strong leader in thought or action. On the other hand they explain in part also cases where a law is enacted readily but enforced with difficulty; for the law may be carried through by a comparatively small body of very earnest men, who produce a disproportionate effect by the heat of their conviction; while the bulk of the people are apathetic and unwilling to support the effort required to overcome a steady passive resistance to the enforcement of the law.

The problem of intensity of belief is connected, moreover, with the fact that different ways of ascertaining the popular will may give different results, in accordance with the larger or smaller proportion of the indifferent who are gathered in to vote. But this is a matter that belongs properly to a later discussion of the methods of expressing public opinion. We are dealing here only with its essential nature.

To sum up what has been said in this chapter: public opinion to be worthy of the name, to be the proper motive force in a democracy, must be really public; and popular government is based upon the assumption of a public opinion of that kind. In order that it may be public a majority is not enough, and unanimity is not required, but the opinion must be such that while the minority may not share it, they feel bound, by conviction not by fear, to accept it; and if democracy is complete the submission of the minority must be given ungrudgingly. An essential difference between government by public opinion as thus defined and by the bare will of a selfish majority has been well expressed by President Hadley. After saying that laws imposed by a majority on a reluctant minority are commonly inoperative, he adds, "It cannot be too often repeated that those opinions which a man is prepared to maintain at another's cost, but not at his own, count for little in forming the general sentiment of a community, or in producing any effective public movement."

# Nations and Classes:
# The Symbols of Identification

HAROLD D. LASSWELL

WHEN ERNST WERNER TECHOW, Erwin Kern, and Hermann Fischer assassinated Walther Rathenau in 1922, they invoked the name of the Fatherland, the monarchy, the spirit of Potsdam. When Friedrich Adler shot the Austrian Prime Minister in 1916, he said it was not because he desired publicity, or because he enjoyed the pleasure of murdering his fellow man, but because the working classes required it. When Pilsudski and Stalin robbed banks in the years before 1917, they said it was not because they needed money and adventure for themselves, but because the overthrow of czarism and the liberation of the oppressed working masses of the world demanded it. When the Paris commune was drowned in blood, it was because the interests of "patriotism" and of "civilization" required it. The millions who struggled from 1914 to 1918 in the thin zones which surrounded the Central Powers were fighting for "God," "country," "civilization," "humanity," "international law," "a war to end war," and a "lasting peace."

The role of these justifying symbols in politics is one of the principal topics of analytic inquiry. With which acts are particular symbols connected? How are the justifying symbols grouped geographically throughout the world? How are they related to one another and to the whole context of political change? The embittered paranoiac who slays the first passer-by whom he suspects of turning destructive rays upon him is of mediocre interest to the student of politics, though a paranoiac like Gorgulov who kills the President of France as the "enemy" of his people becomes relevant on account of

Reprinted from *World Politics and Personal Insecurity: A Contribution to Political Psychiatry* (1935), pp. 29–51, through the courtesy of Luis Kutner as Executor. Copyright 1935, by McGraw-Hill.

the target of his act and the accompanying verbalizations. The person who views himself as representative of a larger unity has widened the configuration against which his act is to be construed. To be of greatest interest to us, the act of demolishing another must be enshrined in justifications. The muscle movements must occur in a context of verbal legitimacy. There must be evidence of the process of self-justification by referring to entities larger than the self, another contribution to the voluminous chapter of human history entitled "The Story of Man and His Justifications."

A satisfactory geography of politics would chart the symbols which men invoke to justify their pretensions, and disclose the nature of the acts with which each symbol is affiliated.[1] Our usual maps show the world of "states," but the world of politics is richer, including acts justified in the name of churches, races, nationalities, tribes, classes, and dynasties. From the study of psychological areas we can often surmise the nature of coming changes in the activity and organization areas. Particularistic expressions in the old Dual Monarchy presaged the approaching end of the state and no doubt the spread of class symbols in the contemporary world is the precursor of drastic changes of boundary lines.

If we look with fresh naïveté at the distribution of persons who use common identifying symbols, many anomalies appear. How does it happen that a man living by Lake Michigan identifies himself with a name that includes the population of New York, a thousand miles east, and of San Diego, several thousand miles west, and yet excludes the population of Winnipeg and Toronto? How does he come to associate himself with the "poor white trash" of the South, and not with the farmers of Alberta; or with the blacks of Georgia, and not with the whites of Quebec?

The relationship between geographical features and symbols seems fast and loose. Australians occupy a continent and the whites, at least, have a unifying term, but the Europeans, Asiatics, Africans, North and South Americans, who occupy continents, are split into parochial groups. Those who live in the Mississippi River Valley call themselves by one inclusive name, but those who are settled in the valley of the Danube use many names. Most of the inhabitants of the principal Japanese islands have a common term, but the North Irelanders are distinct from the South Irelanders.

Symbols do not unite all those who live on the great highlands or in the great lowlands of the earth. If the Italian peninsula is, in a fashion, unified, the Scandinavian peninsula is disunited. Geographical zones which are defined by deciduous or coniferous forests, or by characteristic temperature, rainfall, or barometric ranges, do not neatly coincide with areas of identification. . . .

If we examine the relation between areas of sentiment and of organization, on the one hand, and areas of special activity on the other, instances of noncongruence multiply. The iron and steel manufacturing districts of South Chicago, northern Ohio, and Alabama, together with the Lake Superior ore deposits and various coal and limestone areas, are all included within the United States; but the industrial region of the Rhineland is split between two antagonistic states and nationalities.

The symbols referred to thus far have historically been connected with geographical locations. Another powerful body of symbols has fixed upon some nonspatial characteristic. Most portentous of these is the "proletariat," in whose name various working-class districts of the world are being mobilized to reject the authority of those who use the symbols of "nationalism" or "individualism," and to accept the authority of those who invoke the new verbalism. Even here curious discrepancies reveal themselves, since many of the active proletarians turn out to be lawyers, university graduates, publicists, sons of middle-class or upper-class families, and many of the inactive proletarians prove to be serfs or wage earners in the Southern black belt, in South African mines, or on Caribbean fruit plantations.

No doubt our hypothetically naïve observer would innocently ask why so much stress is put on "place" words or "economic" words as unifying symbols. The wonder grows if one remembers that the number of words which can be used to distinguish one person from another is unlimited. All the curly-haired people might be united in curly-haired consciousness versus all the straight-haired people; all the dry-skinned people might be united against the oily-skinned people; but the words about propinquity and tradition and economic standing have thus far outcompeted physical words in the rivalry for human loyalty. . . . Dr. Carl Jung has done much to create an "introvert" and "extravert" consciousness in mankind, yet the introverts and extraverts are not yet demanding self-determination.[2]

Now this purely schematic consideration of potentialities in human relations may emancipate some of us personally from automatic loyalty to the particular symbolisms which we have incorporated into our personality. Such formalism, however, is far removed from the state of the circumambient world, where specific national and class differences are taken with so much seriousness. For better or worse we are embedded in historical configurations which are characterized by the existence of a large number of comprehensive symbols in the name of which people die or kill. In examining these phenomena, we may in some respects be guided by the results of intensive personality studies which have disclosed so much about the dynamics of the process of identification itself.

We know that the components of behavior which are prominent in the early history of the organism, but which are modified as unacceptable to the environment, persist within the adult structure. . . . We may grasp the hand of the person next to us according to the accepted forms of the social situation, smiling genially; yet repressed hostilities may be expressed in moods of slight depression or constraint, in some speech blocking as one repeats the conventional verbal forms, or in such bodily symptoms as localized skin irritations. The significance of these various formations as compromises between impulses to attack the other person and impulses to inhibit overt hostility can only become manifest when the individual learns how to employ the free-fantasy technique of exposing his reactive structure.[3]

Now what is it that happens when one person becomes emotionally bound to the symbol of another, or to the symbol of the collectivity? An emotional attachment occurs when the symbol of the other is taken as one means of gratifying the affectionate (the libidinal) impulses which are not permitted to exhaust themselves in direct and primitive ways upon the object. Strictly speaking, the symbol of the aspect of the self which is taken by the self to be characterized by an "external" reference secures the libidinal charge.

The emotional relations which are directly relevant to our field of discourse arise in the perception of similarities between an object and ourselves (by partial identification).[4] The necessary prerequisite is the presence of aim-inhibited impulses which are available for redirection toward substitute symbols. We identify with others (a process which is not necessarily accompanied by acute self-awareness) by perceiving that they are from the same college, the same town, the same country; that they admire the same politicians, scientists, or teachers; that they exercise the same skills; that they resemble our past attachments, and so on through an incalculably vast list of possibilities.

The emotional relation to the other is not necessarily positive; we do not invariably remodel ourselves by taking over some feature of his personality pattern. We may react negatively by identifying him with some aspect of our own personality which we deplore as weak or disreputable. In this case we reject the proffered pattern and release profoundly destructive impulses.

Quite often persons are related to the same object (as viewed by a specified observer) without a common externalized symbol of the object, and without a common symbol of all those who are identified with the object. I may be impressed by a stranger whom I see walking alone in the Bois de Boulogne, but my subjective symbol of the stranger may not be related to a name which I could use as an external symbol of the man, or to a symbol of the other people who, unknown to me, have also partially identified with him. This relationship of the man and the several people who have no externalized symbols of him or of one another is one which we shall call *multiple identification.* This condition is highly potential for the more complex identification relationships. The transition to *counteridentification* may be very quickly managed when the multiply identified discover one another and develop external symbols of one another and of the person to whom they occupy a common relation. We may learn that the lone stranger in the Bois de Boulogne is Dr. X, who has new theories of stopping disease through irradiation, and we may be disposed to accept and propagate his methods. The disciples of a political sage or the associates of an active agitator may be bound by the ties of counteridentification.[5]

Of great political relevance is *mutual identification,* whose distinguishing mark is the inclusion of persons within the field of reference of the symbol who are beyond the face-to-face experience of any one person. The term "American" includes persons who are dead and gone and those who are geographically remote, and thus beyond the primary experience of those identified with the word. Interlapping identifications among persons in relation to this symbol make such mutual identifications possible. . . .

The environment of the infant and child is teeming with words of ambiguous reference, which take on positive or negative significance long before there is enough contact with reality either to define their frames of reference, or to distinguish those whose frames of reference are wholly indeterminate. As an "adult" the individual continues to respond to these articulations in many childish and juvenile ways, very often imputing some special and even awesome significance to them. Such words are "law and order," "patriotism," "a gentleman and a soldier," "truth," "justice," "honor," "good," "bad," "loyalty," "duty," "Germans," "French," "Negroes," "national hero," "good citizens," "national interest," "king," "constitution"; but these words do not stand alone in primitive concentrations of irrelevant affect. The whole of our vocabulary, plus our non-verbal symbols, is caught in the mesh of early structuralizations of this kind, so that the inner meaning of our symbols is never revealed except through the technique of free fantasy.

Identification with any particular symbol by any person at any phase of his career line initiates a complex process of symbol elaboration. All the earlier loves tend to be reactivated in relation to the new symbol. The individual who late in life experiences "conversion" and becomes an "American" or a "Czech" or a "Lithuanian" or a "Communist" or a "Socialist" or a "Catholic" reads into this symbol the loves and hopes of his entire personality. His elaborations of the symbol will depend upon the forms of expression with which his personality has been equipped through aptitude and training. If he belongs to those who require large emotional responses from the environment, and if he has a facile technique for the oral or written production of language, he may fill the auditoriums of his vicinity with rhetoric and the printing presses with poetry and prose. When the Dreyfus affair in France awakened the Jewish self-consciousness of Theodor Herzl, he quickly expressed himself in lectures, plays, essays, and programs for the recovery of a national home. These symbol elaborations were also determined by the patterns formed for the glorification of a collective symbol of identification within the culture to which he had been exposed. Hence a "Jewish nation" at such a time and place seemed to Herzl to demand immediate statehood.

The displacement of the infantile, childish, and juvenile affects upon symbols of ambiguous reference has led to the creation of remarkable monuments to human vanity. Nations, classes, tribes, and churches have been treated as collective symbols in the name of which the individual may indulge his elementary urges for supreme power, for omniscience, for amorality, for security.[6]

The examination of such symbol structures became one of the interesting exercises of the eighteenth century intellectuals as the clashes among organization areas broadened into classes among "nations." One of the studies of the day was an *Essay on National Pride,* by Dr. J. G. Zimmerman, physician to His Britannic Majesty at Hanover, and a minor literary light.[7] . . . The principal part of his essay classifies illustrations of national and tribal symbolism, taken from the history and ethnology of the period. He comments upon "the Greenlander, who laps with his dog in the same platter" and holds himself superior to the Danish invader. "Ask the Carribee Indians who live at the mouth of the Orinoque, from what nation they derive their origin; they answer 'Why, we only are men.' ". . . Observing that men prefer the diet to which they are accustomed, the Doctor pungently adds, "The love of our country is little more, in many cases, than the love of an ass for his manger."

The prominence of physical features has prompted innumerable attempts to elaborate the superior claims of collective symbols by imputing special significance to bodily characteristics. It was formerly held that the "inferior races" had "ugly" features, such as slant eyes, large noses, flat noses, thick lips. The Japanese soon presented a special problem here, because they showed as much industrial and fighting ability as many Europeans; but they thought the large eyes and aquiline noses of the West were ugly. The growing recognition of the influence of suggestion on forms of aesthetic taste renders such comparisons of relative "beauty" rather ludicrous. Pigmentation of the skin has also been a focus of "superiority-inferiority" claims, but investigation has revealed that pigmentation scarcely correlates with any agreed index of "capacity.". . .

Each symbol of identification is elaborated according to the patterns already existing in the culture for symbols of that class. There are thus preformed praise patterns of symbol and practice available for application to the new symbol. Since our Western European culture was so long dominated by the symbolism of Christianity, the rising national and proletarian movements, quite without premeditation, look over the Christian patterns. A classical instance of this is the famous procession at the first session of the Legislative Assembly in France in the autumn of 1791, when twelve elderly patriarchs went in search of the Book of the Constitution.

> They came back, having at their head the archivist Camus, who, holding up the Book with his two hands and resting it on his breast, carried with slow and measured tread the new Blessed Sacrament of the French. All the deputies arose and bared their heads. Camus, with meditative mien, kept his eyes lowered.[8]

Writers on many of our contemporary symbols of identification have recently become acutely aware of these connections. It is frequently noted how the principal symbol is endowed with godlike attributes, the collective mission is idealized, an elaborate ritualism is evolved about a banner, pledges of unswerving fidelity are taken ("I pledge allegiance to my flag . . ."), holidays (holy days) are observed, the veneration of statues, pictures, and shrines increases, a body of official doctrines is reverently reiterated and stoutly defended, learned commentators elaborate the subtleties of the official ideology, and devices of popularization are exploited to reach every stratum of the supporting community and to proselyte among the unconverted.[9]

The modern phenomenon of nationalism represents a complicated synthesis of religious, cultural, state, democratic, and allied patterns. Once partly integrated around a particular symbol each new configuration diffused as a culture complex, eliciting fresh acts of identification from some, and provoking decisive acts of rejection from others. Affirmation aroused counteraffirmation, and the outcome of the dialectic was to insure the propagation of the general pattern, subject to profound differentiations in detail.

Since the possession of a distinctive language came to be regarded as one of the details essential to the status of the fully developed national symbol, language revivals became inseparable from the early history of most nationalistic movements. Restrictions of any kind upon the use of the vernacular in schools, universities, law courts, legislatures, forums, churches, or markets were bitterly resented. Intellectuals expanded the national vocabulary as well as the national literature. In Finland the vernacular was fashioned into a literary vehicle on a par with Swedish; in Bohemia the Czech language supplanted the foreign literary speech, which was German; in Albania the nationalists remodeled the crude vernacular into a literary medium. In Greece the artificial "pure" Greek was launched, but failed, the popular "demotike" winning out. Among the Vlachs in Macedonia a national movement got under way with the revival of the vernacular, Roumanian, which the Greeks failed to suppress. In Roumania the spread of nationalism went hand in hand with the expansion of the national tongue. . . .

The general objects of collective effort on behalf of the collective symbol are thus profoundly affected by the patterns conceived to be appropriate in the culture to symbols of this class. Identification with the collective symbol likewise involves identification with many, if not all, of these status symbols, and the discrepancy between the existing position of the collective symbol and the patterns deemed appropriate to the class defines the objectives of concerted effort.

The remodeling of the personality through identification varies from minor changes in vocabulary to profound redefinitions of career, in which individuals devote themselves to the performance of specialized functions in the collective enterprise. They may become devoted missionaries of the cause, exhorting in public and private, or they may carry on the detailed work of administering central office routine, collecting information, soliciting funds, distributing material. The professional revolutionary is one of the most prominent examples of full-time devotion to the expression of the claims of a collective symbol.

The adaptive processes which are initiated in identification modify the relation of the symbol to other symbols in the lives of the persons affected; these other symbols are both "public" and "private" and their interconnections may be infinitely complex. The symbol of the local merchants' association may be reenforced to strengthen the symbol of the nation; but this process of redefinition may involve the inclusion of certain commercial policy demands into the national symbol. This latter process, by means of which special and private demands are legitimized in terms of the more inclusive symbol, adds greatly to the acceptability of the latter. A central core of allusion is sustained and redefined in terms of "tactical" or "strategical" considerations. Personalities display prodigious skill in justifying private goals in terms of master symbols; insofar as this process is unconscious, it is rationalization; insofar as it is conscious, it is justification.

The relation between symbols of identification and of demand, which have just been indicated, may be amplified by noticing the relations between symbols of identification and of expectation. Identification with collective symbols usually modifies the outlook of the person on the future of the world. Expectations are generated about the benevolent implications of future history for cherished aspirations. The result is over-optimism about the future status of the master symbol. . . . The redefinition of future expectations is in part due to the relatively exclusive preoccupation of the individual with the fate of the master symbol. The whole meaning of history is sharpened into some simplified struggle between Good and Evil, bourgeois and proletarian, oppressor and oppressed. The future derives its portentous quality from the fact that it alone can disclose the fate of the contending symbols.

Symbols of identification, demand, and expectation reciprocally influence one another, and interplay with changes in the division of labor. Optimism and devotion may affect the work rate and the birth rate, modifying the value hierarchy. The development of power machinery may cheapen production and lead to the expansion of the market. Demands which are serviceable in extending the market may be redefined in terms of the master symbols of nation or state. Such dynamic interrelations between "material" and "ideological" continue to redefine areas of activity, sentiment, and organization.

From the foregoing it is evident that the spread of any master identifying symbol depends upon the connections among details of great apparent diversity. The success of any symbol in competition with other symbols depends upon frequency of exposure in forms capable of eliciting favorable response, and upon presentation at times when the readjustive possibilities of the population are high. . . .

All research confirms the importance of exposing the specific sequence through which symbol clusters pass. When did a national symbol of identification become associated with demands to oust foreigners from jobs in the army and the bureaucracy? When did sensitiveness to being ruled by executives of foreign origin develop? When did it cease to be good form to speak a foreign tongue? When did it become socially necessary to patronize native art? When did it become imperative to "buy Chinese" or "sell Chinese?" When did it become socially advisable to name children after political heroes? When did it become disloyal to accept favors in return for exercising an official duty?[10]

Recent social science has undertaken to follow and to explain the speedy diffusion of nationalism since the later years of the eighteenth century.[11] In the foreground appears the rapid application of modern technology to production, profoundly altering the life situation of many members of the community. Perceiving new possibilities of profit, self-selected enterprisers took the initiative in demanding many modifications in traditional ways of life, clashing with the symbols and practices favorable to the landed property group. Finding themselves in organization areas where decision making was a restricted privilege, needing ways and means of rendering themselves effective at the centers of dominance, they responded positively to symbols of protest and plan which were circulated by specialized verbalizers. Gradually the ideology of the ruling élite was called into question in the name of mankind as a whole. Democratic language assisted in mobilizing the animosities of the "underprivileged" in mass action which finally altered the methods of élite recruitment and the language of justification. Where members of the bourgeoisie got control of the government, as in France, they transformed their earlier antistate orientation into a pro-state and pro-governmental ideology. Nationalism became henceforth a means of nullifying proletarian challenges from within, and of fostering the power of the state in the world balance. Where the bourgeoisie was particularly weak, and an older social formation needed military support from the masses to defend itself from invasion, the older élite exploited as much as possible of the place-, time-, and tradition-bound symbolism at hand. In Prussia the bourgeoisie never succeeded in capturing the language of nationalism from the monarchy and the feudality that rallied to repulse the French.

In the competition of merely local enterprises with one another, merely local differences are emphasized; hence effective nationalism could not appear until the expansion of the market made possible the concentrating of strong initiative in the hands of enterprisers who were situated at the principal metropoles.

The upper bourgeoisie at the chief marketing centers were receptive to the elaborated symbols of nationalism as they were developed by orators, journalists, poets, novelists, essayists, and systematists. The ideological incorporation of the lesser centers and the back country into the policy of the bourgeois state spread from the centers of dominance by means of the propagation of literacy and by the expansion of such secondary means of incessant stimulation as the press. The expansion of capitalist enterprise tended to promote the active widening of the marketing area for certain goods, like textiles, and, later, iron and steel products. The result was to facilitate the growth of a world-marketing area, which in turn set up many dialectical processes in the form of local opposition to foreign competition. These acute localistic reactions created groups which were favorably disposed toward new local nationalistic expressions. We notice the discovery of local identities throughout Europe, and beyond, as the nineteenth century wore on. The multiplication of state organization areas at the end of the World War is one of the residues of this process.

The emergence in an old organization area of a new élite which speaks in the name of the proletariat challenges the official symbolism of the ruling élites elsewhere. Unity of action would seem to be advantageous among these various élites in the face of the new threat, but intercapitalistic conflicts are still fostered by the importance of safeguarding foreign economic outlets and of uniting the community around nationalistic symbols; there is also a general tendency to doubt the immediate acuteness of the crisis.[12]

The calculation of pecuniary advantage is a highly "rational" process; yet the social patterns which permit this rational process to go on must be sustained by an irrational consensus. Hence the tension between the rational and the traditional is peculiarly high under capitalism, which requires consensus, yet fosters the rational analysis of every acquired symbol and practice. The rationalism of capitalism has rendered it peculiarly dependent for positive values, ethical imperatives, and unifying goal sumbols upon its legacies from previous cultures. The vestiges of primitive folk culture *(Gemeinschaft)* have been drags upon the completely ruthless application of the principle of calculated pecuniary advantage in The Great Society.[13] The insecurities arising from the changes in the material environment have been augmented by the stresses arising from the decline in potency of the older religious symbols and practices. Nationalism and proletarianism are secularized alternatives to the surviving religious patterns, answering to the need of personalities to restabilize themselves in a mobile world.

The emergence of the last world-revolutionary pattern has intensified appeals to parochialism in the postwar world.[14] The older middle-class formations have revivified the national symbols at the expense of class or world symbols, and supplied blood, money, and applause to programs which have been designed to curb the "alien" and "radical" elements in the community. German Nationalism Socialism relies on the older middle classes. If proletarian strategists can devise ways and means of disintegrating the loyalties of the middle classes, proletarian struggles might in time of advancing economic distress eventuate successfully, short of the demoralization involved in prolonged or unsuccessful war.

## Notes

1. Concerning the theory of the symbol in the logical, psychological, and sociopolitical sense, see E. Cassirer, *Philosophie der symbolischen Formen,* 2 vols., Berlin,

1923–1925; C. I. Lewis, *The Mind and World Order*, New York, 1929; A. N. Whitehead, *Symbolism, Its Meaning and Effect*, Cambridge, Mass., 1928; Charles W. Morris, *Six Theories of Mind*, Chicago, 1932; C. K. Ogden and I. A. Richards, *The Meaning of Meaning*, New York, 1925; the forthcoming posthumous publications of George Herbert Mead; Charles E. Merriam, *The Making of Citizens*, Chicago, 1931; Isidor Ginsburg, "National Symbolism," Chap. 17 in Paul Kosok, *Modern Germany*, Chicago, 1933; John F. Markey, *The Symbolic Process and Its Integration in Children*, New York, 1928.

2. *Psychological Types*, New York, 1924. For the growth of the identification symbolism, reference might be made to Dow Thompson, *A Mind That Was Different*, Harlow Publishing Co., Oklahoma City, 1931.

3. See my *Psychopathology and Politics*, Chaps. 2 and 3, Chicago, 1930.

4. The identification dynamisms are summarized in S. Freud, *Group Psychology and the Analysis of the Ego*, Chap. 7, London, 1922.

5. *Identification* is to be distinguished from *affiliation*, in which the conscious components are preponderant.

6. The developmental formula of the political personality has been stated as follows:

$$p\} \ d\} \ r = P$$

The symbol *p* represents private motives, *d* displacement on to public objects, *r* rationalization in terms of public interest; *P* signifies the political man. The *d* and the *r* are mainly derived from the contact of the personality with secondary group symbols. See my *Psychopathology and Politics*, pp. 261–263, Chicago, 1930.

7. First Edition, Zurich, 1758. English by Samuel H. Wilcocke, New York. Printed by M. L. and W. A. Davis for H. Caritat, Bookseller and Librarian, 1799. See my "Two Forgotten Studies in Political Psychology," *American Political Science Review*, 19 (1925):707–717.

8. A. Mathiez, *Les origines des cultes révolutionnaires*, Paris, 1904, p. 27.

9. Religion and nationalism is extensively discussed in the works of Carlton J. H. Hayes, Hans Kohn, and Charles E. Merriam previously referred to. For religion and proletarianism, see Werner Sombart, and also Waldemar Gurian, *Bolshevism; Theory and Practice*, New York, 1932.

10. See the studies in the history of patriotism by Roberto Michels and Carlton J. H. Hayes; the Civic Training Series edited by Charles E. Merriam; Charles A. Beard and G. H. E. Smith, *The Idea of National Interest: An Analytical Study in American Foreign Policy*, New York, 1934.

11. In addition to the literature previously cited, see Friedrich Hertz, "Wesen und Werden der Nation," *Nation und Nationalität*, Erg.- Bd., *Jahrbuch für Soziologie*, Karlsrühe, 1927; H. O. Ziegler, *Die Moderne Nation, Ein Beitrag zur politischen Soziologie*, Tübingen, 1931; R. Johannet, *Le principe des nationalités*, Paris, 1923; *Verhandlungen des zweiten deutschen Soziologentages vom 20. bis 22. Oktober, 1912, in Berlin*, Tübingen, 1913; Otto Bauer, *Die Nationalitätenfrage und die Sozialdemokratie*, Vienna, 1924; Karl Renner, *Der Kampf der österreichischen Nationen um den Staat*, 2 vols., Vienna, 1902; Karl Renner, *Der nationale Streit um die Aemter und die Sozialdemokratie*, Vienna, 1908; Koppel S. Pinson, *Biblio-*

*graphical Introduction to Nationalism* (announced); and various books of Harry Elmer Barnes.

12. Many of the economic aspects of nationalism are well handled in Waldemar Mitscherlich, *Nationalismus: Die Geschichte einer Idee,* Leipzig, 1929; R. G. Hawtrey, *Economic Aspects of Sovereignty,* London, 1930; Walter Sulzbach, *Nationales Gemeinschaftsgefühl und wirtschaftliches Interesse,* Leipzig, 1929; József Eötvös, *Der Einfluss der herrschenden Ideen des 19 Jahrhunderts auf den staat* (from Hungarian), Leipzig, 1854; and in the writings of Bukharin, Lenin, and other historical materialists.

13. The relations between *Gemeinschaft* and *Gesellschaft,* first extensively developed by Ferdinand Tönnies, are carefully restated in Hans Freyer, *Soziologie als Wirlichkeitswissenschaft,* pp. 230–252, Leipzig and Berlin, 1930.

14. See Helen Martin, *Nationalism and Children's Books* (University of Chicago Ph. D. dissertation, 1934), which applies a rigorous technique to the study of the factors affecting the diffusion of children's books throughout the world.

# Stereotypes

## WALTER LIPPMANN

EACH OF US LIVES AND WORKS on a small part of the earth's surface, moves in a small circle, and of these acquaintances knows only a few intimately. Of any public event that has wide effects we see at best only a phase and an aspect. This is as true of the eminent insiders who draft treaties, make laws, and issue orders, as it is of those who have treaties framed for them, laws promulgated to them, orders given at them. Inevitably our opinions cover a bigger space, a longer reach of time, a greater number of things, than we can directly observe. They have, therefore, to be pieced together out of what others have reported and what we can imagine.

Yet even the eyewitness does not bring back a naïve picture of the scene.[1] For experience seems to show that he himself brings something to the scene which later he takes away from it, that oftener than not what he imagines to be the account of an event is really a transfiguration of it. Few facts in consciousness seem to be merely given. Most facts in consciousness seem to be partly made. A report is the joint product of the knower and known, in which the rôle of the observer is always selective and usually creative. The facts we see depend on where we are placed, and the habits of our eyes.

An unfamiliar scene is like the baby's world, "one great, blooming, buzzing confusion."[2] This is the way, says Mr. John Dewey,[3] that any new thing strikes an adult, so far as the thing is really new and strange. "Foreign languages that we do not understand always seem jibberings, babblings, in which it is impossible to fix a definite, clearcut, individualized group of sounds. The countryman in the crowded street, the landlubber at sea, the ignoramus in sport at a contest between experts in a complicated game, are further instances. Put an inexperienced man in a factory, and at first the work seems

Reprinted with permission of Macmillan Publishing Co., Inc., from *Public Opinion* (1922), pp. 59–70. Copyright 1922, renewed 1950 by Walter Lippmann.

to him a meaningless medley. All strangers of another race proverbially look alike to the visiting stranger. Only gross differences of size or color are perceived by an outsider in a flock of sheep, each of which is perfectly individualized to the shepherd. A diffusive blur and an indiscriminately shifting suction characterize what we do not understand. The problem of the acquisition of meaning by things, or (stated in another way) of forming habits of simple apprehension, is thus the problem of introducing (1) *definiteness* and *distinction* and (2) *consistency* or *stability* of meaning into what is otherwise vague and wavering."

But the kind of definiteness and consistency introduced depends upon who introduces them. In a later passage[4] Dewey gives an example of how differently an experienced layman and a chemist might define the word metal. "Smoothness, hardness, glossiness, and brilliancy, heavy weight for its size . . . the serviceable properties of capacity for being hammered and pulled without breaking, of being softened by heat and hardened by cold, of retaining the shape and form given, of resistance to pressure and decay, would probably be included" in the layman's definition. But the chemist would likely as not ignore these esthetic and utilitarian qualities, and define a metal as "any chemical element that enters into combination with oxygen so as to form a base."

For the most part we do not first see, and then define, we define first and then see. In the great blooming, buzzing confusion of the outer world we pick out what our culture has already defined for us, and we tend to perceive that which we have picked out in the form stereotyped for us by our culture. Of the great men who assembled at Paris to settle the affairs of mankind, how many were there who were able to see much of the Europe about them, rather than their commitments about Europe? Could anyone have penetrated the mind of M. Clemenceau, would he have found there images of the Europe of 1919, or a great sediment of stereotyped ideas accumulated and hardened in a long and pugnacious existence? Did he see the Germans of 1919, or the German type as he had learned to see it since 1871? He saw the type, and among the reports that came to him from Germany, he took to heart those reports, and, it seems, those only, which fitted the type that was in his mind. If a junker blustered, that was an authentic German; if a labor leader confessed the guilt of the empire, he was not an authentic German.

At a Congress of Psychology in Göttingen an interesting experiment was made with a crowd of presumably trained observers.[5]

> Not far from the hall in which the Congress was sitting there was a public fête with a masked ball. Suddenly the door of the hall was thrown open and a clown rushed in madly pursued by a negro, revolver in hand. They stopped in the middle of the room fighting; the clown fell, the negro leapt over him, fired, and then both rushed out of the hall. The whole incident hardly lasted twenty seconds.

The President asked those present to write immediately a report since there was sure to be a judicial inquiry. Forty reports were sent in. Only one had less than 20% of mistakes in regard to the principal facts; fourteen had 20% to 40% of mistakes; twelve from 40% to 50%; thirteen more than 50%. Moreover in twenty-four accounts 10% of the details were pure inventions and this proportion was exceeded in ten accounts and diminished in six. Briefly a quarter of the accounts were false.

It goes without saying that the whole scene had been arranged and even photographed in advance. The ten false reports may then be relegated to the category of tales and legends; twenty-four accounts are half legendary, and six have a value approximating to exact evidence.

Thus out of forty trained observers writing a responsible account of a scene that had just happened before their eyes, more than a majority saw a scene that had not taken place. What then did they see? One would suppose it was easier to tell what had occurred, than to invent something which had not occurred. They saw their stereotype of such a brawl. All of them had in the course of their lives acquired a series of images of brawls, and these images flickered before their eyes. In one man these images displaced less than 20% of the actual scene, in thirteen men more than half. In thirty-four out of the forty observers the stereotypes preëmpted at least one-tenth of the scene.

A distinguished art critic said[6] that "what with the almost numberless shapes assumed by an object. . . . What with our insensitiveness and inattention, things scarcely would have for us features and outlines so determined and clear that we could recall them at will, but for the stereotyped shapes art has lent them." The truth is even broader than that, for the stereotyped shapes lent to the world come not merely from art, in the sense of painting and sculpture and literature, but from our moral codes and our social philosophies and our political agitations as well. Substitute in the following passage of Mr. Berenson's the words 'politics,' 'business,' and 'society,' for the word 'art' and the sentences will be no less true: ". . . unless years devoted to the study of all schools of art have taught us also to see with our own eyes, we soon fall into the habit of moulding whatever we look at into the forms borrowed from the one art with which we are acquainted. There is our standard of artistic reality. Let anyone give us shapes and colors which we cannot instantly match in our paltry stock of hackneyed forms and tints, and we shake our heads at his failure to reproduce things as we know they certainly are, or we accuse him of insincerity."

Mr. Berenson speaks of our displeasure when a painter "does not visualize objects exactly as we do," and of the difficulty of appreciating the art of the Middle Ages because since then "our manner of visualizing forms has changed in a thousand ways."[7] He goes on to show how in regard to the human figure we have been taught to see what we do see. "Created by Donatello and Masaccio, and sanctioned by the Humanists, the new canon of the human figure, the new cast of features . . . presented to the ruling classes of that time the type of human being most likely to win the day in the combat of human forces. . . . Who had the power to break through this new standard of vision and, out of the chaos of things, to select shapes more definitely expressive of reality than those fixed by men of genius? No one had such power. People had perforce to see things in that way and in no other, and to see only the shapes depicted, to love only the ideals presented. . . ."[8]

If we cannot fully understand the acts of other people, until we know what they think they know, then in order to do justice we have to appraise not only the information which has been at their disposal, but the minds through which they have filtered it. For the accepted types, the current patterns, the standard versions, intercept information on its way to consciousness. Americanization, for example, is superficially at least the substitution of American for European stereotypes. Thus the peasant who might see his landlord as if he were the lord of the manor, his employer as he saw the local magnate, is taught by Americanization to see the landlord and employer according to American standards. This constitutes a change of mind, which is, in effect, when the inoculation succeeds, a change of vision. His eyes see differently. One kindly gentlewoman has confessed that the stereotypes are of such overwhelming importance, that when hers are not indulged, she at least is unable to accept the brotherhood of man and the fatherhood of God: "we are strangely affected by the clothes we wear. Garments create a mental and social atmosphere. What can be hoped for the Americanism of a man who insists on employing a London tailor? One's very food affects his Americanism. What kind of American consciousness can grow in the atmosphere of sauerkraut and Limburger cheese? Or what can you expect of the Americanism of the man whose breath always reeks of garlic?"[9]

This lady might well have been the patron of a pageant which a friend of mine once attended. It was called the Melting Pot, and it was given on the Fourth of July in an automobile town where many foreign-born workers are employed. In the center of the baseball park at second base stood a huge wooden and canvas pot. There were flights of steps up to the rim on two sides. After the audience had settled itself, and the band had played, a procession came through an opening at one side of the field. It was made up of men of all the foreign nationalities employed in the factories. They wore their native costumes, they were singing their national songs; they danced their folk dances, and carried the banners of all Europe. The master of ceremonies was the principal of the grade school dressed as Uncle Sam. He led them to the pot. He directed them up the steps to the rim, and inside. He called them out again on the other side. They came, dressed in derby hats, coats, pants, vest, stiff collar and polka-dot tie, undoubtedly, said my friend, each with an Eversharp pencil in his pocket, and all singing the Star-Spangled Banner.

To the promoters of this pageant, and probably to most of the actors, it seemed as if they had managed to express the most intimate difficulty to friendly association between the older peoples of America and the newer. The contradiction of their stereotypes interfered with the full recognition of their common humanity. The people who change their names know this. They mean to change themselves, and the attitude of strangers toward them.

There is, of course, some connection between the scene outside and the mind through which we watch it, just as there are some long-haired men and short-haired women in radical gatherings. But to the hurried observer a slight connection is enough. If there are two bobbed heads and four beards in the audience, it will be a bobbed and bearded audience to the reporter who knows beforehand that such gatherings are composed of people with these tastes in the management of their hair. There is a connection between our vision and the facts, but it is often a strange connection. A man has rarely looked at a landscape, let us say, except to examine its possibilities for division into building lots, but he has seen a number of landscapes hanging in the parlor. And from them he has learned to think of a landscape as a rosy sunset, or as a country road with a church steeple and a silver moon. One day he goes to the country, and for hours he does not see a single landscape. Then the sun goes down looking rosy. At once he recognizes a landscape and exclaims that it is beautiful. But two days later, when he tries to recall what he saw, the odds are that he will remember chiefly some landscape in a parlor.

Unless he has been drunk or dreaming or insane he did see a sunset, but he saw in it, and above all remembers from it, more of what the oil painting taught him to observe, than what an impressionist painter, for example, or a cultivated Japanese would have seen and taken away with him. And the Japanese and the painter in turn will have seen and remembered more of the form they had learned, unless they happen to be the very rare people who find fresh sight for mankind. In untrained observation we pick recognizable signs out of the environment. The signs stand for ideas, and these ideas we fill out with our stock of images. We do not so much see this man and that subject; rather we notice that the thing is man or sunset, and then see chiefly what our mind is already full of on those subjects.

There is economy in this. For the attempt to see all things freshly and in detail, rather than as types and generalties, is exhausting, and among busy affairs practically out of the question. In a circle of friends, and in relation to close associates or competitors, there is no shortcut through, and no substitute for, an individualized understanding. Those whom we love and admire most are the men and women whose consciousness is peopled thickly with persons rather than with types, who know us rather than the classification into which we might fit. For even without phrasing it to ourselves, we feel intuitively that all classification is in relation to some purpose not necessarily our own; that between two human beings no association has final dignity in which each does not take the other as an end in himself. There is a taint on any contact between two people which does not affirm as an axiom the personal inviolability of both.

But modern life is hurried and multifarious, above all physical distance separates men who are often in vital contact with each other, such as employer and employee, official and voter. There is neither time nor opportunity for intimate acquaintance. Instead we notice a trait which marks a well known type, and fill in the rest of the picture by means of the stereotypes we carry about in our heads. He is an agitator. That much we notice, or are told. Well, an agitator is this sort of person, and so *he* is this sort of person. He is an intellectual. He is a plutocrat. He is a foreigner. He is a "South European." He is from Back Bay. He is a Harvard Man. How different from the statement: he is a Yale Man. He is a regular fellow. He is a West Pointer. He is an old army sergeant. He is a Greenwich Villager: what don't we know about him then, and about her? He is an international banker. He is from Main Street.

The subtlest and most pervasive of all influences are those which create and maintain the repertory of stereotypes. We are told about the world before we see it. We imagine most things before we experience them. And those preconceptions, unless education has made us acutely aware, govern deeply the whole process of perception. They mark out certain objects as familiar or strange, emphasizing the difference, so that the slightly familiar is seen as very familiar, and the somewhat strange as sharply alien. They are aroused by small signs, which may vary from a true index to a vague analogy. Aroused, they flood fresh vision with older images, and project into the world what has been resurrected in memory. Were there no practical uniformities in the environment, there would be no economy and only error in the human habit of accepting foresight for sight. But there are uniformities sufficiently accurate, and the need of economizing attention is so inevitable, that the abandonment of all stereotypes for a whole innocent approach to experience would impoverish human life.

What matters is the character of the stereotypes, and the gullibility with which we employ them. And these in the end depend upon those inclusive patterns which constitute our philosophy of life. If in that philosophy we assume that the world is codified according to a code which we possess, we are likely to make our reports of what is going on describe a world run by our code. But if our philosophy tells us that each man is only a small part of the world, that his intelligence catches at best only phases and aspects in a coarse net of ideas, then, when we use our stereotypes, we tend to know that they are only stereotypes, to hold them lightly, to modify them gladly. We tend, also, to realize more and more clearly when our ideas started, where they started, how they came to us, why we accepted them. All useful history is antiseptic in this fashion. It enables us to know what fairy tale, what school book, what tradition, what novel, play, picture, phrase, planted one preconception in this mind, another in that mind.

Those who wish to censor art do not at least underestimate this influence. They generally misunderstand it, and almost always they are absurdly bent on preventing other people from discovering anything not sanctioned by them. But at any rate, like Plato in his argument about the poets, they feel vaguely that the types acquired through fiction tend to be imposed on reality. Thus there can be little doubt that the moving picture is steadily building up imagery which is then evoked by the words people read in their newspapers. In the whole experience of the race there has been no aid to visualization comparable to the cinema. If a Florentine wished to visualize the saints, he could go to the frescoes in his church, where he might see a vision of saints standardized for his time by Giotto. If an Athenian wished to visualize the gods he went to the temples. But the number of objects which were pictured was not great. And in the East, where the spirit of the second commandment was widely accepted, the portraiture of concrete things was even more meager, and for that reason perhaps the faculty of practical decision was by so much reduced. In the western world, however, during the last few centuries there has been an enormous increase in the volume and scope of secular description, the word picture, the narrative, the illustrated narrative, and finally the moving picture and, perhaps, the talking picture.

Photographs have the kind of authority over imagination to-day, which the printed word had yesterday, and the spoken word before that. They seem utterly real. They come, we imagine, directly to us without human meddling, and they are the most effortless food for the mind conceivable. Any description in words, or even any inert picture, requires an effort of memory before a picture exists in the mind. But on the screen the whole process of observing, describing, reporting, and then imagining, has been accomplished for you. Without more trouble than is needed to stay awake the result which your imagination is always aiming at is reeled off on the screen. The shadowy idea becomes vivid; your hazy notion, let us say, of the Ku Klux Klan, thanks to Mr. Griffiths, takes vivid shape when you see *The Birth of a Nation.* Historically it may be the wrong shape, morally it may be a pernicious shape, but it is a shape, and I doubt whether anyone who has seen the film and does not know more about the Ku Klux Klan than Mr. Griffiths, will ever hear the name again without seeing those white horsemen.

And so when we speak of the mind of a group of people, of the French mind, the militarist mind, the bolshevik mind, we are liable to serious confusion unless we agree to separate the instinctive equipment from the stereotypes, and the formulae which play so decisive a part in building up the mental world to which the native character is adapted and responds. Failure to make this distinction accounts for oceans of loose talk about collective minds, national souls, and race psychology. To be sure a stereotype may be so consistently and authoritatively transmitted in each generation from parent to child that it seems almost like a biological fact. In some respects, we may indeed have become, as Mr. Wallas says,[10] biologically parasitic upon our social heritage. But certainly there is not the least scientific evidence which would enable anyone to argue that men are born with the political habits of the country in which they are born. In so far as political habits are alike in a nation, the first places to look for an explanation are the nursery, the school, the church, not in that limbo inhabited by Group Minds and National Souls. Until you have thoroughly failed to see tradition being handed on from parents, teachers, priests, and uncles, it is a solecism of the worst order to ascribe political differences to the germ plasm.

It is possible to generalize tentatively and with a decent humility about comparative differences within the same category of education and experience. Yet even this is a tricky enterprise. For almost no two experiences are exactly alike, not even of two children in the same household. The older son never does have the experience of being the younger. And therefore, until we are able to discount the difference in nurture, we must withhold judgment about differences of nature. As well judge the productivity of two soils by comparing their yield before you know which is in Labrador and which is in Iowa, whether they have been cultivated and enriched, exhausted, or allowed to run wild.

# Notes

1. *E.g. cf.* Edmond Locard, *L'Enquête Criminelle et les Méthodes Scientifiques.* A great deal of interesting material has been gathered in late years on the credibility of the witness, which shows, as an able reviewer of Dr. Locard's book says in *The Times* (London) Literary Supplement (August 18, 1921), that credibility varies as to classes of witnesses and classes of events, and also as to type of perception. Thus, perception of touch, odor, and taste have low evidential value. Our hearing is defective and arbitrary when it judges the sources and direction of sound, and in listening to the talk of other people "words which are not heard will be supplied by the witness in all good faith. He will have a theory of the purport of the conversation, and will arrange the sounds he heard to fit it." Even visual perceptions are liable to great error, as in identification, recognition, judgment of distance, estimates of numbers, for example, the size of a crowd. In the untrained observer the sense of time is highly variable. All these original weaknesses are complicated by tricks of memory, and the incessant creative quality of the imagination. *Cf.* also Sherrington, *The Integrative Action of the Nervous System,* pp. 318–327.

   The late Professor Hugo Münsterberg wrote a popular book on this subject called *On the Witness Stand.*

2. Wm. James, *Principles of Psychology,* Vol. I, p. 488.

3. John Dewey, *How We Think,* p. 121.

4. *Op. cit.*, p. 133.

5. A von Gennep, *La formation des légendes*, pp. 158–159. Cited F. van Langenhove, *The Growth of a Legend*, pp. 120–122.

6. Bernard Berenson, *The Central Italian Painters of the Renaissance*, pp. 60, *et seq.*

7. *Cf.* also his comment on *Dante's Visual Images, and his Early Illustrators* in *The Study and Criticism of Italian Art* (First Series), p. 13. "*We* cannot help dressing Virgil as a Roman, and giving him a 'Classical profile' and 'statuesque carriage,' but Dante's visual image of Virgil was probably no less mediaeval, no more based on a critical reconstruction of antiquity, than his entire conception of the Roman poet. Fourteenth Century illustrators make Virgil look like a mediaeval scholar, dressed in cap and gown, and there is no reason why Dante's visual image of him should have been other than this."

8. *The Central Italian Painters*, pp. 66–67.

9. Cited by Mr. Edward Hale Bierstadt, *New Republic*, June 1, 1921, p. 21.

10. Graham Wallas, *Our Social Heritage*, p. 17.

# The Functional Approach to the Study of Attitudes

## DANIEL KATZ

THE STUDY OF OPINION FORMATION and attitude change is basic to an understanding of the public opinion process even though it should not be equated with this process. The public opinion process is one phase of the influencing of collective decisions, and its investigation involves knowledge of channels of communication, of the power structures of a society, of the character of mass media, of the relation between elites, factions and masses, of the role of formal and informal leaders, of the institutionalized access to officials. But the raw material out of which public opinion develops is to be found in the attitudes of individuals, whether they be followers or leaders and whether these attitudes be at the general level of tendencies to conform to legitimate authority or majority opinion or at the specific level of favoring or opposing the particular aspects of the issue under consideration. The nature of the organization of attitudes within the personality and the processes which account for attitude change are thus critical areas for the understanding of the collective product known as public opinion.

## Early Approaches to the Study of Attitude and Opinion

There have been two main streams of thinking with respect to the determination of man's attitudes. The one tradition assumes an irrational model of

Reprinted by permission of the publisher from "The Functional Approach to the Study of Attitudes," by Daniel Katz, *Public Opinion Quarterly* Vol. XXIV (Summer 1960), pp. 163–176.

man: specifically it holds that men have very limited powers of reason and reflection, weak capacity to discriminate, only the most primitive self-insight, and very short memories. Whatever mental capacities people do possess are easily overwhelmed by emotional forces and appeals to self-interest and vanity. The early books on the psychology of advertising, with their emphasis on the doctrine of suggestion, exemplify this approach. One expression of this philosophy is in the propagandist's concern with tricks and traps to manipulate the public. A modern form of it appears in *The Hidden Persuaders,* or the use of subliminal and marginal suggestion, or the devices supposedly employed by "the Madison Avenue boys." Experiments to support this line of thinking started with laboratory demonstrations of the power of hypnotic suggestion and were soon extended to show that people would change their attitudes in an uncritical manner under the influence of the prestige of authority and numbers. For example, individuals would accept or reject the same idea depending upon whether it came from a positive or a negative prestige source.[1]

The second approach is that of the ideologist who invokes a rational model of man. It assumes that the human being has a cerebral cortex, that he seeks understanding, that he consistently attempts to make sense of the world about him, that he possesses discriminating and reasoning powers which will assert themselves over time, and that he is capable of self-criticism and self-insight. It relies heavily upon getting adequate information to people. Our educational system is based upon this rational model. The present emphasis upon the improvement of communication, upon developing more adequate channels of two-way communication, of conferences and institutes, upon bringing people together to interchange ideas are all indications of the belief in the importance of intelligence and comprehension in the formation and change of men's opinions.

Now either school of thought can point to evidence which supports its assumptions, and can make fairly damaging criticisms of its opponent. Solomon Asch and his colleagues, in attacking the irrational model, have called attention to the biased character of the old experiments on prestige suggestion which gave the subject little opportunity to demonstrate critical thinking.[2] And further exploration of subjects in these stupid situations does indicate that they try to make sense of a nonsensical matter as far as possible. Though the same statement is presented by the experimenter to two groups, the first time as coming from a positive source and the second time as coming from a negative source, it is given a different meaning dependent upon the context in which it appears.[3] Thus the experimental subject does his best to give some rational meaning to the problem. On the other hand, a large body of experimental work indicates that there are many limitations in the rational approach in that people see their world in terms of their own needs, remember what they want to remember, and interpret information on the basis of wishful thinking. H. H. Hyman and P. Sheatsley have demonstrated that these experimental results have direct relevance to information campaigns directed at influencing public opinion.[4] These authors assembled facts about such campaigns and showed conclusively that increasing the flow of information to people does not necessarily increase the knowledge absorbed or produce the attitude changes desired.

The major difficulty with these conflicting approaches is their lack of specification of the conditions under which men do act as the theory would predict. For the facts are that people do act at times as if they had been decorticated and at times with intelligence and comprehension. And people themselves do recognize that on occasion they have behaved blindly, impulsively, and thoughtlessly. A second major difficulty is that the rationality-irrationality dimension is not clearly defined. At the extremes it is easy to point to examples, as in the case of the acceptance of stupid suggestions under emotional stress on the one hand, or brilliant problem solving on the other; but this does not provide adequate guidance for the many cases in the middle of the scale where one attempts to discriminate between rationalization and reason.

## Reconciliation of the Conflict in a Functional Approach

The conflict between the rationality and irrationality models was saved from becoming a worthless debate because of the experimentation and research suggested by these models. The findings of this research pointed toward the elements of truth in each approach and gave some indication of the conditions under which each model could make fairly accurate predictions. In general the irrational approach was at its best where the situation imposed heavy restrictions upon search behavior and response alternatives. Where individuals must give quick responses without adequate opportunities to explore the nature of the problem, where there are very few response alternatives available to them, where their own deep emotional needs are aroused, they will in general react much as does the unthinking subject under hypnosis. On the other hand, where the individual can have more adequate commerce with the relevant environmental setting, where he has time to obtain more feedback from his reality testing, and where he has a number of realistic choices, his behavior will reflect the use of his rational faculties.[5] The child will often respond to the directive of the parent not by implicit obedience but by testing out whether or not the parent really meant what he said. . . .

The theory of psychological consonance, or cognitive balance, assumes that man attempts to reduce discrepancies in his beliefs, attitudes, and behavior by appropriate changes in these processes. While the emphasis here is upon consistency or logicality, the theory deals with all dissonances, no matter how produced. Thus they could result from irrational factors of distorted perception and wishful thinking as well as from rational factors of realistic appraisal of a problem and an accurate estimate of its consequences. Moreover, the theory would predict only that the individual will move to reduce dissonance, whether such movement is a good adjustment to the world or leads to the delusional system of the paranoiac. In a sense, then, this theory would avoid the conflict between the old approaches of the rational and the irrational man by not dealing with the specific antecedent causes of behavior or with the particular ways in which the individual solves his problems. . . .

Another point of departure is represented by two groups of workers who have organized their theories around the functions which attitudes perform for the personality. Sarnoff, Katz, and McClintock, in taking this functional approach, have given primary attention to the motivational bases of attitudes and the processes of attitude change.[6] The basic assumption of this group is that both attitude formation and attitude change must be understood in terms of the needs they serve and that, as these motivational processes differ, so too will the conditions and techniques for attitude change. Smith, Bruner, and White have also analyzed the different functions which attitudes perform for the personality. Both groups present essentially the same functions, but Smith, Bruner, and White give more attention to perceptual and cognitive processes and Sarnoff, Katz, and McClintock to the specific conditions of attitude change.

This article will provide a detailed analysis of the four major functions which attitudes can serve, but it is appropriate first to consider the nature of attitudes, their dimensions, and their relations to other psychological structures and processes. . . .

## Nature of Attitudes: Their Dimensions

Attitude is the predisposition of the individual to evaluate some symbol or object or aspect of his world in a favorable or unfavorable manner. Opinion is the verbal expression of an attitude, but attitudes can also be expressed in nonverbal behavior. Attitudes include both the affective, or feeling core of liking or disliking, and the cognitive, or belief, elements which describe the object of the attitude, its characteristics, and its relations to other objects. All attitudes thus include beliefs, but not all beliefs are attitudes. When specific attitudes are organized into a hierarchical structure, they comprise *value systems*. Thus a person may not only hold specific attitudes against deficit spending and unbalanced budgets but may also have a systematic organization of such beliefs and attitudes in the form of a value system of economic conservatism.

The dimensions of attitudes can be stated more precisely if the above distinctions between beliefs and feelings and attitudes and value systems are kept in mind. The *intensity* of an attitude refers to the strength of the *affective* component. In fact, rating scales and even Thurstone scales deal primarily with the intensity of feeling of the individual for or against some social object. The cognitive, or belief, component suggests two additional dimensions, the *specificity* or *generality* of the attitude and the *degree of differentiation* of the beliefs. Differentiation refers to the number of beliefs or cognitive items contained in the attitude, and the general assumption is that the simpler the attitude in cognitive structure the easier it is to change.[7] For simple structures there is no defense in depth, and once a single item of belief has been changed the attitude will change. A rather different dimension of attitude is the *number and strength of its linkages to a related value system*. If an attitude favoring budget balancing by the Federal government is tied in strongly with a value system of economic conservatism, it will be more difficult to change than if it were a fairly isolated attitude of the person. Finally, the relation of the value system to the personality is a consideration of first importance. If an attitude is tied to a value system which is closely related to, or which consists of, the individual's conception of himself, then the appropriate change procedures become more complex. The *centrality* of an attitude refers to its role as part of a value system which is closely related to the individual's self-concept.

An additional aspect of attitudes is not clearly described in most theories, namely, their relation to action or overt behavior. Though behavior related to the attitude has other determinants than the attitude itself, it is also true that some attitudes in themselves have more of what Cartwright calls an action structure than do others.[8] Brewster Smith refers to the dimension as policy orientation[9] and Katz and Stotland speak of it as the action component.[10] For example, while many people have attitudes of approval toward one or the other of the two political parties, these attitudes will differ in their structure with respect to relevant action. One man may be prepared to vote on election day and will know where and when he should vote and will go to the polls no matter what the weather or how great the inconvenience. Another man will only vote if a party worker calls for him in a car. Himmelstrand's work is concerned with all aspects of the relationship between attitude and behavior, but he deals with the action structure of the attitude itself by distinguishing between attitudes where the affect is tied to verbal expression and attitudes where the affect is tied to behavior concerned with more objective referents of the attitude.[11] In the first case an individual derives satisfaction from talking about a problem; in the second case he derives satisfaction from taking some form of concrete action.

Attempts to change attitudes can be directed primarily at the belief component or at the feeling, or affective, component. Rosenberg theorizes that an effective change in one component will result in changes in the other component and presents experimental evidence to confirm this hypothesis.[12] For example, a political candidate will often attempt to win people by making them like him and dislike his opponent, and thus communicate affect rather than ideas. If he is successful, people will not only like him but entertain favorable beliefs about him. Another candidate may deal primarily with ideas and hope that, if he can change people's beliefs about an issue, their feelings will also change.

## Four Functions Which Attitudes Perform for the Individual

The major functions which attitudes perform for the personality can be grouped according to their motivational basis as follows:

*1. The instrumental, adjustive, or utilitarian function* upon which Jeremy Bentham and the utilitarians constructed their model of man. A modern expression of this approach can be found in behavioristic learning theory.

*2. The ego-defensive function* in which the person protects himself from acknowledging the basic truths about himself or the harsh realities in his external world. Freudian psychology and neo-Freudian thinking have been preoccupied with this type of motivation and its outcomes.

*3. The value-expressive function* in which the individual derives satisfactions from expressing attitudes appropriate to his personal values and to his concept of himself. This function is central to doctrines of ego psychology which stress the importance of self-expression, self-development, and self-realization.

*4. The knowledge function* based upon the individual's need to give adequate structure to his universe. The search for meaning, the need to understand, the trend toward better organization of perceptions and beliefs to provide clarity and consistency for the individual, are other descriptions of this function. The development of principles about perceptual and cognitive structure have been the contributions of Gestalt psychology.

Stated simply, the functional approach is the attempt to understand the reasons people hold the attitudes they do. The reasons, however, are at the level of psychological motivations and not of the accidents of external events and circumstances. Unless we know the psychological need which is met by the holding of an attitude we are in a poor position to predict when and how it will change. Moreover, the same attitude expressed toward a political candidate may not perform the same function for all the people who express it. And while many attitudes are predominantly in the service of a single type of motivational process, as described above, other attitudes may serve more than one purpose for the individual. A fuller discussion of how attitudes serve the above four functions is in order.

### 1.  The Adjustment Function

Essentially this function is a recognition of the fact that people strive to maximize the rewards in their external environment and to minimize the penalties. The child develops favorable attitudes toward the objects in his world which are associated with the satisfactions of his needs and unfavorable attitudes toward objects which thwart him or punish him. Attitudes acquired in the service of the adjustment function are either the means for reaching the desired goal or avoiding the undesirable one, or are affective associations based upon experiences in attaining motive satisfactions.[13] The attitudes of the worker favoring a political party which will advance his economic lot are an example of the first type of utilitarian attitude. The pleasant image one has of one's favorite food is an example of the second type of utilitarian attitude.

In general, then, the dynamics of attitude formation with respect to the adjustment function are dependent upon present or past perceptions of the utility of the attitudinal object for the individual. The clarity, consistency, and nearness of rewards and punishments, as they relate to the individual's activities and goals, are important factors in the acquisition of such attitudes. Both attitudes and habits are formed toward specific objects, people, and symbols as they satisfy specific needs. The closer these objects are to actual need satisfaction and the more they are clearly perceived as relevant to need satisfaction, the greater are the probabilities of positive attitude formation. These principles of attitude formation are often observed in the breach rather than the compliance. In industry, management frequently expects to create favorable attitudes toward job performance through programs for making the company more attractive to the worker, such as providing recreational facilities and fringe benefits. Such programs, however, are much more likely to produce favorable attitudes toward the company as a desirable place to work than toward performance on the job. The company benefits and advantages are applied across the board to all employees and are not specifically relevant to increased effort in task performance by the individual worker.

Consistency of reward and punishment also contributes to the clarity of the instrumental object for goal attainment. If a political party bestows recognition and favors on party workers in an unpredictable and inconsistent fashion, it will destroy the favorable evaluation of the importance of working hard for the party among those whose motivation is of the utilitarian sort. But, curiously, while consistency of reward needs to be observed, 100 percent consistency is not as effective as a pattern which is usually consistent but in which there are some lapses. When animal or human subjects are invariably rewarded for a correct performance, they do not retain their learned responses as well as when the reward is sometimes skipped.[14]

## 2.  The Ego-Defensive Function

People not only seek to make the most of their external world and what it offers, but they also expend a great deal of their energy on living with themselves. The mechanisms by which the individual protects his ego from his own unacceptable impulses and from the knowledge of threatening forces from without, and the methods by which he reduces his anxieties created by such problems, are known as mechanisms of ego defense. A more complete account of their origin and nature will be found in Sarnoff's article in this issue.[15] They include the devices by which the individual avoids facing either the inner reality of the kind of person he is, or the outer reality of the dangers the world holds for him. They stem basically from internal conflicts with its resulting insecurities. In one sense the mechanisms of defense are adaptive in temporarily removing the sharp edges of conflict and in saving the individual from complete disaster. In another sense they are not adaptive in that they handicap the individual in his social adjustments and in obtaining the maximum satisfactions available to him from the world in which he lives. The worker who persistently quarrels with his boss and his fellow workers, because he is acting out some of his own internal conflicts, may in this manner relieve himself of some of the emotional tensions which beset him. He is not, however, solving his problem of adjusting to his work situation and thus may deprive himself of advancement or even of steady employment.

Defense mechanisms, Miller and Swanson point out, may be classified into two families on the basis of the more or less primitive nature of the devices employed.[16] The first family, more primitive in nature, are more socially handicapping and consist of denial and complete avoidance. The individual in such cases obliterates through withdrawal and denial the realities which confront him. The exaggerated case of such primitive mechanisms is the fantasy world of the paranoiac. The second type of defense is less handicapping and makes for distortion rather than denial. It includes rationalization, projection, and displacement.

Many of our attitudes have the function of defending our self-image. When we cannot admit to ourselves that we have deep feelings of inferiority we may project those feelings onto some convenient minority group and bolster our egos by attitudes of superiority toward this underprivileged group. The formation of such defensive attitudes differs in essential ways from the formation of attitudes which serve the adjustment function. They proceed from within the person, and the objects and situation to which they are attached are merely convenient outlets for their expression. Not all targets are equally satisfactory for a given defense mechanism, but the point is that the attitude is not created by the target but by the individual's emotional conflicts. And when no convenient target exists the individual will create one. Utilitarian attitudes, on the other hand, are formed with specific reference to the nature of the attitudinal object. They are thus appropriate to the nature of the social world to which they are geared. The high school student who values high grades because he wants to be admitted to a good college has a utilitarian attitude appropriate to the situation to which it is related.

All people employ defense mechanisms, but they differ with respect to the extent that they use them and some of their attitudes may be more defensive in function than others. It follows that the techniques and conditions for attitude change will not be the same for ego-defensive as for utilitarian attitudes.

Moreover, though people are ordinarily unaware of their defense mechanisms, especially at the time of employing them, they differ with respect to the amount of insight they may show at some later time about their use of defenses. In some cases they recognize that they have been protecting their egos without knowing the reason why. In other cases they may not even be aware of the devices they have been using to delude themselves.

## 3.  The Value-Expressive Function

While many attitudes have the function of preventing the individual from revealing to himself and others his true nature, other attitudes have the function of giving positive expression to his central values and to the type of person he conceives himself to be. A man may consider himself to be an enlightened conservative or an internationalist or a liberal, and will hold attitudes which are the appropriate indication of his central values. Thus we need to take account of the fact that not all behavior has the negative function of reducing the tensions of biological drives or of internal conflicts. Satisfactions also accrue to the person from the expression of attitudes which reflect his cherished beliefs and his self-image. The reward to the person in these instances is not so much a matter of gaining social recognition or monetary rewards as of establishing his self-identity and confirming his notion of the sort of person he sees himself to be. The gratifications obtained from value expression may go beyond the confirmation of self-identity. Just as we find satisfaction in the exercise of our talents and abilities, so we find reward in the expression of any attribute associated with our egos.

Value-expressive attitudes not only give clarity to the self-image but also mold that self-image closer to the heart's desire. The teenager who by dress and speech establishes his identity as similar to his own peer group may appear to the outsider a weakling and a craven conformer. To himself he is asserting his independence of the adult world to which he had rendered childlike subservience and conformity all his life. Very early in the development of the personality the need for clarity of self-image is important—the need to know "who I am." Later it may be even more important to know that in some measure I am the type of person I want to be. Even as adults, however, the clarity and stability of the self-image is of primary significance. Just as the kind, considerate person will cover over his acts of selfishness, so too will the ruthless individualist become confused and embarrassed by his acts of sympathetic compassion. One reason it is difficult to change the character of the adult is that he is not comfortable with the new "me."

Group support for such personality change is almost a necessity, as in Alcoholics Anonymous, so that the individual is aware of approval of his new self by people who are like him.

The socialization process during the formative years sets the basic outlines for the individual's self-concept. Parents constantly hold up before the child the model of the good character they want him to be. A good boy eats his spinach, does not hit girls, etc. The candy and the stick are less in evidence in training the child than the constant appeal to his notion of his own character. It is small wonder, then, that children reflect the acceptance of this model by inquiring about the characters of the actors in every drama, whether it be a television play, a political contest, or a war, wanting to know who are the "good guys" and who are the "bad guys." Even as adults we persist in labeling others in the terms of such character images. Joe McCarthy and his cause collapsed in fantastic fashion when the telecast of the Army hearings showed him in the role of the villain attacking the gentle, good man represented by Joseph Welch. . . .

## 4. The Knowledge Function

Individuals not only acquire beliefs in the interest of satisfying various specific needs, they also seek knowledge to give meaning to what would otherwise be an unorganized chaotic universe. People need standards or frames of reference for understanding their world, and attitudes help to supply such standards. The problem of understanding, as John Dewey made clear years ago, is one "of introducing (1) definiteness and distinction and (2) consistency and stability of meaning into what is otherwise vague and wavering."[17] The definiteness and stability are provided in good measure by the norms of our culture, which give the otherwise perplexed individual ready-made attitudes for comprehending his universe. Walter Lippmann's classical contribution to the study of opinions and attitudes was his description of stereotypes and the way they provided order and clarity for a bewildering set of complexities.[18] The most interesting finding in Herzog's familiar study of the gratifications obtained by housewives in listening to daytime serials was the unsuspected role of information and advice.[19] The stories were liked "because they explained things to the inarticulate listener."

The need to know does not of course imply that people are driven by a thirst for universal knowledge. The American public's appalling lack of practical information has been documented many times. In 1956, for example, only 13 percent of the people in Detroit could correctly name the two United States Senators from the state of Michigan and only 18 percent knew the name of their own Congressman.[20] People are not avid seekers after knowledge as judged by what the educator or social reformer would desire. But they do want to understand the events which impinge directly on their own life.

Moreover, many of the attitudes they have already acquired give them sufficient basis for interpreting much of what they perceive to be important for them. Our already existing stereotypes, in Lippmann's language, "are an ordered, more or less consistent picture of the world, to which our habits, our tastes, our capacities, our comforts and our hopes have adjusted themselves. They may not be a complete picture of the world, but they are a picture of a possible world to which we are adapted."[21] It follows that new information will not modify old attitudes unless there is some inadequacy or incompleteness or inconsistency in the existing attitudinal structure as it relates to the perceptions of new situations.

# Notes

1. Muzafer Sherif, *The Psychology of Social Norms*, New York, Harper, 1936.
2. Solomon E. Asch, *Social Psychology*, New York, Prentice-Hall, 1952.
3. *Ibid.*, pp. 426–427. The following statement was attributed to its rightful author, John Adams, for some subjects and to Karl Marx for others: "those who hold and those who are without property have ever formed distinct interests in society." When the statement was attributed to Marx, this type of comment appeared: "Marx is stressing the need for a redistribution of wealth." When it was attributed to Adams, this comment appeared: "This social division is innate in mankind."
4. Herbert H. Hyman and Paul B. Sheatsley, "Some Reasons Why Information Campaigns Fail," *Public Opinion Quarterly*, Vol. 11, 1947, pp. 413–423.
5. William A. Scott points out that in the area of international relations the incompleteness and remoteness of the information and the lack of pressures on the individual to defend his views result in inconsistencies. Inconsistent elements with respect to a system of international beliefs may, however, be consistent with the larger system of the personality. "Rationality and Non-rationality of International Attitudes," *Journal of Conflict Resolution*, Vol. 2, 1958, pp. 9–16.
6. Irving Sarnoff and Daniel Katz, "The Motivational Bases of Attitude Change," *Journal of Abnormal and Social Psychology*, Vol. 49, 1954, pp. 115–124.
7. David Krech and Richard S. Crutchfield, *Theory and Problems of Social Psychology*, New York, McGraw-Hill, 1948, pp. 160–163.
8. Dorwin Cartwright, "Some Principles of Mass Persuasion," *Human Relations*, Vol. 2, 1949, pp. 253–267.
9. M. Brewster Smith, "The Personal Setting of Public Opinions: A Study of Attitudes Toward Russia," *Public Opinion Quarterly*, Vol. 11, 1947, pp. 507–523.
10. Daniel Katz and Ezra Stotland, "A Preliminary Statement to a Theory of Attitude Structure and Change," in Sigmund Koch, editor, *Psychological Study of a Science*, Vol. 3, New York, McGraw-Hill, 1959, pp. 423–471.
11. Ulf Himmelstrand, "Verbal Attitudes and Behavior: A Paradigm for the study of Message Transmission and Transformation," *Public Opinion Quarterly*, Vol. XXIV (1960), pp. 224–250.

12. Milton J. Rosenberg, "A Structural Theory of Attitude Dynamics," *Public Opinion Quarterly,* Vol. XXIV (1960), pp. 319–340.

13. Katz and Stotland, *op. cit.,* pp. 434–443.

14. William O. Jenkins and Julian C. Stanley, "Partial Reinforcement: Review and Critique," *Psychological Bulletin,* Vol. 47, 1950, pp. 193–214.

15. Irving Sarnoff, "Psychoanalytic Theory and Social Attitudes," *Public Opinion Quarterly,* Vol. XXIV (1960), pp. 251–279.

16. Daniel R. Miller and Guy E. Swanson, *Inner Conflict and Defense,* New York, Holt, 1960, pp. 194–288.

17. John Dewey, *How We Think,* New York, Macmillan, 1910.

18. Walter Lippmann, *Public Opinion,* New York, Macmillan, 1922.

19. Herta Herzog, "What Do We Really Know about Daytime Serial Listeners?" in Paul F. Lazarsfeld and Frank N. Stanton, editors, *Radio Research 1942–1943,* New York, Duell, Sloan & Pearce, 1944, pp. 3–33.

20. From a study of the impact of party organization on political behavior in the Detroit area, by Daniel Katz and Samuel Eldersveld, in manuscript.

21. Lippmann, *op. cit.,* p. 95.

# 2

# Formation of Public Opinion

The process by which citizens acquire their political attitudes and opinions is enormously complex, involving a continuous interplay among institutional sources of information and persuasion, interpersonal contacts, and ideological and personality factors. The absence of a widely accepted model of how public opinion is formed illustrates the difficulty of achieving a theoretical consensus about the many topics on which opinions are held and on which mass media provide information. As we noted earlier, what has developed in place of a single paradigm is a variety of approaches, each of which directs its scholarly adherents to different aspects of the process. One area of recent widespread agreement, reflected in the selections to follow, is the proposition that mass media exert a major influence on public opinion formation.

A major concern voiced by Kelman is that the survey methods used to guage public attitudes fail to yield sufficient cognitive and motivational information about respondents from which to draw meaningful inferences about how individuals reason in forming opinions about politics. Using interviewing techniques, he develops a typology of three forms of "social influence" to explain the individual's involvement in the process of public opinion formation: *compliance, identification,* and *internalization.*

Like the classical theorists Bryce and Lowell (in Section 1), Tocqueville is more interested in the institutional bases of public opinion formation than in how it crystallizes in the psychologies of individuals. In these passages taken from his classic *Democracy in America,* Tocqueville discusses the reciprocal and symbiotic relationship between newspapers and "public associations" in nineteenth-century America. We must bear in mind that two features of modern social life often taken for granted now, namely, democratic politics and an integrated national society, were new to the world in Tocqueville's day and very much in the process of formation. Quite understandably, then, a certain amount of puzzlement over these developments often shows through his remarkable insights. Note later that Tocqueville is at one with Bagdikian (Section 4) in explaining the profusion of newspapers in the United States as largely a result of the country's *political* decentralization.

The process by which children acquire the knowledge and competence to participate in the civic life of their society is called political socialization— an area of considerable interest to public opinion researchers. Students of political socialization have typically focused their efforts on determining the relative importance of the family, school, and peer group as agencies in the process. Chafee et al. try to assess the mass media's contribution to the youngster's acquisition of a political identity. Sampling high school and junior high school students, they found that students who used the media more were generally better informed but that the media had no clear impact on their attitudes or political behavior.

Mueller traces the sources of support and opposition to the Korean and Vietnam wars, carefully distinguishing between popular opinion as a whole and the activities of smaller partisan groups. Differences in the magnitude of opposition to the two wars were not so great as is often believed, he finds. The level of popular disapproval of the Vietnam War may be exaggerated because organized opposition was more vocal, a development that resulted from the efforts of the "intellectual Left" to oppose the Vietnam War more forcefully than they had the Korean War.

Mueller also notes that people are seldom willing to pay "high information costs" to decide their opinion on an issue but usually are willing to decide on the basis of information from institutions they *trust.* We may wish to ask what implications this has for a period such as the 1970s, when polls showed that confidence in nearly *all* of society's major institutions was in decline.

Finally, in his impressive review of the twenty-year period from 1956 to 1976, M. Robinson assesses television's relationship to the political process. He discusses the major political events of this period—civil rights, the Kennedy assassination, Vietnam, Watergate—and describes television's "deromanticizing" influence on them all. He concludes that while entertainment programs provided models for more liberal life-styles, television's news coverage encouraged the growth of politically conservative views and opinions.

# Processes of Opinion Change

## HERBERT C. KELMAN

A PERSISTENT CONCERN in the analysis of public opinion data is the "meaning" that one can ascribe to the observed distributions and trends—and to the positions taken by particular individuals and segments of the population. Clearly, to understand what opinion data mean we have to know considerably more than the direction of an individual's responses or the distribution of responses in the population. We need information that will allow us to make some inferences about the characteristics of the observed opinions—their intensity, their salience, the level of commitment that they imply. We need information about the motivational bases of these opinions—about the functions that they fulfill for the individual and the motivational systems in which they are embedded.[1] We need information about the cognitive links of the opinions—the amount and the nature of information that supports them, the specific expectations and evaluations that surround them.

The need for more detailed information becomes even more apparent when we attempt to use opinion data for the prediction of subsequent behavior. What is the likelihood that the opinions observed in a particular survey will be translated into some form of concrete action? What is the nature of the actions that people who hold a particular opinion are likely to take, and how are they likely to react to various events? How likely are these opinions to persist over time and to generalize to related issues? What are the conditions under which one might expect these opinions to be abandoned and changed? Such predictions can be made only to the extent to which we are informed about the crucial dimensions of the opinions in question, about the motivations that underlie them, and about the cognitive contexts in which they are held.

Reprinted by permission of the publisher from "Processes of Opinion Change," by Herbert Kelman, *Public Opinion Quarterly*, Vol. XXV (Spring 1961), pp. 57–78.

## Inferring the Meaning of Opinions

In a certain sense, the need for more detailed information about opinions can (and must) be met by improvements and refinements in the methodology of opinion assessment. A great deal of progress in this direction has already been made in recent years. Thus, many widely accepted features of interviewing technique are specifically designed to elicit information on which valid inferences about the meaning of opinions can be based: the creation of a relaxed, nonjudgmental atmosphere; the emphasis on open-ended questions; the progressive funneling from general to specific questions; the use of probes, of indirect questions, and of interlocking questions; and so on. These procedures facilitate inferences (1) by maximizing the likelihood that the respondent will give rich and full information and thus reveal the motivational and cognitive structure underlying the expressed opinions, and (2) by minimizing the likelihood that the respondent will consciously or unconsciously distort his "private" opinions when expressing them to the interviewer. . . .

There is no question about the importance of these methodological advances, but in and of themselves they do not solve the problem of inference. They increase the investigator's ability to obtain rich and relatively undistorted information on which he can then base valid inferences. But, no matter how refined the techniques, they do not provide direct information about the meaning of the opinions and do not permit automatic predictions to subsequent behavior: the investigator still has to make inferences from the data.

To make such inferences, the student of public opinion needs a theoretical framework which accounts for the adoption and expression of particular opinions on the part of individuals and groups. Such a framework can serve as a guide in the collection of data: it can provide a systematic basis for deciding what information is relevant and what questions should be asked in order to permit the drawing of inferences. Similarly, it can serve as a guide for interpreting data and deriving implications from them.

The need for such a framework is particularly apparent when one attempts to make predictions about subsequent behavior on the basis of opinion data. For example, in a relaxed interview situation a particular respondent may express himself favorably toward socialized medicine. What are the chances that he will take the same position in a variety of other situations? To answer this, we would need a theoretical scheme for the analysis of interaction situations, in terms of which we could make some inferences about the structure and meaning of this particular interview situation as compared to various other situations in which the issue of socialized medicine might arise. . . .

The model that I shall present here emerged out of the study of social influence and behavior change. It is, essentially, an attempt to conceptualize the processes of opinion formation and opinion change. It starts with the assumption that opinions adopted under different conditions of social influence, and based on different motivations, will differ in terms of their qualitative characteristics and their subsequent histories. Thus, if we know something about the determinants and motivational bases of particular opinions, we should be able to make predictions about the conditions under which they are likely to be expressed, the conditions under which they are likely to change, and other behavioral consequences to which they are likely to lead. Ideally, such a model can be useful in the analysis of public opinion by suggesting relevant variables in terms of which opinion data can be examined and predictions can be formulated.

## The Study of Social Influence

Social influence has been a central area of concern for experimental social psychology almost since its beginnings. Three general research traditions in this area can be distinguished: (1) the study of social influences on judgments, stemming from the earlier work on prestige suggestion;[2] (2) the study of social influences arising from small-group interaction;[3] and (3) the study of social influences arising from persuasive communications.[4] In recent years, there has been a considerable convergence between these three traditions, going hand in hand with an increased interest in developing general principles of social influence and socially induced behavior change.

One result of these developments has been that many investigators found it necessary to make qualitative distinctions between different types of influence. In some cases, these distinctions arose primarily out of the observation that social influence may have qualitatively different effects, that it may produce different kinds of change. For example, under some conditions it may result in mere public conformity—in superficial changes on a verbal or overt level without accompanying changes in belief; in other situations it may result in private acceptance—in a change that is more general, more durable, more integrated with the person's own values.[5] Other investigators found it necessary to make distinctions because they observed that influence may occur for different reasons, that it may arise out of different motivations and orientations. For example, under some conditions influence may be primarily informational—the subject may conform to the influencing person or group because he views him as a source of valid information; in other situations influence may be primarily normative—the subject may conform in order to meet the positive expectations of the influencing person or group.[6]

My own work can be viewed in the general context that I have outlined here. I started out with the distinction between public conformity and private acceptance, and tried to establish some of the distinct determinants of each. I became dissatisfied with this dichotomy as I began to look at important examples of social influence that could not be encompassed by it. I was especially impressed with the accounts of ideological conversion of the "true believer" variety, and with the recent accounts of "brainwashing," particularly the Chinese Communist methods of "thought reform."[7] It is apparent that these experiences do not simply involve public conformity, but that indeed they produce a change in underlying beliefs. But it is equally apparent that they do not produce what we would usually consider private acceptance—changes that are in some sense integrated with the person's own value system and that have become independent of the external source. Rather, they seem to produce new beliefs that are isolated from the rest of the person's values and that are highly dependent on external support.

These considerations eventually led me to distinguish three processes of social influence, each characterized by a distinct set of antecedent and a distinct set of consequent conditions. I have called these processes *compliance, identification,* and *internalization.*[8]

## Three Processes of Social Influence

*Compliance* can be said to occur when an individual accepts influence from another person or from a group because he hopes to achieve a favorable reaction from the other. He may be interested in attaining certain specific rewards or in avoiding certain specific punishments that the influencing agent controls. For example, an individual may make a special effort to express only "correct" opinions in order to gain admission into a particular group or social set, or in order to avoid being fired from his government job. Or, the individual may be concerned with gaining approval or avoiding disapproval from the influencing agent in a more general way. . . . What the individual learns, essentially, is to say or do the expected thing in special situations, regardless of what his private beliefs may be. Opinions adopted through compliance should be expressed only when the person's behavior is observable by the influencing agent.

*Identification* can be said to occur when an individual adopts behavior derived from another person or a group because this behavior is associated with a satisfying self-defining relationship to this person or group. By a self-defining relationship I mean a role relationship that forms a part of the person's self-image. Accepting influence through identification, then, is a way of establishing or maintaining the desired relationship to the other, and the self-definition that is anchored in this relationship. . . .

The behavior of the brainwashed prisoner in Communist China provides one example of this type of identification. By adopting the attitudes and beliefs of the prison authorities—including *their* evaluation of *him*—he attempts to regain his identity, which has been subjected to severe threats. But this kind of identification does not occur only in such severe crisis situations. It can also be observed, for example, in the context of socialization of children, where the taking over of parental attitudes and actions is a normal, and probably essential, part of personality development. The more or less conscious efforts involved when an individual learns to play a desired occupational role and imitates an appropriate role model would also exemplify this process. Here, of course, the individual is much more selective in the attitudes and actions he takes over from the other person. What is at stake is not his basic sense of identity or the stability of his self-concept, but rather his more limited "professional identity."

The self-defining relationship that an individual tries to establish or maintain through identification may also take the form of a reciprocal role relationship—that is, of a relationship in which the roles of the two parties are defined with reference to one another. An individual may be involved in a reciprocal relationship with another specific individual, as in a friendship relationship between two people. Or he may enact a social role which is defined with reference to another (reciprocal) role, as in the relationship between patient and doctor. A reciprocal-role relationship can be maintained only if the participants have mutually shared expectations of one another's behavior. Thus, if an individual finds a particular relationship satisfying, he will tend to behave in such a way as to meet the expectations of the other. . . .

Identification may also serve to maintain an individual's relationship to a group in which his self-definition is anchored. Such a relationship may have elements of classical identification as well as of reciprocal roles: to maintain his self-definition as a group member an individual, typically, has to model his behavior along particular lines and has to meet the expectations of his fellow members. An example of identification with a group would be the member of the Communist Party who derives strength and a sense of identity from his self-definition as part of the vanguard of the proletarian revolution and as an agent of historical destiny. A similar process, but at a low degree of intensity, is probably involved in many of the conventions that people acquire as part of their socialization into a particular group.

Identification is similar to compliance in that the individual does not adopt the induced behavior because its content per se is intrinsically satisfying. Identification differs from compliance, however, in that the individual actually believes the opinions and actions that he adopts. The behavior is accepted both publicly and privately, and its manifestation does not depend on observability by the influencing agent. It does depend, however, on the role that an individual takes at any given moment in time. Only when the appropriate role is activated—only when the individual is acting within the relationship upon which the identification is based—will the induced opinions be expressed. The individual is not primarily concerned with pleasing the other, with giving him what he wants (as in compliance), but he is concerned with meeting the other's expectations for his own role performance. Thus, opinions adopted through identification do remain tied to the external source and dependent on social support. They are not integrated with the individual's value system, but rather tend to be isolated from the rest of his values—to remain encapsulated.

Finally, *internalization* can be said to occur when an individual accepts influence because the induced behavior is congruent with his value system. It is the content of the induced behavior that is intrinsically rewarding here. The individual adopts it because he finds it useful for the solution of a problem, or because it is congenial to his own orientation, or because it is demanded by his own values—in short, because he perceives it as inherently conducive to the maximization of his values. The characteristics of the influencing agent do play an important role in internalization, but the crucial dimension here—as we shall see below—is the agent's credibility, that is, his relation to the content.

The most obvious examples of internalization are those that involve the evaluation and acceptance of induced behavior on rational grounds. A person may adopt the recommendations of an expert, for example, because he finds them relevant to his own problems and congruent with his own values. Typically, when internalization is involved, he will not accept these recommendations *in toto* but modify them to some degree so that they will fit his own unique situation. . . .

Internalization, however, does not necessarily involve the adoption of induced behavior on rational grounds. I would not want to equate internalization with rationality, even though the description of the process has decidedly rationalist overtones. For example, I would characterize as internalization the adoption of beliefs because of their congruence with a value system that is basically *irrational*. Thus, an authoritarian individual may adopt certain racist attitudes because they fit into his paranoid, irrational view of the world. Presumably, what is involved here is internalization, since it is the content of the induced behavior and its relation to the person's value system that is satisfying. Similarly, it should be noted that congruence with a person's value system does not necessarily imply logical consistency. Behavior would be congruent if, in some way or other, it fit into the person's value system, if it seemed to belong there and be demanded by it.

It follows from this conception that behavior adopted through internalization is in some way—rational or otherwise—integrated with the individual's existing values. It becomes part of a personal system, as distinguished from a system of social-role expectations. Such behavior gradually becomes independent of the external source. Its manifestation depends neither on observability by the influencing agent nor on the activation of the relevant role, but on the extent to which the underlying values have been made relevant by the issues under consideration. This does not mean that the individual will invariably express internalized opinions, regardless of the social situation. In any specific situation, he has to choose among competing values in the face of a variety of situational requirements. It does mean, however, that these opinions will at least enter into competition with other alternatives whenever they are relevant in content.

It should be stressed that the three processes are not mutually exclusive.

While they have been defined in terms of pure cases, they do not generally occur in pure form in real-life situations. The examples that have been given are, at best, situations in which a particular process predominates and determines the central features of the interaction.

## Antecedents and Consequents of the Three Processes

For each of the three processes, a distinct set of antecedents and a distinct set of consequents have been proposed. These are summarized in the table below. First, with respect to the antecedents of the three processes, it should be noted that no systematic quantitative differences between them are hypothesized. The probability of each process is presented as a function of the same three determinants: the importance of the induction for the individual's goal achievement, the power of the influencing agent, and the prepotency of the induced response. For each process, the magnitude of these determinants may vary over the entire range: each may be based on an induction with varying degrees of importance, on an influencing agent with varying degrees of power, and so on. The processes differ only in terms of the *qualitative* form that these determinants take. They differ, as can be seen in the table (p. 60), in terms of the *basis* for the importance of the induction, the *source* of the influencing agent's power, and the *manner* of achieving prepotency of the induced response.

1. The processes can be distinguished in terms of the basis for the importance of the induction, that is, in terms of the nature of the motivational system that is activated in the influence situation. What is it about the influence situation that makes it important, that makes it relevant to the individual's goals? What are the primary concerns that the individual brings to the situation or that are aroused by it? The differences between the three processes in this respect are implicit in the descriptions of the processes given above: (a) To the extent that the individual is concerned—for whatever reason—with the *social effect* of his behavior, influence will tend to take the form of compliance. (b) To the extent that he is concerned with the *social anchorage* of his behavior, influence will tend to take the form of identification. (c) To the extent that he is concerned with the *value congruence* of his behavior (rational or otherwise), influence will tend to take the form of internalization.

2. A difference between the three processes in terms of the source of the influencing agent's power is hypothesized. (a) To the extent that the agent's power is based on his *means control,* influence will tend to take the form of compliance. An agent possesses means control if he is in a position to supply or withhold means needed by the individual for the achievement of his goals. The perception of means control may depend on the agent's *actual* control over specific rewards and punishments, or on his *potential*

## Summary of the Distinctions between the Three Processes

| | COMPLIANCE | IDENTIFICATION | INTERNALIZATION |
|---|---|---|---|
| **Antecedents** | | | |
| 1. Basis for the *importance of the induction* | Concern with social effect of behavior | Concern with social anchorage of behavior | Concern with value congruence of behavior |
| 2. Source of *power of the influencing agent* | Means control | Attractiveness | Credibility |
| 3. Manner of achieving *prepotency of the induced response* | Limitation of choice behavior | Delineation of role requirements | Reorganization of means-ends framework |
| **Consequents:** | | | |
| 1. Conditions of performance of induced response | Surveillance by influencing agent | Salience of relationship to agent | Relevance of values to issue |
| 2. Conditions of change and extinction of induced response | Changed perception of conditions for social rewards | Changed perception of conditions for satisfying self-defining relationships | Changed perception of conditions for value maximization |
| 3. Type of behavior system in which induced response is embedded | External demands of a specific setting | Expectations defining a specific role | Person's value system |

control, which would be related to his position in the social structure (his status, authority, or general prestige). (b) To the extent that the agent's power is based on his *attractiveness*, influence will tend to take the form of identification. An agent is attractive if he occupies a role which the individual himself desires[9] or if he occupies a role reciprocal to one the individual wants to establish or maintain. . . . (c) To the extent that the agent's power is based on his *credibility*, influence will tend to take the form of internalization. An agent possesses credibility if his statements are considered truthful and valid, and hence worthy of serious consideration. . . .

3. It is proposed that the three processes differ in terms of the way in which prepotency is achieved. (a) To the extent that the induced response becomes prepotent—that is, becomes a "distinguished path" relative to alternative response possibilities—because the individual's choice behavior is limited, influence will tend to take the form of compliance. This may happen if the individual is pressured into the induced response, or if alternative responses are blocked. The induced response thus becomes prepotent because it is, essentially, the only response permitted: the individual sees himself as having no choice and as being restricted to this particular alternative. (b) To the extent that the induced response becomes prepotent because the requirements of a particular role are delineated, influence will tend to take the form of identification. This may happen if the situation is defined in terms of a particular role relationship and the demands of that role are more or less clearly specified. . . . (c) Finally, to the extent that the induced response becomes prepotent because there has been a reorganization in the individual's conception of means-ends relationships, influence will tend to take the form of internalization. This may happen if the implications of the induced response for certain important values—implications of which the individual had been unaware heretofore—are brought out, or if the advantages of the induced response as a path to the individual's goals, compared to the various alternatives that are available, are made apparent. . . .

Depending, then, on the nature of these three antecedents, the influence process will take the form of compliance, identification, or internalization. Each of these corresponds to a characteristic pattern of internal responses— thoughts and feelings—in which the individual engages as he accepts influence. The resulting changes will, in turn, be different for the three processes, as indicated in the second half of the table. Here, again, it is assumed that there are no systematic quantitative differences between the processes, but rather qualitative variations in the subsequent histories of behavior adopted through each process.

1. It is proposed that the processes differ in terms of the subsequent conditions under which the induced response will be performed or expressed. (a) When an individual adopts an induced response through compliance, he tends to perform it only under conditions of *surveillance* by the influencing agent. These conditions are met if the agent is physically present, or if he

is likely to find out about the individual's actions. (b) When an individual adopts an induced response through identification, he tends to perform it only under conditions of *salience* of his relationship to the agent. That is, the occurrence of the behavior will depend on the extent to which the person's relationship to the agent has been engaged in the situation. Somehow this relationship has to be brought into focus and the individual has to be acting within the particular role that is involved in the identification. This does not necessarily mean, however, that he is consciously aware of the relationship; the role can be activated without such awareness. (c) When an individual adopts an induced response through internalization, he tends to perform it under conditions of *relevance of the values* that were initially involved in the influence situation. The behavior will tend to occur whenever these values are activated by the issues under consideration in a given situation, quite regardless of surveillance or salience of the influencing agent. This does not mean, of course, that the behavior will occur every time it becomes relevant. It may be outcompeted by other responses in certain situations. The probability of occurrence with a given degree of issue relevance will depend on the strength of the internalized behavior.

2. It is hypothesized that responses adopted through the three processes will differ in terms of the conditions under which they will subsequently be abandoned or changed. (a) A response adopted through compliance will be abandoned if it is no longer perceived as the best path toward the attainment of social rewards. (b) A response adopted through identification will be abandoned if it is no longer perceived as the best path toward the maintenance or establishment of satisfying self-defining relationships. (c) A response adopted through internalization will be abandoned if it is no longer perceived as the best path toward the maximization of the individual's values.

3. Finally, it is hypothesized that responses adopted through the three processes will differ from each other along certain qualitative dimensions. These can best be summarized, perhaps, by referring to the type of behavior system in which the induced response is embedded. (a) Behavior adopted through compliance is part of a system of external demands that characterize a specific setting. In other words, it is part of the rules of conduct that an individual learns in order to get along in a particular situation or series of situations. The behavior tends to be related to the person's values only in an instrumental rather than an intrinsic way. As long as opinions, for example, remain at that level, the individual will tend to regard them as not really representative of his true beliefs. (b) Behavior adopted through identification is part of a system of expectations defining a particular role—whether this is the role of the other which he is taking over, or a role reciprocal to the other's. This behavior will be regarded by the person as representing himself, and may in fact form an important aspect of himself. It will tend to be isolated, however, from the rest of the person's values—to have little interplay with them. In extreme cases, the system in which the induced response is embedded may be encapsulated and function almost like a foreign body within the person. The induced responses here will be relatively inflexible and stereo-

typed. (c) Behavior adopted through internalization is part of an internal system. It is fitted into the person's basic framework of values and is congruent with it. This does not imply complete consistency: the degree of consistency can vary for different individuals and different areas of behavior. It does mean, however, that there is some interplay between the new beliefs and the rest of the person's values. The new behavior can serve to modify existing beliefs and can in turn be modified by them. As a result of this interaction, behavior adopted through internalization will tend to be relatively idiosyncratic, flexible, complex, and differentiated.

## Research Based on the Model

The model itself and its possible implications may be seen more clearly if I present a brief summary of the research in which it was used. This research has moved in three general directions: experimental tests of the relationships proposed by the model, application of the model to the study of personality factors in social influence, and application of the model to the analysis of a natural influence situation.

### Experimental Tests of the Proposed Distinctions between the Three Processes

. . . the experimental situation involved the use of tape-recorded communications. Three versions of the communication were used, each presented to a different group of college students. In each of the communications a novel program of science education was described and the rationale behind it was outlined. The basic message was identical in all cases, but the communications differed in terms of certain additional information that was included in order to produce different orientations. In one communication (*role-orientation* condition) the additional information was designed to spell out the implications of the induced opinions for the subject's relationship to certain important reference groups. Positive reference groups were associated with acceptance of the message, and—in a rather dramatic way—negative reference groups were associated with opposition to it. The intention here was to create two of the postulated antecedents for *identification:* a concern with the social anchorage of one's opinions, and a delineation of the requirements for maintaining the desired relationship to one's reference groups (see the table). In the second communication (*value-orientation* condition) the additional information was designed to spell out the implications of the induced opinions for an important value—personal responsibility for the consequences of one's actions. The communication argued that acceptance of the message would tend to maximize this value. The intention here was to create two of the postulated antecedents of *internalization:* a concern with the value congruence of one's opinions, and a reorganization of one's conception of means-ends relationships. The third communication was introduced for purposes of comparison and contained only the basic message.

On the basis of the theoretical model it was predicted that the nature of the attitude changes produced by the two experimental communications would differ. Role orientation would presumably produce the consequences hypothesized for identification, while value orientation would produce the consequences hypothesized for internalization. A number of measurement situations were devised to test these predictions: (1) In each group, half the subjects completed attitude questionnaires immediately after the communication, under conditions of salience, and half completed them a few weeks later, under conditions of nonsalience. As predicted, there was a significant difference between these two conditions of measurement for the role-orientation group but not for the value-orientation group. (2) The generalization of the induced attitudes to other issues involving the same values, and to other situations involving similar action alternatives, was measured. The prediction that the value-orientation group would show more generalization than the role-orientation group on the value dimension tended to be confirmed. The prediction that the reverse would be true for generalization along the action dimension was not upheld. (3) Flexibility of the induced attitudes was assessed by asking subjects to describe their doubts and qualifications. As predicted, the value-orientation group scored significantly higher on this index. (4) Complexity of the induced attitudes was assessed some weeks after the communication by asking subjects to list the things they would want to take into account in developing a new science education program. The total number of items listed was greater for the role-orientation group, but the number of items showing an awareness of relevant issues (as rated by a naïve judge) was clearly greater in the value-orientation group. (5) Half the subjects in each group were exposed to a countercommunication presenting a new consensus, the other half to a countercommunication presenting new arguments. It was predicted that the role-orientation group would be relatively more affected by the first type of countercommunication, and the value-orientation group by the second. The predicted pattern emerged, though it fell short of statistical significance.

The results of this study are not entirely unambiguous. They are sufficiently strong, however, to suggest that it should be possible to develop a number of criteria by which identification-based and internalized attitudes can be distinguished from one another. On the basis of such distinctions, one can then make certain inferences about the meaning of these attitudes and further predictions about their future course. . . .

### The Application of the Model to the Analysis of a Natural Influence Situation

We are currently engaged in an extensive study of Scandinavian students who have spent a year of study or work in the United States.[10] We are interested in the effects of their stay here on their self-images in three areas: nationality, profession, and interpersonal relations. Our emphasis is on learning about the processes by which changes in the self-image come about or, conversely, the processes by which the person's existing image maintains itself in the face of new experiences. Our subjects were questioned at the beginning of their stay in the United States and at the end of their stay, and once again a year after their return home.

This study was not designed as a direct test of certain specific hypotheses about the three processes of influence. In this kind of rich field situation it seemed more sensible to allow the data to point the way and to be open to different kinds of conceptualizations demanded by the nature of the material. The model of influence did, however, enter into the formulation of the problem and the development of the schedules and is now entering into the analysis of the data.

In a preliminary analysis of some of our intensive case material, for example, we found it useful to differentiate four patterns of reaction to the American experience which may affect various aspects of the self-image: (1) An individual may change his self-image by a reorganization of its internal structure; here we would speak of a change by means of the process of *internalization*. (2) His self-image may be changed by a reshaping of the social relationships in which this image is anchored; here we would speak of a change by means of *identification*. (3) The individual may focus on the internal structure of the self-image but maintain it essentially in its original form; here we would speak of the process of *confirmation*. Finally, (4) he may maintain his self-image through a focus on its original social anchorage; here maintenance by the process of *resistance* would be involved. We have related these four patterns to a number of variables in a very tentative way, but the analysis will have to progress considerably farther before we can assess the usefulness of this scheme. It is my hope that this kind of analysis will give us a better understanding of the attitudes and images that a visitor takes away from his visit to a foreign country and will allow us to make some predictions about the subsequent history of these attitudes and images. Some of these predictions we will be able to check out on the basis of our post-return data.

# Conclusion

There is enough evidence to suggest that the distinction between compliance, identification, and internalization is valid, even though it has certainly not been established in all its details. The specification of distinct antecedents and consequents for each of the processes has generated a number of hypotheses which have met the experimental test. It seems reasonable to conclude, therefore, that this model may be useful in the analysis of various influence situations and the resulting opinion changes. It should be particularly germane whenever one is concerned with the quality and durability of changes and with the motivational conditions that produced them.

I have also attempted to show the implications of this model for the analysis of public opinion. By tying together certain antecedents of influence with certain of its consequents, it enables us to infer the motivations underlying a particular opinion from a knowledge of its manifestations, and to predict the future course of an opinion from a knowledge of the conditions under which it was formed. Needless to say, the usefulness of the model in this respect is limited, not only because it is still in an early stage of development but also because of the inherent complexity of the inferences involved. Yet it does suggest an approach to the problem of meaning in the analysis of public opinion data.

## Notes

1. For discussions of the different motivational bases of opinion see I. Sarnott and D. Katz, "The Motivational Bases of Attitude Change," *Journal of Abnormal and Social Psychology,* Vol. 49, 1954, pp. 115–124; and M. B. Smith, J. S. Bruner, and R. W. White, *Opinions and Personality,* New York, Wiley, 1956.

2. See, for example, S. E. Asch, *Social Psychology,* New York, Prentice-Hall, 1952.

3. See, for example, D. Cartwright and A. Zander, editors, *Group Dynamics,* Evanston, Ill., Row, Peterson, 1953.

4. See, for example, C. I. Hovland, I. L. Janis, and H. H. Kelley, *Communication and Persuasion,* New Haven, Yale University Press, 1953.

5. See, for example, L. Festinger, "An Analysis of Compliant Behavior," in M. Sherif and M. O. Wilson, editors, *Group Relations at the Crossroads,* New York, Harper, 1953, pp. 232–256; H. C. Kelman, "Attitude Change as a Function of Response Restriction," *Human Relations,* Vol. 6, 1953, pp. 185–214; J. R. P. French, Jr., and B. Raven, "The Bases of Social Power," in D. Cartwright, editor, *Studies in Social Power,* Ann Arbor, Mich., Institute for Social Research, 1959, pp. 150–167; and Marie Jahoda, "Conformity and Independence," *Human Relations,* Vol. 12, 1959, pp. 99–120.

6. See, for example, M. Deutsch and H. B. Gerard, "A Study of Normative and Informational Social Influence upon Individual Judgment," *Journal of Abnormal and Social Psychology,* Vol. 51, 1955, pp. 629–636; J. W. Thibaut and L. Strickland, "Psychological Set and Social Conformity," *Journal of Personality,* Vol. 25, 1956, pp. 115–129; and J. M. Jackson and H. D. Saltzstein, "The Effect of Person–Group Relationships on Conformity Processes," *Journal of Abnormal and Social Psychology,* Vol. 57, 1958, pp. 17–24.

7. For instance, R. J. Lifton, " 'Thought Reform' of Western Civilians in Chinese Communist Prisons," *Psychiatry,* Vol. 19, 1956, pp. 173–195.

8. A detailed description of these processes and the experimental work based on them will be contained in a forthcoming book, *Social Influence and Personal*

*Belief: A Theoretical and Experimental Approach to the Study of Behavior Change,* to be published by John Wiley & Sons.

9. This is similar to John Whiting's conception of "Status Envy" as a basis for identification. See J. W. M. Whiting, "Sorcery, Sin, and the Superego," in M. R. Jones, editor, *Nebraska Symposium on Motivation,* Lincoln, University of Nebraska Press, 1959, pp. 174–195.

10. Lotte Bailyn and H. C. Kelman, "The Effects of a Year's Experience in America on the Self-image of Scandinavians: Report of Research in Progress," paper read at the meetings of the American Psychological Association, Cincinnati, 1959.

*This paper is based on a research program on social influence and behavior change, supported by grant M-2516 from the National Institute of Mental Health.*

# Newspapers and Public Associations in the United States

## ALEXIS DE TOQUEVILLE

## Of the Relation Between Public Associations and the Newspapers

When men are no longer united amongst themselves by firm and lasting ties, it is impossible to obtain the co-operation of any great number of them, unless you can persuade every man whose help you require that his private interest obliges him voluntarily to unite his exertions to the exertions of all the others. This can be habitually and conveniently effected only by means of a newspaper: nothing but a newspaper can drop the same thought into a thousand minds at the same moment. A newspaper is an adviser who does not require to be sought, but who comes of his own accord, and talks to you briefly every day of the common weal, without distracting you from your private affairs.

Newspapers therefore become more necessary in proportion as men become more equal, and individualism more to be feared. To suppose that they only serve to protect freedom would be to diminish their importance: they maintain civilization. I shall not deny that, in democratic countries, newspapers frequently lead the citizens to launch together into very ill-digested schemes; but if there were no newspapers, there would be no common activity. The evil which they produce is therefore much less than that which they cure.

Reprinted from "Newspapers and Public Associations in the United States," in *Democracy in America*, edited by Richard D. Heffner, The New American Library, 1956.

The effect of a newspaper is not only to suggest the same purpose to a great number of persons, but to furnish means for executing in common the designs which they may have singly conceived. The principal citizens who inhabit an aristocratic country discern each other from afar; and if they wish to unite their forces, they move towards each other, drawing a multitude of men after them. It frequently happens, on the contrary, in democratic countries, that a great number of men who wish or who want to combine cannot accomplish it, because, as they are very insignificant and lost amidst the crowd, they cannot see, and know not where to find, one another. A newspaper then takes up the notion or the feeling which had occurred simultaneously, but singly, to each of them. All are then immediately guided towards this beacon; and these wandering minds, which had long sought each other in darkness, at length meet and unite. The newspaper brought them together, and the newspaper is still necessary to keep them united.

In order that an association amongst a democratic people should have any power, it must be a numerous body. The persons of whom it is composed are therefore scattered over a wide extent, and each of them is detained in the place of his domicile by the narrowness of his income, or by the small unremitting exertions by which he earns it. Means must then be found to converse every day without seeing each other, and to take steps in common without having met. Thus, hardly any democratic association can do without newspapers.

There is, consequently, a necessary connection between public associations and newspapers: newspapers make associations, and associations make newspapers; and if it has been correctly advanced, that associations will increase in number as the conditions of men become more equal, it is not less certain that the number of newspapers increases in proportion to that of associations. Thus it is, in America, that we find at the same time the greatest number of associations and of newspapers.

This connection between the number of newspapers and that of associations leads us to the discovery of a further connection between the state of the periodical press and the form of the administration in a country, and shows that the number of newspapers must diminish or increase amongst a democratic people, in proportion as its administration is more or less centralized. For, amongst democratic nations, the exercise of local powers cannot be intrusted to the principal members of the community, as in aristocracies. Those powers must either be abolished, or placed in the hands of very large numbers of men, who then in fact constitute an association permanently established by law, for the purpose of administering the affairs of a certain extent of territory; and they require a journal, to bring to them every day, in the midst of their own minor concerns, some intelligence of the state of their public weal. The more numerous local powers are, the greater is the number of men in whom they are vested by law; and as this want is hourly felt, the more profusely do newspapers abound.

The extraordinary subdivision of administrative power has much more to do with the enormous number of American newspapers, than the great political freedom of the country and the absolute liberty of the press. If all the inhabitants of the Union had the suffrage,—but a suffrage which should extend only to the choice of their legislators in Congress,—they would require but few newspapers, because they would have to act together only on very important, but very rare, occasions. But within the great national association, lesser associations have been established by law in every county, every city, and indeed in every village, for the purposes of local administration. The laws of the country thus compel every American to co-operate every day of his life with some of his fellow-citizens for a common purpose, and each one of them requires a newspaper to inform him what all the others are doing.

I am of opinion that a democratic people, without any national representative assemblies, but with a great number of small local powers, would have in the end more newspapers than another people governed by a centralized administration and an elective legislature. What best explains to me the enormous circulation of the daily press in the United States is, that, amongst the Americans, I find the utmost national freedom combined with local freedom of every kind.

There is a prevailing opinion in France and England, that the circulation of newspapers would be indefinitely increased by removing the taxes which have been laid upon the press. This is a very exaggerated estimate of the effects oɪ such a reform. Newspapers increase in numbers, not according to their cheapness, but according to the more or less frequent want which a great number of men may feel for intercommunication and combination.

In like manner, I should attribute the increasing influence of the daily press to causes more general than those by which it is commonly explained. A newspaper can only subsist on the condition of publishing sentiments or principles common to a large number of men. A newspaper, therefore, always represents an association which is composed of its habitual readers. This association may be more or less defined, more or less restricted, more or less numerous; but the fact that the newspaper keeps alive, is a proof that at least the germ of such an association exists in the minds of its readers.

This leads me to a last reflection . . . the more equal the conditions of men become, and the less strong men individually are the more easily do they give way to the current of the multitude, and the more difficult it is for them to adhere by themselves to an opinion which the multitude discard. A newspaper represents an association; it may be said to address each of its readers in the name of all the others, and to exert its influence over them in proportion to their individual weakness. The power of the newspaper press must therefore increase as the social conditions of men become more equal. . . .

# Liberty of the Press in the United States

The influence of the liberty of the press does not affect political opinions alone, but extends to all the opinions of men, and modifies customs as well as laws. . . . I confess that I do not entertain that firm and complete attachment to the liberty of the press which is wont to be excited by things that are supremely good in their very nature. I approve of it from a consideration more of the evils it prevents, than of the advantages it insures. If any one could point out an intermediate and yet a tenable position between the complete independence and the entire servitude of opinion. I should, perhaps, be inclined to adopt it; but the difficulty is, to discover this intermediate position. Intending to correct the licentiousness of the press, and to restore the use of orderly language, you first try the offender by a jury; but if the jury acquits him, the opinion which was that of a single individual becomes the opinion of the whole country. Too much and too little has therefore been done; go farther, then. You bring the delinquent before permanent magistrates; but even here, the cause must be heard before it can be decided; and the very principles which no book would have ventured to avow are blazoned forth in the pleadings, and what was obscurely hinted at in a single composition is thus repeated in a multitude of other publications. The language is only the expression, and (if I may so speak) the body, of the thought, but it is not the thought itself. Tribunals may condemn the body, but the sense, the spirit, of the work is too subtile for their authority. Too much has still been done to recede, too little to attain your end; you must go still farther. Establish a censorship of the press. But the tongue of the public speaker will still make itself heard, and your purpose is not yet accomplished; you have only increased the mischief. Thought is not, like physical strength, dependent upon the number of its agents; nor can authors be counted like the troops which compose an army. On the contrary, the authority of a principle is often increased by the small number of men by whom it is expressed. The words of one strong-minded man, addressed to the passions of a listening assembly, have more power than the vociferations of a thousand orators; and if it be allowed to speak freely in any one public place, the consequence is the same as if free speaking was allowed in every village. The liberty of speech must therefore be destroyed, as well as the liberty of the press. And now you have succeeded, everybody is reduced to silence. But your object was to repress the abuses of liberty, and you are brought to the feet of a despot. You have been led from the extreme of independence to the extreme of servitude, without finding a single tenable position on the way at which you could stop. . . .

The small influence of the American journals is attributable to several reasons, amongst which are the following.

The liberty of writing, like all other liberty, is most formidable when it is a novelty; for a people who have never been accustomed to hear state affairs discussed before them, place implicit confidence in the first tribune who presents himself. The Anglo-Americans have enjoyed this liberty ever since the foundation of the Colonies; moreover, the press cannot create human passions, however skillfully it may kindle them where they exist. In America, political life is active, varied, even agitated, but is rarely affected by those deep passions which are excited only when material interests are impaired: and in the United States, these interests are prosperous. A glance at a French and an American newspaper is sufficient to show the difference which exists in this respect between the two nations. In France, the space allotted to commercial advertisements is very limited, and the news-intelligence is not considerable; but the essential part of the journal is the discussion of the politics of the day. In America, three quarters of the enormous sheet are filled with advertisements, and the remainder is frequently occupied by political intelligence or trivial anecdotes: it is only from time to time, that one finds a corner devoted to passionate discussions, like those which the journalists of France every day give to their readers.

It has been demonstrated by observation, and discovered by the sure instinct even of the pettiest despots, that the influence of a power is increased in proportion as its direction is centralized. In France, the press combines a two-fold centralization; almost all its power is centered in the same spot, and, so to speak, in the same hands; for its organs are far from numerous. The influence of a public press thus constituted, upon a sceptical nation, must be almost unbounded. It is an enemy with whom a government may sign an occasional truce, but which it is difficult to resist for any length of time.

Neither of these kinds of centralization exists in America. The United States have no metropolis; the intelligence and the power of the people are disseminated through all the parts of this vast country, and instead of radiating from a common point, they cross each other in every direction; the Americans have nowhere established any central direction of opinion, any more than of the conduct of affairs. This difference arises from local circumstances, and not from human power; but it is owing to the laws of the Union that there are no licenses to be granted to printers, no securities demanded from editors, as in France, and no stamp duty, as in France and England. The consequence is, that nothing is easier than to set up a newspaper, as a small number of subscribers suffices to defray the expenses.

Hence the number of periodical and semi-periodical publications in the United States is almost incredibly large. The most enlightened Americans attribute the little influence of the press to this excessive dissemination of its power; and it is an axiom of political science in that country, that the only way to neutralize the effect of the public journals is to multiply their number. I cannot see how a truth which is so self-evident should not already have been more generally admitted in Europe. I can see why the persons who hope to bring about revolutions by means of the press, should be desirous of confining it to a few powerful organs; but it is inconceivable that the official partisans of the existing state of things, and the natural supporters of the laws, should attempt to diminish the influence of the press by concentrating its power. The governments of Europe seem to treat the press with the courtesy which the knights of old showed to their opponents; having found from their own experience that centralization is a powerful weapon, they have furnished their enemies with it, in order doubtless to have more glory for overcoming them.

In America, there is scarcely a hamlet which has not its newspaper. It may readily be imagined, that neither discipline nor unity of action can be established among so many combatants; and each one consequently fights under his own standard. All the political journals of the United States are, indeed, arrayed on the side of the administration or against it; but they attack and defend it in a thousand different ways. They cannot form those great currents of opinion which sweep away the strongest dikes. This division of the influence of the press produces other consequences scarcely less remarkable. The facility with which newspapers can be established produces a multitude of them; but as the competition prevents any considerable profit, persons of much capacity are rarely led to engage in these undertakings. Such is the number of the public prints, that, even if they were a source of wealth, writers of ability could not be found to direct them all. The journalists of the United States are generally in a very humble position, with a scanty education and a vulgar turn of mind. The will of the majority is the most general of laws, and it establishes certain habits to which every one must then conform; the aggregate of these common habits is what is called the class-spirit *(esprit de corps)* of each profession; thus there is the class-spirit of the bar, of the court, &c. The class-spirit of the French journalists consists in a violent, but frequently an eloquent and lofty, manner of discussing the great interests of the state: and the exceptions to this mode of writing are only occasional. The characteristics of the American journalist consist in an open and coarse appeal to the passions of his readers; he abandons principles to assail the characters of individuals, to track them into private life, and disclose all their weaknesses and vices. . . .

But although the press is limited to these resources, its influence in America is immense. It causes political life to circulate through all the parts of that vast territory. Its eye is constantly open to detect the secret springs of political designs, and to summon the leaders of all parties in turn to the bar of public opinion. It rallies the interests of the community round certain principles, and draws up the creed of every party; for it affords a means of intercourse between those who hear and address each other, without ever coming into immediate contact. When many organs of the press adopt the same line of conduct, their influence in the long run becomes irresistible; and public opinion, perpetually assailed from the same side, eventually yields to the attack. In the United States, each separate journal exercises but little authority; but the power of the periodical press is second only to that of the people. . . .

# Mass Communication and Political Socialization

STEVEN H. CHAFFEE
L. SCOTT WARD
LEONARD P. TIPTON

ANALYSES OF THE AGENCIES of political socialization generally relegate the mass media to a secondary role at best. While the media are often listed as socialization agents alongside parents, schools and peers, there has been little evidence for mass communication as a casual element in a child's development of political cognitions and behaviors.[1] Debate usually centers around the relative effects of the schools *vs.* the family; the media are considered sources of reinforcement of processes initiated by the more primary agents; peer political influences are assumed to be important but have not been studied directly.[2]

Attempts by Jennings and his colleagues to demonstrate the impact of parents and schools on political socialization have yielded little, however.[3] They have found only minor evidence that the child models his political orientations on those of his parents; differences accounted for by variations in school curricula appear negligible. The basis for minimizing the role played by mass media, by contrast, has not been based on this kind of empirical test, but on generalizations from research on processes other than political socialization.

The most complete exposition of the view that the media have little direct effect on social attitudes and behavior has been presented by Klapper.[4] Citing a wide range of evidence and invoking psychological principles of learning

Extract from Steven H. Chaffee, L. Scott Ward and Leonard P. Tipton, "Mass Communication and Political Socialization," in *Journalism Quarterly*, Vol. 47 (1970), pp. 647–659, 666. Reprinted by permission.

and dissonance theory, Klapper proposes that the effects of mass communication are a) mostly simple reinforcement of existing predispositions due to "selective exposure," and b) largely neutralized by interpersonal influences in a "two-step flow" of communication. Klapper offered his generalizations quite tentatively and stressed that there is a small residuum of conditions under which the media have direct effects. But his generalizations are often cited as evidence (rather than hypothesis), primarily by network executives, that the media do not have substantial harmful effects on children.[5] In the political socialization literature, Dawson and Prewitt have cited Klapper's generalizations, which is reasonable enough, in the absence of evidence pro or con; they assert that media content mainly reinforces the child's political predispositions and that its effect is mediated by subsequent influences from interpersonal sources at home and in school.[6]

The "reinforcement" portion of this view seems shortsighted on at least two counts. First, the whole point of research on political socialization is that the child does not have political predispositions at the outset; thus, the question is not whether the media "convert" him to new attitudes, but whether he develops any attitudes at all. It is irrelevant to argue that the media reinforce political predispositions where none yet exist. If the child is politically aware enough to expose himself selectively to reinforcing media messages, he is already socialized. Secondly, Klapper's generalizations are based mainly on studies of opinions on controversial issues, whereas the most likely effects of the media in political socialization are in the acquisition of political knowledge and the building of interest in public affairs. The mass media institutions attempt, in the main, to provide information and stimulate interest, but to avoid taking sides or to present several sides for public examination. Knowledge and interest are important indices of political socialization, and should (hopefully) precede the development of particular opinions. Thus, one might find evidence of "direct" effects of mass communication if he looks for the kinds of influences the media are trying to provide, rather than those the media are supposed to avoid.

The "two-step flow" portion of the argument is perhaps even less persuasive when applied to political socialization. For reasons similar to those advanced in the preceding paragraph, the media have repeatedly been found to have a direct role in providing information; the "two-step flow" is considered one of attitudinal influence specifically.[7] Further, if mass communication induces youngsters to discuss public affairs among themselves or with their parents, as the "two-step" model says, that in itself would seem to be a major direct effect of the mass media. As the authors of the classic Elmira election campaign study noted, it is heartening for democratic theory to find that voters discuss the ideas they acquire via mass media, before translating them into votes.[8] If mass communication has this kind of social effect on the developing child, it is indeed serving as an important agent of political socialization. Significant peergroup discussion of politics is unlikely, of course, until the group reaches a maturational level where most of its members have been politically socialized. But ultimately, the knotty question of the relative contributions of mass vs. interpersonal sources is one for empirical research, not argument and analogy.

Although there has been a great deal of research on adolescent media use, and on political socialization, these areas rarely overlap. Media-use studies usually only peripherally examine consumption of public affairs and political content, often because the research involves younger children. Studies of political socialization usually compare age groupings on such measures as political knowledge and trust in government; media use is treated as either an added dependent variable or as a secondary agent of socialization, as discussed above.[9] One study that has attempted to relate adolescent media use to political socialization is that of Jennings and Niemi; they treat media use for political news as a form of political activity, rather than as an agent of political socialization.[10] In a national sample of high school seniors and their parents, they found that 83% of the high school seniors and 87% of their parents report following public affairs at least "some" of the time. . . .

Antecedent socialization variables that might account for differential adolescent political media use have been examined by several communication researchers. Clarke's work indicates that parent-child "identification," "independence training" and reading skills are all related to public affairs reading among 10th grade boys.[11]

McLeod, Chaffee and Wackman have inferred that the structure of parent-child communication is a major determinant of both media use patterns and other indicators of political socialization.[12] They find the greatest attention to media public affairs reports by adolescents whose parents have stressed "concept orientations" but not "social harmony."

Schramm, Lyle and Parker found considerable public affairs viewing among adolescents but not among younger children.[13] Schramm also found significant relationships between reactions to 1958 election coverage, based on a scale in the form "not seen; saw but didn't particularly like; saw and particularly liked," and mental ability and grade. Predictably, intelligent 12th graders were more likely to have seen the election coverage and to have liked it, than 10th or 8th graders of any intelligence level.

Byrne examined media use and socio-economic status, race and residence.[14] He concluded that children with primarily television news exposure (over newspapers) tend to think favorably about government and feel it is effective. These children tend to be black, low SES and rural.

Hess and Torney show evidence that by the time they reach adolescence youths have attained considerable political knowledge, have discussed conditions and issues and have worn campaign buttons and passed out literature.[15] However, the mass communication research literature suggests that purposive use of media for public affairs and/or political information is virtually nonexistent until late in the high school years.

In summary, there are major gaps in the empirical picture. Specific use of the media for public affairs content has not been examined in relation to cognitive or behavioral indicators of political socialization. The "developmental" studies consist of comparisons of age groups at a single point in time, rather than making repeated measurements on the same children longitudinally so that time order could be assessed and "processes" traced. Research has rarely been timed to coincide with major political events, such as election campaigns, when public affairs media use is likely to be greatest and political socialization probably proceeds most rapidly. To the extent that the question of mass *vs.* interpersonal sources has been considered an empirical one at all, it has been approached only indirectly as a matter of "which measures explain more variance," instead of explicit comparisons among the various sources. And there is no real evidence on the most basic question: can it be shown that the mass media have *any* direct effect on political socialization?

This study is an attempt to fill those research gaps. In contrast to the approach of most mass communication researchers, we treat media use as an independent variable and look at changes over time in consumption of media public affairs content during the 1968 national election campaign, and their relationship to changes in political cognitions and behaviors. In contrast to the developmental approach of most political socialization researchers, we are looking at a relatively short time period—albeit one in which we expect a great deal of political socialization to occur—on the assumption that socialization is a cumulative process (*i.e.* that a significant portion of the changes we trace will endure).

The general hypothesis is that public affairs media consumption accounts for some change in political cognitions and behavior by comparison with three other agencies of political socialization: parents, teachers and peers.

## Study Design

The study was conducted in five Wisconsin cities, selected to provide socio-economic and political diversity in the total sample. The cities, located in Milwaukee and Fox River Valley regions, ranged in population from 18,000 to 68,000 (1960 census). In the 1968 general election, two of these cities gave large majorities to Hubert Humphrey, two to Richard Nixon, and the fifth gave Nixon a slight edge. In the April 1968 Wisconsin primary, Senator Eugene McCarthy easily defeated President Lyndon Johnson in three of the cities; the McCarthy–Johnson vote was close in the other two.

Data were collected by self-administered questionnaires filled out at school, in May (about one month after the primary election), and again in November (within two weeks after the general election). The eventual sample consisted of a panel of 1,291 students, about equally divided between two grade levels. The junior high sample consists of 639 who were 7th grade students in

May and 8th graders in November. . . . The senior high group (N = 652) was in the 10th grade in May, 11th in November.

In our analyses, data from these two age groups are presented separately. Comparisons between them should be made guardedly, however, since they do not represent identical universes. We sampled only in public schools, and parochial school enrollment is much heavier at the junior high level; thus our senior high sample includes substantially more Roman Catholics. . . .

This lack of comparability was not serious for our purposes. While we expect differences between grade levels in the *absolute level* on many measures, we hypothesize that the political socialization process, as indicated by the *relationships among* these measures, will be about the same at either grade level. Therefore we treat the two grade-level samples as separate replications of the same study. In each of our tables, the junior high and senior high data are juxtaposed so that the similarity of process can be assessed.

Although we have "Time 1-Time 2" measures taken six months apart, this should not be interpreted as a "before-after" study. The election campaign had begun in Wisconsin in January, aiming at the April primary. Many of our young respondents participated actively in the McCarthy campaign (sometimes called a "children's crusade") in early spring. Our May questionnaires reached the students during a lull in the year's campaigning, and the design can probably be best described as a "during-after" one.

Three kinds of measures were made in both May and November: mass media use, political knowledge and campaigning activity. Thus we focus on behavior rather than inferred cognitive states such as attitudes, although our estimates of behavior are necessarily based on self-report for media use and campaigning activity. Only political knowledge was tested directly—and this was the only measure for which we could not use identical questionnaire items in the two time periods. Because of elections, assassinations and other "real world" events, most of the knowledge questions we asked in May were not relevant in November—or the answers to them had changed. Therefore, no direct May–November comparison of knowledge could be made. Table 1 shows changes in the other variables, which are discussed below.

A 22-item factual knowledge test was administered in May, and a 29-item test in November. The May test asked for identification of the countries of four leaders; the parties and present jobs of five presidential candidates and three Wisconsin politicians; the local congressman; and the number of U.S. Senators from Wisconsin. The November test asked for the names and parties of the winning and losing candidates in the presidential, gubernatorial and senatorial elections; names of the winner and loser in the congressional election; the parties, states and jobs of Nelson Rockefeller and Eugene McCarthy; names of at least six cabinet-level departments of the U.S. government, and whether U.S. Supreme Court justices are elected or appointed. . . .

Although adolescents are not permitted to participate formally in the political process by voting, they are not barred from attempting to influence those who do vote. We asked about a number of possible types of campaigning activity in the spring; three items were reported frequently enough to be repeated in the fall. These items (all forms of communicative output) provide a four-level index of campaign activism: wearing a campaign button, distributing campaign leaflets and trying to talk someone into liking a candidate.

Changes in the total score on this index are shown at the top of Table 1. There was a marked increase in campaigning among the junior high students, but no overall change for the senior high sample.

**TABLE 1.   May–November Changes in Campaigning and Media Use Indices**

| INDEX | GRADE | MAY MEAN | NOVEMBER MEAN | NET CHANGE | CORRELATION MAY VS. NOVEMBER |
|---|---|---|---|---|---|
| Campaign | Jr.Hi | .74 | 1.16 | +.42 | .31 |
| Activity | Sr.Hi | 1.02 | 1.02 | none | .47 |
| TV Entertainment | Jr.Hi | 2.21 | 1.77 | −.44 | .33 |
| Viewing | Sr.Hi | 1.92 | 1.29 | −.63 | .40 |
| Newspaper Enter- | Jr.Hi | 1.97 | 1.82 | −.15 | .31 |
| tainment Reading | Sr.Hi | 2.04 | 1.97 | −.07 | .46 |
| TV Public | Jr.Hi | .51 | .55 | +.04 | .37 |
| Affairs Viewing | Sr.Hi | .51 | .52 | +.01 | .51 |
| Newspaper Public | Jr.Hi | 1.42 | 1.52 | +.10 | .50 |
| Affairs Reading | Sr.Hi | 1.63 | 1.70 | +.07 | .53 |
| Total Public | Jr.Hi | 1.93 | 2.07 | +.14 | .53 |
| Affairs Media Use | Sr.Hi | 2.14 | 2.23 | +.09 | .63 |

Table 1 also shows that the May–November correlations between the two activity indices were rather low. This is probably due both to unreliability (a measure that correlates only .31 with itself over time is unlikely to correlate significantly with another variable) and real change in terms of who is active.

Ten questions were asked about the content the student regularly consumes via the mass media. Five dealt with specific types of television programing and five with specific types of newspaper content. From these items, we constructed four indices of mass media use, representing consumption of Entertainment *vs.* Public Affairs content, via newspapers *vs.* television. The Public Affairs content indices were later combined into a single total use index to provide our best measure of mass media public affairs consumption. The following items were used in these measures:

a) TV Entertainment Viewing: regularly watching comedies, westerns and spy-adventure shows.
b) TV Public Affairs Viewing: regularly watching news specials and national news shows.

c) Newspaper Entertainment Reading: regular reading of comics and sports.

d) Newspaper Public Affairs Reading: regular reading of the front page, news about politics and news about the Vietnam war.

e) Total Public Affairs Media Use: sum of scores from *(b)* and *(d)*.

The Entertainment content indices were intended as "control" categories; that is, we expected that they would not be related to changes in political socialization, whereas the Public Affairs categories would. It is conceivable, however, that Entertainment content could serve to attract the youngster to the media, after which he would be exposed to Public Affairs content. Therefore, we have retained the Entertainment categories throughout our analysis, even though we did not expect that they would account for political socialization directly.

Table 1 shows changes in these indices during the campaign. There was a self-reported decrease in Entertainment consumption via both newspapers and television, and a reported increase in Public Affairs consumption. Whether these represent real changes or a tendency to give more socially desirable responses in the retest is debatable. Comparison of the junior high *vs.* senior high means would suggest that there are no lasting trends away from Newspaper Entertainment Reading or toward TV Public Affairs Viewing. There may have been temporary changes of these types during the campaign, simply because the media are saturated with political material just before an election. The question of shifts in media habits during adolescent development awaits more thorough study; we are more interested here in the ways in which these indices relate to other variables.

The chance of our finding strong correlations is not great, however, to judge from the May–November correlations. All are rather low, and their depression cannot be plausibly attributed solely to massive real changes. It is not surprising that reliability is low, since most of our measures consist of only two or three items each. Fortunately, our Ns are large enough so that rather small correlations will be statistically significant; this factor helps to balance the unreliability of many of our measures.

It should also be noted in Table 1 that the May–November correlations are higher for the senior high than the junior high group, on every index. Most of these differences are statistically significant. Although it is conceivable that older youths are more consistent in these behaviors over time, the most likely explanation of these differences is again measurement reliability. The senior high students are more experienced at test-taking, and thus there is probably less error in their responses to our questions.

As is so often the case in studies of this sort, we found that "almost everything correlated with everything else." But we are interested here in more than simple statistical associations among variables. We hope to develop some picture of the *process* of politicization during the campaign. This implies that we should arrive at statements about the *time order* of events. If use of mass media public affairs content "causes" political socialization, then it should (a) be correlated with the criterion measures, (b) precede them in time and (c) be functionally, not fortuitously, related to them.

To test this kind of hypothesis, we used a variant of "cross-lagged" correlation, partialing for initial scores on the dependent variable. Figure 1 shows schematically the six correlations that are possible in a two-variable study when measures are taken at two different times. A simple cross-lagged test consists of the difference between the hypothesized time-order correlation *(f)* and the reverse time-order correlation *(e)*. If there is no difference between these two correlations, then one has no evidence of a process in which the hypothesized independent variable precedes the dependent variable. However, the reverse does not necessarily hold; the simple cross-lagged test $(f - e < 0)$ is not in itself sufficient evidence to infer the hypothesized time order. One should also show that the hypothesized correlation *(f)* exceeds the static correlations within time periods (*c* and *d*).[16]

Finally, it is preferable to have a test of the explained change in the dependent variable that is independent of the initial level on that measure; this, in effect, controls for other possible independent variables, which might account for initial differences. One method would be to use gain scores, but these tend to be unreliable and poorly distributed and leave open the threat of a regression effect. A more satisfactory procedure is partial correlation, controlling for initial (Time 1) scores on the dependent variable. In terms of Figure 1, the standard partial formula would be

$$r_p = \frac{f - cb}{\sqrt{1 - c^2}\sqrt{1 - b^2}}.$$

However, it provides a better test of the time-order hypothesis if we build the cross-lagged test *(f − e)* into this formula. Accordingly, we have combined the standard partial correlation formula and the cross-lagged factor into the single computation

$$rp = \frac{f - eb}{\sqrt{1 - c^2}\sqrt{1 - b^2}}$$

by substituting the cross-lagged test for the more usual $f - c$ portion of the numerator.[17]

## Findings

The main results of our study are shown in Table 2, where political knowledge is the dependent variable, and in Table 3, where campaigning activity is the dependent variable. The independent variables include the five media use indices, plus (in Table 2 only) campaigning activity. Wherever

**FIGURE 1.**   Possible Correlations in a Two-Variable, Two-Time Study

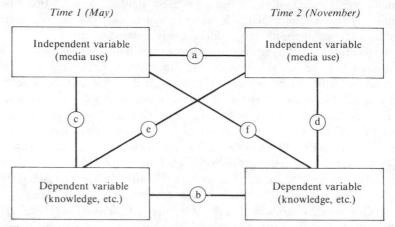

Note: The encircled letters a, b, . . . f indicate correlations. These letters are entered into the formulas described in the text, and in Tables 2 and 3.

asterisks appear in these tables, they indicate evidence contrary to the general hypothesis.

The only relationships in these tables that are totally free of counter-hypothetical evidence are those between Public Affairs media use (either TV or newspapers, or the two combined) and increased political knowledge (Table 2). Remarkably similar data at the two grade levels show the hypothe-

**TABLE 2.**   Correlations of Communication Indices with Political Knowledge

| INDEPENDENT VARIABLE | GRADE LEVEL | HYPOTH-ESIZED $r(f)$ | REVERSE $r(e)$ | MEAN STATIC $r(c\ \&\ d)$ | PARTIAL $r$ | PARTIAL $r$ SIG. LEVEL |
|---|---|---|---|---|---|---|
| Campaign Activity | Jr.Hi | .20 | .18 | .23[b] | .10 | .01 |
|  | Sr.Hi | .27 | .25 | .28[b] | .13 | .001 |
| TV Entertainment | Jr.Hi | .00 | −.12 | −.05 | .12 | .01 |
| Viewing | Sr.Hi | −.24 | −.09 | −.15 | −.25 | .001[d] |
| Newspaper Enter- | Jr.Hi | .18 | .11 | .17 | .15 | .001 |
| tainment Reading | Sr.Hi | .07 | .08[a] | .09[b] | .01 | [c] |
| TV Public Affairs | Jr.Hi | .26 | .18 | .23 | .20 | .001 |
| Viewing | Sr.Hi | .29 | .21 | .25 | .21 | .001 |
| Newspaper Public | Jr.Hi | .29 | .18 | .25 | .23 | .001 |
| Affairs Reading | Sr.Hi | .27 | .17 | .24 | .23 | .001 |
| Total Public | Jr.Hi | .33 | .22 | .29 | .26 | .001 |
| Affairs Media Use | Sr.Hi | .33 | .23 | .30 | .26 | .001 |

[a] Reject hypothesis, since reverse correlation exceeds hypothesized correlation.
[b] Hypothesis is dubious, since hypothesized correlation does not exceed mean static correlation.
[c] Reject hypothesis, since partial correlation is non-significant.
[d] Data indicate a negative inference, that media use lowers knowledge.

sized correlation considerably higher than the reverse correlation, higher than the mean of the two static correlations, and highly significant when partialed on initial scores. Both media predict knowledge fairly well, and the combination of the two into a composite index yields even better prediction.

Two other relationships in Table 2 hold for the junior high group only. There are significant partial correlations between Entertainment use via both media, and political knowledge. In the case of TV Entertainment Viewing, the partialing technique seems to have uncovered a relationship that was not apparent from the raw hypothesized correlation alone. These findings suggest that, for the young junior high students, *any* use of the mass media tends to expose them to sources of increased political knowledge. By senior high age, however, these side-effects of non-selective media use disappear. In the case of TV Entertainment Viewing, there is a highly significant senior high negative relationship with political knowledge, as well as a mild negative relationship with campaigning activity (Table 3). (It is noteworthy that these two negative effects of TV Entertainment Viewing at the senior high level pass all our tests for time-order inference, *in the wrong direction*. Therefore, we should accept a negative causal inference and have not otherwise asterisked those rows in Table 2 and 3.)

**TABLE 3.  Correlations of Communication Indices with Campaign Activity**

| INDEPENDENT VARIABLE | GRADE LEVEL | HYPOTH-ESIZED $r(f)$ | REVERSE $r(e)$ | MEAN STATIC $r(c\ \&\ d)$ | PARTIAL $r$ | PARTIAL $r$ SIG. LEVEL |
|---|---|---|---|---|---|---|
| TV Entertainment | Jr.Hi | .02 | .07[a] | .05[b] | −.01 | c |
| Viewing | Sr.Hi | −.09 | −.03 | −.07 | −.08 | .05[d] |
| Newspaper Enter- | Jr.Hi | .11 | .11[a] | .08 | .08 | .05 |
| tainment Reading | Sr.Hi | .04 | −.02 | .04[b] | .04 | c |
| TV Public Affairs | Jr.Hi | .13 | .17[a] | .16[b] | .08 | .05 |
| Viewing | Sr.Hi | .19 | .20[a] | .20[b] | .11 | .01 |
| Newspaper Public | Jr.Hi | .22 | .11 | .20 | .20 | .001 |
| Affairs Reading | Sr.Hi | .25 | .20 | .27[b] | .18 | .001 |
| Total Public | Jr.Hi | .21 | .17 | .22[b] | .17 | .001 |
| Affairs Media Use | Sr.Hi | .27 | .25 | .29[b] | .18 | .001 |

[a] Reject hypothesis, since reverse correlation exceeds hypothesized correlation.
[b] Hypothesis is dubious, since hypothesized correlation does not exceed mean static correlation.
[c] Reject hypothesis, since partial correlation is non-significant.
[d] Data indicate a negative inference, that media use lowers campaigning.

Campaigning Activity does not appear to enter into time-order relationships as either an independent variable (Table 2) or a dependent variable (Table 3). Rather consistently, the static within-time correlations of this variable with knowledge and media use are greater than the hypothesized time-lagged correlation. There is one exception, in Table 3, where Newspaper Public Affairs Reading predicts Campaigning Activity, at least for the junior high group. Since we consider the static-*vs.*-hypothesized correlation comparison our weakest test against a causal inference (see note 16), we could tentatively infer that Newspaper Public Affairs Reading leads to greater Campaigning Activity regardless of grade level. It should be stressed that this inference does not extend to TV Public Affairs Viewing, which appears to retard Campaigning Activity, if anything. In this connection, note that the Composite Public Affairs Use index predicts Campaigning Activity less well than Newspaper Public Affairs Reading alone (Table 3), despite presumed greater reliability.

In sum, the use of newspapers for public affairs news inputs emerges as an important functional variable in the process of political socialization. This behavior increases in incidence during the campaign, it is more frequent among the older adolescents and it appears to precede increased knowledge and activity. Television has a more mixed effect and may even deter active campaigning behavior. But specific viewing of public affairs programing does lead to knowledge gain.

It would be unremarkable if we were to infer simply that those who follow media public affairs reports know more about current events than do those who ignore these reports. But our findings indicate a more global process in our young respondents during the campaign. The hypothesized time-lagged correlations in Table 2 that exceed the corresponding mean static correlations can be interpreted operationally in this way: attention to media public affairs reports in May predicts the youth's November knowledge ranking better than it predicts his May knowledge ranking. This occurs despite the fact that the May knowledge measure tested information about matters that were in May's news, whereas the November knowledge measure tested information that was in the November media reports. As an "information gain" inference we can say that high media use during the campaign predicted a large relative *future* gain in knowledge better than it explained current knowledge.

This interpretation encourages the general inference that mass communication plays a causal role in the political socialization process. But the relationship is somewhat reciprocal, too. If there were no causal relationship between these two variables, the time-lagged correlations would be .19 and .21 for the junior and senior high samples, respectively.[18] The hypothesized *(f)* correlations are clearly above those "null hypothesis" levels, but so are the reverse *(e)* correlations (to a lesser extent). This means that high initial media public affairs use predicts later gains in knowledge *and* that high initial knowledge predicts later gains in public affairs media use. The total effect of mass communication then is to widen the gap between the informed youngsters and others.

For our last set of analyses, we turn to a variable that was measured only in the November questionnaire; therefore it is open only to static analysis. We do, however, relate it to the process variables that have already been analyzed.

Rather than attempt to assess indirectly the relative impact of different agents of political socialization, we asked our respondents to make this comparison themselves. We listed the four sources that are commonly thought to be important: parents, friends, teachers and mass media. We asked each respondent to rate each of these on two bases: how much information he gets from the source and how much his personal opinions issue from it. Separate sets of questions requested this assessment for two current news topics: student conduct and student demonstrations at the University of Wisconsin, and the bombing halt in Vietnam and the peace talks. Ratings for these two topics were summed to provide index scores.

The results for this set of questions are presented in Table 4. The junior high and senior high data are quite similar with two exceptions. Parents are rated as a more important source of information and opinions for the junior high group. And there is a tendency for senior high students to rate the mass media higher as a source of information.

**TABLE 4.    Mean Ratings of Sources of Information and Opinions about Current Affairs**

|  | GRADE LEVEL | SOURCE RATED | | | |
|---|---|---|---|---|---|
|  |  | Parents | Friends | Teachers | Mass Media |
| Rating as Source | Jr.Hi | 3.7 | 2.4 | 3.9 | 5.4 |
| of Information | Sr.Hi | 2.8 | 2.7 | 3.8 | 5.7 |
| Rating as Source | Jr.Hi | 3.7 | 2.5 | 3.3 | 4.5 |
| of Opinions | Sr.Hi | 2.8 | 2.6 | 3.1 | 4.5 |

Comparing the sources, the mass media are clearly rated as the most important source of information and (albeit to a lesser extent) personal opinions. Friends are the least important source. Teachers appear to be more a source of information than of opinion.

These self-report ratings contravene the prevailing view that inter-personal sources are more important than formal channels. The credence given to such data depends, of course, on the degree to which one is willing to trust a person's introspective inference about the influences on his thinking. Some researchers would prefer their own assumptions. . . .

## Conclusions

In all, our data point to the inference that mass communication plays a role in political socialization insofar as political knowledge is concerned, but its influence does not extend to overt behavior such as campaigning activity. Not surprisingly, this effect is a specific function of attention to public affairs content in the media, although entertainment content may "attract" younger children to the media so that they learn something about politics without necessarily intending to. . . .

High media use during the campaign predicts high knowledge (relative to the student's age-peers) after the campaign—even when those factors that account for Time-1 knowledge are partialed out. This time-order evidence indicates that media use should be considered as an independent (or intervening) variable in the political socialization process, not merely as one of many dependent variables. . . .

Our young respondents clearly attribute both informative and opinion-making powers to the media. The more knowledgeable are more likely to say they rely on the media, whereas the less knowledgeable turn to more personal sources for their information and opinions. Perhaps our most surprising finding is the extent to which the youngsters feel their opinions (as distinct from information) are based on mass media reports. They rate the media as more influential than parents, teachers or peers. . . .

We should consider the attitudinal effects of the mass media on political socialization as an open question. There is solid evidence of informational effects; beyond attitudes, there is little evidence of effects on overt political behavior. And of course there is much yet to be learned about other factors that account for differences in media public affairs use and consequent knowledge. Meanwhile, while media influences may be to an extent modified by intervening personal interactions, there can be little doubt that mass communication has some direct effects on the developing adolescent.

## Notes

1. See, *e.g.* Herbert Hyman, *Political Socialization* (Glencoe, Ill.: Free Press, 1959); Richard E. Dawson and Kenneth Prewitt, *Political Socialization* (Boston: Little, Brown and Co., 1969).

2. Robert D. Hess and Judith V. Torney, *The Development of Political Attitudes in Children* (Chicago: Aldine Publishing Co., 1967); Hyman, *op. cit.;* Dawson and Prewitt, *op. cit.*

3. M. Kent Jennings and Richard Niemi, "Patterns of Political Learning," *Harvard Educational Review*, 38:443–67 (Summer 1968); Jennings and Niemi, "The Transmission of Politcal Values from Parent to Child," *American Political Science Review*, 62:169–84 (March 1968); Kenneth P. Langton and Jennings, "Political Socialization and the High School Civics Curriculum," *American Political Science Review*, 62:852–67 (September 1968); Langton, *Political Socialization* (New York: Oxford University Press, 1969).

4. Joseph T. Klapper, *The Effects of Mass Communication* (New York: Free Press, 1960).

5. Including Klapper, who in 1962 was appointed director of social research for the Columbia Broadcasting System, and has since testified frequently in that

capacity before governmental bodies concerned about possible detrimental effects of television on children.

6. Dawson and Prewitt, *op. cit.*

7. Paul J. Deutschmann and Wayne A. Danielson, "Diffusion of Knowledge of the Major News Story," JOURNAL QUARTERLY, 37:345–55 (Summer 1960); Wilbur Schramm, "Communication and Change," in Daniel Lerner and Wilbur Schramm, eds., *Communication and Change in the Developing Countries* (Honolulu: East-West Center Press, 1967), pp. 5–32; Bradley S. Greenberg, "Person-to-Person Communication in the Diffusion of News Events," JOURNALISM QUARTERLY, 41:489–94 (Autumn 1964); Verling C. Troldahl, "A Field Test of a Modified 'Two-Step Flow of Communication' Model," *Public Opinion Quarterly,* 30:609–23 (Winter 1966–67). The direct power of the media to inform without converting opinions is discussed in Klapper, *op. cit.,* pp. 84–90.

8. Bernard R. Berelson, Paul F. Lazarsfeld and William N. McPhee, *Voting: A Study of Opinion Formation in a Presidential Campaign* (Chicago: University of Chicago Press, 1954), pp. 305–23.

9. For a thorough analysis of the various components of political socialization from a systems-theory viewpoint, see David Easton and Jack Dennis, *Children in the Political System* (New York: McGraw-Hill, 1969).

10. Jennings and Niemi, "Patterns of Political Learning," *loc. cit.*

11. Peter Clarke, "A Study of Children's Reading Behavior," report to U.S. Department of Health, Education and Welfare, Office of Education Bureau of Research, March 1969 (Project No. 7–1069).

12. Jack M. McLeod, Steven H. Chaffee and Daniel B. Wackman, "Family Communication: An Updated Report," paper presented to Communication Theory and Methodology Division of AEJ at Boulder, Colo., 1967; Chaffee, McLeod and Wackman, "Family Communication Patterns and Adolescent Political Participation," in Jack Dennis, ed., *Socialization to Politics: A Reader* (New York: Wiley, 1973).

13. Wilbur Schramm, Jack Lyle and Edwin B. Parker, *Television in the Lives of Our Children* (Stanford, Calif.: Stanford University Press, 1961).

14. Gary C. Byrne, "Mass Media and Political Socialization of Children and Pre-Adults," JOURNALISM QUARTERLY, 46:140–2 (Spring 1969).

15. Hess and Torney, *supra,* 2.

16. Failure to pass this test is inconclusive, especially if the hypothesized correlation is close to the static correlations. The latter will tend to be greater simply because of homogeneity of testing conditions, which enhances the associations between measures taken in a single reactive measurement administration—such as our self-administered questionnaires.

17. For this partialing technique, we have relied heavily on the reasoning of George W. Bohrnstedt, "Observations on the Measurement of Change," in Edgar F. Borgatta, ed., *Sociological Methodology 1969* (San Francisco: Jossey-Bass, 1969) pp. 113–33. The formula we have used differs from that given by Bohrnstedt, but is consistent with his line of argument. By partialing out the initial scores on the dependent variable, our analysis explains only *change* in that variable, which is our main interest. This method controls for the influence of external

variables that might account for initial differences in the dependent variable. Substitution of the reverse *(e)* correlation for the static *(c)* correlation is based on the assumption of null conditions, and therefore does not prejudice the data against the null hypothesis.

18. These "baseline" correlations, which would be expected under null conditions only, were calculated as proposed in R. M. Rozelle and D. T. Campbell, "More Plausible Rival Hypotheses in the Cross-Lagged Panel Correlation Technique," *Psychological Bulletin* 71:74–80 (1969). For a thorough methodological analysis of cross-lagged techniques from a path-analytic perspective, see D. R. Heise, "Causal Inference from Panel Data," in E. F. Borgatta and G. W. Bohrnstedt (eds.), *Sociological Methodology 1970* (San Francisco: Jossey-Bass, 1970).

# Popular Support for the Wars in Korea and Vietnam

## JOHN E. MUELLER

WHEN ONE TAKES SUPPORT or opposition for the wars in Korea or Vietnam and correlates either of them (1) with the casualties suffered at the time the poll was conducted or (2) with the duration of the war at the time of the survey, one gets, at least, a reasonably good fit—as would be the case if one correlated support or opposition with *any* variable that increased (or decreased) continually during the wars. But in all cases, correlating the *logarithm* of the number of casualties suffered at the time of the poll gives the best fit. . . .

What this suggests, then, is that *Americans, in the aggregate, reacted in similar ways to the two wars.* While they did weary of the wars, they generally seem to have become hardened to the wars' costs: they are sensitive to relatively small losses in the early stages, but only to large losses in later stages. Another way of looking at the trends is to see subgroups of the population dropping off sequentially from the war's support as casualties mount. In the early stages the support of those with considerable misgivings is easily alienated; in later stages the only advocates left are the relatively hardened supporters whose conversion to opposition proves to be more difficult.

Although the casualty figures can be taken to be a good composite indicator of the intensity and costs of the wars as well as their length, and although public opinion seems to relate to these figures, it should not be assumed that Americans are reacting in a direct sense to the numbers themselves. On occasion, the public has been asked to estimate the American casualty or death figures for a war, and it is possible to compare these estimates with the respondents' policy preferences on the war. Four surveys of this kind were investigated: two taken at the beginning of the Vietnam War, one from the midst of the Korean War, and one from shortly after World War II. No consistent patterns could be found. There was no clear tendency for high (or low) estimators to support or oppose the wars, and few demographic relations of interest emerged. . . .

The situation with regard to the data from Korea and Vietnam is rather extraordinary. . . . The amount of *vocal* opposition to the war in Vietnam was vastly greater than that for the war in Korea. Yet it has now been found that support for the wars among the general public followed a pattern of decline that was remarkably similar. Although support for the war in Vietnam did finally drop below those levels found during Korea, it did so only after the war had gone on considerably longer and only after American casualties had far surpassed those of the earlier war. . . .

This similarity of support might seem surprising, for grand proclamations about the extreme unpopularity of the war in Vietnam are common. James Reston once called it "the most unpopular American war of this century"; a study group for the National Commission on the Causes and Prevention of Violence has declared that it "commands less popular support than any previous American international war"; and journalist David Wise has disclosed that in the Vietnam War, the nation entered "the most unpopular war in its history."[1] The poll evidence suggests that Vietnam has, at least, one rival for these unhappy distinctions.[2]

Vietnam is seen by some to be a more unpopular war than Korea, even from its beginning, probably because . . . *vocal* opposition as judged by demonstrations, petitions, and organized political campaigns was far greater during the later war. Of course all the anti-Vietnam demonstrators, petition-signers, and campaign workers together represent only a few percent of the American adult population, and thus cannot be expected, by themselves, to exert a measurable effect in a cross-sectional poll. But one might expect their existence to be symptomatic of a much larger discontent. The data suggest, however, that although the opposition to the war in Vietnam may have been more vocal than that in Korea, it was not more extensive until the war had far exceeded the Korean War in casualties.

## Some Explanations

One must account, therefore, not for increased *popular* opposition in the Vietnam case, but for increased *vocal* opposition. Several suggestions can be made.

### 1. The Intellectual Left

. . . Most of the vocal opposition to the war in Vietnam seems to have come from the intellectual, nonunion Left. For the reasons discussed there, it seems likely that this small group did view the wars differently: Korea seemed an unpleasant, but necessary, episode in the cold war against Stalinist Russia; however, an anti-Communist war in Vietnam, under the substantially altered cold war atmosphere of the mid-1960s, was not found to be worthy of support. . . .

The years between the Korean and Vietnam wars had seen the gradual emergence of the intellectual Left as a force with political, though not necessarily electoral impact. This seems to have grown out of the opposition to McCarthy and then developed in the late 1950s with movements urging arms-control measures such as atomic test bans, unilateral disarmament initiatives, and alliance readjustments. In the early 1960s it had as a major inspiration the opposition to President Kennedy's fallout shelter program (see Levine 1963).

Around 1963, the intellectual Left moved from a preoccupation with international cold war issues to an alignment with the fast-emerging civil rights forces. In part, this was a result of the attractive dynamism of the movement and of its aggressive and inspired leadership. And, in part, it was due, after the 1962 Cuban missile crisis, to the notable thaw in the cold war. This seemed to make international threats and issues less pressing. The near evaporation of the arms control movement at this point is quite ironic, since the improved diplomatic atmosphere made it likely that pressure for arms-control measures would finally prove effective.[3]

In its association with the civil rights movement, the intellectual Left picked up and helped develop effective new techniques for political expression: passive disobedience, peaceful mass protest, the use of the media, and obstructionism.

As important legislative and judicial victories were won in the civil rights struggle, as the issue became more technical and cloudy, as blacks showed themselves capable of handling their own movement and, in some quarters, became rather resentful of (even friendly) white interference, and as the movement developed into the destructive, but possibly cathartic and vital, riot stage—as these developments occurred, the civil rights issue became less attractive to the intellectual Left.

Vietnam became at first a competitive cause, then a dominating one, until by 1968 the intellectual Left was almost entirely preoccupied with it. The new techniques of political expression were refashioned and redeveloped to fit the new cause and were put into action. The seeming efficacy of the movement generated a certain attractive inertia, swelling the ranks.

Thus *the "new Left" of the late 1960s seems, in this analysis, to be the old Left with new methods of expression, a new vocalism.* It is not "young people" brought up in the shadow of the bomb or of John Dewey. . . . In fact, it was found that young people were generally more inclined to support the wars than their elders. . . .

This is not simply to say that the intellectual Left is fickle about its causes. Rather, because it is limited in size and energy, it does not seem able effectively to fight full force on two fronts at the same time and must choose its priorities: the race issue, it was common to hear in the late 1960s, can never be solved until the war in Vietnam is brought to an end.

Thus the difference in vocal opposition between the wars can be traced in part to a shift in attitude by one political group and to the effective use by that group of newly learned techniques of expression. However, none of this is to deny the political impact of the agitation on important elite groups, including those that finance political campaigns (Robinson 1970:9). The message here is simply to warn against the assumption that intellectual agitation is the same thing as a mass movement.[4]

## 2. McCarthyism, the Korean War, and Academic Economics

If there were people on the Left in opposition to the Korean War, their expression of dissent may have been smothered by the pall of McCarthyism.[5] In the early 1950s, a war opponent risked the danger of being labeled a Communist. In the 1960s the climate had changed enough so that such labeling was less likely to occur and, more importantly, less likely to be effective if applied.

For academicians, an important element of the intellectual Left, economic considerations may have reinforced these pressures, thus discouraging any inclined to oppose the Korean War from loudly voicing their point of view. The academic marketplace of the early 1950s was an extreme buyers' market as the generation born in predepression days, embellished by somewhat older people whose graduate education had been postponed by World War II, entered the academic profession to find only the depression generation to teach. Thus job insecurity may have made political protest economically unwise and may have made the academic profession peculiarly susceptible to McCarthyite intimidation.

By the mid-1960s, however, the situation was reversed. The post-World War II babies were going to college while depression babies were entering the academic profession which then became a sellers' market. Thus academicians could protest, threaten to resign, and speak freely and impertinently, always aware that jobs were open somewhere. In part, therefore, academic courage may have an economic base.

While the fear of McCarthyite attack might have kept Korean War opponents from publicly expressing a point of view that could be interpreted as pro-Communist, it does not appear that the McCarthy camp was a notable source of support for the war. . . . Those who adopted a McCarthy point of view were no more likely than others to find the war worthwhile either while it was being fought or after it was over, although (at least in 1953) they did have an escalatory vision of what strategy should be pursued there.

A 1954 survey by National Opinion Research Center (NORC) included a large number of questions concerning areas of foreign policy other than

Korea. By and large, they show little difference between approvers and disapprovers of McCarthy—even on such issues as trusting Yugoslavia, defending Formosa if under Communist attack, or recognizing Communist China. Nor do the groups differ markedly on their willingness to volunteer whether "most people can be trusted." Similar results are generated by a NORC survey conducted in the last months of the Korean War. . . . While those intent on rooting out domestic Communists were, comparatively, somewhat opposed to dealing with and compromising with the Russians, they did not differ from others on trading with Communist China or on the wisdom of intervening militarily in other countries to stop international Communism.

## 3. The Attentive Public

It may be the case, as James Rosenau has suggested, that the size of the attentive public has been increasing in response to advances in education, technology, and communication. These increases would not be enough to register markedly in public opinion polls, but they might show themselves in the increased scope of organized political protest (Rosenau 1968).

## 4. The Vietnam Protest as Counterproductive

Finally, it should be considered that the protest against the war in Vietnam may have been counterproductive in its impact on public opinion: that is, the war might have been somewhat *more* unpopular if the protest had not existed. . . .

Many people, in arriving at a position on an issue, do not cue on the elements of the issue itself so much as on the expressed preferences of various opinion leaders. Instead of paying high information costs by sorting through the intricacies of argument of the issue, they prefer to take the word of people and institutions that they have reason to trust. Thus the public does not view an issue in the simple debating-manual sense with arguments pro and con neatly arranged. Rather the issue comes attended by certain public figures who array themselves on various sides and whose visible presence at an issue position may influence public opinion more than any element of the issue itself.

For a war, then, public opinion is going to be influenced by who is for it and who is against it. Now it happens that the opposition to the war in Vietnam came to be associated with rioting, disruption, and bomb throwing, and war protesters, as a group, enjoyed negative popularity ratings to an almost unparalleled degree. This has been shown in a number of studies and is, perhaps, most dramatically evident in the public's reaction to the 1968 Democratic Convention disorders, which was overwhelmingly favorable to the Chicago police (Robinson 1970; Converse et al. 1969:1087–88).

That negative reference groups can harm a cause's impact, a sort of negative follower effect, is quite clear. Cantril reports a poll from 1940, before the United States entered World War II, in which it was found that 57 percent of the American public expressed its agreement with the idea that the country should try to have friendly relations with Germany if she won the war in Europe. However, when the name of Charles Lindbergh, a prominent isolationist leader, was associated with this idea, support for it dropped to 46 percent while opposition climbed 16 percentage points (1947:41).

Thus it seems entirely possible that, because their cause became associated with an extraordinarily unpopular reference group, any gain the opposition to the war in Vietnam may have achieved by forcefully bringing its point of view to public attention was nullified. But, again, it must be observed that the protest may still have been effective in a general political sense if it was successful in altering attitudes among elites and decision-makers.

## Sources of the Anti-Vietnam Protest

Studies indicate quite clearly that the young people who did oppose the war, as well as their well-educated older colleagues, were very disproportionately associated with the "better" colleges in the country (Converse and Schuman 1970:23–25). In cross-sectional polls, however, their attitudes are overwhelmed by the legions among the young and the educated who enjoy no such association. It is of interest to consider why these associations should correspond with opposition to the war and the president's policy there.

One element in the explanation concerns the relatively liberal and left-liberal atmosphere at the better universities. Since, as noted above, political liberals were inclined to oppose the Vietnam War, it is not surprising to find opposition to the war in Vietnam centered at places where liberals are concentrated: the better universities (see Armor et al. 1967).

But in part this begs the question. What must be discussed is why the better universities are relatively liberal places. It could be that the more intelligent a person is, the more likely he is to adopt the liberal philosophy. However comforting this thought may be to liberals, it is of questionable validity, since in decades past the better universities were often bastions of conservatism. Or, it may be that pliable student minds are being bent to the Left by a band of liberal professors. But this explanation fits poorly with studies that find student values and attitudes in the aggregate not to be affected in any such gross way, if indeed they are affected at all, by the college experience (Jacob 1957; Goldsen et al. 1960; Feldman and Newcomb 1969). Nor does it fit with those that find faculty members to be particularly ineffective when changes do occur (Feldman and Newcomb 1969:330–31 et passim.). Nor does it fit with those that find college-bound high school seniors already to differ markedly in attitude from their peers (Langton and Jennings 1968:866).

A better explanation might draw on an observation . . . about the liberalism of Jews. Outside of a few sections in a few cities, the only easily identifiable places that Jews are found in strikingly disproportion are the colleges and universities of the land—and very particularly the better ones. Thus the liberalism of those associated with the better universities may not derive from anything endemic in the university situation. Rather, it may stem from the influence of a major subpopulation in the university community inclined toward liberalism and war opposition regardless of its association with the college.[6]

## TV

Many have seen Vietnam as a "television war" and argue that the vivid and largely uncensored day-by-day television coverage of the war and its brutalities made a profound impression on public attitudes.

The poll data used in this study do not support such a conclusion. They clearly show that whatever impact television had, it was not enough to reduce support for the war below the levels attained by the Korean War, when television was in its infancy, until casualty levels had far surpassed those of the earlier war.[7] Furthermore the television coverage of the 1968 Democratic Convention, although favorable to the demonstrators, was not capable of generating popular sympathy for them or their cause. . . .

A study conducted by NORC during World War II seems to be consonant with these findings. In the study realistic war pictures were shown to 112 respondents. Their reactions to a number of poll questions were then ascertained and compared to a matched sample of unexposed respondents. The exposure seems to have increased favorable attitudes toward a realistic news policy, but it affected attitudes toward the war itself not at all (NORC 1944).

## Notes

1. *New York Times,* June 21, 1968; *ibid.,* June 6, 1969; Wise (1968:27). All these statements were made before Vietnam support fell below that of Korea.

2. On the other hand, one possible indicator, the morale of American troops, would suggest that the earlier war was the more unpopular. Social commentators during the Korean War were fond of attributing the low morale they discerned to miscellaneous notions about the crusading spirit of the American people, who were unable to support a war unless there were some Great Ideal at stake. . . . See *New York Times,* February 14, 1968.

3. Indicative of the change was the collapse of the *Journal of Arms Control* after two issues in 1963. It proved to be the wrong journal at the wrong time on the wrong subject.

4. That demonstrators have not been representative either of the general public or of nondemonstrating activists in their attitudes toward the war in Vietnam is suggested by the evidence presented by Verba and Brody (1970).

5. It has been suggested that the fear politicians had of McCarthy was somewhat unrealistic. See Polsby (1960).

6. A survey conducted by the President's Commission on Campus Unrest found that campus disturbances occurred most often at large, eastern, liberal arts colleges with high admissions standards (*New York Times,* November 5, 1970).

7. For an excellent discussion, see Arlen (1969). The Harris Poll once reported, "For most Americans television helps simplify the enormous complexities of the war and the net effect is that when they switch off their sets, 83 percent feel more hawkish than they did before they turned them on" (*Newsweek,* July 10, 1967, p. 22). The question on which this observation is based, however, was "Has the television coverage of the war made you feel more like you ought to back up the boys fighting in Vietnam or not?" (Letter from Louis Harris Political Data Center, University of North Carolina, September 10, 1969.)

# References

ARLEN, MICHAEL J., *1969. Living-room War* (New York: Viking).

ARMOR, DAVID J., JOSEPH B. GIACQUINTA, R. GORDON McINTOSH, and DIANA E. H. RUSSELL, *1967.* "Professors' Attitudes Toward the Vietnam War" 31 *Public Opinion Quarterly* 159–75 (Summer).

CANTRIL, HADLEY and ASSOCIATES, *1947. Guaging Public Opinion* (Princeton, N.J.: Princeton University Press).

CONVERSE, PHILIP E. and HOWARD SCHUMAN, *1970.* " 'Silent Majorities' and the Vietnam War." *Scientific American* 17–25 (June).

CONVERSE, PHILIP E., WARREN E. MILLER, JERROLD G. RUSK, and ARTHUR C. WOLFE, *1969.* "Continuity and Change in American Politics: Parties and Issues in the 1968 Elections" 63 *American Political Science Review* 1083–1105 (December).

FELDMAN, KENNETH A. and THEODORE M. NEWCOMB, *1969. The Impact of College on Students,* Vol. 1 (San Francisco: Jassey-Bass).

GOLDSEN, ROSE K., MORRIS ROSENBERG, ROBIN M. WILLIAMS, JR., And EDWARD A. SUCHMAN, *1960. What College Students Think* (Princeton, N.J.: Van Nostrand).

JACOB, PHILIP E., *1957. Changing Values in College* (New York: Harper and Row).

LANGTON, KENNETH P. and M. KENT JENNINGS, *1968.* "Political Socialization and the High School Civics Curriculum in the United States" 62 *American Political Science Review* 852–67 (September).

LEVINE, ROBERT A., *1963. The Arms Debate* (Cambridge, Mass.: Harvard University Press).

NATIONAL OPINION RESEARCH CENTER, *1944.* "The Effect of Realistic War Pictures," *Report EW 20,* March 13.

POLSBY, NELSON W., *1960.* "Toward an Explanation of McCarthyism" 8 *Political Studies* 250–71 (October).

ROBINSON, JOHN P., *1970.* "Public Reaction to Political Protest: Chicago 1968" 34 *Public Opinion Quarterly* 1–9 (Spring).

ROSENAU, JAMES N., *1968.* "The Attentive Public and Foreign Policy: A Theory of Growth and Some New Evidence" Research Monograph No. 31, Center of International Studies, Princeton University.

VERBA, SYDNEY and RICHARD BRODY, *1970.* "Participation, Policy Preferences, and the War in Vietnam" 34 *Public Opinion Quarterly* 325–32 (Fall).

WISE, DAVID, *1968.* "The Twilight of a President," *New York Times Magazine,* November 3, p. 27 ff.

# Television and American Politics: 1956–1976

MICHAEL J. ROBINSON

TELEVISION HAS CHANGED MARKEDLY during the last two decades. And so has American politics. Since 1956, public opinion in the United States has in many ways come full circle—from conservative to liberal and back to conservative (or at least "neo-conservative") once again. And in many respects, television has gone through the same changes. Indeed, one of the main arguments in this article is that television and politics have gone through this metamorphosis together, and that television has been a major factor in the political changes that have taken place since the 1950's.

But the crucial point is not merely that television began as a conservative influence, then became a liberal influence, and eventually emerged as a conservative influence once more. Equally important is that in the 1950's television was a *reflection* of our social and political opinions, but by the 1960's it was an important *cause* of them.

This fundamental shift—from effect to cause—makes my intention somewhat different from that of most essays about television. My purpose is both to explain much of the last 20 years of politics by explaining the changes in American television and to explain why television itself changed during those years. This will eventually lead to the following conclusions: 1) that until 1960, television was an institution with little or no major political impact; 2) that since 1960, television has pushed politics back and forth, between left and right, liberal and conservative; and 3) that *since 1968, television in its total effect has been simultaneously fostering social liberalism and political conservatism.*

Reprinted with permission of the author from *The Public Interest,* No. 48 (Summer 1977). © 1977 by National Affairs, Inc.

## The Two Modes of Television

To understand all of this, one must keep in mind that there are, and have always been, two modes of television: entertainment and information. Sometimes the distinction between the two is not as great as the network news departments might pretend. . . . The distinction was perhaps not so important back in 1956, when shows like *December Bride, I Love Lucy,* and the *$64,000 Question* were the backbone of programming, and almost all television merely served to reinforce the social conventionalism and political conservatism of the time. Television journalism was working in an opposite direction, perhaps—but only ever so slightly, and only occasionally. . . .

But during the 1960's, the distinction became quite meaningful, as entertainment television and television journalism both became politically important and powerful. By then, the principal political message and images of the two broadcasting modes had begun to diverge: Entertainment television and its themes began moving us toward social and political liberalism; television journalism and its themes began doing just the opposite—moving us toward social and political conservatism.

If this theory is correct—and it certainly has its share of detractors— the irony is striking. That part of television most closely and accurately identified with Madison Avenue and the business community would be the fomenter of a more "open" and liberal set of social-political values—what might best be described in 1977 as "Sonny-and-Cherism." In contrast, that part of the industry regularly attacked for being an electronic sounding board of "Eastern establishment liberalism" would be a major cause of the political retrenchmen that occurred during the last years of the 1960's, when the most rapidly growing form of conservatism resembled something akin to the combined philosophies of Paul Harvey and Archie Bunker.

Although his theory is not without missing pieces, enough of it fits together that I think it deserves consideration. The best way to consider this theory is to divide the last two decades into four distinct phases, nearly equal in length, and to look at the major developments in each period—developments crucial for television, for politics, or for both. I will begin by returning to the 1950's, the most quiescent, least politicized period of postwar America— Happy Days, so to speak.

## Television as a Commercial Toy: 1956–1960

In retrospect, the 1950's look very much like the era of the politics of happiness, even if we didn't know it then. The Suez crisis, the Polish rebellion, the Hungarian revolution, Eisenhower's heart attack, and even the sinking of the Andrea Doria all occurred within an eight-month period during 1956. Yet by contemporary standards, we were politically inert. Social scientists were asserting both the "end of ideology" (hiatus, as it turned out) and a new middle-class American concensus.

Social scientists were also demonstrating, with newly acquired statistical techniques, that television had almost no impact whatsoever on voters in Presidential or Congressional elections: The University of Chicago, the University of Michigan, and Miami University all released major studies in the 1950's strenuously denying the alleged omnipotence of television. This first wave of research from prestigious universities and by renowned social scientists produced a school of thought that regarded television as having no more political influence than radio or newspapers, and probably less than personal communication. That school, founded in the 1950's on data from the first large-scale survey-research projects, still represents—and still misguides—mainstream academic opinion about the impact of television. . . .

To be sure, entertainment television of the "Golden Age" (as the 1950's have inappropriately been labeled) was undeniably irrelevant. From the list of the top-rated programs in this period (see the table on page 112), it is easy to understand the total frustration of anyone who even dreamed of using television as a mechanism for stimulating political awareness—let alone political change—at this time. Entertainment television had nothing whatever to offer beyond the social clichés of the period—the inevitability of marriage, the frivolousness of womanhood, the desirability of youthfulness, and the necessity of material abundance. . . .

If entertainment television was almost wholly without political substance or impact—save for its ability to make the suburbs and stainless-steel barbecue sets look good, while making the Russians look bad—television journalism had only slightly more impact. With a few important exceptions—the Murrow-McCarthy case on *See It Now* and the Army-McCarthy hearings have since become romantic legends—television news and documentaries were not major social or political forces during the middle 1950's.

Electronic campaigning, however, had started to come of age. The 1956 election witnessed the first comprehensive effort at Presidential advertising on television. But just as in 1952, the "scientific" literature demonstrated that television was anything but a powerful campaign tool. After the 1956 campaign, it became almost an article of faith among social scientists that the supposed political power of television was only an illusion of the unscientific laity.

One question that continued to surface at this time was whether television was a major cause of widespread conformity to middle-class social values. Or was television merely the effect? I think that the question is important now because the answer itself varies over time. At one time, television was the effect—the 1950's. Since then, however, television has transformed itself into a *cause* of social values and philosophy. But what produced this crucial transformation? The first and more important answer emphasizes the basic changes that were inevitable in an industry like television. The second answer involves a poignant historical incident that was to network television in the 1950's what Watergate was to the Presidency in the 1970's.

## The Great Change

In its first 10 years, television was an organization working toward two goals—saturation and acceptance. It was a new medium, and considerably less diverse in its composition and motives than older, more established media, like radio and the movies. Television was scared of radio, scared of the movies, and even scared of its own sponsors.

Television, so new and so expensive, could be—and was—intimidated. There were few within the industry who seriously regarded television as a political instrument, and even fewer who felt that the industry had any right, let alone a responsibility, to do anything "meaningful." In its prepubescence, television was extraordinarily "uptight." Of course, to some degree, so was everything else in the 1950's—escept for the greasers, beatniks, and Elvis Presley. . . .

One other factor seems important in understanding the inability of early television to do anything but reinforce the status quo. Until the 1960's, advertisers produced programs. Independent packaging and packagers came later. Advertisers—still remembering vividly the days in which the undershirt went out of style simply because Clark Gable chose not to wear one in the movies—were the least likely of all the industry people to use television entertainment for any purpose but commercial sales, or in ways that could possibly offend any prospective buyer.

A final factor, of course, was the nature of the times. The "witch hunt" in Hollywood and, more importantly, the publication of *Red Channels: The Report of Communist Influence in Radio and Television* made virtually everyone connected with the industry terribly reticent about doing politically controversial programming (unless it was controversially anti-Communist).

But within 10 years the industry and the country inexorably and inevitably changed and matured. Investments in television proved sound—very sound. With financial security came less anxiety about controversial programming. Advertisers and sponsors became subordinated to the newly developing program packagers. And, of course, as McCarthyism and the cold war began to wane, television had greater license to do less insipid programming, or at least less irrelevant programming.

All these changes meant that a more pluralistic institution would emerge, and it did. But that evolutionary process was hastened by an event that nobody had really anticipated, and nobody really wanted.

In November 1956, on NBC's quiz show, *Twenty-One,* the country saw for the first time a young, scholarly, and handsome English professor from Columbia. In a matter of weeks, Charles Van Doren became a kind of national hero. But it was soon revealed that he, like so many other quiz-show contestants before him, had participated in a cruel national hoax: Several contestants, like Van Doren, had been given at least partial answers to the questions before the shows ever began, as producers fed the answers selectively and secretly to especially attractive contestants, those whom the audience would love to watch week by week. The subsequent public confession by Van Doren of such cheating delt a terrible blow to the industry; television quickly came to be regarded as the force that seduced both Robin Hood and Einstein at the same time.

The effect of the quiz-show scandals was what might have been expected from an industry committed to corporate profits and extending itself geographically and financially. The networks and affiliates immediately sought to shore up their image. Within a year the National Association of Broadcasters (NAB) had established the Television Information Office (TIO), the public-relations arm for the industry. TIO immediately commissioned the Roper organization to assess the damage that the scandals had caused. This was the beginning of the Roper pool on television and other media—the most comprehensive set of surveys ever conducted.

In part, TIO did its original surveys hoping to show that the public, despite the scandals, still loved television. But in fact, despite loaded questions on the topic of quiz-show scandals, the Roper survey indicated that television had been hurt badly. More importantly, according to the Roper data, in 1959 clear pluralities believed that newspapers were *more* important and *more* credible than television as a source of information. It became essential to the industry that those pluralities be reversed. To accomplish that, the networks embarked on a campaign to increase the size and quality of their news and public-affairs divisions. The quiz-show scandals thus led to the policy of using news as the principal vehicle for improving the corporate image of television—an industry that is literally nothing without its image. . . .

## Television as a Political Instrument: 1960–1964

It should come as no surprise that television journalism reached puberty before entertainment television did. After all, public-affairs television was actually born first (1939). And despite what Fred Friendly or Sander Vanocur might say, public-affairs television has had fewer popular or commercial restraints upon it from the start—in part because it represented so small a proportion of the entire industry, and in part because the Paleys and Sarnoffs of this world *did* believe in informing people (within limits). So by 1960, although the top three shows were *Gunsmoke, Wagon Train,* and *Have Gun, Will Travel,* television journalism was clearly beginning to count.

Without doubt, the single most important development during these years was the Kennedy-Nixon debates. And if the "Great Debates" were a boon to John Kennedy, they were an even bigger bonanza for the media professionals who had services to sell. Indeed, because of the debates, the amount expended by Presidential candidates for radio and television increased by nearly 300 percent between 1960 and 1964, a rate of increase never achieved before or since. The Kennedy-Nixon debates signaled the beginning of the audio-visual orgy of the 1960's, which finally slowed in 1971 when Congress first limited the amount candidates could spend on television campaigning. . . .

The early 1960's also witnessed another new political function for television. Kennedy, so pleased with the medium that everyone agreed had helped elect him, quickly tried to convert the networks into a large Presidential megaphone. Eisenhower had never liked television and had done badly with it, but Kennedy reveled in it, more than tripling his predecessor's rate of monthly network appearances and, quite surprisingly, building a record that even Lyndon Johnson could not match. Only Carter has managed to surpass Kennedy's zeal for and attachment to television.

Kennedy gave the networks their first real opportunity to televise the President in his office, at work, and during his press conferences. In return, Kennedy tacitly accepted the unstated privilege of using the networks to build a more plebiscitary Presidency than any since that of Franklin Roosevelt. There is some irony here, in that Kennedy's innovative use of television—which generally served both the desires of the network news departments and the tastes of the correspondents—helped expand the "imperial Presidency" more quickly than most television journalists would care to admit. Under Kennedy, television overwhelmingly concentrated on the Presidency for the first time. By the time of his death, Kennedy had helped to make both network journalism and the Presidency more powerful forces in American politics. . . .

## The Civil-Rights Movement

Television in the early 1960's was not wholly concerned with the debates or John Kennedy. In fact, during the early part of the decade, television seemed to be shifting power not just *upward* toward the Presidency, but also *downward* toward the photogenic.

Consider the Southern civil-rights movement, the first real issue that television news ever covered on a recurring basis. The movement became the first continuing saga of network journalism because it was so much an audio-visual phenomenon. . . . It was a basic constitutional and human issue, with easily distinguishable and very photogenic heroes and villains: Martin Luther King, Bull Connor, Orville Faubus, and the inimitable George Corley Wallace. . . .

At a minimum, television coverage of the early civil-rights movement altered the public's notions as to what the political agenda should be. In that regard, the "March on Washington" in August 1963 was the greatest public-relations gambit ever staged—staged as it was for television. Between the spring and summer of 1963, the percentage of people regarding civil rights as "the most important problem facing America" increased by a factor of 13—from four percent to 52 percent, a shift in perceived public priorities never achieved before or since in so short a time.

One of the most important lessons of this period was that television news and television documentaries provided a new and powerful political resource. Television allowed for a previously unattainable level of governmental access for groups who had few of the traditional resources. *Television became an important means for redistributing political power from the haves to the have-nots.* All the media do this to some extent—but none to the degree possible with network television. The have-nots could quickly reach the government by doing something literally visible enough to merit attention. Obviously, sensationalism has always meant press coverage, but television made the principal criterion a visual one. That inevitably meant a shift in power toward those groups wretched or angry or clever enough to do what was needed to become photogenic. . . .

## Videopolitics: 1963–1972

Most Americans, young or old, probably remember 1963 as the year that John Kennedy was assassinated. But media freaks remember it as the year that CBS, NBC, and eventually ABC switched from a 15-minute to a 30-minute format for evening news. I think that a case can be made that the latter development was, in the long run, every bit as important in our political development as the former—that the 30-minute news program that began in 1963 altered the basic process of political communication in the United States. Given the events of the next 10 years, one can make a case that the emergence of the television news system after 1963 was probably among the two or three most important political phenomena during the period 1963–1972. . . .

To understand the effects of the television news system, it is essential to understand its attributes, some of which are unique, some of which are merely extraordinary. One unique characteristic is that its audience is an *inadvertent* one—which, in large proportion, does not come purposely to television for news, but arrives almost accidentally, watching the news because it is "on" or because it leads into or out of something else. . . . In what is probably the most thorough investigation ever conducted into the motives for watching television news, Richard Hofstetter, at San Diego State, found that 87 percent of the television audience watches network news for "non-political" reasons. . . .

This inadvertent audience is enormous—40 million viewers nightly. But the size of this audience is not as important as its composition. *Compared with all other news audiences, the television news audience is disproportionately drawn from the low end of the social spectrum.* The people who watch the most television news, in absolute *and* in proportional terms, are among the least well-educated and least "connected" individuals in our mass society. This is unprecedented for a news audience, and completely reverses the general pattern of high correlation between news consumption and socio-economic status. . . .

Because of its size, composition, and constancy, the evening news audience is singularly vulnerable to the messages it receives. Before the advent of the television news system, the inadvertent audience was *potentially* vulnerable to a host of politically relevant influences through various news media. But without television news, not enough information reached this audience to realize its potential. Consequently, *before the television news system, those who consumed meager amounts of news proved to be both highly stable in their political opinions and very passive in their pattern of political behavior.* This audience was, at that early stage, literally a silent majority. *But with television, this formerly quiescent political stratum could become—and did, for a short while—one of the least stable and least quiescent portions of the public, as television news came to act as a stimulus.* That was perhaps the inevitable outcome of bringing political information—especially the kind of information the 1960's provided—to those previously connected to politics by civics books, by headlines, or by precinct workers.

## Television News Is Different

Even if the messages of television journalism had been precisely the same as those of the print media, we might still have expected that the television news system would have had special impact—simply because so many more "unconnected" people would have been receiving information about politics than before. But the messages are not and have not been the same. Television news has always been different from print—even in the Swayze era—and the differences between the two have in some respects become more important since 1963.

First, television news is national news; print news is not, and has not been. We have never had a national daily newspaper, except for the *Wall Street Journal,* and the focus of news had always been local until the coming of the television news system. But the focus is now unmistakably national.

This national orientation may seem trivial at first. But in a system in which news is defined as that which is extraordinary, sensational, abnormal, or bad—which is undoubtedly the American definition of news—the geographic focus is per se extremely important. *When television shifted its focus*

*toward Washington, it was only a matter of time before "Washington news"*
*would also shift our political frustrations toward Washington,* instead of toward
city government or the state capitals. Perhaps one of the least observed but
most important trends in public opinion during the years following the establishment of the television news system was that the public confidence in
state and local government remained constantly low (as the negative information about those levels of government continued at the same absolute levels)
but that confidence in the federal government declined—and presumably at
a rate inversely related to the emerging preeminence of network news.

Television news differs from print news in several other respects. Television
tends to be more "intense" than print news—selecting a few topics, issues,
or areas for coverage and returning to them incessantly. My analysis of news
coverage of the 1976 Presidential campaign indicated that, compared with
the print media, television concentration on far fewer primaries, even adjusting
for the greater "length" of newspaper coverage. In fact, in the early campaign,
television devoted more than half of all its coverage to one state alone—
New Hampshire. Newspapers—both chain newspapers and prestige newspapers—allocated far smaller amounts of their "news hole" to New Hampshire. . . . In absolute terms, the election returns from New Hampshire
received almost four times as much coverage as the returns from New
York. . . .

A good deal has also been made of the alleged partisan differences between
television news and the print media. On balance, it is probably fair to say
that news people on television tend to be more liberal than those in print
journalism. But the news itself does not always or does not generally reflect
this—especially if we contrast the networks with the major newspapers. If
we define "partisan" or "liberal" merely in terms of party affiliation, it is
not so clear that there is a consistent pro-Democratic bias in network news.
With respect to the 1972 election, in the longest, most comprehensive content
analysis even done of television news, Richard Hofstetter demonstrated that
Nixon got *significantly more positive coverage on television* than did McGovern.
And if news time alone is any indication, my data show that Ronald Reagan
was the network "darling" during the early phases of the 1976 campaign.
In short, the issue of "bias" remains open.

But even ignoring the question of "partisan" bias between the two media—
print and television—the remaining list of contrasts is still quite long. Television news is more *thematic* than other types of news; only the shortest items—
those less than 30 seconds—lack a didactic conclusion or message. Especially
since the development of the 30-minute newscast, television tends to offer
us "stories," not news items. Television news also tends to concentrate more
on personalities. The tendency to "Kissingerize" foreign policy—to regard
it as one man acting alone—was even more pronounced on television than
in print, if not so pronounced in either medium as in the former Secretary's
mind. . . .

Finally, television has an audio-visual quality the other media lack. Most of the research in this field indicates that this obvious and unique quality makes the content of television more memorable and evocative, if not necessarily more persuasive. And seeing journalists, as opposed to reading them, makes anchormen and correspondents both more familiar and more credible. Walter Cronkite is more likely believed because he is seen, than seen because he is believed.

## Videopolitics and the Party System

What have been the effects of the first 10 years of the television news system—the decade of videopolitics? One must begin by conceding the difficulty of saying what was causing what between 1963 and 1972—regardless of the type or quality of data chosen. Nonetheless, several types of data suggest that television journalism, as a whole, did engender some fundamental political changes during this period—changes in our political institutions, our traditional patterns of voting, our public opinions, and our political ethos.

The effects of television on our institutions have been evolving for some time, beginning well before 1963. Keeping in mind that the media may affect either the *internal workings* or *external significance* of any institution, I believe that the influence television has had on the internal operations of our major institutions has been a direct function of the amount of coverage each has either attracted or allowed to take place. Beyond that, I believe that the real significance an institution has in the political process, in a television age, is related to its ability to attract television coverage and *at the same time* to maintain one or more critical activities distinct from the coverage it attracts. All this means is that an institution that can attract lots of television coverage, knows how to accommodate such coverage, and maintains an important area of authority beyond that coverage will grow more powerful. The Presidency is the obvious case. But an institution with few resources to begin with, which attracts or solicits television in order to build a new political resource for itself, will inevitably *lose* power. The political parties seem to be in precisely this predicament. . . .

Perhaps the most interesting example of the parasitic relationship between television and the parties (especially the Democratic party) involves the marked tendency of state legislatures since 1964 to seek national network coverage of primary elections so aggressively that even the state parties have suffered somewhat as a consequence. Television networks do overload heavily on primary states during Presidential elections, and state legislatures do what they can to attract as much network news coverage for their states as possible. Switching from conventions or caucuses to Presidential primaries is something state legislatures can do to increase their visibility with little *immediate* cost. Between 1964 and 1972, the number of primary states doubled, at least in part because television news made primary politics so much more attractive in terms of television coverage. . . .

One important outcome of this usurpation of the parties by the media has been that network news has emerged as "the loyal opposition," more so than even the party out of office. *It is now the networks that act as the shadow cabinet.* . . .

## Television, the "Imperial Presidency," and Congress

The Presidency, of course, is at the other end of the continuum. Singular and bristling with Constitutional authority, the Presidency has always been the likely place for political power to accumulate, and the media to congregate. . . . The Presidency has the unique mix of media attractiveness and clearly defined institutional authority that virtually insures an advantage for the office itself. . . . There is another possible, paradoxical, and unsettling ramification of the television news system for the Presidency. While television, through its nearly compulsive predilection for the Presidency, has probably made the office more powerful, it may also have rendered the authority of the President less legitimate. We see, close-up, all the shortcomings of the successive incumbents. The result may be a new sort of equilibrium in Presidential power, in which *television helps move power toward the office but detracts from the legitimacy of the officeholder.* Whatever the final balance, it is interesting that our communications system may centralize authority while rendering the authorities themselves less respectable. . . .

The only conclusion that seems certain is that *the television news system has a symbiotic relationship with the strong institutions and a parasitic relationship with the weak.* Among the major non-elective institutions, only the courts have been able simply to refuse to accommodate themselves to television without paying a price.

## Videopolitics and the Electoral Connection

The impact of the television news system on the electorate has been much more radical than its impact on institutions. I would guess that 1963 was once again the pivotal year.

Through 1960, the standard pattern of voting was to support the nominee of the party to which one felt the greater psychological and sentimental attachment—almost regardless of the issues or the candidates. That pattern existed throughout the 1930's, 1940's, and even the 1950's. In 1960, psychological attachment to party was statistically as great a factor in voting choice as it had been in 1940. But by 1964, in the first Presidential election held under the television news system, images and issues, according to Herbert Asher at Ohio State, were almost three times as important a predictor of vote as they had been in 1960. Goldwater's candidacy no doubt played some role in this, but it was as much a function of the changing communications process as anything else. In 1964, for the first time, it was the *least* politically involved who were *most likely* to vote "issues" instead of "party," and this development was surely an outgrowth of the "inadvertent" television news audience and of the special concerns of network news.

Nonetheless, in one sense, the greatest electoral change that emerged in this period was not simply the growth in "issue voting." Nor was it the unprecedentedly rapid increase in the number and percentage of political independents, another crucial post-1963 phenomenon in which network journalism played a role. (By covering both parties in a less than favorable light, and by giving viewers more information about candidates than they would otherwise have received, network news made partisan loyalty both less desirable and less useful.) *The greatest change was the shift toward a more plebiscitary process of electing leaders—in which television journalism provided a more direct link between the public and the candidates than had ever existed.* The direct contact between electorate and elected was obviously little more than an illusion, but it was, for the first time since the colonial period, unfettered and unmediated by party or any other large political organization. The contact was made instead through media consultants, professional campaign coordinators, and especially through network news. For good or ill, this is nothing less than a quiet revolution in the traditional American idea of representative democracy. At a minimum, this new system has rendered obsolete the old theory of a "two-step flow" of communication—the widely held notion that political information flows from the source to opinion leaders, and only then to the public. The television news system circumvented both party and opinion leaders, and in the process not only rendered the electorate less committed to partisan identification but also left it considerably more sensitive to images and issues. . . .

Nonetheless, in perhaps the three most important pieces of research done in the last five years in this thankless area of assessing the electoral impact of campaign television—by Richard Hofstetter at San Diego State, Robert McClure and Thomas Patterson at Syracuse, and Gary Jacobson at Trinity College—the findings have been reasonably consistent. As a rule, *ad campaigns do not directly buy many votes.* For obvious reasons, most of the "bought" votes come in primary elections—or, for less obvious reasons, in Senatorial campaigns. At the Presidential level, in the general election, the effects are minimal. McClure and Patterson estimate that in the 1972 Presidential election only *one percent* of the eligible voters were "manipulated" by television advertising. The belief that television ads directly buy many voters is as unsophisticated as the notion that lobbyists directly buy many Congressmen. The process of influence in both exchanges is much more subtle. . . .

Significantly, it was the Ford-Carter debates—especially the "Polish freedom" debate—that showed once again the greater potential electoral effect of network journalism than of ad campaigns. The second debate confirmed what no spot could do by itself: It made people feel that Ford might not be competent to be President. The real impact of network journalism, however, is demonstrated not by the second debate alone, but by the *development* of the public response to it. The survey data show unambiguously that *the public did not realize how serious and significant the "Polish blunder" was until network news told them.* According to Robert Teeter, on the night of the second debate, Ford actually held an 11-percentage-point lead over Carter (as measured by responses to the question about "who won"). Twenty-four hours later, Ford was 45 points behind Carter—a net loss of 56 percentage points!

On balance, the 1976 election revealed once again that television news is the crucial mechanism for determining the candidate's image, and that the television news system has made image more important than ever before. But the election also demonstrated again that ad campaigns are not the major determinant of the vote—or anything close to it. Carter has even conceded that Ford won the television ad campaign; Carter, on the other hand, won the election.

On final point about television and electoral politics: By 1968 television journalism had become not just the primary source of campaign news, but to ever increasing degrees, the *only* source of campaign news, as older viewers came to regard television news as "enough" and younger viewers matured under a system in which Cronkite, Brinkley, Chancellor, and Reasoner *were* journalism. Quite remarkably, between 1964 and 1972 the percentage of people relying *solely* on television for information about national campaigns doubled. By 1972 television had unquestionably become the electoral connection. . . .

## Politically "Relevant" Prime Time

The social forces unleashed in the mid-1960's did to entertainment television what the early part of the decade had done to television news. Television programmers and their shows grew more political, as Burbank learned about war, racism, and radical chic. By the late 1960's, the new generation of television producers began to wear their "relevant" programming like a badge. Social status became a function, to a growing degree, of the ability to produce a hit with a "message."

*Laugh-In* was a breakthrough in this regard, and so to a lesser extent was the *Smothers Brothers* program. Why variety programming led the way toward "openness" in television is hard to explain, but by 1968 politically "relevant" variety shows were a recognizable genre, and their messages were,

I think, doing what the network journalists were secretly hoping to do—move audiences toward social, sexual, and even political liberalism, or at the very least toward "secularism."

As the decade changed, this "message" genre became even more popular and less direct—or at least more subtle, as the slapstick relevance of variety programs spilled over into situation comedies. Norman Lear and his friends—*All in the Family, Maude, The Jeffersons*—were the first family of politically relevant situation-comedy spinoffs, and since 1969 Lear has continued to win the favor of most of the critics. But Mary Tyler Moore and Grant Tinker perhaps represent a more important case. Less political *but more socially "relevant"* than most of Lear's programs, the MTM programs made the cultural and sexual values of the liberal establishment look both cute and responsible at the same time.

After Lear and MTM came the action-adventure people. As early as the late 1960's, the dramatic shows tried to pick up on political "relevance": *Store Front Lawyers, The Young Lawyers, Mod Squad,* etc. Most of those failed in the ratings, or started out big, and then petered out in the second season. But following the modern situation comedies, producers of prime-time drama discovered the salability of sexually oriented plots. By 1976 it became almost a cliché to see action-adventure television featuring rape, bisexuality, homosexuality, abortion—week by week. Traditional sexual attitudes were conspicuously absent in such programs. By 1974, nobody in television could attack homosexuality as wrong and get away with it—not even Anita Bryant, as it now turns out.

One trend given legitimacy by virtually all prime-time television was the inchoate women's movement. Mary Tyler Moore and "Mary Tyler Moore-ism" seem to have been unusually effective in "consciousness-raising." Between 1958 and 1969, the percentage of women accepting the idea that a woman could serve effectively as President actually *declined* by three percent. But between 1969 and 1972, the proportion of women who came to accept the idea of a female President *increased* by 19 percent. The National Organization for Women (NOW), which had been established in 1966, had had little or no effect on women's attitudes during its first three years; if anything, NOW merely provoked the development of an anti-feminist backlash among women. But during those first two seasons in which Mary Richards and Rhoda Morgenstern came to television, the level of public support among women for a female President increased more than during any other two-year—or 10-year—period since the 1930's.

The trend toward "secularizing" social values may have reached its peak in 1975, with the reunification of Sonny and Cher on network television—not as husband and wife, but as a formerly married couple, with the wife pregnant by her second husband.

It is almost impossible to demonstrate the dramatic shift in entertainment television without listing the leading programs. On the next page are the top prime-time shows from five typical years: 1953, 1959, 1966, 1972, and 1975. From 1953 through 1966, not a single program in this list could have been regarded at the time as politically or socially "relevant." But by 1972, five of the top 10 could have conceivably been so regarded—and their themes were always "establishment-liberal" or "establishment-swinger."

**Leading Programs on Network Television (Selected Years)**

| 1953 | 1959 |
|---|---|
| 1. *I Love Lucy* | 1. *Gunsmoke* |
| 2. *Dragnet* | 2. *Wagon Train* |
| 3. *Arthur Godfrey's Talent Scouts* | 3. *Have Gun Will Travel* |
| 4. *You Bet Your Life* | 4. *The Danny Thomas Show* |
| 5. *The Bob Hope Show* | 5. *The Red Skelton Show* |
| 6. *The Milton Berle Show* | 6. *Father Knows Best* |
| 7. *Arthur Godfrey and Friends* | 7. *77 Sunset Strip* |
| 8. *The Ford Show* | 8. *The Price is Right* |
| 9. *The Jackie Gleason Show* | 9. *Wanted: Dead or Alive* |
| 10. *Fireside Theatre* | 10. *Perry Mason* |

| 1966 | 1972 |
|---|---|
| 1. *Bonanza* | 1. *All in the Family* |
| 2. *The Red Skelton Hour* | 2. *Sanford & Son* |
| 3. *The Andy Griffith Show* | 3. *Hawaii Five-O* |
| 4. *The Lucy Show* | 4. *Maude* |
| 5. *The Jackie Gleason Show* | 5. *Bridget Loves Bernie* |
| 6. *Green Acres* | 6. *The NBC Sunday Night Mystery Movie* |
| 7. *Daktari* | 7. *The Mary Tyler Moore Show* |
| 8. *Bewitched* | 8. *Gunsmoke* |
| 9. *The Beverly Hillbillies* | 9. *The Wonderful World of Disney* |
| 10. *Gomer Pyle, USMC* | 10. *Ironside* |

| 1975 |
|---|
| 1. *All in the Family* |
| 2. *Laverne and Shirley* |
| 3. *Rich Man, Poor Man* |
| 4. *Maude* |
| 5. *The Bionic Woman* |
| 6. *Phyllis* |
| 7. *The Six Million Dollar Man* |
| 8. *Sanford & Son* |
| 9. *Rhoda* |
| 10. *Happy Days* |

Source: A. C. Nielsen Company.

It is in these programs and this period that I find some explanation for the growing . . . liberalism . . . regarding premarital sexual relations, divorce, feminism, and interracial personal relations. This trend *needs* explanation, since during this same period, public-opinion polls consistently showed a slow but significant increase in the percentage of Americans regarding themselves as political conservatives. So I return to my original thesis here—that political conservatism was in part a consequence of the "new" prime-time entertainment programming.

But how does one explain the striking paradox that the liberal television journalists were producing "backlash," while at the same time the handmaidens of Madison Avenue were producing "openness" and "relevance"? The answer lies in some fundamental differences between network journalism and entertainment television. The liberal themes in entertainment television are indirect—although they are not subliminal, they are not the essence of the content. These messages embody some of the finest techniques of commercial advertising: They are present without being real or upsetting. And since the themes come across through fictitious characters and situations, they do not assault viewers, but rather live "with" them.

Moreover, entertainment television—especially in these serial presentations—has developed a kind of credibility for its characters and heroes that even Walter Cronkite could envy. After establishing what amounts to a direct and personal relationship with Mary Richards or even Sonny Bono, television can use these characters as models for behavior or thought. This is not exactly credibility—it is something like *personability,* and it cause the viewers to accept the themes that are connected with the characters.

Television news has none of this. The messages are in the action, not in the personalities. The action is "real"—sordidly so. And the journalists do not offer us—as the stars of entertainment television do—a model for behavior, or any tangible theory of politics or society. Indeed, what does Walter Cronkite really think? Television journalists should be pleased, in fact, to hear that their alleged "nonpartisanism" can be, and is, observed—even though the consequences of nonpartisan news seem not to be altogether nonpartisan.

Despite the liberal values of the people who produce the news, the effect of television news has been pretty much in the opposite direction of entertainment television—and pretty much in the opposite direction of the secret hopes of the news people themselves. By 1972, the images on network news were pushing us toward a desire for authoritative, centralized political control, while the images on prime-time entertainment shows were pushing us toward social hedonism and libertarianism. This tension, though still unresolved, represents a revolutionary change from the 1950's. . . .

## "Neo-conservatism" as a Video Byproduct

Since 1972, the two realms of television—news and entertainment—have been finding new themes and achieving a new equilibrium, and have therefore been producing a new kind of political effect. The emphasis of network news—

again with events serving as a guide—began to change once again, this time from an intense focus on *social disintegration,* which had produced during the 1960's a backlash-conservatism among the inadvertent audience, to a more subtle concern for *governmental incapacity,* which I believe has tended to produce a bit of political "neo-conservatism" in us all.

It may well be only coincidence that Jimmy Carter based his campaign on solving government inefficiency and ending bureaucratic waste. But I think not. I believe that by 1972 the new themes of network journalism had once again set in motion a shift toward conservatism—but not backlash conservatism so much as neo-conservatism. This new trend, unlike the video backlash of the 1960's, is as evident among the higher social strata as the lower, and is considerably less "reactive." And once again, this development tends to run counter to the political inclinations of the news staffs and producers, although not quite so starkly as in the case of "videomalaise."

"Bad government" is a time-honored theme in what one might call journalistic populism—the political philosophy of the press corps that distrusts all political authority unless it is used to redistribute wealth. But this now popular focus of network journalism on insensible or corrupt government stems as much from the need for changing themes as anything else. For while it is obvious that the end of the social-disintegration theme fits the facts of the case—there was indeed less rioting, looting, and sniping by 1972—it cannot be easily demonstrated that government is less competent, compassionate, or decent now than it was in 1956. The networks may not have told us directly that government and authority are bad, or dumb, or getting worse—but they have certainly "shown" us. And we have watched fairly closely, all of us. The recent growth in political "conservatism," self-defined, may be as much a media phenomenon as the growth of Wallacism. If George Wallace was the unintended beneficiary of television journalism then, the *Wall Street Journal* and *The Public Interest* may be the unintended beneficiaries now.

One recent development in prime-time entertainment television has had the unusual effect of reinforcing rather than countering the news-induced tendency toward political "neo-conservatism." This development is the obvious and marked increase in police-action programming during the last four years. In 1975, eight of the top 20 programs were crime-detective serials of one form or another. (By 1976, the number had slipped to five.)

Although they vary widely in quality from *Kojak* down through *Charlie's Angels,* the themes of these programs are mostly the same: Heinous, unregenerate, professional criminals are apprehended and incarcerated through the guile or zeal of one or more iconoclastic, anti-heroic—but basically good—cops or detectives. Such themes, one would surmise, tend to sharpen public concern about crime, and public support for strong-armed law-enforcement officals. Quite remarkably, this theory has recently been supported by scientific evidence. George Gerbner, at the Annenberg School of Communication, who has monitored the trend toward tough-cop heroes on prime-time television, has demonstrated that heavy consumption of prime-time television produces attitudes about society that fall somewhere between "backlash" and "neoconservative." His data show that heavy viewers, more than light viewers, tend to exaggerate the incidence of criminal behavior in the United States, and to overestimate the likelihood of being victimized by crime. Gerbner suggests that recent prime-time television programming tends to make society look worse than it is and, as a consequence, engenders support for vesting greater power in the state—a tendency that "fits" with the kinds of effects news programming may have fostered during the 1960's. On balance, then, since the early 1970's prime-time television has probably been producing more support for Kojak than for Archie Bunker.

This tendency toward political conservatism, however, is still being countered somewhat by the continued predilection for "liberal" comedy (not to mention the social and racial liberalism of today's television cops, like Kojak). Despite the inroads made by ABC with its nostalgic programming *(Happy Days, Laverne and Shirley)*, Lear and MTM continue to stay at or near the top in public approval, and there has been no real abatement in the general evolution of network television toward "social openness" and unfettered personal expression.

If there is a pattern since 1972, it would seem to be that television continues to pull us in opposite directions. Prime-time entertainment programming still seems to be edging society toward social and personal "liberation," even if the police-action shows have created a public opinion in favor of broader state authority to deal with specifically criminal behavior. And as has been the case since 1963, television journalism seems still to be producing a conservative reaction to itself, a "modern" conservatism focusing more on the inadequacies of the state than anything else. The new equilibrium achieved by network television since 1972 would help explain three . . . political phenomena: the growth in political conservatism; the concommitant growth in social, racial, and personal liberalism; and the unanticipated but very real appeal of Jimmy Carter, a unique if enigmatic blend of the two tendencies. . . .

If there is a common denominator between the effects of television journalism and entertainment television, it is perhaps that television in general has been *de-romanticizing* both government and social institutions for a long time. Television obviously does not offer reality, but it now moves more and more away from romanticism in news and entertainment. Interestingly enough, de-romanticizing government gets billed as conservatism; de-romanticizing society gets labeled as liberalism. But what is crucial is the tendency to denigrate, overtly in news or covertly in drama, the notion that either government or our common American social institutions are virginal. The final irony may be that television, on balance, has been "bipartisan" in its de-romanticizing. A little left socially and a little right politically puts us somewhere near the place we started. . . .

Perhaps the one conclusion that should be drawn is that in a free society, *the medium providing the major source of both news and entertainment must fundamentally influence the public, the government, and the relationship between them.* It would be hard to argue that television has not profoundly altered our politics in the last two decades. It would be ludicrous to think that television will not be a major factor in the next two decades as well, as it moves itself and us from theme to theme.

# 3

# Public Opinion and the Political Process

In Section I we saw that public opinion is accorded an important role in democratic theory. In principle, public opinion should act as one of democracy's self-regulating mechanisms, yet its actual suitability to this role is an open empirical question. What is the character of public opinion, once formed? To what degree do citizens exhibit predictable and consistent ideological orientations? How durable is public opinion in the face of the media's power to alter or modify it? These are the issues addressed in this section.

Communications researchers have been concerned for decades with the mass media's political "effects," conceived as the ability to *change* political behavior, votes, or attitudes. While the weight of this research suggests the media's power to alter opinions and voting behavior directly is quite limited, many analysts believe the media's real political influence lies in their ability to *shape* political discourse by differential coverage and exposure of various issues (cf. the Langs' article in Section 7). Here, McCombs and Shaw propose that mass media set the "agenda" for political campaigns by their emphasis on and style of reporting different issues. In comparing the content of campaign reporting with the opinions of prospective voters, they find significant correspondence between the points most salient to individual citizens and those highlighted in news reports. They suggest that news media have considerable power to determine which topics will be most important in political campaigns even if they do not substantially alter voters' choices concerning outcomes.

Blumler's article concentrates on individuals' patterns of information-seeking and the informal "division of labor" between television and the press with respect to news reporting in Britain. He examines the intrinsic, organizational and historical features of these two media to explain why each serves a different reportorial function and why, on the whole, television is the preferred source of news for most people. He sees less editorializing on television than in newspapers and finds the popular press in Britain less informative than television in its coverage of political news.[1] Moreover, television is more "linear" than newspapers, whose spatial layout allows readers selectivity in which items they attend to. Consequently, television news is seen as more credible by its audience. People are drawn to it for putatively objective "guidance" on political issues and to newspapers more for reinforcement of views they already have formulated. Newspapers and television thus serve different and complementary functions for news audiences.

Studies of individuals' belief systems by Phillip Converse[2] and others have found surprisingly little "ideological consistency" among mass publics. As Nie and Anderson point out, however, most of these studies were conducted at approximately the same time during the late 1950s, a period known for its relative political quiescence. Using what they consider comparable data for 1956, 1964, and 1972, they compare attitude clusters for several "issue areas" in each of these years to determine if the changing political context of the 1960s brought about a rebirth of "ideological thinking." They find, as previous studies have, that ideological consistency, conceived in terms of clustering along a traditional liberal-to-conservative continuum, was low in 1956, suggesting perhaps that ideology had, in Daniel Bell's words, indeed "ended," if only momentarily.[3] However, attitudes did tend to assemble along more traditional liberal/conservative lines in 1964 and 1972. Nie and Anderson conclude that ideological inconsistency is not an inveterate feature of mass politics but varies according to the political context.

However, in all scientific communities, findings are subject to methodological scrutiny, reanalysis, replication, and reinterpretation. In one of the field's most interesting debates, Bishop et al. argued that Nie and Andersen's findings for the different time points are incomparable because of differences in the way the survey questions used were worded for each year. The finding of attitudinal consistency for 1964 and 1972, they argue, is an "artifact" of *question wording*, not necessarily a product of attitudinal change. Finally, Nie et al. contend in their rebuttal that this possibility, while important, is insufficient for explaining the sheer weight of evidence that is not affected by question wording, and argue that such criticisms do not damage their thesis significantly.

# Notes

1. It might be interesting to compare the British press with the American press, as the latter is not so sharply differentiated into popular and elite newspapers and provides a higher proportion of political reporting, on average. Also, American television provides an interesting comparison with British broadcasting since editorial commentaries have become a more standard feature in the U.S.

2. Phillip E. Converse, "The Nature of Belief Systems, David Apter, ed., in *Ideology and Discontent* (New York: Free Press, 1964).

3. Daniel Bell, *The End of Ideology* (New York: Free Press, 1960).

# The Press, Television, and Democracy

JAY BLUMLER

DEMOCRACY DEPENDS uniquely on mass communications. Rulers, who may use coercion only exceptionally, must rely mainly on persuasion for cultivating the public support they need. Citizens, who know that their rulers are fallible, must depend on the mass media for independent comment about the affairs of state. Thus the mass media have become keys to democracy.

Among those keys, the two most important of course, are the press and television. How should we interpret their respective roles in British political life? This question can be approached from at least three angles. First, there is the consumer's own perspective: What do readers and viewers seek from the mass media? Second, we can cast an eye on recent controversies: How are television and the press treated as objects of public debate? And third, there is the standpoint of the political system as a whole: What political functions do the newspapers and television serve?

First, then, how do citizens aim to use their newspapers and television sets when following politics? There is a wide overlap, of course. On a typical day most people glance at a newspaper and tune in to a TV news bulletin. Fans of some special topic are particularly likely to follow it in all the available media. The avid reader of his newspaper's sports page will probably be a regular patron of *Match of the Day* as well. Nevertheless, certain complementary patterns of media use spring from the different characteristics of television and the press. For example, up-to-the-minute news is sought mainly from the broadcast bulletins. Curiosity about political personalities is satisfied mainly through TV. For a fuller account of political events, people tend to

Extracted from a BBC broadcast script which later appeared in *The Listener* (July 3, 1969), pp. 4–5. Used by permission of *The Listener* and the copyright holder, Jay Blumler.

rely on the newspapers, which can devote more wordage to interpretation and analysis. But television is favored when a window seat on political actuality is wanted—an impression, say, of a demonstration, a political convention, or a Congressional Committee investigating the conduct of the Vietnam War.

Perhaps three features of this division of labor are politically most significant. First, whereas newspapers may print opinions of their own, broadcasters must refrain from editorializing. This matches a similar distinction which applies to the ordinary citizen's approach to politics. On any single issue, some people mainly seek support for the opinions they already hold, while others welcome its exploration in a several-sided perspective. Moreover, a hint of an empirical connection between these distinctions emerged from a survey of Leeds voters that Denis McQuail and I carried out during the 1964 election. We found that those individuals who wished mainly to be reminded of their parties' strong points had also followed the campaign extensively in their newspapers; those electors who wanted guidance in deciding how to vote had relied heavily on television.

Second, voters not only think TV is more impartial than the press, they also rate it a more reliable source of information. As Jack Gould, an American newspaperman, has put it, "the greatest asset of broadcasting is the public belief that for the most part the medium does try to be fair." This is important because many men in the street perceive the political arena as teeming with axe-grinding spokesmen, whose claims are intrinsically unreliable. No wonder that they latch onto TV's supposed authenticity as a trusty sheet-anchor in an untrustworthy political world.

Third, the press can be used more flexibly than television. On opening his newspaper, the reader can pick and choose what to consult. When watching a TV bulletin, however, the viewer is more or less in the hands of the newscaster. The significance of this difference stems from the uneven distribution of political interest throughout the population. The same political item, which an indifferent voter can ignore in his newspaper, may get through to him over television. In other words, political materials tend to reach a pre-selected readership in the press, while the audience for political television is much less selective.

Television and the press are not only complementary news media: To many members of the more attentive public, they are also centers of debate about how political communications should be organized. It is noticeable that television and the press have been treated rather differently in the ensuing controversy. While the sins of the British press have virtually escaped notice, political television has recently attracted a heavy fire of criticism.

What exactly does the concentration of this bombardment on television signify? In my view, it shows again, with the press, in politics we know more or less where we stand, but with television we don't know quite what to expect. We have learned to live with present levels of political reporting in our newspapers and few of us are inclined to ask now for something quite different. Most proposals for reform are concerned merely to stem the tide of prospective press closures or mergers. But television stands apart as the focus of several mixtures of still unresolved expectations. One such mixture reflects certain hopes and misgivings that are reposed in television journalism. Unlike the privately owned press, television is essentially a public medium: Its operators are licensed. This has helped to generate demands that broadcasting should be used to promote civic enlightenment. But many of TV's resources are devoted to mass entertainment. And this has aroused fears that the seriousness of its public affairs coverage may be compromised.

Another tension springs from the desire, on the one hand, of many reporters and producers to serve the TV audience with a vigorous and critical brand of journalism, and from their subjection, on the other hand, in the norm of impartiality, which counsels restraint and can even be interpreted as imposing the rather colorless function of merely passing on information. A politician who has figured unflatteringly in some critical piece of television journalism may conclude, therefore, not only that the reporter had somehow got his facts wrong or had misjudged their significance, but also that he had stepped outside the bounds of his proper sphere. Yet a journalist who knuckles under to a demand to sidestep controversy will feel guilty about a betrayal of his professional conscience.

A deeply ambivalent streak in Britain's political culture introduces yet a third set of unresolved expectations into the equation. In this country, predemocratic attitudes of deference towards holders of high positions coexist with democratic norms that legitimize the accountability of rulers to the mass electorate. Thus, a deferential outlook upholds the simultaneous screening of party broadcasts on all available channels without competition from other programs; but democratic values provoke complaints about the paternalistic implications of this arrangement. Democratic attitudes have nourished demands for the televising of Parliament; but deferential caution mananged in late 1966 to resist such pressure by the margin of one vote in the House of Commons. Political interviewers are particularly exposed to the crossfires that emanate from these diverse sources. When they are not being rebuked for impertinence (for insufficient deference), they are being criticized for having pulled their punches (for having neglected their democratic duty).

So television is a more controversial political medium than the press. This is not because it engages more boldly in controversy, but because its rights in the political field are less clearly defined.

But perhaps what matters most are the functions that the press and television serve in the wider political system. In his recently published book, Mr. Colin Seymour-Ure has provided a lucid analysis of the political role of the newspaper industry.[1] He claims that two chastening facts emerge from a close look at the most widely circulated newspapers and their readers. First, the strictly political content of the popular press is slight. Second, most readers pay only a faint and sporadic attention to such content. Mr.

Seymour-Ure concludes from this that certain functions, which democratic political theory had traditionally assigned to the newspapers, can no longer be taken for granted. It is doubtful whether the press acts as a neutral conveyor of much political information to the mass electorate. It is also doubtful whether it is a major influence on voters' ideas, encouraging them to favor certain policies and parties rather than others.

Does it follow that the press plays only a marginal part in political life? No, says Mr. Seymour-Ure, who draws attention to the importance of what he calls its watchdog function. This influences the workings of politics by threat of exposure. It is channeled, however, mainly through a horizontal process of communication. That is, the watchdog function of the press depends less on the direct impact of exposure on the mass public than on the effects of publicity on a politician's own colleagues and opponents.

It is intriguing to ask whether a similar picture would emerge from an equivalent analysis of television. In my opinion, its political functions must be conceived along different lines. For one thing, the political reach of television is more wide-ranging than that of most newspapers. I have already pointed out that it is easier for the apathetic citizen to evade political items in his newspaper than on his television screen. In addition, survey results have repeatedly shown that television is the more popular source of political information among less educated householders. It does not follow from this that many viewers actually learn anything about civic issues from watching political programs. But it is worth mentioning that when Dennis McQuail and I divided our 1964 sample into five descending groups of voters according to a measure of their interest in politics, we found signs of a gain in political knowledge through exposure to election television in even the most indifferent body of captive viewers. On this kind of evidence we are certainly not entitled to dismiss television out of hand as a potential instrument of mass political education.

Neither should we sell television short as an influence on viewers' political ideas. This assertion may shock some listeners who have been taught by other communications specialists to accept the so-called doctrine of the political impotence of television. Let me hasten to add that if we are concerned only with voting behavior, then television must still be regarded as impotent. Most electors simply do not wear their votes on their political sleeves, and those who do are more likely to be swayed by their relations, neighbors, and workmates than by any mass medium. Casting a vote is typically a highly involving political act. But what about all the other dimensions of political outlook that engage a person's emotions, group loyalties, and sense of commitment far less deeply?

A provocative answer emerged from the results of our election survey of 1964. We found that a substantial swing of sentiment in favor of the Liberal Party had marched hand in hand with the number of political programs that the viewers had seen during the campaign. The most significant feature of this effect was its incidence. It was not dispersed throughout the whole sample. Instead it was concentrated entirely among those voters whose motivations for following the election we had previously measured as only moderate or weak. In other words, televised propaganda had influenced the attitudes of those viewers whose presence in the audience was due not to their zest for politics but to their attachment to television.

Notice how this finding underlines again the long arm of television—or rather how it confirms the vulnerability of the less selective part of its audience. To clarify the extent of this source of TV's political power, much more research will be needed. But we can already draw up an impressive list of those topics where it would make sense to seek evidence of the impact of television: on new issues that erupt unexpectedly onto the political scene; impressions of foreign affairs; perceptions of those domestic groups that viewers rarely meet in person—like University students among the elderly, and racial minorities in areas little penetrated by immigration; or even on impressions of their own organizations that have been formed by the less involved body of rank-and-filers—like card-carrying trade unionists or nominal members of the Church of England.

The last specific difference between television and the press to which I will refer may also be introduced by citing a finding from our 1964 survey. (When the respondents were asked about the program forms in which they preferred politicians to appear on TV, 18 percent opted for a debate between opponents, 39 percent chose an interview with a reporter, and only 10 percent preferred a straight talk. Further analysis suggested that this pattern of response arose from the voter's need to probe the reliability of the information supplied by politicians.) In a simple world the viewer could put his own questions and challenges directly to the politician, but in modern society this is impossible. So the viewer expects reporters working in television journalism to challenge the politician for him instead. This differs significantly from the watchdog function of the press. As Mr. Seymour-Ure has pointed out, the key polarities of newspaper work are secrecy and publicity, and the reporter's role resembles that of a detective. But investigative reporting features much less prominently in the output of television. Instead of a watchdog function, then, television discharges what may be called an accountability function; it sets out to hold politicians to account for their decisions on behalf of the public by proxy.

Evidently television should not be portrayed as merely a horizontal medium of political communication. In outlining its functions, I have noted, first, that its political reach is extensive; second, that it attracts the more susceptible voter; and third, that many viewers regard it as an instrument for requiring politicians to account for themselves to the electorate. It follows from this combination of characteristics that television has injected a powerful agent of vertical communication into the British political system.

Unfortunately, many intellectuals still project onto television their own preferences for a more horizontal medium. In his contribution to the debate about political broadcasting last autumn, for example, Mr. Crossman was mainly preoccupied with TV's failure to serve the minority of activists, participators and opinion-formers. I would strongly endorse his plea for the screening of more specialist political programs. But since the interests of the active minority are already catered for by the quality press, by many political weeklies and monthlies, and even by Third Program talks, I found Mr. Crossman's priorities rather odd. After all, a healthy democracy depends not only on the faith and understanding of its activists but also on the expectations of its masses.

I am equally impatient with those who dismiss television as the source of a vicarious but illusory participation in public events. Playing an active part in politics has always been a minority taste, and TV has not changed this for better or worse. The mainsprings of apathy or a disposition to participate in public affairs lie, not in any of the mass media, but in a whole host of deep-seated attitudes, including an individual's image of himself as the kind of person who is, or is not, suited to active civic work. Television trades not in participation, then, but in awareness. Instead of deploring this, we should be asking how TV's inevitable involvement in mass politics could be more constructively exploited.

It will not be easy to find an acceptable answer to this question. But perhaps we should seek it in the type of democracy we so often claim to be—a polity that values pragmatism, freedom, and the availability of alternatives. From this point of view, it is surprising that the journalistic profession is not more obviously concerned to portray politics as an arena of choice. It is naive to expect television to foster among viewers an awareness of the existence and implications of political choices? Such an objective would be compatible with the medium's technical capacity to combine elements from diverse sources in a single program format, and consistent, too, with the recognized traditions of public service broadcasting in Britain.

## Note

1. Colin Seymour-Ure, *The Press, Politics, and the Public* (London: Methuen, 1968).

# The Agenda-Setting Function of Mass Media

MAXWELL E. McCOMBS
DONALD L. SHAW

IN OUR DAY, more than ever before, candidates go before the people through the mass media rather than in person.[1] The information in the mass media becomes the only contact many have with politics. The pledges, promises, and rhetoric encapsulated in news stories, columns, and editorials constitute much of the information upon which a voting decision has to be made. Most of what people know comes to them "second" or "third" hand from the mass media or from other people.[2]

Although the evidence that mass media deeply change attitudes in a campaign is far from conclusive,[3] the evidence is much stronger that voters learn from the immense quantity of information available during each campaign.[4] People, of course, vary greatly in their attention to mass media political information. Some, normally the better educated and most politically interested (and those least likely to change political beliefs), actively seek information; but most seem to acquire it, if at all, without much effort. It just comes in. As Berelson succinctly puts it: "On any single subject many 'hear' but few 'listen'." But Berelson also found that those with the greatest mass media exposure are most likely to know where the candidates stand on different issues.[5] Trenaman and McQuail found the same thing in a study of the 1959 General Election in England.[6] Voters do learn.

They apparently learn, furthermore, in direct proportion to the emphasis

Reprinted by permission of the publisher from "The Agenda-Setting Function of Mass Media," by Maxwell McCombs and Donald Shaw, in *Public Opinion Quarterly*, Vol. 36 (Summer 1972), pp. 176–87.

placed on the campaign issues by the mass media. Specifically focusing on the agenda-setting function of the media, Lang and Lang observe:

> The mass media force attention to certain issues. They build up public images of political figures. They are constantly presenting objects suggesting what individuals in the mass should think about, know about, have feelings about.[7]

Perhaps this hypothesized agenda-setting function of the mass media is most succinctly stated by Cohen, who noted that the press "may not be successful much of the time in telling people what to think, but it is stunningly successful in telling its readers what to think *about*."[8] While the mass media may have little influence on the direction or intensity of attitudes, it is hypothesized that *the mass media set the agenda for each political campaign, influencing the salience of attitudes toward the political issues.*

## Method

To investigate the agenda-setting capacity of the mass media in the 1968 presidential campaign, this study attempted to match what Chapel Hill voters *said* were key issues of the campaign with the *actual content* of the mass media used by them during the campaign. Respondents were selected randomly from lists of registered voters in five Chapel Hill precincts economically, socially, and racially representative of the community. By restricting this study to one community, numerous other sources of variation—for example, regional differences or variations in media performance—were controlled.

Between September 18 and October 6, 100 interviews were completed. To select these 100 respondents a filter question was used to identify those who had not yet definitely decided how to vote—presumably those more open or susceptible to campaign information. Only those not yet fully committed to a particular candidate were interviewed. Borrowing from the Trenaman and McQuail strategy, this study asked each respondent to outline the key issues as he saw them, regardless of what the candidates might be saying at the moment.[9] Interviewers recorded the answers as exactly as possible.

Concurrently with the voter interviews, the mass media serving these voters were collected and content analyzed. A pretest in spring 1968 found that for the Chapel Hill community almost all the mass media political information was provided by the following sources: Durham *Morning Herald,* Durham *Sun,* Raleigh *News and Observer,* Raleigh *Times,* New York *Times, Time, Newsweek,* and NBC and CBS evening news broadcasts.

The answers of respondents regarding major problems as they saw them and the news and editorial comment appearing between September 12 and October 6 in the sampled newspapers, magazines, and news broadcasts were coded into 15 categories representing the key issues and other kinds of campaign news. Media news content also was divided into "major" and "minor" levels to see whether there was any substantial difference in mass media emphasis across topics.[10] For the print media, this major/minor division was in terms of space and position; for television, it was made in terms of position and time allowed. More specifically, *major* items were defined as follows:

1. Television: Any story 45 seconds or more in length and/or one of the three lead stories.
2. Newspapers: Any story which appeared as the lead on the front page or on any page under a three-column headline in which at least one-third of the story (a minimum of five paragraphs) was devoted to political news coverage.
3. News Magazines: Any story more than one column or any item which appeared in the lead at the beginning of the news section of the magazine.
4. Editorial Page Coverage of Newspapers and Magazines: Any item in the lead editorial position (the top left corner of the editorial page) plus all items in which one-third (at least five paragraphs) of an editorial or columnist comment was devoted to political campaign coverage.

*Minor* items are those stories which are political in nature and included in the study but which are smaller in terms of space, time, or display than major items.

## Findings

Our analysis of the over-all *major* item emphasis of the selected mass media on different topics and candidates during the campaign . . , indicates that a considerable amount of campaign news was *not* devoted to discussion of the major political issues but rather to *analysis of the campaign itself.* This may give pause to those who think of campaign news as being primarily about the *issues.* Thirty-five percent of the major news coverage of Wallace was composed of this analysis ("Has he a chance to win or not?"). For Humphrey and Nixon the figures were, respectively, 30 percent and 25 percent. . . .

Table 1 focuses on the relative emphasis of each party on the issues, as reflected in the mass media. The table shows that Humphrey/Muskie emphasized foreign policy far more than did Nixon/Agnew or Wallace/Lemay. In the case of the "law and order" issue, however, over half the Wallace/Lemay news was about this, while less than one-fourth of the Humphrey/Muskie news concentrated upon this topic. With Nixon/Agnew it was almost a third—just behind the Republican emphasis on foreign policy. Humphrey of course spent considerable time justifying (or commenting upon) the Vietname War; Nixon did not choose (or have) to do this.

**TABLE 1. Mass Media Report on Issues, by Parties**

| ISSUES | REPUBLICAN Nixon/Agnew | | | DEMOCRATIC Humphrey/Muskie | | | AMERICAN Wallace/Lemay | | |
|---|---|---|---|---|---|---|---|---|---|
| | MAJOR | MINOR | TOTAL | MAJOR | MINOR | TOTAL | MAJOR | MINOR | TOTAL |
| Foreign policy | 34% | 40% | 38% | 65% | 63% | 64% | 30% | 21% | 26% |
| Law and order | 26 | 36 | 32 | 19 | 26 | 23 | 48 | 55 | 52 |
| Fiscal policy | 13 | 1 | 6 | 10 | 6 | 8 | — | — | — |
| Public welfare | 13 | 14 | 13 | 4 | 3 | 4 | 7 | 12 | 10 |
| Civil rights | 15 | 8 | 11 | 2 | 2 | 2 | 14 | 12 | 13 |
| Total percent[a] | 101% | 99% | 100% | 100% | 100% | 101% | 99% | 100% | 101% |
| Total number | 47 | 72 | 119 | 48 | 62 | 110 | 28 | 33 | 61 |

[a] Some columns do not sum to 100% because of rounding.

The media appear to have exerted a considerable impact on voters' judgments of what they considered the major issues of the campaign (even though the questionnaire specifically asked them to make judgments without regard to what politicians might be saying at the moment). The correlation between the major item emphasis on the main campaign issues carried by the media and voters' independent judgments of what were the important issues was +.967. Between minor item emphasis on the main campaign issues and voters' judgments, the correlation was +.979. In short, the data suggest a very strong relationship between the emphasis placed on different campaign issues by the media (reflecting to a considerable degree the emphasis by candidates) and the judgments of voters as to the salience and importance of various campaign topics.

But while the three presidential candidates placed widely different emphasis upon different issues, the judgments of the voters seem to reflect the *composite* of the mass media coverage. This suggests that voters pay some attention to all the political news *regardless* of whether it is from, or about, any particular favored candidate. Because the tables we have seen reflect the composite of *all* the respondents, it is possible that individual differences, reflected in party preferences and in a predisposition to look mainly at material favorable to one's own party, are lost by lumping all the voters together in the analysis. Therefore, answers of respondents who indicated a preference (but not commitment) for one of the candidates during the September–October period studied (45 of the respondents; the others were undecided) were analyzed separately. Table 2 shows the results of this analysis for four selected media.

The table shows the frequency of important issues cited by respondents who favored Humphrey, Nixon, or Wallace correlated *(a)* with the frequency of *all* the major and minor issues carried by the media and *(b)* with the frequency of the major and minor issues oriented to *each party* (stories with a particular party or candidate as a primary referent) carried by each of the four media. For example, the correlation is .89 between what Democrats see as the important issues and the New York *Times's* emphasis on the issues in *all* its major news items. The correlation is .79 between the Democrats' emphasis on the issues and the emphasis of the New York *Times* as reflected *only* in items about the Democratic candidates.

If one expected voters to pay more attention to the major and minor issues oriented to their own party—that is, to read or view *selectively*—the correlations between the voters and news/opinion about their own party should be strongest. This would be evidence of selective perception.[11] If, on the other hand, the voters attend reasonably well to *all* the news, *regardless* of which candidate or party issue is stressed, the correlations between the voter and total media content would be strongest. This would be evidence of the agenda-setting function. The crucial question is which set of correlation is stronger.

TABLE 2.  Intercorrelations of Major and Minor Issue Emphasis by Selected Media with Voter Issue Emphasis

| Selected Media | MAJOR ITEMS | | MINOR ITEMS | |
| --- | --- | --- | --- | --- |
| | All News | News Own Party | All News | News Own Party |
| New York *Times* | | | | |
| Voters (D) | .89 | .79 | .97 | .85 |
| Voters (R) | .80 | .40 | .88 | .98 |
| Voters (W) | .89 | .25 | .78 | −.53 |
| Durham *Morning Herald* | | | | |
| Voters (D) | .84 | .74 | .95 | .83 |
| Voters (R) | .59 | .88 | .84 | .69 |
| Voters (W) | .82 | .76 | .79 | .00 |
| CBS | | | | |
| Voters (D) | .83 | .83 | .81 | .71 |
| Voters (R) | .50 | .00 | .57 | .40 |
| Voters (W) | .78 | .80 | .86 | .76 |
| NBC | | | | |
| Voters (D) | .57 | .76 | .64 | .73 |
| Voters (R) | .27 | .13 | .66 | .63 |
| Voters (W) | .84 | .21 | .48 | −.33 |

In general, Table 2 shows that voters who were not firmly committed early in the campaign attended well to *all* the news. For major news items, correlations were more often higher between voter judgments of important issues and the issues reflected in all the news (including of course news about their favored candidate/party) than were voter judgments of issues reflected in news *only* about their candidate/party. For minor news items, again voters more often correlated highest with the emphasis reflected in all the news than with the emphasis reflected in news about a favored candidate. Considering both major and minor item coverage, 18 of 24 possible comparisons show voters more in agreement with all the news rather than with news only about their own party/candidate perference. This finding is better explained by the agenda-setting function of the mass media than by selective perception.

Although the data reported in Table 2 generally show high agreement between voter and media evaluations of what the important issues were in 1968, the correlations are not uniform across the various media and all groups of voters. The variations across media are more clearly reflected in Table 3, which includes all survey respondents, not just those predisposed toward a candidate at the time of the survey. There also is a high degree of consensus among the news media about the significant issues of the campaign, but again there is not perfect agreement. Considering the news media as mediators between voters and the actual political arena, we might interpret the correlations in Table 4 as reliability coefficients, indicating the extent of agreement among the news media about what the important political events are. To the extent that the coefficients are less than perfect, the pseudo-environment reflected in the mass media is less than a perfect representation of the actual 1968 campaign.

**TABLE 3.    Correlations of Voter Emphasis on Issues with Media Coverage**

|  | NEWSWEEK | TIME | NEW YORK TIMES | RALEIGH TIMES | RALEIGH NEWS AND OBSERVER |
|---|---|---|---|---|---|
| Major Items | .30 | .30 | .96 | .80 | .91 |
| Minor Items | .53 | .78 | .97 | .73 | .93 |

|  | DURHAM SUN | DURHAM MORNING HERALD | NBC NEWS | CBS NEWS |  |
|---|---|---|---|---|---|
| Major Items | .82 | .94 | .89 | .63 |  |
| Minor Items | .96 | .93 | .91 | .81 |  |

Two sets of factors, at least, reduce consensus among the news media. First, the basic characteristics of newspapers, television, and newsmagazines differ. Newspapers appear daily and have lots of space. Television is daily but has a severe time constraint. Newsmagazines appear weekly; news therefore cannot be as "timely." Table 4 shows that the highest correlations tend to be among like media; the lowest correlations, between different media.

Second, news media do have a point of view, sometimes extreme biases. However, the high correlations in Table 4 (especially among like media) suggest consensus on news values, especially on major news items. Although there is no explicit, commonly agreed-upon definition of news, there is a professional norm regarding major news stories from day to day. These major-story norms doubtless are greatly influenced today by widespread use of the major wire services—especially by newspapers and television—for much political information.[12] But as we move from major events of the campaign, upon which nearly everyone agrees, there is more room for individual interpretation, reflected in the lower correlations for minor item agreement among media shown in Table 4. Since a newspaper, for example, uses only about 15 percent of the material available on any given day, there is considerable latitude for selection among minor items.

In short, the political world is reproduced imperfectly by individual news media. Yet the evidence in this study that voters tend to share the media's *composite* definition of what is important strongly suggests an agenda-setting function of the mass media.

TABLE 4. Intercorrelation of Mass Media Presidential News Coverage for Major and Minor Items

| | NEWS-WEEK | TIME | NEW YORK TIMES | RALEIGH TIMES | RALEIGH NEWS & OBSERVER | DURHAM SUN | DURHAM MORNING HERALD | NBC | CBS |
|---|---|---|---|---|---|---|---|---|---|
| | | | | *Major Items* | | | | | |
| Newsweek | | .99 | .54 | .92 | .79 | .81 | .79 | .68 | .42 |
| Time | .65 | | .51 | .90 | .77 | .81 | .76 | .68 | .43 |
| New York Times | .46 | .59 | | .70 | .71 | .66 | .81 | .66 | .66 |
| Raleigh Times | .73 | .66 | .64 | | .85 | .89 | .90 | .72 | .62 |
| Raleigh News and Observer | .84 | .49 | .60 | .74 | | .84 | .93 | .82 | .60 |
| Durham Sun | .77 | .47 | .47 | .70 | .80 | | .94 | .91 | .77 |
| Durham Morning Herald | .89 | .68 | .68 | .80 | .93 | .73 | | .89 | .76 |
| NBC News | .81 | .65 | .38 | .87 | .73 | .84 | .75 | | .82 |
| CBS News | .66 | .60 | .83 | .88 | .79 | .76 | .78 | .72 | |
| | | | | *Minor Items* | | | | | |

134

# Discussion

The existence of an agenda-setting function of the mass media is not *proved* by the correlations reported here, of course, but the evidence is in line with the conditions that must exist if agenda-setting by the mass media does occur. This study has compared aggregate units—Chapel Hill voters as a group compared to the aggregate performance of several mass media. This is satisfactory as a first test of the agenda-setting hypothesis, but subsequent research must move from a broad societal level to the social psychological level, matching individual attitudes with individual use of the mass media. Yet even the present study refines the evidence in several respects. Efforts were made to match respondent attitudes only with media actually used by Chapel Hill voters. Further, the analysis includes a juxtaposition of the agenda-setting and selective perception hypotheses. Comparison of these correlations too supports the agenda-setting hypothesis.

Interpreting the evidence from this study as indicating mass media influence seems more plausible than alternative explanations. Any argument that the correlations between media and voter emphasis are spurious—that they are simply responding to the same events and not influencing each other one way or the other--assumes that voters have alternative means of observing the day-to-day change in the political arena. This assumption is not plausible; since few directly participate in presidential election campaigns, and fewer still see presidential candidates in person, the information flowing in interpersonal communication channels is primarily relayed from, and based upon, mass media news coverage. The media are the major primary sources of national political information; for most, mass media provide the best—and only--easily available approximation of ever-changing political realities.

It might also be argued that the high correlations indicate that the media simply were successful in matching their messages to audience interests. Yet since numerous studies indicate a sharp divergence between the news values of professional journalists and their audiences, it would be remarkable to find a near perfect fit in this one case.[13] It seems more likely that the media have prevailed in this area of major coverage. . . .

Future studies of communication behavior and political agenda-setting must consider both psychological and sociological variables; knowledge of both is crucial to establishment of sound theoretical constructs. Considered at both levels as a communication concept, agenda-setting seems useful for study of the process of political consensus. . . .

# Notes

1. See Bernard R. Berelson, Paul F. Lazarsfeld, and William N. McPhee, *Voting,* Chicago, University of Chicago Press, 1954, p. 234. Of course to some degree

candidates have always depended upon the mass media, but radio and television brought a new intimacy into politics.

2. Kurt Lang and Gladys Engel Lang, "The Mass Media and Voting," in Bernard Berelson and Morris Janowitz, eds., *Reader in Public Opinion and Communication,* 2d ed., New York, Free Press, 1966, p. 466.

3. See Berelson *et al., op. cit.,* p. 223; Paul F. Lazarsfeld, Bernard Berelson, and Hazel Gaudet, *The People's Choice,* New York, Columbia University Press, 1948, p. xx; and Joseph Trenaman and Denis McQuail, *Television and the Political Image,* London, Methuen and Co., 1961, pp. 147, 191.

4. See Bernard C. Cohen, *The Press and Foreign Policy,* Princeton, Princeton University Press, 1963, p. 120.

5. Berelson *et al., op. cit.,* pp. 244, 228.

6. Trenaman and McQuail, *op. cit.,* p. 165.

7. Lang and Lang, *op. cit.,* p. 468. Trenaman and McQuail warn that there was little evidence in their study that television (or any other mass medium) did anything other than provide information; there was little or no attitude change on significant issues. . . .

8. Cohen, *op. cit.,* p. 13.

9. See Trenaman and McQuail, *op. cit.,* p. 172. The survey question was: "What are you *most* concerned about these days? That is, regardless of what politicians say, what are the two or three main things which you think the government *should* concentrate on doing something about?"

10. Intercoder reliability was above 90 for content analysis of both "major" and "minor" items. Details of categorization are described in the full report of this project. A small number of copies of the full report is available for distribution and may be obtained by writing the authors.

11. While recent reviews of the literature and new experiments have questioned the validity of the selective perception hypothesis, this has nevertheless been the focus of much communication research. For example, see Richard F. Carter, Ronald H. Pyszka, and Jose L. Guerrero, "Dissonance and Exposure to Arousive Information," *Journalism Quarterly,* Vol. 46, 1969, pp. 37–42; and David O. Sears and Jonathan L. Freedman, "Selective Exposure to Information: A Critical Review," *Public Opinion Quarterly,* Vol. 31, 1967, pp. 194–213.

12. A number of studies have focused on the influence of the wire services. For example, see David Gold and Jerry L. Simmons, "News Selection Patterns among Iowa Dailies," *Public Opinion Quarterly,* Vol. 29, 1965, pp. 425–430; Guido H. Stempel III, "How Newspapers Use the Associated Press Afternoon A-Wire," *Journalism Quarterly,* Vol. 41, 1964, pp. 380–384; Ralph D. Casey and Thomas H. Copeland Jr., "Use of Foreign News by 19 Minnesota Dailies," *Journalism Quarterly,* Vol. 35, 1958, pp. 87–89; Howard L. Lewis, "The Cuban Revolt Story: AP, UPI, and Three Papers," *Journalism Quarterly,* Vol. 37, 1960, pp. 573–578; George A. Van Horn, "Analysis of AP News on Trunk and Wisconsin State Wires," *Journalism Quarterly,* Vol. 29, 1952, pp. 426–432; and Scott M. Cutlip, "Content and Flow of AP News—From Trunk to TTS to Reader," *Journalism Quarterly,* Vol. 31, 1954, pp. 434–446.

13. Furthermore, five of the nine media studied here are national media and none of the remaining for four originate in Chapel Hill. It is easier to argue that Chapel Hill voters fit their judgments of issue salience to the mass media than the reverse. An interesting study which discusses the problems of trying to fit day-to-day news judgments to reader interest is Guido H. Stepel III, "A Factor Analytic Study of Reader Interest in News," *Journalism Quarterly*, Vol. 44, 1967, pp. 326–330. An older study is Philip F. Griffin, "Reader Comprehension of News Stories: A Preliminary Study," *Journalism Quarterly*, Vol. 26, 1949, pp. 389–396.

# Mass Belief Systems Revisited: Political Change and Attitude Structure

NORMAN H. NIE
with
KRISTI ANDERSEN

MODERN SURVEY TECHNIQUES have often been most fruitful in undercutting common wisdom about politics. These techniques—more precise than the impressionistic techniques of earlier observers—have shown that some common understandings of the nature of mass political beliefs have been wrong. But one must approach survey-based findings with caution. Surveys too can distort, particularly if one assumes that a pattern that is found at one point in time represents a general, long-term tendency extending beyond the specific time period in which the research was conducted. We must be careful that we do not replace a common wisdom of impressionistic political science by a common wisdom based on a precise, but time-bound, research technique.

One of the newer "common wisdoms" derived from survey techniques has to do with the absence of ideology in the American public. Ideology has many meanings, but one of its components is usually a high degree of consistency among political attitudes—attitudes on a wide range of issues falling into clear liberal and conservative tendencies.[1] And this component has been found to be particularly lacking in the American mass public.

The mass public has usually been contrasted with more elite publics—for example, politicians, journalists and academics. In elite publics, attitudes

Reprinted from "Mass Belief Systems Revisited: Political Change and Attitude Structure," by Norman H. Nie with Kristi Andersen, in *The Journal of Politics,* Vol. 36 (August 1976), pp. 540–587, by permission of the authors and publisher.

on a wide variety of issues are bound together in highly predictable ways. Attitudes on welfare measures, government spending, and taxation are usually highly intercorrelated, reflecting a general position on the proper scope of government activity. Furthermore, attitudes on issues such as race, civil liberties, and foreign policy also tend to be related to each other as well as to attitudes on domestic economic policies. This relationship across a wide range of issues enables us to identify many members of political elite groups as liberals or conservatives.

Studies of the interrelationship of opinions among mass publics, on the other hand, have found little evidence for this kind of ideological structuring. The citizenry at large has not organized its political beliefs along liberal/conservative lines. Within a given issue-domain there is some evidence of attitude consistency—for example, positions on governmental responsibility for providing employment are related to those on governmental responsibility in the areas of medicine and housing. However, attitudes in separate issue-spheres appear to bear little or no relationship to each other. Attitudes on welfare, taxation, government spending, as well as those on other domestic economic policies show only minor relationships to each other. And attitudes on the more remote issues of race, civil liberties, and foreign policy have virtually no relationship to each other or to positions on welfare or economic liberalism. In short, available studies indicate that there is little or no interdependence or opinion constraint, to use Converse's term, in mass attitudes.[2]

The explanation usually given for the difference in the structure of beliefs between elite and mass emphasizes certain critical limitations inherent in mass publics. The mass public has neither the educational background, the contextual knowledge, nor the capacity to deal with abstract concepts that sustain an organized set of beliefs over a wide range of political issues.[3]

There is, however, one major problem with these descriptions of the state of mass belief systems: the studies on which they are based are all from a single historical period some 15 to 20 years ago. V. O. Key's major work on attitude consistency is based on data gathered during the 1956 presidential election. Philip Converse's seminal article on "The Nature of Belief Systems in Mass Publics," though published somewhat later, uses data collected in 1958 and 1960. Most of the other studies which contribute to our knowledge of mass ideology, such as *The American Voter* and McClosky's study of party elites and regulars, are also based on data gathered around 1960.

But American politics in the 60s and early 70s were not the same as those of the 1950s. The quiescent Eisenhower years were followed by turmoil on many fronts: the civil-rights movement, black militancy and urban violence, a protracted and divisive war, campus unrest, changing morals and life-styles—all interspersed with a tragic series of political assassinations. This change in the nature of American politics provides a crucial test of the analysis of mass-belief systems. If the lack of organization of mass political attitudes is based on enduring characteristics of the mass public, it should be relatively insensitive to such changes in the world of politics. But if we find that the structure of mass attitudes has been affected by the political upheavals of the 1960s, we may have to reconsider the character of mass attitudes and the factors which affect their structure.

In this paper we propose to examine the structure of mass attitudes over the past 16 years. We will show that there have been major increases in the levels of attitude consistency within the mass public.[4] Not only has the constraint among traditional issues such as those examined by Converse and Key increased substantially, but new issues as they have emerged in the 60s have been incorporated by the mass public into what now appears to be a broad liberal/conservative ideology.

We should note here that our definition of liberal/conservative consistency is not based on a priori logical relationships between political attitudes; in fact, none of the issues with which we are concerned, though they may share common symbols, bear any strictly logical relationship to one another.[5] Instead, our definition of consistency is based upon the political context in which attitudes are formed. Regardless of whether issues are logically connected, liberal and conservative positions on a wide variety of issues are established over a period of time and come to constitute the ideological "cues" of the political system. It is in this way that on such logical distant issues as the conduct of the Vietnam War and attitudes toward school integration, "liberal" and "conservative" stances are clearly defined and accepted.

## The Data

The analysis is based on data gathered by the Survey Research Center at the University of Michigan in conjunction with its national election studies. Between 1952 and 1972, the Survey Research Center (SRC) has interviewed a representative sample of some 1,500 to 2,700 adult Americans in each of the presidential elections and in several of the off-year congressional elections. The respondents in each of these surveys were asked questions about their attitudes on a wide variety of political issues. Many of these opinion questions appear in only one or two of the surveys, but a set of questions covering five basic issue-areas is available for each of the presidential election years from 1956 through 1972 and for the 1958 congressional election. Similar questions were asked of a national sample in a survey which was administered by the National Opinion Research Center (NORC) in the spring of 1971.

The five issue-areas for which we have comparable data over the entire time period are:

(1) *Social Welfare.* The questions elicit the respondent's attitudes on the federal government's responsibility to provide welfare programs in the areas of employment, of education, and of medical care.

(2) *Welfare Measures Specific for Blacks.* Respondents were asked whether they thought the federal government should provide special welfare programs for blacks in the areas of jobs and housing.

(3) *The Size of Government.* From 1956 through 1960 respondents were asked whether they thought it best that the federal government be kept out of areas such as housing and electric power generation that were traditionally handled by private industry. From 1964 through 1972, respondents were asked a slightly more general question concerning whether they thought the federal government was already too big and involved in too many areas. (This question is not asked in the 1971 NORC study.)

(4) *Racial Integration in the Schools.* The questions asked whether the federal government ought to enforce school integration or stay completely out of that problem.

(5) *The Cold War.* These questions vary from period to period as the nature of the cold war changed, but they are all concerned with the toughness of the United States toward communism and the desirability of military intervention. In 1956, 1958, and 1960, respondents were asked whether they thought the government ought to send soldiers abroad to aid countries fighting communism. The 1964 and '68 surveys asked whether the United States government should sit down and talk to Communist leaders to settle differences. In 1968, '71, and '72, the questions asked whether we should pursue a military victory against the Communists in Vietnam or withdraw our forces.

With the exceptions mentioned above, the questions to be used in the analysis are, with minor variations in wording and coding, identical at all points in time. To make interpretation easier, coding categories were reordered wherever necessary to range from conservative to liberal. For purposes of statistical comparability, answers to questions which originally permitted more than three codes were collapsed so that responses to all questions conformed to a unified trichotomous format of: 1) conservative; 2) centrist; 3) liberal.[6] Refusals, those with no opinions, and those giving "don't know" responses were always excluded from the analysis.

## The Emergence of Mass Ideology: Over-Time Comparisons of Attitude Consistency

Figure 1 presents a comparison of levels of attitude consistency among the five issue-areas in 1956, 1964, and 1972—the beginning, middle and end points of the period under investigation. . . . The indicators of attitude constraint in 1956 are presented on the left-hand vertical line; those for 1964 on the vertical line in the middle, and those for 1972 on the line to the right. The data points represent the relationship of attitudes (measured by Gammas)[7] across pairs of issues—there being ten such paired relationships for the five issues.

FIGURE 1.   Comparison of Attitude Consistency in 1956, 1964, and 1972: Average
Gammas Between Five Issue Areas

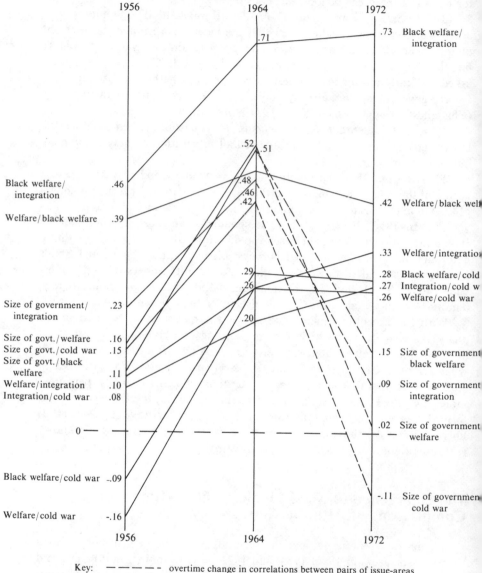

Key:   — — — — —   overtime change in correlations between pairs of issue-areas
       ———————   1964-1972 change in correlation between size of government
                  issue and other issue areas

The coefficients tell us how much of a relationship there is between the
questions in any two issue-areas. Positive correlations indicate the presence
of at least some liberal/conservative opinion consistency. Zero or low correlations indicate an absence of liberal/conservative consistency, while negative

coefficients signify that those giving liberal responses to questions within one issue-area are more likely to give conservative responses to questions in the other.

For those issue-areas where more than one question is available—namely social welfare and the cold war—the correlations presented are an average of the gammas between each of the questions in that issue-area and the question or questions in the other area. In those cases where there is only one question for each of the two issue-areas the simple correlation between those two questions is presented. . . .

Thus our findings closely parallel those reported in the earlier studies. As of 1956, there is little evidence of any unified liberal/conservative attitude continuum, and with only two exceptions—involving questions which share common symbols—there appears to be little or no opinion structure.

A quick glance at the parallel figures for 1964 reveals a dramatic change in levels of attitude consistency. The degree of association between attitudes on each of the five issues has increased, and in almost all cases the increases are quite substantial. There are no longer any negative correlations and in contrast to 1956 where only two of the ten coefficients were greater than .25, we now find just the opposite—only one of the ten is less than .25. What is truly impressive about the pattern of consistency in 1964 is not only the magnitude of the over-all increase in consistency, but also the number of different issue-domains which have come to be bound together. In 1956, moderate to high levels of attitude consistency were encountered on only two pairs of domestic issues. In 1964, on the other hand, not only has the relationship between attitudes on these increased substantially but attitudes on *all* of the domestic issues are highly intercorrelated and appear to reflect the kind of over-arching liberal/conservative ideology which is, the theory of mass beliefs suggests, beyond the capacity of the mass public. Furthermore, in 1964, there is considerable consistency between attitudes on domestic issues and positions on the conduct of the cold war.

The pattern for 1972 is more complicated. At first glance, there appears to be a substantial decline in the level of attitude constraint compared to 1964, but on closer inspection of the data, we can see that all relationships not involving size of government have (within the range of sampling error) maintained themselves or increased. Correlations among all issue-areas, both domestic and foreign, with the exception of size of government are above .25 in 1972.[8]

The important point, then, is that the pattern of attitudes found among Americans in the 1950s was a transient phenomenon and not an inevitable characteristic of mass politics. Of course, the pattern that emerged in the 1960s may be transient as well, but that does not change our argument about the lack of inevitability of the earlier pattern. Indeed, our data suggest that not only specific political attitudes but the *structure* of mass attitudes may be affected by politics in the real world. The average citizen may not be as apolitical as has been thought. The persistence of attitude consistency among the mass public will depend—as we have demonstrated—on the character of the American political experience in the 1970s.

## Notes

1. The empirical study of ideology in the mass public has proceeded along three lines. First, researchers have investigated the degree to which citizens conceptualize politics in ideological terms, either by deciding whether their spontaneous evaluations of political objects have ideological content or by directly determining their knowledge of ideological terms. (Cf. Angus Campbell et al., *The American Voter*, New York: John Wiley & Sons, Inc., 1960; and Philip Converse, "The Nature of Belief Systems in Mass Publics," chap. 6 in *Ideology and Discontent*, David Apter, ed., New York: Free Press, 1964). Second, students of mass opinion have looked for a coherent structure among citizens' attitudes on political issues which would suggest that they organize their political beliefs on a broad ideological continuum such as liberalism/conservatism. Finally, other students of ideology—operating on a somewhat different level and with a completely different methodology— have attempted to probe for deeper and more personal ways in which citizens make order of the political world around them. (Cf. especially Robert Lane, *Political Ideology* [New York: Free Press, 1962]).

2. This discussion of the difference between the organization of attitudes in elites and mass publics has drawn heavily on the following works: Converse, "Belief Systems," 227–231 particularly; Herbert McClosky, "Consensus and Ideology in American Politics," *American Political Science Review*, 58 (June 1964), 361–382; McClosky, Paul J. Hoffman, and Rosemary O'Hara, "Issue Conflict and Consensus among Leaders and Followers," *American Political Science Review*, 54 (June 1960), 419; James W. Prothro and C. W. Grigg, "Fundamental Principles of Democracy: Basis of Agreement and Disagreement," *Journal of Politics*, 22 (May 1969), 276– 294. The specific description of the relationship among opinions in the mass public relies upon the analysis of V. O. Key, Jr., in *Public Opinion in American Democracy* (New York: Alfred A. Knopf, 1961), chap. 7, 153–181.

3. This explanation for the structure of mass beliefs is most coherently stated by Converse, "Belief Systems." However, it is explicit or implicit in most of the other studies citied.

4. Throughout this paper we use the terms attitude consistency and attitude constraint interchangeably. For us, both terms simply imply predictability of liberal/conservative attitudes across issue areas.

5. For example, respondents were asked whether they thought the federal government ought to play an active role in seeing to it that black and white children go to the same schools. They were also asked whether they thought the government should devise special programs to help blacks economically. While both questions share the symbol of blacks, it would not be illogical for a respondent to be against government enforcement of integration, but at the same time favor economic assistance to blacks. The issues may be symbolically related, but there is no formal logical connection between them.

6. Because Tau-gamma is used as our basic measure of association and because it is somewhat sensitive to the number of degrees of freedom in a table, recoding was required in order to get an unbiased estimation of the relationship between the various attitudes and between the same attitudes across time. In the recoding of the data, two guidelines were followed: (1) to make as even as possible the proportions of the population in each of the three categories, while (2) not permitting the first guideline to place respondents on the agree and disagree side of an issue in the same category. The rationale for the second recoding guideline is obvious in any attempt to classify responses as basically liberal or conservative. The rationale for the first guideline again relates to the use of gamma as the measure of association because it is highly sensitive and unreliable when there are extreme margins.

7. Tau-gamma was chosen as the measure of association because it is sensitive to attitude consistency of the scalar as well as the correlational type. Further, of the ordinal measures with this property it is the one most widely understood, and therefore the one most easy to interpret.

8. Given that the major shifts in levels of attitude constraint take place between 1960 and 1964, coinciding with some subtle and perhaps important shifts in the question format used by the SRC, the issue arises as to whether or not any of the observed increase in attitude consistency is an artifact of questionnaire design. A number of different types of evidence suggest that this is not the case. 1) While the '64 question format utilizes a stronger screener to deter those who "have not thought about the issue" from responding than was used in the '56, '58, and '60 studies, there is no appreciable increase in the average number of "no opinion" responses between the pre- and post-1964 periods. Increased attitude consistency is therefore not simply a function of screening out a larger proportion of the less interested and articulate segment of the population. 2) While the timing of changes in levels of constraint and question format coincide between '60 and '64, there have been two subsequent question format changes of equal significance since 1968, and neither of these seems to have had any bearing on the level of attitude consistency. The NORC '71 study utilizes a seven-point liberal to conservative scale much closer in format to the SRC pre-1964 Likert-type questions than to the dichotomous choices used by the SRC in '64 and '68. Furthermore, the questions in the NORC study make no explicit attempt to screen out those who had "perhaps not thought enough about the issues" to have an opinion. In 1972, the SRC itself adopted a seven-point scale, similar to that used in the NORC '71 study, for a number of the opinion questions we use. However, the SRC continued to follow its practice of attempting to deter from responding those who claimed to have thought little about individual issues. There has, in other words, been a continuous modification of question format from '68 onward, yet levels of attitude constraint have remained more or less constant in that period. In short, we have one instance—that is, between '60 and '64—where a significant shift in attitude constraint coincided with a basic change in question format. But from '64 onward we find a virtually constant level of attitude consistency in the face of two equally dramatic variations in question format. 3) Finally, it has long been a tenet of survey research that changes in question wording and format are most likely to affect the response of those who are least interested and concerned with the subject matter and thus who are least likely to have strong positions. Conversely, respondents who are

highly interested and concerned, and who are most likely to take intense positions, have been found to be much less affected by the types of question changes described above. In order to provide a further test of the artifact hypothesis, we created a pool of respondents whose attitude structure should have been least susceptible to changes in question wording and format. This subset of the population was composed of those in each year who claimed to be: (a) strong partisan identifiers; (b) highly concerned with the election outcome; and (c) greatly interested in the campaign. Our findings about the levels of attitude constraint in this group are unambiguous. The largest increase in levels of attitude consistency within the population are found within this group, which is least likely to be affected by changes in the wording and coding of questions.

The arguments countering the artifact hypothesis briefly discussed above are presented in greater depth in a document entitled, "Levels of Attitude Consistency and Changes in Question Format: An Analysis of the Problem of Artifact," which can be obtained upon request from the authors. This document more fully elaborates the changes in the question formats and their significance and presents, as well, the supporting data alluded to in points 1 and 3 above.

Finally, NORC has a study currently in the field containing a full methodological experiment which should provide more definitive data on the actual impact of questionnaire wording and format on the intercorrelation among political attitudes of the type under investigation.

# The Changing Structure of Mass Belief Systems: Fact or Artifact?

GEORGE F. BISHOP
ROBERT W. OLDENDICK
ALFRED J. TUCHFARBER
STEPHEN E. BENNETT

IN THEIR HIGHLY ACCLAIMED VOLUME, *The Changing American Voter*, and in an earlier article, Norman Nie and his colleagues have presented seemingly incontrovertible evidence of monumental shifts in the structure of mass belief systems: the breakdown of partisanship, the emergence of ideological thinking or "consistency," and the growth of issue voting.[1] In this brief report, however, we will describe findings on one of these major trends—the rise of issue consistency—which will tell us there has been little or no change since the "non-ideological" 1950s. Furthermore, we will make the case that much of the apparent shift in mass sophistication is due to a basic methodological artifact: changes in question wording and format.

The first of these changes took place at the time of the 1964 American national election when the Survey Research Center (SRC) converted the issue questions used by Nie and other researchers from a five-point Likert format (i.e., strongly agree—strongly disagree) to a dichotomous choice between relatively well-defined substantive alternatives. Interestingly, this is also the point at which the trend line for issue consistency (and issue voting) takes a sharp upward turn. In 1968 the SRC began to experiment with still another format, a seven-point semantic differential type of scale anchored at each end by opposing policy statements of the kind used in the dichotomous-choice questions. And by 1972 almost all of the issue questions that have

Reprinted by permission of the publisher from *The Journal of Politics*, Vol. 40 (August 1978), pp. 781–787.

figured so prominently in the secondary analyses of the Michigan Electoral Series appear in this form. But however desirable these modifications might have been at the time from a technical standpoint (i.e., to improve reliability, maximize variance), they have only confounded the trend analysis of changes in the structure of mass political attitudes. For we now know that even minor variations in the wording of survey questions can produce significant discrepancies not just in the marginals but also in the magnitude of association among items—i.e., in our measures of "constraint."[2]

An opportunity for a direct test of the artifact hypothesis became available when the National Opinion Research Center recently released data from a national amalgam survey designed, among other things, to assess the effects of the various question formats that have operationalized issue attitudes in the SRC/CPS election series.[3]

## Data and Findings

In December of 1973 NORC interviewers administered three different forms of the Michigan issue questions to randomized subgroups of a national sample. The first group (N = 501) received the items in the five-point Likert format used by the SRC prior to 1964; the second group (N = 495), the dichotomous-choice format instituted in 1964; and the third group (N = 493), the more recent seven-point scales.[4] Juxtaposing the data from these "replicated" items in the 1973 NORC experiment with those from the SRC surveys of the fifties and sixties allows us to answer the question of whether the American voter of the 1970s is any more consistent, attitudinally, than his or her counterpart of the 1950s and early 1960s.[5]

The figures in Table 1, describing the trends in issue consistency for *21* pairs of issues from 1956 to 1973, leave little doubt that the structure of American political attitudes has remained remarkably stable since the Eisenhower years. Averaging over the issue pairs, in fact, yields identical values for 1960 and 1973 (.22) and one that is nearly so for 1956 (.20). Granted there are a few issue pairs that deviate from the general pattern of small differences. But if the readers will scrutinize these instances closely, they will find about as many cases where issue consistency is higher in the earlier period (e.g., black welfare—school integration in 1958; employment–school aid in 1960) as in the more recent period (e.g., school aid–black welfare and school integration–electric power and housing in 1973). The important point, though, is that there is no discernible pattern to these few deviations and that, by and large, the amount of constraint among issue beliefs is about as high as it ever was.

Turning to the trends for the dichotomous issue questions from 1964 to 1973, we find further support for the question wording thesis, but also some apparent evidence of real substantive change when the questions are held

TABLE 1.  Gamma Coefficients for Pairs of Five-Point Issue Questions in 1956, 1958, 1960 and 1973

| Issue Pair | SRC 1956 | SRC 1958 | SRC 1960 | NORC 1973 |
|---|---|---|---|---|
| Employment–School Aid | .41 | .46 | .56 | .40 |
| Employment–Medicare | .50 | —[a] | .55 | .57 |
| Employment–Black Welfare | .40 | .33 | .32 | .33 |
| Employment–School Integration | .09 | .12 | .19 | .02 |
| Employment–Elec. Power & Housing | .13 | .07 | .12 | .12 |
| Employment–U.S. Soldiers overseas | .06 | .12 | .01 | .08 |
| School Aid–Medicare | .37 | —[a] | .48 | .53 |
| School Aid–Black Welfare | .34 | .29 | .31 | .49 |
| School Aid–School Integration | .11 | .14 | .22 | .10 |
| School Aid–Elec. Power & Housing | .13 | .10 | .15 | .14 |
| School Aid–U.S. Soldiers overseas | .13 | .13 | .15 | .03 |
| Medicare–Black Welfare | .29 | —[a] | .30 | .42 |
| Medicare–School Integration | .08 | —[a] | .12 | .02 |
| Medicare–Elec. Power & Housing | .24 | —[a] | .16 | .19 |
| Medicare–U.S. Soldiers overseas | .04 | —[a] | .08 | .12 |
| Black Welfare–School Integration | .41 | .58 | .49 | .26 |
| Black Welfare–Elec. Power & Housing | .10 | .05 | .07 | .16 |
| Black Welfare–U.S. Soldiers overseas | .11 | .11 | .13 | .01 |
| School Integration–Elec. Power & Housing | .19 | .15 | .16 | .37 |
| School Integration–U.S. Soldiers overseas | .05 | .00 | .04 | .17 |
| Elec. Power & Housing–U.S. Soldiers overseas | .10 | .02 | .06 | .14 |
| X = | .20 | -- | .22 | .22 |

[a] The question on medicare was not asked in 1958.

constant (see Table 2). If we were to focus only on the average of the coefficients at the bottom of Table 2, however, we would draw the conclusion that the levels of issue connectedness in 1964 and 1968 (both of which greatly exceed that found for the 1956–1960 timespan, thus demonstrating the dramatic effects of the changes in wording and format) were essentially equivalent, but that they declined rather sharply sometime between 1968 and 1973. But as Nie and his associates have taken great pains to point out, much of the decline in the aggregate stems from the loss of predictive power on one particular issue: the question of whether the federal government is getting too powerful, a question which the SRC first introduced in 1964 and which Nie and his co-workers inexplicably substituted into their trend analysis in place of the earlier item on the government's involvement in electric power and housing (see Table 1).[6] This substitution, along with the replacement of the "cold war" (1956–1960) question on keeping U.S. soldiers overseas to help anti-communist nations by the 1964 item on whether we should negotiate our differences with Communist countries, has, in fact, produced much of the noncomparability that plagues the analysis by Nie and his associates. Unfortunately, we are unable to make cross-time comparisons through 1973 for the issue of relations with Communist countries since the NORC experiment did not replicate the previous SRC item on this topic; it includes, instead, a dichotomous version of the earlier SRC five-point question on keeping troops overseas to help countries opposed to Communism. Nonetheless, we think it is worthwhile to note that, with very minor exceptions, neither the five-point item on troops abroad (Table 1) nor the dichotomous version (Table 2) displayed any more constraint with other issues in 1973 than did the original question on this policy back in the fifties, a continuity which reaffirms our thesis about the enduring structure of American political attitudes.

When we look at the remaining issue pairs, two relatively distinct patterns emerge: (a) pairs combining the issues of employment, school aid, medicare

TABLE 2.    Yule's Q Coefficients for Pairs of Dichotomous Issue Questions in 1964, 1968, 1972 and 1973

| Issue Pair | SRC 1964 | SRC 1968 | CPS 1972 | NORC 1973 |
|---|---|---|---|---|
| Employment–School Aid | .60 | .61 | — | .55 |
| Employment–Medicare | .80 | .76 | — | .87 |
| Employment–Black Welfare | .68 | .74 | — | .74 |
| Employment–School Integration | .33 | .65 | — | .68 |
| Employment–Size of Govt. | −.55 | −.52 | — | −.12 |
| Employment–Communist Relations | .22 | .15 | — | — |
| Employment–U.S. Soldiers Overseas | — | — | — | .01 |
| School Aid–Medicare | .71 | .69 | — | .85 |
| School Aid–Black Welfare | .56 | .64 | — | .68 |
| School Aid–School Integration | .33 | .69 | — | .58 |
| School Aid–Size of Govt. | −.65 | −.65 | — | −.11 |
| School Aid–Communist Relations | .38 | .28 | — | — |
| School Aid–U.S. Soldiers Overseas | — | — | — | .14 |
| Medicare–Black Welfare | .59 | .53 | — | .69 |
| Medicare–School Integration | .37 | .51 | — | .46 |
| Medicare–Size of Govt. | −.71 | −.55 | — | .10 |
| Medicare–Communist Relations | .23 | .05 | — | — |
| Medicare–U.S. Soldiers Overseas | — | — | — | .05 |
| Black Welfare–School Integration | .83 | .84 | .84 | .85 |
| Black Welfare–Size of Govt. | −.63 | −.47 | −.18 | −.22 |
| Black Welfare–Communist Relations | .42 | .50 | — | — |
| Black Welfare–U.S. Soldiers Overseas | — | — | — | .11 |
| School Integration–Size of Govt. | −.55 | −.53 | −.11 | −.28 |
| School Integration–Communist Relations | .23 | .52 | — | — |
| School Integration–U.S. Soldiers Overseas | — | — | — | .26 |
| Size of Govt.–Communist Relations | −.41 | −.36 | — | — |
| Size of Govt.–U.S. Soldiers Overseas | — | — | — | .18 |
| $\bar{X}$ = | .51 | .53 | — | .41 |

and black welfare with each other, the coefficients for which tend to be fairly similar over the nine-year interval (within the expected range of sampling error for multistage designs) and (b) pairs containing the school integration issue, most of which increase rather substantially between 1964 and 1968 and then level off from 1968 to 1973. Tempting as it might be to say . . . "here at last is a bona fide instance of increased attitudinal integration"— with question wording indeed held constant, we have reason to believe, once again, that things are not quite as they seem. For one thing, there is no parallel evidence from our analysis of the five-point items (Table 1) that school integration attitudes have become more interconnected with other issue beliefs since the fifties. Furthermore, we have difficulty understanding why the school integration issue should have become as highly constrained, proportionately speaking, with an issue like relations with Communist countries (1964–1968)—to which it is theoretically and psychologically rather distant—as with issues like federal aid to education, medicare, or employment which are at least superficially relevant in that they fall within the same general domain of domestic issues. What then accounts for the changes in the magnitude of the gamma coefficients for the school integration pairs?

Not so surprisingly, perhaps, it has little or nothing to do with the psychodynamic process of resolving cognitive inconsistencies on the part of the mass public, but rather to another very fundamental factor: shifts in the marginals of one item, namely, the school integration question. Between 1964 and 1968, the mass public became, for whatever reason, significantly less liberal and more conservative (about a 10% overall swing) on the issue of integrating schools; and this turnover merely happened to coincide with relatively stable marginals for the other issues, such that the cells for "consistent cases" in the crosstabulations swelled to boost the size of the gamma coefficients.[7] In other words the change in constraint was largely a by-product of what was probably a very real movement in public sentiment about the desirability of integrating schools and did not necessarily reflect any deliberate thinking on the part of respondents about how their new feelings about this question related to a host of other issues, especially such remote items as settling our differences with Communist countries.

What we are saying in a nutshell is that, when we take into account the variations in question wording that have occurred in the SRC electoral series, many of the apparent changes in the quality of mass belief systems since the fifties disappear or become negligible; and that where they do appear to persist in the face of comparable questions, it is more likely the result of subtle and not so subtle shifts in the marginals which may have very little connection with the processes observed in laboratory studies of cognitive consistency. It is, to coin an expression, more a matter of what is "coincident" than what is "consistent."

Finally, though this report has clearly focused on the methodological problems afflicting the analysis of attiudinal constraint by Norman Nie and his associates, we have good reason to believe that our findings apply just as well to the equally acclaimed work by Gerald Pomper and others on issue voting, particularly when we remember that the trend lines for all these phenomena parallel each other rather closely over time.[8] So we must ask once more: Has the American voter truly changed?

## Notes

1. Norman H. Nie, Sidney Verba and John R. Petrocik, *The Changing American Voter* (Cambridge, Mass.: Harvard University Press, 1976); see also Norman H. Nie with Kristi Andersen "Mass Belief Systems Revisited: Political Change and Attitude Structure," *Journal of Politics*, 36 (August 1974), 540–587.

2. Howard Schuman and Otis D. Duncan, "Questions about Attitude Survey Questions," in *Sociological Methodology 1973–1974*, ed. Herbert L. Costner (San Francisco: Jossey-Bass, 1974), 232–251; Howard Schuman and Stanley Presser, "Question Wording as an Independent Variable in Survey Analysis," *Sociological Methods and Research*, 6 (Fall 1977), 151–170.

3. We would like to thank Norman Nie, the principal investigator on the 1973 NORC experiment, for releasing these data into the public domain.

4. For the exact wording of the replicated issue questions, see the original SRC/CPS codebooks for the 1956–1974 American national election studies, Inter-University Consortium for Political and Social Research (Ann Arbor: University of Michigan).

5. In this paper we present only trend analyses for the five-point issue questions from 1956 to 1973 and for the dichotomous issue items from 1964 to 1973. No data is shown for the seven-point scales because they would represent a trend for just one year and for only one CPS item asked in comparable 7-point form in the 1972 election—the question on whether the government should guarantee employment (and the standard of living). The NORC experiment also failed to properly replicate the CPS 7-point issue scales by not including the standard filter question, a factor which would make any comparison between these datasets inappropriate, even if a longer trend period were available for items of similar content.

6. Nie *et al.*, *The Changing American Voter*, 125–128.

7. If the increase in the size of the gamma coefficients resulted from more integrated ideological thinking by the electorate, we would have expected simultaneous movement of the marginals in a liberal or conservative direction on several issues bearing some conceptual relevance to one another. Or perhaps a more convincing pattern would have been a substantial rise in the magnitude of the various coefficients coupled with fairly stable marginals on all of the items, which would suggest that the mass public had resolved some of the attitudinal inconsistencies observed in the 1964 election.

8. See Gerald Pomper, *Voters' Choice: Varieties of American Electoral Behavior* (New York: Dodd, Mead Company, 1975); and "Toward a More Responsive Two-Party System: What, Again?" *Journal of Politics*, 33 (November 1971), 916–940; "From Confusion to Clarity: Issues and American Voters, 1956–1962," *American Political Science Review*, 66 (June 1972), 415–428.

# "Reply to Bishop *et al.*"

NORMAN H. NIE
SIDNEY VERBA
JOHN H. PETROCIK

WHETHER THE ELECTORATE was ever as consistent in their responses to these issues as is shown here (see Figure 1) for 1964 through 1972 has been a matter of considerable debate. The SRC/CPS election studies changed the format and, in a couple of instances, the content of these questions for the 1964 election study. Since the correlation among these items increased substantially in the 1964 data, many scholars have attributed virtually all of the change to measurement factors rather than to substantive variables.

The analysis upon which the competing interpretation rests appears in George Bishop and others, "Change in the Structure of American Political Attitudes: The Nagging Question of Question Wording," *American Journal of Political Science,* 22 (May 1978), 250–269; George Bishop and others, "Effects of Question Wording and Format on Political Attitude Consistency," *Public Opinion Quarterly* (forthcoming); George Bishop and others, "The Changing Structure of Mass Belief Systems: Fact or Artifact?" *Journal of Politics,* 40 (August 1978), 781–790; Alfred J. Tuchfarber and George F. Bishop, "Trends in the Structure of American Political Attitudes, 1956–1976: Change or Stability?" paper presented at the Annual Meeting of the Midwest Political Science Association, Chicago, 1978; and George Bishop and others, "Questions About Question Wording: A Rejoinder to Revisiting Mass Belief Systems Revisited," *American Journal of Political Science,* 23 (February 1979), 187–192. All of these papers by Bishop and his colleagues present the same basic data and argument. The rejoinder cited last is slightly different from the others.

Extracted from Norman H. Nie, Sidney Verba, and John H. Petrocik, "Reply to Bishop et al.," in *The Changing American Voters,* enlarged edition (1979), note on pp. 367–370, by permission of the authors and Harvard University Press. Copyright © 1976, 1979 by the Twentieth Century Fund.

FIGURE 1.   Ideological Evaluation of Candidates, 1952–1976

Percent

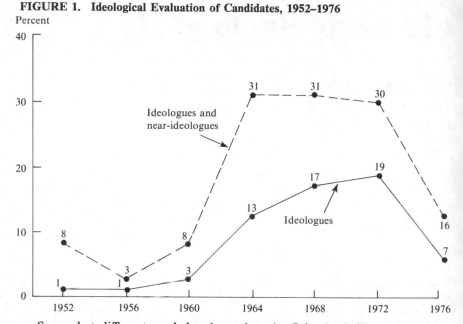

Somewhat different work has been done by John L. Sullivan, James E. Piereson, and George E. Marcus in "Ideological Constraint in the Mass Public: A Methodological Critique and Some New Findings," *American Journal of Political Science,* 22 (May 1978), pp. 233–249, and "The More Things Change, The More They Remain the Same: The Stability of Mass Belief Systems," *American Journal of Political Science,* 23 (February 1979). Gregory Brunk has addressed the same concerns in his "The 1964 Attitude Consistency Leap Reconsidered," *Political Methodology* (1979), 176–186. Hugh L. LeBlanc and Mary Beth Merrin treat the data in a slightly different way, but they also question the extent to which issue consistency has increased. See "Mass Belief Systems Revisited," *Journal of Politics,* 39 (November 1977), 1082–1087. Another critique appears in Eric R. A. Smith, "The False Measures of the Levels of Conceptualization," paper presented at the Annual Meeting of the Pacific Chapter, American Association for Public Opinion Research, Lake Arrowhead, California, 1979.

We have attempted to answer these criticisms in Norman Nie and James N. Rabjohn, "Revisiting Mass Belief Systems Revisited: Or, Why Doing Research Is Like Watching a Tennis Match," *American Journal of Political Science,* 23 (February 1979), 139–175; John Petrocik, "Comment: Reconsidering the Reconsiderations of the 1964 Change in Attitude Consistency," *Political Methodology,* 5 (Winter 1978), 361–368; and John Petrocik, "The Changeable American Voter: Some Revisions of the Revision," paper presented at the Annual Meeting of the American Political Science Association, New York, 1978, a revised version of which will appear in *The Electorate*

*Reconsidered,* ed. John C. Pierce and John L. Sullivan (Beverly Hills, Calif.: Sage Publications).

This epilogue provides particularly important data for the debate. Despite constant questions in the 1972 and 1976 surveys, the average intercorrelation among the items dropped off considerably in 1976. This decline is consistent with our expectation. We assume that attitude consistency responds as much to the political context as it does to individual psychological properties. The different candidates and a vastly different political atmosphere in 1976 explain the lower correlation, just as more ideological candidates and a more heated political context after 1960, we believe, precipitated greater issue consistency. Our substantive explanation accounts for the increase and the decline in the correlations. The methodological argument explains the increase, but it does not have any provision for the downward trend of 1976. Unless there is a measurement change that has been overlooked, the artifact explanation for our data, while plausible, is not sufficiently supported to dislodge our thesis.

Furthermore, our argument on the change in 1964 is based not only upon a change in the level of issue consistency but also upon a number of changes in other measures not affected by variation in format. In particular, the change in the types of answers given to open-ended candidate and party evaluation questions —a change that is coterminous with the issue consistency change—corroborates our belief that a real change took place in 1964. Both issue consistency and the open-ended answers change back again in 1976. Finally, as we shall see, the pattern of issue voting also changes in a similar manner. Thus, our argument as to the reality of change does not depend on any single measure.

# 4

# Mass Media: Organization Structure and Control

In addition to producing and distributing culture and information, American mass media are formal organizations staffed by professionals, owned by stockholders, and regulated by government. The mass communications system plays a critical part in the economic and political structure of society. Its centrality directs scholarly attention to linkages between it and other institutions as well as to its internal process and structure.

As Hirsch notes in his selection, American mass media are organized more along the lines of private enterprise and the market place than has been the case in most other countries, even other Western industrialized nations. The prevailing pattern has been one of private ownership, relatively little state regulation, and a flexible definition of the "public interest" on the government's part. These characteristics raise pointed questions concerning the power of the media, and the extent to which these aspects of organization and control influence media content. How, if at all, do the profit-making requirements of media organizations influence the character of entertainment or patterns of news coverage? How do organizational structures shape and constrain the work of professional artists and journalists? Also, we may wish to know how the introduction of new technologies affects these arrangements or how the concentration of media technology in the hands of Western countries determines patterns of international media flow and the cultural and political organization of mass communication in developing nations.

While there is little consensus about the answers to these questions, few researchers doubt the importance of better understanding the organization and control of the media and their consequences. These topics have generated considerable discussion and research, as we shall see in the articles selected for this section.

News distribution in the United States is unique in its high degree of decentralization. Bagdikian's essay explains why America has such a diminutive national press compared with other countries. In the United States, even the most centralized news gathering organizations, Associated Press, United Press International, and the three major broadcasting networks, operate through local distributional channels of independently managed radio, television, and newspaper outlets. This unique localism stretches back to pre-Revolutionary America, when newspapers emerged as merchandising organs whose chief function was to link prospective consumers with local commercial traders. This function continues today because personal consumption in the United States is high enough to support large numbers of local merchants, whose advertising represents the chief source of revenue for local newspapers. The principal reason for the localism of American news, however, is the decentralized nature of the American government, whose local units are powerful enough to continually generate news of importance to citizens living within their jurisdictions. The local press is sustained, therefore, by the continuous occurrence of newsworthy events that only it can cover.

However, a heightened awareness of the importance of national government, and the regional and national standardization of retail outlets by a shrinking number of large firms, have partially undercut the social bases of the local press. Bagdikian nevertheless insists that America still needs its local press and warns that the diminishing number of daily newspapers threatens to create a void that no other institution is at present able to fill.

Phenomenological sociology has gradually gained acceptance over the last decade. It stresses that laypersons' understanding of society is organized not around abstract, theory-like principles so much as practical, normative rules of procedure derived from personal experience. Tuchman applies this approach to the professional world of newspaper journalists. The "raw material" of reporting consists of unpredictable and unanticipated events. Tuchman shows how newsworkers develop classifications that reduce the great variability of these events to a small and manageable number of types, thereby allowing them to convert the unusual into news copy. She emphasizes that these classifications, or "typifications," break down not along substantive lines but according to the practical tasks associated with the organizational requirements of news production. Thus, newsworkers learn to translate their own perceptions into news categories compatible with the processes of complex organizations, in order to optimize their control over the work flow. As a contribution to our understanding of the mass media, Tuchman's approach interfaces with organizational analysis and the sociology of work and may be fruitfully applied to other work settings.

Tunstall reviews the "television imperialism" thesis that American programs shown abroad constitute a cultural arm of American domination over large parts of the world. He finds the argument deficient on several counts. He notes, for example, that it is in their ability to regulate the flow of *news*, rather than entertainment, that the "Anglo-American" media exercise their greatest measure of control. Although worldwide reliance of the American newsweeklies *Time* and *Newsweek* is considerable, the United States shares supremacy in this area with Western Europe, whose news agencies originated in the nineteenth century. Tunstall's article also provides a succinct introduction to debates over the relative merits of imported symbols versus "authentic" local culture for developing countries struggling to build a national cultural and social identity. He points out that much indigenous culture is ill suited to promote such goals, because it reinforces local or tribal allegiances at the expense of national identifications.

The nature and functions of American television must be understood in terms of the medium's history, technological prowess, and industrial character. Hirsch demonstrates that television's status as an industry whose principal mission is the "delivery" of audiences to advertisers explains much about its program content. Since most of the products advertised are purchased in urban areas, program content is primarily geared to attract the city dweller. Hirsch also traces the history of television's institutional matrix, showing that its relative exemption from government regulation derives from a set of arrangements which evolved during earlier periods for radio, film, and newspapers. At the same time, the rise of television as the foremost mass medium, in turn, facilitated specialization of these older media. Television's technical superiority for culturally unifying large, heterogeneous audiences permitted it to supplant these older media, forcing them to differentiate their programming. Here again, in the case of radio and magazines, broadcast and publication policies were tied to the media's "audience delivery" function, so these specialized media now act to link advertisers of products with limited appeal to members of those subgroups at whom new radio formats and specialized magazines are directed. Finally, Hirsch's article reviews arguments for dismantling television networks and finds them wanting.

# The Political Basis for Local Newspapers and Broadcast Licenses

BEN H. BAGDIKIAN

AMONG WORLD NEWS SYSTEMS, America's is peculiar.

In other countries there are national newspapers issued in one or two important urban centers and distributed as the primary serious journals throughout the country. Local papers are marginal and parochial, classified geographically and culturally as "the provincial press."

In most countries radio and television also are centralized, with few local originating facilities. Programs typically emanate from a central studio owned and controlled by a government monopoly.

In the United States, the typical American consumer receives all his daily printed and broadcast news from a local private enterprise. There are historical reasons for this unique pattern in the United States and social reasons why it should continue. Though there are contemporary trends diminishing local independence, compared to world systems the American news continues to be rooted in the local community.

The American news is even at odds with its own technological and corporate environment. It transmits most of its information through national monopolies, the telephone and telegraph systems. Its major suppliers of national and world news are two highly centralized national services, the Associated Press and United Press International. The newspaper industry as a whole is one of the country's largest and as such operates in an economic environ-

Abridged from Chapter 4, "Some Peculiarities of American News," pp. 69–87 in *The Information Machines* by Ben H. Bagdikian. Copyright © 1971 by The RAND Corporation. Reprinted by permission of Harper & Row, Publishers, Inc.

ment of corporate giantism and oligopoly. Yet the news itself continues to be dispensed through a highly fragmented collection of local firms. . . .

No other country approaches this degree of localism in news institutions. In Russia, for example, metropolitan Moscow has less than 3 percent of total U.S.S.R. population, but Moscow-based dailies have 87 percent of all Russian daily circulation. In Japan, metropolitan Tokyo has 11 percent of national population, but Tokyo-based dailies have 70 percent of national circulation. In Britain, metropolitan London has 14 percent of population, but its dailies have 70 percent of national circulation.

In contrast, metropolitan New York and Washington, D.C., together have 6.6 percent of national population and together their daily papers supply only 9.6 percent of daily papers throughout the country.

Technical innovations in the coming years could change the fundamental pattern of public information distribution in the United States, and it is logical to ask whether the unique localism in the United States can or should be preserved. This question is worth asking because prevailing explanations for the absence of national news media in the United States seldom touch on its profound social basis.

The usual explanation for the lack of national newspapers is that the United States is so large geographically that it has been impossible to transport a paper speedily from its city of origin to all other cities. This has been one influence. But if it were the controlling factor, it would be predictable that new technology would quickly eliminate the pattern of local newspapers, since remote reproduction of large quantities of documents will become increasingly fast and inexpensive. One need not even wait for future developments. Present technology permits effective centralized control of newspaper production over great distances. Russia is two and a half times larger than the United States but manages to control most of its papers from Moscow.

Still another explanation usually offered is national affluence that can support many papers. This, like geographical size, is a factor but not a controlling one. A number of countries have a higher rate of per-capita newspaper buying but support fewer individual papers. . . .

The American broadcasting news system follows somewhat the same pattern, with a large number of individual radio and television stations spread throughout the country. This is primarily the result of governmental regulatory policy rather than market mechanisms that govern placement of newspapers. But it is significant that government policy places a high value on localized radio and television stations. Governments of other industrialized countries favor centralized systems.

Centralizing radio broadcasting would be technically simple. Commercial radio signals ricochet between the surface of the earth and layers of the atmosphere during the evening, propelling themselves over very long distances in every direction. Thus, it would not be difficult to produce nighttime coverage of the entire continental United States from a single transmitter. As a matter of fact, this was done from 1934 to 1938 when WLW in Cincinnati was permitted to operate at 500,000 watts.

Daytime radio signals fade more quickly, but with easily achieved power and selected frequencies a single station can still be heard within ranges of several hundreds of miles, so that a few stations could easily cover the entire United States.

Despite this technical feasibility of a few stations covering the entire country, there are 6,200 commercial AM and FM radio stations operating in 2,672 separate American communities. The largest number of radio stations in a single area is 34.

If the only desired end in the distribution of radio stations were diversity on a national scale, this could be achieved more easily, economically, and with greater variety than the present scattered locations. It would be possible, for example, to have 100 powerful radio transmitters that could reach every radio in the United States, rather than 6200 weaker ones reaching only their own locales. And the 100 centralized ones would provide more choice for the average listener, whose present maximum local stations are 34, with most communities able to receive far fewer. But the 100 centralized stations would not conform to the special force of localism in the United States.

Television cannot be so easily propagated from a few national transmitters because its carrier wave has a range less than a hundred miles and is even more disturbed than radio by intervening masses. But if national coverage with several channels were desired, it could be produced by several centralized studios whose programs would be relayed to each locality by relatively simple translator stations that are automatic. Instead, there are 639 commercial television transmitters in operation in 285 metropolitan areas, each with facilities for originating its own programs, rather than merely relaying national ones.

The fundamental reason for this persistent localism in American news institutions is a peculiarity in American political organization and the prevailing pattern of family money spending.

More governmental functions are left to the local level in the United States than in other developed countries. Schools, property taxes, land use, public health, large areas of business regulation, and many other political and social activities are controlled by locally elected and locally controlled bodies in the United States, while in other countries many of these are controlled by national governments or administered by national bureaucracies.

These locally controlled policies have maximum immediate impact on family life, such as schooling for children, design and location of homes, routes of local highways, and rates of personal property taxes. Such decisions are made by a complicated but highly localized set of political bodies. There are 18,000 municipalities and 17,000 townships. Within these are 500,000 local government units of one kind or another directly elected by local residents, 100,000 of these being directly elected local school boards, and 70,000 of the local jurisdictions possessing the power to impose taxes on their constituents.

No national newspaper or national broadcast news program can tell the local citizen what he needs or wants to know about these local activities that affect his family life. Furthermore, what is relevant to one local jurisdiction is only minimally significant for the next, since school systems, property taxes, and similar matters follow strictly local lines and cease to apply across the local boundary. Continuing information from relatively small districts is a unique imperative of the American social system.

Another powerful force for localism in the mass media is the large amount of local money spending by the average family. Mass purchasing power requires enough spending decisions to support advertising as a major economic activity. . . .

The great majority of this family money spending is done locally among competing enterprises. There are 1,700,000 retail stores in the United States. The average American family spends $5,000 a year in them. Many of these stores advertise in competition for this disposable family income, and most of their advertising is in the general locality of their stores, in the mass media of the region.

Thus, there is both a political and an economic base for the localized pattern of American news media.

But there are conflicting forces at work, some in the direction of the traditional fragmentation of news firms, and some in the direction of a more homogenized, national pattern of a few organizations dominating the country. At present, there seems to be a tenuous equilibrium between the forces, with a surprising degree of stability among small journalism units despite the national trend toward large national corporations. The nature of new technology and the way it is organized could be crucial to the fate of this equilibrium.

The stability and profit of small, local journalism firms are remarkable, considering their rarity in other countries. In the daily-newspaper business, for example, there is a common pattern of a few large firms controlling a disproportionate share of the total market. In the United States, 8 percent of the largest papers have over half of all circulation. The smaller papers, those under twenty-five thousand circulation, constitute 70 percent of all daily newspaper firms but they have less than 20 percent of national circulation. . . .

Location of broadcasting stations is decided by the Federal Communications Commission, and though these decisions are influenced by market demand, they are more influenced by limitations of positions on the dial. And, since there is no simple measure of "customers" for broadcasting because the consumer does not pay directly for his broadcast, determining how stations share their market is somewhat blurred. Here, as with newspapers, one sees advantages with domination of larger markets, with profit margins being generally higher for stations in densely populated areas.

The pattern of economic activity of television stations by size is difficult to discern in official data, since the Federal Communications Commission does not issue comparable information for television. There are fewer television stations nationally, and fewer per market. There are over two hundred television markets; the top ten markets have more than a third of all TV households in the country and the top forty markets have two-thirds.

The news media from the start were carriers of local merchandising information. The newspaper in the United States began as a printed extension of bulletin boards of taverns and coffeehouses, its content mainly of ship arrivals and their offerings of cargo. These papers sold for six cents each, a very high price in the eighteenth century, designed for the affluent in the local population. The nonadvertising content consisted largely of reprinted stories from the English papers which arrived on the same ship as the merchandise. Until the Revolution, the most common name for American newspapers was *Advertiser*.

This pattern was enhanced by the absence of very large cities in the eighteenth-century North American continent. When the first dailies were established, the two largest cities, New York and Philadelphia, each had twenty-five thousand population. . . .

As the country grew it developed a different demographic pattern from Europe, which already had its population clustered around large cities. The American frontier expanded and its population kept proliferating outward to virgin territory. A lively apprentice system produced many printers who had a reputation for itchy feet and parched throats, drifting drinkers who fell out of one job to another just beyond their reputation, but leaving behind the idea of a locally printed sheet.

Other factors helped create many small papers instead of a few large ones. One was the absence of a tax on papers. The European attempt to control the press through stamp taxes was so burdensome in many countries that it inhibited new papers. This concentrated circulation in the few papers that were rich and stable enough to pay the heavy duty on individual editions, and that tended to be very establishmentarian.

In the United States there was both constitutional and statutory encouragement for a free and growing press. Congress was forbidden to make any law abridging the freedom of the press. And the new postal system set up by Benjamin Franklin, an ex-printer, and William Hunter favored local printers. Each subscriber to a newspaper was charged nine pence sterling a year for every fifty miles the paper had to be carried by the postal system. On the other hand, papers sent from one printer to another went free. Thus, the individual subscriber was penalized by distance while his local printer was not; this encouraged printers to clip and paste other papers from distant cities and reprint locally. . . .

The most spectacular burgeoning of the press came in midnineteenth century, largely because of new communications technology, like paper production from wood, high-speed presses, railroads, and the telegraph. The prices of many papers dropped. It became possible to buy a daily paper for a penny. In 1800, there had been 235 individual newspapers in the country, by 1850, 2,300. By 1860, there were more than three times as many papers in the United States as in England and France. Always local merchandising and local government stimulated indigenous papers, and the number of dailies rose to a peak of 2,461 in 1916.

But with World War I the number of newspapers in the country began to decline and has continued to decline until today there are 1,750 papers, a drop of 30 percent. And since that time there has been a rise in strictly national news media, separate or nearly separate from the local papers and broadcast stations. The rise was slow until the last twenty years, during which it has become marked.

Since 1940, total daily newspaper circulation in the United States has risen about 50 percent, roughly the same as population. But the carriers of daily national news have outpaced this. The *Wall Street Journal's* circulation in its home state increased 2,100 percent, but outside New York it went up 4,700 percent. The *New York Times's* circulation in greater New York rose 30 percent, outside its own city, 165 percent. The *Christian Science Monitor's* circulation in its home city, Boston, actually dropped slighly, but elsewhere in the country it rose 26 percent.

National news magazines, an invention of the period, have gained even more rapidly. In the 1940–1968 period, *Time, Newsweek,* and *U.S. News and World Report* increased their circulation 585 percent. . . .

Commercial pressures for ever wider jurisdictions, made all the more tempting by easier and cheaper long-distance transmission of information, raise the possibility of increasing separation between local media and national.

Two factors push in this direction. One is the growth in popular consciousness of national and world affairs, the result both of increased cosmopolitanism and education and the enlargement of the role of the national government and world events in the life of the average family.

The other factor is the trend in contemporary advertising and merchandising reversing the historic role of rooting the local media to their immediate communities.

In the late nineteenth century, newspapers for the first time took seriously the possibility that at least one newspaper could be sold to each household each day. By then it was technically possible to manufacture enough papers for this kind of saturation. Advertising was becoming an important national economic activity and assuming an ever larger share of the newspaper's revenues. In 1867 $50 million a year was spent on ads; in 1900 this had gone up ten times, by 1950 a hundred times.

Merchants generally buy space or broadcasting time on the basis of the cost of exposing their advertising to a thousand persons, or cost-per-thousand. As individual newspaper production plants developed the capacity to print one complete newspaper for every house in the community, and advertisers clearly became indirect subsidizers of these plants, the working of the market-place made it inevitable that it would be less expensive for the advertisers to support one plant in a community instead of two or three or a dozen. Even with the increased advertising rates that a local monopoly could charge, the cost-per-thousand was cheaper than advertising in two or more competing papers.

Since World War I the number of individual newspapers has declined, though the surviving papers have become fatter and devote a larger percentage of their space to advertisements. Since World War II advertising content in daily papers has gone from 52 percent to 61 percent, the size of papers from twenty-two pages a day, of which eleven were ads, to fifty pages in 1965 for the average daily, of which thirty were ads.

Fatter papers meant larger plants, more presses, more typesetting machines, and larger work forces. Processing of advertising is more demanding and expensive than that of news matter. Costs rose. But, once plates were on the presses, labor costs remained relatively level and the cost of added circulation was largely the cost of paper and ink. And, since advertising was placed more on the basis of cost-per-thousand than any other single factor, it was advantageous for a paper to increase its production, even if it meant extending its sales beyond the limits of its immediate city.

Conversion of newspapers into substantial manufacturing plants inhibited growth of new papers in new communities. Surviving papers gained monopolies in their own communities and pushed beyond the city limits to nearby communities. Consequently, the cost of starting new papers in the new communities at the edges of the metropolises was unattractive, since the established nearby papers were always prepared to produce papers for the new communities at small incremental cost. The country created more and more communities, and served them with fewer and fewer newspapers.

The consequences of this reversal of the traditional American tendency for each community to serve its self-governing functions with its own news medium are difficult to measure. But the change from 90 percent of urban places with their own daily paper to less than 30 percent is a radical one, and it may have radical consequences. It could be a contributing factor to the growing inability of municipalities to control their social and political affairs, to the psychological loss of community identity characteristic of newer towns and cities, and to the sluggishness with which urban governments responded to postwar social pathologies and the slowness with which this pathology, once felt, came to national attention. . . .

The basic causes for present community malaise in the United States can hardly be laid at the door of absent or delinquent news media. Even with ideal local attention to civic affairs, it would be difficult to cope with the bewildering maze of governmental and quasi-governmental units, often uncoordinated and frequently at cross purposes. But apathy or frustration produced by this random agglomeration of civic functions is deepened by the lack of locally based news media that even try to follow and publicize systematically the more important developments. In a country of 100,000 autonomous school districts and 400,000 other local governmental units, it is significant that fewer than 30 percent of the communities in whose boundaries they lie has any locally based news medium.

This poor fit between community units and news media comes largely because newspapers and radio and television stations, even though they carry a place name in their identification, do not arrange their output by civic boundaries but instead by merchandising territories. As the automobile determines the range for shopping, merchandising territories increasingly ignore civic boundaries. And, as these shopping territories enlarge, the growing production power of the mass media follows them through communities whose civic affairs they largely ignore.

The effective boundary line of most newspapers is a territory called "retail trade zone," which varies in definition from place to place but commonly ends in neighborhoods where the paper's daily sales fall to between 5 and 20 percent of the total households.

Broadcasting stations occupy territories called "markets," which are usually the area of the effective range of their broadcast signal.

About 400 markets are calculated for daily newspapers and about 230 markets for broadcasting stations. Within these are most of the 500,000 units of local government. Given the total space for serious local news in newspapers, and the total time devoted in typical broadcasting stations, it would be impossible to give systematic reportage of all the important public-affairs developments in each of the significant public bodies within the market areas of individual news media.

In 1969 a majority of the FCC raised questions about the transfer in ownership of the only television station in Hutchinson, Kansas, KTVH, Channel 12. The Commission was concerned with concentration of ownerships, but KTVH is typical of other television stations in its jurisdiction, which represents problems regardless of ownership.

KTVH covers about 18,000 square miles with its strongest signal, with average penetration of 90 percent of the 344,000 homes. If the 23 counties for which KTVH is the primary station have their share of all local governmental units in Kansas, they contain over 800 different governmental bodies, including 210 municipalities and 110 school boards. About 350 of them levy taxes.

If the station devotes typical TV time to local news (not including sports), and if each of the governmental bodies in its area made only one newsworthy decision a month, and if the station happened to cover this decision, and if the station devoted all of its local newscasts exclusively to the deliberations of these public bodies, each would have reportage of thirty seconds a month.

KTVH is part of the Kansas Broadcasting System for the purpose of selling commercials. This network of television stations advertises itself as "a 93 county major television market of 403,400 television homes, 1.3 million people in a five state area with a consumer spendable income of over $3.5 billion. . . ."

For merchandisers, such a network is effective. As reporters of events within their boundaries, it reduces each civic function to a fraction of a minute per month.

Yet the merchandising function continues to favor ever larger geographical territories, so that the cost of reaching each consumer will drop. This is impelled not only by the larger shopping ranges made possible by the automobile, but also by the growth of unified national brands, commonly available "at your local" (anonymous) drug, department, or grocery store. Standard-brand cosmetics, food, and cigarettes do not need to specify particular stores or addresses in order to stimulate sales by wide-area broadcasting or newspaper advertising.

Among newspapers, two categories of standardized retail goods make up 42 percent of all newspaper advertising: automobiles with 28 percent, and foods with 14 percent. In television, in 1970, four categories of nationally standard brands made up almost 60 percent of all television advertising: foods with 19 percent; toiletries, 17 percent; tobacco, 12 percent; and drugs, 11 percent.

The retail outlets for these standardized items are also becoming regionally and nationally standardized by a relatively small number of recognizable and dominant firms. The combination of near-universal recognition of both store names and brand names means that broad, homogenized advertising becomes more effective, and the small medium with a special audience less competitive.

Especially with broadcasting, whose entertainment and news also are increasingly produced in a national source, the financial rewards lie with enlargement of area and of gross population, even to the deliberate exclusion of a station's immediate home base.

The Federal Communications Commission recently took note of this tendency. "We have . . . noted that there is a tendency on the part of stations in suburban communities in metropolitan areas, to identify themselves with the entire metropolitan area rather than with the particular needs of their communities." The FCC intervened when the only full-time radio station in Camden, New Jersey, was about to be sold to a Texas corporation which intended to eliminate all local programming serving the 117,000 population of Camden in order to attract advertising for programming designed for the metropolitan Philadelphia area across the Delaware River, although Philadelphia already had twenty-eight of its own radio stations.

Technology helped eliminate the idea of every community with a news medium of its own. But even broadcasting once started as a local service. When the British Broadcasting Corporation started in 1922, there was no practical network system in existence. Consequently it established twenty strictly local stations with only ¼ kw power (American communities now have stations with many times that power). When communications technology improved, the BBC became a centralized operation out of London. Frank Gillard, managing director of radio for the BBC, says that the result has been that the former development of local talent in discussion, entertainment, and culture atrophied as only the highly professionalized work of London reached the air, and that "democracy in the country breaks down at the local level.". . .

The ability of a community to keep in touch with itself began to deteriorate when populations became so large that it was no longer possible for all voters to fit in the small hall. Community identity, self-knowledge, and cohesion have been worsening ever since.

The technical innovations of the next generation could evolve in a way that would make local self-government more chaotic and community identity more damaged, leaving ever more communities lost to the world of modern communications. The further homogenizing of mass communications could produce deeper pathology in neighborhood life and community government, with little information on how national ideas can be applied at the local level.

On the other hand, future technology could provide a restoration of community communications resembling the New England town meeting. New methods have the capacity, the low cost-per-channel, and the ability to limit particular programs to small areas like neighborhoods. But if they are to do this they will have to be driven by something different from the present commercial mass-market mechanisms. For all practical purposes, "the audience" for the news media today is first a collection of people with money to spend and only second a specific collection of citizens with private and public problems to solve. New techniques of communications can reverse that order but this will require basic changes in public and corporate policies that shape the distribution of information.

# Making News by Doing Work: Routinizing the Unexpected

GAYE TUCHMAN

ONE THEME DOMINANT in the sociology of work is the "control" of work. Proponents of the structural and technological approach (Perrow 1967; Thompson 1967; March and Simon 1958) stress that organizations routinize tasks if possible, for routinization facilitates the control of work. As discussed by Hughes (1964) and others of the Chicago school (Becker, Geer, and Hughes 1961), persons at work always have too much work to do. To cope with this problem, they try to control the flow of work and the amount of work to be done.

Prompted, possibly, by a view of routine as negotiated process (Bucher 1970), members of the Chicago school extend the discussion of work to the handling of emergencies. For instance, Everett Hughes (1964, pp. 55–56) suggests that the professional's "struggle . . . to maintain control over [his or her] decisions of what work to do and over the disposition of [his or her] time and [his or her] routine of life" may be particularly acute for workers who "deal routinely with what are emergencies to the people who receive their services." He speaks of this situation as introducing a "chronic tension" between worker and client, and, in an often quoted passage, explains: ". . . the person with the crisis feels that the other is trying to belittle his trouble. The physician plays one emergency off against the other; the reason he can't run right up to see Johnny who may have the measles is that he is, unfortunately right at that moment, treating a case of the black plague" (p. 55). Hughes's example suggests that, in handling some types of emergen-

Reprinted from Gaye Tuchman, "Making News by Doing Work: Routinizing the Unexpected," *American Journal of Sociology*, Vol. 79, No. 1, pp. 110–131, by permission of The University of Chicago Press. Copyright © 1973 by University of Chicago Press.

cies, specialists seek to impose priorities and routines upon them. It also implies that some workers, such as doctors, lawyers, and firemen, may profitably be viewed as specialists in handling *specific* kinds of emergencies.

Sociologists have paid scant attention to workers who routinely handle nonspecialized emergencies, ranging from fires and legal cases to medical problems. Yet, some workers do precisely this task. News workers (and they are still overwhelmingly men) stand out as workers called upon to give accounts (for a discussion of accounts, see Scott and Lyman [1968]) of a wide variety of disasters—*unexpected* events—on a *routine* basis. News work thrives upon processing unexpected events, events that "burst to the surface in some disruptive, exceptional (and hence newsworthy)" manner (Noyes 1971). As Helen Hughes (1940) noted, "Quickening urgency" is the "essence of news" (p. 58).

That workers impose routines upon their work poses a problem concerning nonspecialized unexpected events: how can an organization routinize the processing of unexpected events? Specifically, how do newsmen routinize the handling of a variety of unexpected events in order to process and to present accounts and explanations of them? For, without some routine method of coping with unexpected events, news organizations, as rational enterprises, would flounder and fail.

To answer these questions, this article uses two ideas developed in the sociology of work. (1) Routinization is impeded by variability in raw material (an idea in the organizational literature [Perrow 1967]). (2) Persons categorize the objects of their work to control it (an idea in the literature on occupations and professions [Becker et al. 1961]). Together these ideas suggest that the way [newsmen] classify events-as-news decreases the variability of the raw material processed by news organizations and facilitates routinization. . . .

The data presented here were gathered by participant observation at two sites. They were a local independent television station affiliated with a major network and a daily morning newspaper with a circulation of about 250,000. Both had substantial competition within their own medium and from other media. Both are located in the same city, a major television market. Research at these two sites lasted a little over two years. Informants knew me to be a sociologist engaged in research. . . .

## News Workers on Categories of News

At work, news workers use five terms to differentiate categories of news: hard news, soft news, spot news, developing news, and continuing news. Journalism texts and informants explain that these terms differentiate *kinds of news content* or the *subject* of events-as-news. Asked for definitions of their categories, news workers fluster, for they take these categories so much for granted that they find them difficult to define. To specify definitions,

newsmen offer examples of the stories that fall within a category. They tend to classify the same stories in the same manner, and some stories are cited with such frequency that they may be viewed as prototypes. This section reviews the prototypical cases mentioned by informants.

## Hard News Versus Soft News

The informants' main distinction was between hard news and its antithesis, soft news. As they put it, hard news concerns events potentially available to analysis or interpretation and consists of "factual presentations" of events deemed newsworthy (for a discussion of "factual presentations" and analysis, see Tuchman [1972]). When pressed, informants indicated that hard news is "simply" the stuff news presentations are made of. For instance, asked for a definition of hard news, a television editor offered the following catalog of basic news stories: "Hard news is the gubernatorial message to the legislature, the State of the Union Address to Congress, the train-truck accident or the murder, the bank hold-up, the legislative proposal . . . and the fire tomorrow."

This editor and other informants voluntarily contrasted hard news with soft news, also known as the feature or human interest story. Some examples of soft news stories are: an item about a big-city bus driver who offers a cheery "good morning" to every passenger on his early morning run, a feature about a lonely female bear, a story about young adults who rent for a month a billboard proclaiming "Happy Anniversary Mom and Dad."

News workers distinguish between these two lists by saying that a hard news story is "interesting to human beings" and a soft news story is "interesting because it deals with the life of human beings" (Mott 1952, p. 58). Or, they state that hard news concerns information people should have to be informed citizens and soft news concerns human foibles and the "texture of our human life" (Mott 1952, p. 58). Finally, they may simply summarize, hard news concerns important matters and soft news, interesting matters. . . .

## Spot News and Developing News

Difficulties also appear in the news workers' distinctions between spot news and developing news. The most important of these difficulties is that the news workers partially abandon the statement that the categories are based upon the content or subject matter of events-as-news.

Asked to discuss spot news, newsmen replied that spot news is a type (subclassification) of hard news. News workers cited the fire as a prototypical example of spot news. (Occasionally, informants added a second example, either a robbery, murder, accident, tornado, or earthquake.) The subject matter of all examples was conflicts with nature, technology, or the penal code.

Asked about developing news (another subclassification of hard news), the newsmen cited the same examples. Asked, then, to distinguish between spot news and developing news, informants introduced a new element, the amount of information that they have about an event-as-news at a given point in time. When they learned of an unexpected event, it was classed "spot news." If it took a while to learn the "facts" associated with a "breaking story," it was "developing news." It remained "developing news" so long as "facts" were still emerging and being gathered. When I pressed by pointing to previous statements that the subject of the story determined that story's classification, the news workers insisted that both statements were correct. In essence, they countered, the subject matter of certain kinds of events-as-news had a tendency to occur in specific ways (e.g., fires break out unexpectedly; many demonstrations are preplanned). And so, newsmen happen to learn of them in certain ways.

### Continuing News

Asked to define continuing news, informants reverted to discussing the subject matter of an event-as-news. As the newsmen put it, continuing news is a series of stories *on the same subject* based upon events occurring over a period of time. As a prototype, the newsmen cited the legislative bill. The passage of a bill, they explained, is a complicated process occurring over a period of time. Although news of the bill's progress through the legislative maze may vary from day to day, all stories about the bill deal with the same content—the bill's provisions and whether they will be enacted. In this sense, they said, the story about the legislative bill continues as news. (Other examples cited by informants included trials, politics, economics, diplomacy, and war. Almost all examples were confrontations within or among recognized institutions.) . . .

### From Category to Typification

Examination of the newsmen's definitions of their categories had been prompted by the notion that the categories would enable the routinization of work. To be sure, the definitions, prototypical examples, and lists of events decrease the variability of events as the raw material of news. Yet they are problematic: the newsmen state that their categories are based upon the subject matter of events-as-news. But it is difficult to apply consistently their distinctions between hard news and soft news. Also, discussing spot news, developing news, and continuing news, the informants introduced a *seemingly* extraneous element: the subject matter of certain kinds of events-as-news tends to happen in certain kinds of ways. And so, newsmen "just happen" to be alerted to the need to process them in different ways.

The news workers' insistence that the way something happens is important to their classificatory system suggests a reconsideration of the relevance of classifications to the organization of work. The need for a reanalysis is supported by attempts to discuss events that become news (Boorstin 1964; Molotch and Lester 1972) and by research on disasters (Bucher 1957). For, like the newsmen, this research insists that the way an event happens influences accounts of it. For example, discussing a plane crash, Bucher (1957) argues that, faced with a disaster, persons try to locate the point in the process that "caused" the accident so they may prevent future accidents from happening in the same manner. Bucher's findings suggest that the way in which an event happens, the classifications used to describe the event, and the work done to prevent a recurrence are related. They prompt the proposal that newsmen do not categorize events-as-news by distinguishing between kinds of subject matter. Rather, they typify events-as-news according to the way these happen and according to the requirements of the organizational structure within which news stories are constructed.

The theoretical distinction between "category" and "typification" is crucial, for "typification" implies a phenomenological perspective.[1] "Category" refers to classification of objects according to one or more relevant characteristics ruled salient by the classifiers, frequently by what anthropologists term a "formal analysis." (For a discussion of categories and formal analysis, see Tyler [1969, pp. 2, 194–342].) The use of "category" connotes a request for definitions from informants and a sorting of those definitions along dimensions specified by the researcher. "Typification" refers to classification in which the relevant characteristics are central to the solution of practical tasks or problems at hand and are constituted in and grounded in everyday activity. The use of "typification" connotes an attempt to place informants' classifications in their everyday context; typifications are embedded in and take their meaning from the settings in which they are used and the occasions that prompt their use. (Anthropologists use "componential analysis" to discover meaning in context [see Tyler 1969, pp. 255–88, 396–432].)

## Typifications of News

Because typifications are embedded in practical tasks in everyday life, they provide a key to understanding how news workers decrease the variability of events as the raw material of news. This section argues that news organizations routinize the processing of unexpected events by typifying them along dimensions that reflect practical tasks associated with their work. These tasks are related to both organizational structure and the manner in which an event occurs. As summarized in table 1, news workers' distinctions between hard news and soft news reflect questions of scheduling; the news workers' distinctions between spot news and developing news pertain to the allocation of resources and vary in their application according to the technology being used; and the typification "continuing news" is based upon problems in predicting the course of events-as-news.

**TABLE 1.   Practical Issues in Typifying News***

| TYPIFICATION | HOW IS AN EVENT SCHEDULED? | IS DISSEMINATION URGENT? | DOES TECHNOLOGY AFFECT PERCEPTION? | ARE FUTURE PREDICTIONS FACILITATED? |
|---|---|---|---|---|
| Soft news .......... Nonscheduled | | No | No | Yes |
| Hard news ......... Unscheduled and prescheduled | | Yes | Sometimes | Sometimes |
| Spot news ........ Unscheduled | | Yes | No | No |
| Developing news . . Unscheduled | | Yes | Yes | No |
| Continuing news . . Prescheduled | | Yes | No | Yes |

* As McKinney and Bourque note (1972, p. 232), typifications are flexible and undergo continual transformation. Technically, then, as noted by Lindsay Churchill (personal communication), recording typifications in this manner transforms them into components of a typology.

## Hard News: The Flow of News Work and Scheduling

As previously noted, "quickening urgency" is the "essence of news." Because it is timely and urgent, hard news "demands" speed, especially in gathering "facts" and meeting deadlines. Both Breed (1955) and I (1972) have described these processes. We stressed that the need for speed is so overarching that it influences characteristics of news stories. If news workers do not work quickly, the hard news story will be obsolete before it can be distributed in today's newscast or in the newspaper sold tomorrow. As Park wrote (Park and Burgess 1967, p. 19), old news is "mere information."

In contrast, soft news stories do not need to be "timely." The Sunday newspaper is padded with feature stories about events that occurred earlier in the week. Because they are concerned with "timeliness," news workers make fine distinctions. They explain that some kinds of content (hard news stories) become obsolete more quickly than others (soft news items). This distinction is based upon the distribution of nonscheduled, prescheduled, and unscheduled events as hard news and as soft news.

A *non*scheduled event-as-news is an event whose date of dissemination as news is determined by the news workers. A *pre*scheduled event-as-news is an event announced for a future date by its convenors; news of the event is to be disseminated the day it occurs or the day after. An *un*scheduled event-as-news is an event that occurs unexpectedly; news of it is to be disseminated that day or the day after. *The type of scheduling characteristic of an event-as-news affects the organization of work.*

Most hard news stories concern prescheduled events (a debate on a legislative bill) or unscheduled events (a fire). News workers do not decide when stories about prescheduled and unscheduled events-as-news are to be disseminated. News workers do decide when to gather "facts" and to disseminate accounts and explanations of nonscheduled hard news stories. Nonscheduled hard news stories tend to involve investigative reporting. The publication of the Pentagon Papers by the *New York Times* is an example of a nonscheduled hard news story, for the *Times* held the papers three months before it published extracts, digests, and analyses of them. Processing nonscheduled stories, the news organization controls the timing and flow of work.

Members of the news enterprise almost always control the timing and flow of work required to process soft news stories. Few soft news stories concern unscheduled events, as indicated by the previous list of feature stories. Another example is "The Man in the News" series run by the *New York Times.* Like the obituaries of famous men and women, the "facts" can be gathered, written up, and edited in anticipation of future dissemination. Prescheduled soft news also includes such annual "February stories" as an item appropriate to Washington's birthday, another for Lincoln's birthday, and a third for Valentine's Day. A reporter may be assigned to these stories days in advance, and the specific information to be included in the story may be gathered, written, and edited days before its eventual dissemination. . . .

In general, the distinction between hard news and soft news as typifications reflects practical task in news organizations: scheduling work in relation to both the way an event-as-story happens and the way in which a story is to be processed and disseminated.

## Spot News: Allocating Resources and Dealing with Technology

Governing the flow of news work, like the organization of most work, involves more than scheduling. It also involves the allocation of resources and the control of work through prediction. To cope with these tasks, newsmen distinguish among spot news, developing news, and continuing news.

Spot news events are unscheduled; they appear suddenly and must be processed quickly. The examples of spot news offered by informants indicate that spot news is the *specifically unforeseen event-as-news.* For instance, although the news workers may anticipate the probability of a fire, they cannot specifically predict where and when a fire will start. This inability to make a specific prediction concerning some events affects the flow of news work.

If a three-alarm fire starts close to deadline, information must be gathered and edited more quickly than usual to meet that deadline. If a major fire starts 50 miles from the city room, transportation problems influence the time needed to gather and to process "facts" and so influences the allocation of resources to cover the fire. . . .

As one might expect from findings that the organization of work is influenced by its technology (Hage and Aiken 1969; Perrow 1967; Thompson 1967), the allocation of resources in the newspaper newsroom was different from the allocation of resources in the television newsroom. At the newspaper, at least three of the 20-person staff of general reporters and rewrite men were in the city room from 8 A.M. until midnight. Usually, they covered minor stories by telephone, rewrote copy phoned to them by correspondents scattered in small towns around the state, and wrote obituaries. To some extent, this work is essential: the items produced fill small holes in the newspaper and are supposed to be of interest to some readers. To some extent, it is busywork to alleviate the boredom of sitting and waiting for a specifically unforeseen event to happen. If needed, though, this reserve personnel was available to cover spot news.

The television station had few reserve reporters and no reserve cameramen, except from 4 P.M. to 6 P.M. and from 9:30 P.M. until 11:00 P.M. At these times, reporters and cameramen, bringing their film to be processed, had generally returned from their assignments. They would wait either to cover a spot news story or to go off shift. Should a specifically unforeseen event occur at any other time of day, the station had to (1) pay overtime, (2) pull a reporter and a cameraman from a less important story they were already covering, (3) pull a cameraman from a "silent film story" he was covering by himself, (4) hire a free-lance cameraman, (5) pull a staff announcer from his routine duties, such as reading station identification, or (6) assign a newswriter to act as reporter after gaining permission from the appropriate unions. The alternative(s) chosen depended upon the specific situation.

Two points concerning these arrangements are of particular pertinence. First, news workers stress that creating and recreating stable situations to cope with spot news is a continual, ongoing process. As they discuss it, it seems more like a battle. Second, the nature of those created situations depends upon the technology used by the medium.

### Developing News: Technology and the Perception of Events

Practical problems of dealing with a technology are so important that they even affect the news worker's perception of a spot news story, especially whether he [or she] will apply the typification "developing news" to an event-as-story. In the case of developing news, technology provides a lens through which events-as-news are perceived.

Developing news concerns "emergent situations" (for a discussion of emergent situations, see Bucher [1957]), as indicated by the following prototypical example. A plane crashes. Although this event is unexpected, there are, nonetheless, limitations upon the "facts" it can possibly contain. The newsmen would not expect to run a story stating that those reported dead have come to life. Nor would they expect to run a report of an official denial that a crash occurred. The "facts" of the news story are: a plane crashed at 2:00 P.M., in Ellen Park, when an engine caught fire and another went dead, damaging two houses, killing eight people and injuring an additional 15 persons. All else is amplification. Since the plane crash was specifically unexpected, reporters were not present to record "facts" "accurately." "Facts" must be reconstructed, and as more information becomes known, the "facts" will be more "accurate." Although the actual event remains the same, the account of the event changes, or as the news workers put it, "the story develops." Ongoing changes of this sort are called "developing news."

Most spot news stories are developing news. Since both present interrelated work demands, the newspapermen tend to use the terms interchangeably. Television news workers use the term "developing news" in a more restricted manner: they identify some stories as spot news that newspaper workers term "developing news." This variation occurs because of the differing technologies associated with the two media. The process of covering the death of Martin Luther King—an event that raised different practical problems for the two local media—illustrates this variation.

At the local newspaper, King's injury and subsequent death were labeled "developing news." A continual flow of updated copy needed editing and "demanded" constant revision of the planned format. The executive editor learned of the attempted assassination and plotted a format for the front page. King's condition was reported as "grave" by the wire services, and the editor drew another format, including stories about other topics above the fold on page one. A wire service bulletin reported King to be dead; all other stories were relegated below the fold. Every story on page 1 needed a new headline of a different size of type, and lead paragraphs of some stories had to be reset into smaller type. Inside pages were also affected.

The television network with which the observed local station is affiliated reported on King's condition as a developing story. Periodically, it interrupted programs to present bulletins. But, this was a spot news story for the local television station's personnel. Obviously, the format of the 11 P.M. newscast was modified early in the evening. Because of the network's bulletins, the story about King (whatever it might have turned out to be) had to be the program's lead. At the newspaper, the production manager and compositors bemoaned the need to reset the front page three times, each reset accompanying a major development in the story. All production staff worked overtime. At the television station, readjustments in production plans meant less work, not more. By prearrangement, the newwork preempted the first few minutes of the late evening newscast to tell the story, just as it had preempted the same five minutes some months earlier to report the death of three astronauts.

The degree to which resources must be reallocated to meet practical exigencies and the way reallocation is accomplished depends upon both the event being processed and the medium processing it. The technology used by a specific medium does more than "merely" influence the ways in which resources are allocated. It influences the typification of event-as-news or how that news story is perceived and classified.

### Continuing News: Controlling Work through Prediction

Spot news and developing news are constituted in work arrangements intended to *cope* with the amount of information specifically predictable *before* an event occurs. This information is slight or nonexistent, because the events are unscheduled. In contrast, continuing news *facilitates* the control of work, for continuing news events are generally prescheduled. Prescheduling is implicit in the newsmen's definition of continuing news as a "series of stories on the same subject based upon events occurring over a period of time." This definition implies the existence of prescheduled change. For instance, the account of the progress of a legislative bill through Congress is an account of a series of events following one another in a continual temporal sequence. An event occurring at any specific point in the sequence bears consequences for anticipated events.

Because they are prescheduled, continuing news stories help newsmen and news organizations to regulate their own activities; they free newsmen to deal with the exigencies of the specifically unforeseen. Take that legislative bill. It is to be channeled through the House, the Senate, and the executive office. To cover this series of events-as-news, the newsman must be familiar with the legislative process. Such familiarity may even be viewed as part of his "professional stock of knowledge at hand" (a term discussed by Schutz [1962, vol. 2, pp. 29 ff.]). He knows the ideas of pertinent committee members, as well as the distribution of power within the House committee, the Senate committee, and the Senate as a whole. In addition, he also knows the progress being made by other legislative bills. With this cumulative stock of knowledge at hand, he may not only predict the bill's eventual disposition, including the specific route through the legislative process (this bill will be bogged down in the House Ways and Means Committee), but also, he can weigh the need to cover this bill on any one day against the need to cover another bill for which he had comparable information. The newsman's "expert" or "professional" stock of knowledge at hand permits him, other newsmen, and his news organization to control work activities.

This matter of control is a key theme in the study of work, for there is always too much work to be done. In news work, no matter how many reporters from any one news organization may be assigned to a legislature or to work at a specific beat or bureau, newsmen (and news organizations) are inundated with more work than they can do. There are so many bills being introduced, so many committee hearings, so many minute yet potentially important readjustments in the distribution of power. In a sense, the newsmen make more work for themselves by choosing to cover several stories in a cursory manner rather than covering one story intensively. Certainly, such a practice is tempting, for the newsman wants to turn in as much copy as possible and this is accomplished more easily by skimming the surface of many stories than by digging down a potential "blind alley" to provide intensive coverage of one event-as-news. The latter alternative is made even less appealing by the possibility that the news desk will dismiss the story as "illegitimate," as frequently happens to stories about social movements. More important, the news desk, the beat reporters, and the news bureaus are increasingly inundated by larger and larger batches of news releases. Most of these can lay claim to being a legitimate hard news story. As I have discussed elsewhere (1972), hard news is "factual" and news workers are leary of news analysis. As a result of this emphasis upon "facts," newsmen interpret the increasing piles of news releases as more and more stories for them to cover.

Being able to predict the future coverage of a continuing story (whether it concerns a bill, a trial, or a new economic policy) enables an editor, a bureau chief, and, ultimately, a newsman to decide where to go and what to do on any one crowded day. Also, the ability to predict helps the individual newsman to sort out which reportorial technique to use on various stories. For instance, drawing upon the collective professional stock of knowledge shared by newsmen, he can decide which of today's assignments require his presence at hearings, which can be covered by telephone, which can be reconstructed through interviews with key informants, and which "merely" require him to stick his head through a door to confirm that "everything" is as anticipated. The ability to predict enables the news organization in general and a reporter in particular to make choices and still accomplish such mundane but routinely necessay tasks as chatting with potential news sources.

The continuing news story is a boon to the newsman's ability to control his own work, to anticipate specifically and so to dissipate future problems by projecting events into a routine. The newsman's and the news organization's ability to process continuing stories routinely by predicting future outcomes enables the news organization to cope with unexpected events. At the very least, it enables an assignment editor to state, "Joe Smith will not be available to cover spot news stories a week from Tuesday, because he will be covering the $X$ trial." In sum, continuing news typifies events as raw materials to be specifically planned for in advance, and this typification is constituted in practical tasks at work. . . .

## Conclusion

To answer the question of how an organization can process information about unexpected events, I have examined the categories newsmen use to describe events-as-news. Based upon distinctions between and among kinds of news content, the newsmen's categories neither significantly decrease the variability of events as the raw material of news, nor explain the newsmen's activities. However, viewed as typifications, the same classifications reduce the variability of the raw material of news. News organizations can process seemingly unexpected events, including emergencies and disasters, because they typify events-as-news by the manner in which they happen and in terms of the ramifications "this manner of happening" holds for the organization of work. Each of the typifications is anchored in a basic organizational issue concerning the control of work. Further, the news workers' typifications reconstitute the everyday world. They construct and reconstruct social reality by establishing the context in which social phenomena are perceived and defined.

To some extent, the approach used here has roots in past research on news, particularly the work of Lang and Lang (1953, 1968). However, it provides an essential modification, for past research emphasizes the notion "distortion." As Shibutani (1966) implies in his seminal work on rumor, the concept "distortion" is alien to the discussion of socially constructed realities. Each socially constructed reality necessarily has meaning and significance (Berger and Luckmann 1967; Schutz 1962). Elsewhere (1973), I have argued that "distortion" is itself a socially constructed concept. The construction of reality through redefinition, reconsideration, and reaccounting is an ongoing process. The news workers' typifications indicate that it might be valuable to think of news not as distorting, but rather as reconstituting the everyday world.

Second, the arguments presented here, when compared to the Molotch (1970) and Bucher (1957) findings, suggest a tantalizing possibility: individuals, groups, and organizations not only react to and characterize events by typifying *what* has happened, but also they may typify events by stressing the *way* "things" happen. Of particular importance may be the way events may be practically managed, altered, or projected into the future. Recent work on deviance (Emerson and Messinger 1972) and the recent attempts of Molotch and Lester (1972) to analyze public events suggests that such an approach may cut across areas of sociological inquiry and so prove theoretically fruitful.

## Note

1. The phenomenological perspective is not alien to sociological thought. In recent years, researchers (Zimmerman 1970; Cicourel 1968; Emerson 1969; Emerson and

Messinger 1971; Sudnow 1965) have discussed the relationship of typification to practical tasks in people-processing organizations. Examining the production of typifications has enabled labeling theorists to highlight the moral and occupational assumptions underpinning the treatment of deviants: It has enabled them to locate the *practical* considerations that police, judges, doctors, and social workers rely upon to label offenders and clients (for an extended discussion, see Emerson and Messinger [1972] and Freidson [1971]). As Schutz pointed out (1962), typifications help to routinize the world in which we live. They epitomize the routine grounds of everyday life; they enable us to make limited predictions (projections) and thus to plan and to act.

# References

BECKER, HOWARD, BLANCHE GEER, and EVERETT C. HUGHES. 1961. *Boys in White*. Chicago: University of Chicago Press.

BERGER, PETER, and THOMAS LUCKMANN. 1967. *The Social Construction of Reality*. Garden City, N.J.: Anchor.

BOORSTIN, DANIEL. 1964. *The Image: A Guide to Pseudo-Events in America*. New York: Harper & Row.

BREED, WARREN. 1955. "Social Control in the Newsroom." *Social Forces* 33 (May): 326–35.

BUCHER, RUE. 1957. "Blame and Hostility in Disaster." *American Journal of Sociology* 62 (March): 467–75.

———. 1970. "Social Processes and Power in a Medical School." In *Power in Organizations*, edited by Mayer Zald. Nashville, Tenn.: Vanderbilt University Press.

CICOUREL, AARON. 1968. *The Social Organization of Juvenile Justice*. New York: Wiley.

EMERSON, ROBERT. 1969. *Judging Delinquents: Context and Process in Juvenile Court*. Chicago: Aldine.

EMERSON, ROBERT, and SHELDON MESSINGER. 1972. "Deviance and Moral Enterprise." Paper presented at the meeting of the Society for the Study of Social Problems, New Orleans, August 28.

FRIEDSON, ELIOT. 1971. "Deviance as Diagnosis: Defiance, Deficiency, and Disability." Paper presented at the meeting of the American Sociological Association, Denver, September 1.

HAGE, JERALD, and MICHAEL AIKEN. 1969. "Routine Technology, Social Structure and Organizational Goals." *Administrative Science Quarterly* 14 (3): 366–78.

Hughes, EVERETT C. 1964. *Men and Their Work*. Glencoe, Ill.: Free Press.

HUGHES, HELEN MACGILL. 1940. *News and the Human Interest Story*. Chicago: University of Chicago Press.

LANG, KURT, and GLADYS ENGEL LANG. 1953. "The Unique Perspective of Television." *American Sociological Review* 18 (February): 3–12.

———. 1968. *Politics and Television*. New York: Quadrangle.

MCKINNEY, JOHN C., and LINDA BROOKOVER BOURQUE. 1972. "Further Comments on 'The Changing South': A Response to Sly and Weller." *American Sociological Review* 37 (April): 230–36.

MARCH, JAMES, and HERBERT SIMON. 1958. *Organizations.* New York: Wiley.

MOLOTCH, HARVEY. 1970. "Oil in Santa Barbara and Power in America." *Sociological Inquiry* 40 (Winter): 131–44.

MOLOTCH, HARVEY, and MARILYN LESTER. 1972. "Accidents, Scandals, and Routines: Resources for Conflict Methodology." Paper presented at the meeting of the American Sociological Association, New Orleans, August 30.

MOTT, FRANK LUTHER. 1952. *The News in America.* Cambridge, Mass.: Harvard University Press.

NOYES, NEWBOLD. 1971. Extract from speech to the American Society of Newspaper Editors, Washington, D.C., April 14.

PARK, ROBERT, and ERNEST BURGESS. 1967. *The City.* Chicago: University of Chicago Press.

PERROW, CHARLES. 1967. "A Framework for the Comparative Analysis of Organizations." *American Sociological Review* 32 (April): 194–208.

SCHUTZ, ALFRED. 1962. *Collected Papers.* 2 vols. The Hague: Nijhoff.

SCOTT, MARVIN, and STANFORD LYMAN. 1968. "Accounts." *American Sociological Review* 33 (February): 46–62.

SHIBUTANI, TAMOTSU. 1966. *Improvised News: A Sociological Study of Rumor.* Indianapolis: Bobbs-Merrill.

SUDNOW, DAVID. 1965. "Normal Crimes: Sociological Features of the Penal Code in a Public Defender's Office." *Social Problems* 12 (Winter): 255–72.

THOMPSON, JAMES. 1967. *Organizations in Action.* New York: McGraw-Hill.

TUCHMAN, GAYE. 1969. "News, the Newsman's Reality." Ph.D. dissertation, Brandeis University.

———. 1972. "Objectivity as Strategic Ritual: An Examination of Newsmen's Notions of Objectivity." *American Journal of Sociology* 77 (January): 660–70.

———. 1973. "The Technology of Objectivity." *Urban Life and Culture,* vol. 2 (April).

TYLER, STEPHEN A., ed. 1969. *Cognitive Anthropology.* New York: Holt, Rinehart & Winston.

ZIMMERMAN, DON H. 1970. "Record-keeping and the Intake Process in a Public Welfare Organization." In *On Record: Files and Dossiers in American Life,* edited by Stanton Wheeler. New York: Russell Sage.

# Media Imperialism?

JEREMY TUNSTALL

"THE MEDIA ARE AMERICAN, and Vodka's Russian. So what?" commented one American.

An African country of ten million people cannot make all its own feature films—so it imports them from Hollywood. It cannot collect its own international or Pan-African news—so it imports it from Reuters of London. It lacks resources to produce more than very modest quantities of recorded music, television entertainment, paperback books or comic strips; so it imports these things at low prices from American companies like UPI, RCA–NBC, Paramount, King Features and Disney or from British organizations like Reuters, the BBC or EMI.

Even an economically and artistically strong nation like Sweden, complete with its own national language, defended by state subsidies to the arts and media, and surrounded by its own circle of smaller Scandinavian states, even Sweden could not continue with its current level of media consumption without large imports of films, television series, international news, music, comics and so on. And these Swedish media imports come mainly from the United States and Britain.

In most of the world's countries the media are only there at all, on the present scale, as the result of imports in which the American media (with some British support) predominate. One major influence of American imported media lies in the styles and patterns which most other countries in the world have adopted and copied. This influence includes the very definition of what a *newspaper,* or a *feature film,* or a *television set* is.

Does the predominant form of newspaper need to be something which is printed every day and contains numerous pages of which many are advertis-

Extract from Jeremy Tunstall, "Media Imperialism?" in *The Media Are American* (1977), pp. 17–18, 37–63. Reprinted by permission of Constable Publishers.

ing? For the United States, where this format was largely developed, it is convenient and suitable; but for an African nation where transport is slow, literacy low, newsprint scarce and advertising weak, this "daily newspaper" format is less obviously suitable.

Does the predominant form of film have to be the feature film with a fictional story running for two hours or so? No, it does not, but this was the format which Hollywood evolved in the U.S. domestic market and which all other nations including the Soviet Union and China copied, scarcely recognizing that there was a choice.

And television? Does television have to be based on *domestic* sets—a square box which eats electricity and sits in the living room? Would not for many countries some format closer to the village hall movies have been better? Or was television necessary at all, when in many places in the world even village hall movies still have not arrived? But no, virtually every country of even a few million people has adopted the box-in-the-sitting-room concept of television even though the box may cost more than a farm family's annual cash income.

The high tide of American media exports, in their most obvious form, has passed. *I Love Lucy, Peyton Place* and *Mission Impossible* no longer rule the global village quite so masterfully as in the 1960s. But Hollywood is always dying only to be reborn with renewed vigour. And the world, by adopting American media formats, has in practice become hooked on American-style media whether these are homemade or imported. . . .

## The Television Imperialism Thesis

Many people over the last hundred years have pointed out the importance of American (and British) media in the world.[1] The most carefully researched work on this topic is still Thomas Guback's *The International Film Industry* (1969) which analyses Hollywood dominance in the western European film industries since 1945. However, Herbert Schiller's *Mass Communications and American Empire,* also by an American and also published in 1969, is a rare exception to the general lack of Marxist empirical accounts.[2] Schiller's thesis—that American television exports are part of an attempt by the American military industrial complex to subjugate the world—has been followed by other related work. Alan Wells's *Picture Tube Imperialism?* (1972) pursues the television imperialism thesis in Latin America.

Schiller's first contention is that despite the apparently commercial character of United States telecommunications, the American radio spectrum has increasingly come under the control of the federal government in general and the U.S. Secretary of Defense in particular. Domestic American radio and television is concerned with selling receiving sets and advertising goods. The educational stations of early American radio were lost as a consequence of commercialism and greed, and Schiller would like to see a return to a more educational and less commercial emphasis. Since 1950 and increasingly since the Cuban Bay of Pigs fiasco of 1961, Schiller sees American television as having come under the control of Washington; for example RCA (which controls the NBC television and radio networks) is also a major defence contractor—and consequently beholden to, and uncritical of, the federal government.

The great expansion of American television into the world around 1960—equipment, programming and advertising—is seen by Schiller as part of a general effort of the American military industrial complex to subject the world to military control, electronic surveillance and homogenized American commercial culture. American television programme exports, through their close connection with the manufacture of television receiving sets and American advertising agencies, are also seen as the spearhead for an American consumer goods invasion of the world. This export boom has, and is intended to have, the effect of muting political protest in much of the world; local and authentic culture in many countries is driven on to the defensive by homogenized American culture. Traditional national drama and folk music retreat before *Peyton Place* and *Bonanza.* So powerful is the thrust of American commercial television that few nations can resist. Even nations which deliberately choose not to have commercial broadcasting find their policies being reversed by American advertising agencies within their borders and by pirate radio stations from without. Commercial radio and television received from neighbouring countries tend to a "domino effect," by which commercial radio spreads remorselessly into India, while commercial television spreads from one west European country to the next. With the exception of the communist countries, and perhaps Japan, few nations can resist.

During the 1960s, Schiller argued, American policy came to focus even more strongly on subjugating and pacifying the poor nations; and in this strategy space satellites were to play a key part. The United States government handed its telecommunications satellite policy into the hands of the giant electronics companies (ATT, ITT, RCA) and then negotiated with the western nations Intelsat arrangements which gave the United States dominance of world communications; ultimately the policy was to beam American network television complete with commercials straight into domestic television sets around the world. The homogenization of world culture would then be complete. False consciousness would be plugged via satellite into every human home.

Alan Wells elaborates how American television imperialism works in Latin America. Latin American television, since its birth, has been dominated by United States finance, companies, technology, programming—and, above all, dominated by New York advertising agencies and practices. There is a very substantial U.S. direct ownership interest in Latin American television stations. "Worldvision," an ominously titled subsidiary of the U.S. national

ABC network, plays a dominant role in Latin America; American advertising agencies not only produce most of the very numerous commercial breaks but also sponsor, shape and determine the whole pattern of programming and importing from the U.S.A. Indeed, "approximately 80 percent of the hemisphere's current programs—including *The Flintstones, I Love Lucy, Bonanza* and *Route 66*—were produced in the United States."[3] This near monopoly of North American television programming within South America distorts entire economies away from "producerism" and towards "consumerism." Madison Avenue picture tube imperialism has triumphed in every Latin American country except Cuba.

The Schiller–Wells account *exaggerates* the strength of American television, partly because some of their quoted figures are unreliable; they concentrate on the high point of American television exports in the mid-1960s. They also tend to accept too easily the promotional optimism of a company like ABC, whose Worldvision remained a paper 'network' only. Sometimes, too, their logic is faulty. They complain that in the poor countries only the very rich can buy television anyhow, and then they see television as subverting the whole nation. But the American influence on world television—even if not so great as these authors argue—has been very considerable.

These authors' argument is also too *weak*. They scarcely notice the tendency of television merely to repeat a previous pattern of radio and feature films. This television imperialism thesis ignores the much earlier pattern of the press and news agencies which quite unambiguously did have an imperial character—although the empires were European ones, mainly British, but also French, Dutch, Belgian, Portuguese.

Tapio Varis (1974) has produced the first reasonably comprehensive mapping of worldwide television import patterns. Varis found for 1971 (the year before Wells's book was published) that the television channels in the larger Latin American countries (such as Argentina, Colombia and Mexico) imported between 10 percent and 39 percent of programming. The only one of seven Latin American countries in the Varis study to import 80 percent of programming was Guatemala.[4] Varis also found that a substantial proportion of television imports came from countries other than U.S.A., including imports from such Latin American countries as Mexico. . . .

A more recent study by Elihu Katz, George Wedell and their colleagues[5] traces the history of both radio and television in ten Latin American, Asian and African countries plus Cyprus. This study attributes a considerably larger place to British influence. The Katz–Wedell study suggests that the television imperialism thesis takes too little account of radio and of differences both within and between nations. It also strongly confirms that there was a high point of American influence on world television at some point in the 1960s. Central to the Katz–Wedell study is the notion of "phases of institutionalization." First there was a direct transfer or adoption of a metropolitan—usually American, British or French—model of broadcasting, with radio setting the pattern for television. Secondly, there was a phase of adapting this system to the local society. Thirdly, and ultimately, a new 'sense of direction' was introduced by the government—this typically involved removing any remaining vestiges of direct foreign ownership and increasing the direct control of government. This third phase typically occurred around 1970 and thus invalidated some of the Schiller and Wells arguments around the time they were being published. . . .

Katz and Wedell reject any strong television imperialism thesis, and they tend to see the American and British exporters of television models and styles as no less muddled and self-deceiving than the importers.

Nevertheless despite their implicit rejection of much of the television imperialism thesis, Katz and Wedell do provide much descriptive material which fits the thesis quite well. The importance of production (transmission and studio) technology is confirmed. Like the other students of television exports, they look with horror on the weight of commercial advertising, the predominance of American entertainment series and the relative absence in most countries of high quality educational or cultural television programming.

## Expensive Media Product at Low Prices

The economies of scale operate in many manufacturing fields, and especially in fields where the research and development costs are high—such as new drugs, aircraft production or computers. In these three fields the United States has achieved supremacy. But the economies of scale work in an even more extreme way in some media fields. In order to achieve extra overseas sales you have physically to manufacture and sell additional aircraft, or computers or pills—and a similar situation obtains with books or records. But in other media fields the additional cost of extra "copies" is negligible. Only one copy is needed to show on a national television network. Only a smallish number of copies of feature films are required for one country. And—what few television imperialism writers have noticed—news agencies and syndication services are also subject to extreme economies of scale; only you have a news service available in a foreign capital, hooking up additional clients costs a fairly negligible amount.

Such economies of scale operate equally for all large producers, one might think. But this is not quite the case. The standard American practice in all media fields is initially to undercut the opposition through price competition; this follows from the enormous numbers of publications and broadcasts outlets in the U.S.A. The policy is wide sales at low prices. American news agencies adopted this policy when they broke into the world market and they still operate it now. Hollywood did this so successfully with feature films that it could later raise its prices. The same tactics were pursued in television—

but the possibility of greatly raising prices has been defeated by the national television organizations which are typically strong buyers looking for bargains among competing sellers. . . .

Reasonably reliable estimates of the total overseas revenue of United States media are available in some cases, even though the nature of revenue varies greatly between media—as does the ratio of "revenue" to profit. Probably first would come feature films; Hollywood "theatrical" revenues abroad were $592 million in 1975. Approximately second equal would be records (including tapes, etc.) and the overseas revenues (commission, not billings) of American advertising agencies. Next would come the roughly $100 million revenue of U.S. television exports; then the overseas revenue of AP and UPI. These five categories together probably earned revenues of between $1,500 and $2,000 million in 1975.

By 1975 British television exports were probably earning about as much as those of the United States, if feature films on television are excluded. This British success depended heavily on the market of the United States itself. But lacking Hollywood's large theatrical film earnings, Britain must have earned a sizeable fraction of her export media revenue through books and EMI records. In video news exports—Britain's strongest single media export field—revenues were extremely small; Visnews in 1975–6 earned revenues of only £3·8 million and no profit at all.

The tendency of the most obviously politically influential media exports to earn the least revenue is consistent with the non-profit goals which often obtain in news, plus the market strength of such major purchasers of news as national news agencies and broadcasting organizations. Over half American export media revenues are earned from the young people who buy pop records or visit cinemas, and from advertisers, around the world. Or to express the same point in media imperialism terms: Media exporters earn monopoly profits by selling entertainment to young consumers of entertainment and young housewife users of advertised products, while the media exporters dump their products at low prices on national broadcasting organizations and news agencies.

## Importing News

In retrospect it may seem inexplicable that the governments of certain countries ever allowed media importing to take place on the scale of Hollywood film importing around 1920 or American television series importing after 1960. But governments are more interested in news than any other media form; and international arrangements for controlling the trade in news had been established long before 1920.

The main instrument of news trading was the international news agency;

the main exporters of international news around 1870 were Reuters and Havas—and all the other countries were the customers of the British and the French agency. More precisely, the importers were often national news agencies in particular countries; any government could indirectly control the incoming flow of British or French news by controlling or guiding the national agency through which the news was sieved before it reached any domestic newspapers. It was not surprising that the great diplomatic and financial nations, France and Britain, should dominate the world wholesaling of news. Moreover a powerful and rising European nation like Germany was able to get itself included as the third member of the cartel with its own special area in Scandinavia and Russia.

The international dissemination of news thus acquired a strong flavour of free trade—free trade as a doctrine interpreted by Britain and France. One of the contributions of the United States on the world scene was to give this free trade a fresh flavour; the American agencies in the early twentieth century brought an increase in direct competition both amongst themselves and between themselves and the Europeans; the news cartel slowly lost is imperial overtones and incorporated more competition. . . .

At the time of the Hollywood world-wide export dominance of 1920, most of the world's governments were more or less willing to accept the western international news agencies. And this situation has continued ever since. The western agencies have largely maintained their international acceptability despite the emergence of the communist bloc and the independence of ex-colonial nations. Governments in these countries can still control the in-flow of news, and to some extent the out-flow, through the mechanism of their national agency. The world's governments, with almost no exceptions, allow the international agencies to gather news about them for world dissemination. Governments know that it is possible to cover a country from outside—via radio and newspapers, by interviewing plane passengers arriving in neighbouring countries and so on; most governments prefer to have the foreign agency men based in the country, where correspondents often have little alternative to heavy dependence on the local national news agency. International news agencies are partly mere go-betweens for national news agencies. But the two American agencies and the British agency have acquired special international legitimacy. Most governments, politicians and journalists acknowledge that this news—while neither neutral nor always accurate—is at least more neutral and more accurate than any likely alternative. Even though the Anglo-Americans only behave as if neutrality were possible or accuracy meaningful, nevertheless the energy which goes into the "as if" performance is apparently widely thought to be impressive.

These agencies have largely shaped the presentation of international news in all countries around the world; these agencies do not merely play a major part in establishing the international political agenda, but they have done so now for a hundred years. And for a hundred years they have been the main definers of world "news values," of what sort of things become news. . . .

Time and Newsweek are available in most countries in the world; even at the height of the Cold War such American magazines were relatively seldom censored,[6] and in many countries there are now domestic imitations—which often copy the American formats in considerable detail. In western Europe export sales of dailies, weeklies and monthlies are dominated by American and British publications (French and German foreign sales are confined largely to Switzerland, Belgium and Austria).[7] A large number of American technical magazines have significant foreign sales.[8]

"Off-shore" media production, which is especially familiar in the feature film industry, was pioneered in Europe by American tycoon publishers. From 1887 James Gordon Bennett jnr produced a daily edition of the Herald in Paris, and since then—apart from 1940-4— . . . there has always been at least one American daily newspaper published in Paris. These efforts not only directed European attention towards American newspaper tycoons but also brought to Europe many young American journalists, who often later worked on other publications. Bennett's journalists were the first of many succeeding waves of American communicators—others appeared in films (from about 1910 on), in commercial radio (about 1930 on), in television (especially 1955 on). There were also waves of agency journalists and of advertising men. The off-shore style of production led to overseas editions of various magazines of which Reader's Digest is the most famous; women's magazines were another major field later followed by men's magazines. Recently we have seen off-shore American business magazines.

Even those relatively few of the world's newspapers and other news media which have their own staff correspondents tend to station a high proportion of them in New York, Washington and London. Staff correspondents reporting from the United States tend to rely heavily on the dominant U.S. domestic media. Foreign correspondents subscribe to a special American agency wire for such correspondents; every day they read the New York Times and Washington Post and perhaps the Wall Street Journal; every week they plough through piles of magazines—and they follow the networks.[9] The Editor or foreign editor back home in London or Tokyo has often himself previously been stationed in the U.S.A. and he continues to take an active interest in American news—he does this via the London or Tokyo service of the self-same agencies available in the U.S.A., via local editions of the self-same news magazines and so on. Consequently foreign correspondents stationed in the U.S.A. tend to receive enthusiastic requests for reports on the latest White House briefing, the . . . latest dark-horse for the Republican nomination, and requests for the correspondent's own version of Newsweek's fascinating feature on the worse-than-ever difficulties of New York's Mayor. Thus the correspondent finds himself rewriting at source bits and pieces of the very same American national media which in regional versions are on sale around the world. Something similar happens for foreign correspondents based in Britain. . . .

The Anglo-American video news agencies also provide the core of the material for the Eurovision daily news exchange. Visnews alone provided 25·5 percent of all news material on Eurovision in 1973. Eurovision has the most significant and long established daily television news exchange in the world and it is now linked to other regional exchanges; it has a daily exchange with the Soviet and east European Intervision. Its news goes daily from Madrid via Atlantic satellite to Latin America. Its exchange links are also spreading across the Mediterranean into North Africa and the Middle East. In all cases the flow of news is either entirely, or mainly, 'one-way flow' out of Eurovision, and in all cases the Anglo-American video news agencies provide the core of material transmitted. It is thus difficult to exaggerate either the direct presence or the indirect influence of Anglo-American materials and styles on television news throughout the world.

Having shaped the world's print news values, the Anglo-Americans have largely written the international grammar of television news; the main television news bulletin in most countries in the world will normally carry some Visnews material. Why? Audiences in all countries have been taught to expect television news to include an expensive commodity—foreign news film. If you don't buy it cheaply from the Anglo-Americans there is no practical alternative. Moreover, as with newspapers, this foreign coverage is of more visually dramatic material; it is typically of higher technical quality than local material (in most countries) and among television "professionals" it carries more prestige than does domestic material.

Being dependent upon foreign countries for their information about international politics may have been a difficult pill to swallow. But foreign ministries—faced with the alternative of not having the information, or having to rely entirely on their own diplomats—swallowed the pill. After this, accepting entertainment from abroad was easy; foreign advertising, easier still. . . .

## Impact on Domestic Media: A Canadian Example

. . . A study of Canadian responses to the importing of United States magazines is one rare example of a detailed case study of one country's response to a particular media import. Canadian responses are probably more clearly articulated than would be the responses in many other countries. Yet Litvak and Moule's *Cultural Sovereignty: The Time and Reader's Digest Case in Canada,* reveals a situation of great complexity and with quite a chequered history. United States magazines in Canada first became a national Canadian issue around 1920. The issue, as raised by Horatio C. Hocken, a former Mayor of Toronto and an ex-journalist, included these points:

The great bulk of United States magazines consisted of salacious literature that dissipated the morals of Canadian youth.

That American publications were mainly responsible for Canada's "brain drain" by depicting the United States as a land of unlimited promise, higher wages, better living conditions, and "good times.". . .

That United States publications, especially those of the Hearst syndicate, often expressed opinions repugnant to British sentiment in Canada.

That United States magazines posed an economic threat because of the substantial volume of advertising they conveyed, which attracted customers that would otherwise buy from Canadian manufacturers.

That the Canadian magazine industry was fighting a losing battle for its very survival and desperately needed protection or assistance. . . .

That magazines are crucial vehicles in the generation and dissemination of national sentiment and therefore deserve special consideration apart from strictly commercial calculations.[10]

These arguments have a familiar ring—all have been used in many other countries. Most of the arguments against American imports are negative ones; they cover a wide range of concerns—moral, cultural, political and commercial—and some seem to be rather contradictory. The main arguments in favour of media imports into Canada—as elsewhere—were projected on a rather general plane; the entry of United States magazines should be allowed to continue—proponents of this case argued—in the interests of freedom of the press, and freedom of citizen choice. . . .

## Cultural Imperialism Versus Authentic Local Culture

The cultural imperialism thesis claims that authentic, traditional and local culture in many parts of the world is being battered out of existence by the indiscriminate dumping of large quantities of slick commercial and media products, mainly from the United States. Those who make this argument most forcibly tend to favour restrictions upon media imports, plus the deliberate preservation of authentic and traditional culture.

This problem of cultural identity is part of a larger problem of national identity. The United States, Britain and France belong to a minority of the world's nations in having a fairly strong national identity. Almost all their citizens speak roughly the same language; but even in these countries there are major internal frictions—regional, ethnic and language, as well as social class, differences. And even this degree of national identity has only been achieved after several centuries of national existence, including civil war often followed by the brutal subjugation of regional and ethnic minorities. Countries which have an unusually strong national identity—such as U.S.A., Britain and France—also happen to be the very same countries which have the longest traditions of the press and other media, conducted primarily in a single national language.

The strength of national identity is less marked in Latin America either despite, or possibly because of, the use of Spanish as the language of all but one of the main countries. In much of eastern, central, and parts of northern, Europe there are two, three or more separate languages, religions and cultural traditions within a single state. The Soviet Union has this pattern on an even larger scale, as does India and some other Asian countries. There are similarly sharp cleavages within many Arab countries; and Africa is the continent where national identity is least strong of all.

The variety of languages within many nation states is at once a major factor in "cultural imperialism" and in lack of national identity. There are also very big differences between urban and rural areas, a very uneven pattern of development between some backward areas and other areas with exportable resources. Not only peasants' rebellions, guerrilla uprisings and palace revolutions but large-scale civil wars are a recent experience or an immediate realistic prospect in many lands. In the many countries where the prime object of policy is to reduce the threat of armed conflict, the need to strengthen "authentic culture" may not be seen as primary.

The most authentic and traditional culture often seems, and not only to the ruling élite, to be also the most inappropriate. This is not merely because traditional culture sanctions what would now be called civil war. Traditional culture is also typically archaic, does not fit with contemporary notions of justic or equality, and depends upon religious beliefs which have long been in decline. Many traditional cultures were primarily carried by a small élite of scholars and priests, who often used languages which few other people understood. Not only Arab and Hindu cultures but many others ascribed a fixed subservient position to women, the young and the occupationally less favoured. It is precisely these unpopular characteristics of much authentic culture which make the imported media culture so popular by contrast. . . .

The debate about cultural imperialism and authentic culture is reminiscent of, and related to, another debate about "mass society," mass culture and indeed the "mass media." The term "mass" has a long intellectual genealogy of its own and has long been used by both left and right with various shades of meaning and implication.[11] When this debate dealt with Europe and the United States it was confused enough. But the same debate, transposed to Asia and Africa, gets confused even further. It is precisely the highly educated élite in Asian and African countries who are the most active consumers of imported—and presumably "low, brutal and commercial"—media. It is the rural dwellers—short of land, food, literacy, income, life expectation, birth control devices and so on—who are the main consumers of traditional and "authentic" culture.

T. W. Adorno at one time claimed that even a symphony concert when broadcast on radio was drained of significance; many mass culture critics also had very harsh things to say about the large audiences which went to western and crime films in the 1930s—films which yet other cultural experts have subsequently decided were masterpieces after all. Even more bizarre, however, is the western intellectual who switches off the baseball game, turns down the hi-fi or pushes aside the Sunday magazine and pens a terse instruction to the developing world to get back to its tribal harvest ceremonials or funeral music.

Such a caricature illustrates that the real choice probably lies with hybrid forms. In many countries there are older cultural forms which continue in vigorous existence, although modified by western influences. Pop music often takes this form; "eastern westerns" or the Latin American *telenovelas* are other examples. The debate should, then, be about whether such hybrid forms are primarily traditional and "authentic" or whether they are merely translations or imitations of Anglo-American forms.

## Politics and Inequality

How do the Anglo-American media affect politics or inequality within an importing country? Do they, as the Media Imperialism thesis implies, buttress reactionary politicians and solidify inequalities? Or do they have democratic and egalitarian implications?

Among nineteenth-century élites in Europe one of the main anxieties about the American press was its lack of respect for established practices and people. . . .

Responses to imported American media continue to be related to attitudes towards currently prevalent inequalities. But it would be quite misleading to think in terms of media imports always favouring the poor at the expense of the rich. Even within the United States the media are primarily aimed at the middle of the population, not at its very poorest members. In terms of England in 1842, or western Europe today, imports of American media may quite realistically be seen as potentially hostile to established élites. But the emphasis of these media upon success and status favours the new rich more than the old poor. These media also present a heavily *urban* view of life.

In multi-party nations of western Europe, and perhaps to some extent in eastern Europe, imports of American media materials may tend towards democratizing and egalitarian effects. Such commercial infusions will tend to influence, if not the basic substance of political power within importing countries, then at least the *styles* politicians use in presenting themselves to local and national publics. Increased amounts of market oriented media fare— more entertaining entertainment, and more "neutral" news—will tend to make the more obviously political party fare seem less entertaining and more obviously dull and unattractive. Thus politicians try to dress up their political messages in more entertaining and neutral-looking packages. This in turn implies the use of PR and market research skills—in presenting the chief executive and his supporters, but also in presenting and shaping policies in even the most complex and delicate areas.

In multi-party countries, the rise of commercial or mainly advertising-financed media and the decline of party or government-financed media may become cumulative. Politically or government-controlled media tend to become less attractive to audiences, hence less important to politicians, and so on. More and more politicians use the techniques and the advice of advertising, market research and public relations, while argument is heard (and heeded) that media which are obviously controlled by government or party constitute bad political strategy. There is a gradual change by which politicians and governments in multi-party countries seek accommodations within an increasingly commercial pattern of media.

But in poorer African and Asian nations infusions of Western media may indeed buttress and extend existing inequalities. Since these imported media are consumed mainly by the urban and relatively affluent, and since importing becomes a substitute for providing cheap domestic media to most areas, inequality may be increased. In many poor countries, also, the media are controlled by the government; the national media may become a key instrument through which a small affluent élite maintains itself in power. This view of the media as prime defenders of the status quo is often shared by politicans in power and illustrated by the heavy military guard found outside many capital city radio stations.

Thus foreign media may in some affluent countries favour more equality, but in other less affluent countries favour more inequality. In yet other countries, such as those of Latin America both sorts of effects may occur at the same time. For example Wells may be right in believing that the imported media tip the scales away from the country and in favour of the city; but within the heavily populated Latin American cities those same media might have an egalitarian effect.


## One Media Imperialist, or a Dozen?

The media imperialism thesis does not confront the presence of strong regional exporters in various parts of the world. Mexico and Argentina have a tradition of exporting media to their neighbours; Egypt exports to the Arab world, while Indian films and records go to many countries in Africa and Asia. Not only the United States, Britain and France, but also West Germany, Italy, Spain and Japan all export some media. Even Sweden has its own little media empire in Scandinavia. And the Soviet Union has strong media markets in eastern Europe.

This phenomenon can be seen as running counter to the media imperialist thesis—showing that American and British media exports have many substantial rivals. But there are also grounds for seeing Mexican or Egyptian or even Indian exports as an indirect extension of Anglo-American influence. *The countries which are strong regional exporters of media tend themselves to be unusually heavy importers of American media.*

Italy in 1972 was after the U.S.A. the second largest exporter of feature films, with considerable strength in every world region. Yet Italy itself took over half of its imports from the U.S.A., Britain, Mexico and India all took an unusually high proportion of their imports from the U.S.A. Other strong film exporters—Japan, Egypt and West Germany—were strong importers of American films. Only the U.S.S.R., among major film exporters, imports virtually nothing from Hollywood.

By 1972 the majority of films made in Britain were Hollywood financed and distributed; and a substantial proportion of Italian and French films (including Italian-French co-productions subsidized by both governments) were also American-financed and distributed. And all of the major film exporters in the world (except U.S.S.R.) take around three-quarters of their film imports from the U.S.A., U.K., Italy and France combined. Thus almost all significant film exporters in the world are themselves open to heavy current Hollywood influence.

The strength of Soviet film exports in eastern Europe is noticeably weaker than Hollywood's unassisted export strength in all world regions apart from eastern Europe.

These data, incidentally, illustrate that television is not necessarily the best example for the media imperialist thesis. The continuing extent of Hollywood feature film exports around the world is all the more remarkable because Hollywood has here retained its export leadership for 60 years.

The television imperialism thesis cannot be considered merely for television alone. A more historical approach, covering all media, is required. We must also note, for example, both exporters and importers' intentions—as well as recognizing that many social consequences are unintended. Nevertheless the Schiller thesis has a number of strengths. It takes the whole world for its unit of analysis—and Schiller's domino theory of American media influence is one illustration of the benefits of so doing.

In my view the Anglo-American media are connected with imperialism, British imperialism. But these media exports both predate and still run ahead of the general American economic presence overseas or the multi-national company phenomenon. Schiller attributes too many of this world's ills to television. He also has an unrealistic view of returning to cultures many of which although authentic are also dead. In my view a non-American way out of the media box is difficult to discover because it is an American, or Anglo-American, built box. The only way out is to construct a new box, and this, with the possible exception of the Chinese, no nation seems keen to do.

# Notes

1. The present author first came across this phenomenon in the case of British advertising agencies. See Jeremy Tunstall (1964), pp 33–5, 140–1, 156–7, 224–6.

2. The shortage of Marxist empirically based accounts of this topic is illustrated in *Marxism and the Mass Media: Towards a Basic Bibliography 3* (1974) which contains 453 references.

3. Alan Wells (1972), p. 121.

4. Kaarle Nordenstreng and Tapio Varis (1974), p. 14.

5. E. Katz, E. G. Wedell et al. (1977).

6. Michael A. Barkočy (1963).

7. "Profiles of the European Executive Market." Survey conducted in 11 west European countries for Newsweek International by Conrad Jameson Associates (London, 1973).

8. "Foreign Circulation of Representative U.S. Publications 1964–65" (New York: Magazine Publishers' Association).

9. This passage on foreign correspondents in the U.S.A. is based on John Hohenberg's (1967) account of how Asian foreign correspondents operate in the U.S.A., upon the author's experience of interviewing foreign correspondents of British media in New York and Washington in 1965 and upon questionnaires completed by 37 such British correspondents in 1968 and reported in *Journalists at Work* (1971).

10. Isaiah Litvak and Christopher Maule (1974), pp. 19–20.

11. Leon Bramson (1961).

# References

BARKOČY, MICHAEL A. (1963). "Censorship Against *Time* and *Life* International Editions," *Journalism Quarterly* 40, pp. 517–24.

BRAMSON, LEON (1961). *The Political Context of Sociology,* Princeton University Press.

HOHENBERG, JOHN (1967). *Between Two Worlds: Policy, Press, and Public Opinion in Asian-American Relations,* New York: Praeger.

KATZ, E.; WEDELL, E. G.; PILSWORTH, M. J. and SHINAR, D. (1976). *Broadcasting and National Development,* Manuscript.

LITVAK, ISAIAH and MAULE, CHRISTOPHER (1974). *Cultural Sovereignty: The Time and Reader's Digest Case in Canada,* New York: Praeger.

NORDENSTRENG, KAARLE and VARIS, TAPIO (1974). *Television Traffic—A One-Way Street?,* Paris: Unesco.

TUNSTALL, JEREMY (1964). *The Advertising Man in London Advertising Agencies,* London: Chapman & Hall.

VARIS, TAPIO (1974). "Global Traffic in Television," *Journal of Communication* 24, pp. 102–9.

WELLS, ALAN (1972). *Picture-Tube Imperialism? The Impact of U.S. Television on Latin-America,* Maryknoll, N.Y.: Orbis Books.

# Public Policy Toward Television: Mass Media and Education in American Society

PAUL M. HIRSCH

TWO KEY COMPONENTS of an urban industrial society are a common culture and national economy. By presenting popular national symbols, sponsored by nationally advertised brand names, the mass media in the United States have played a major role in encouraging and maintaining each of these. Television, in particular, provides a steady flow of information and images to which all are exposed. These influence our perceptions of the world and touch upon the lives of all Americans. . . . What are some of the meanings of such a successful perpetual image machine, encompassing all cities and communities, for a commercial, urban industrial society? How did it come about and how might it change? How much is known about its effects on society as a whole, and on categories of individual viewers? These are among the questions addressed here. . . .

The character of the American mass media system has been determined largely by its long-standing commitments to private enterprise, local self-government, minimal government regulation, and a tradition of *caveat emptor,* or, let the consumer beware. These commitments, also tied to the constitutional protection of press freedom, account for a tightly organized and highly profitable broadcasting industry, in which stations are licensed to provide service to local communities but may meet this requirement by affiliating with national networks or syndication services which feature national programming. Within this social environment, the provision of mass-communi-

Reprinted from *School Review,* Vol. 85 (August, 1977), pp. 481–511, by permission of The University of Chicago Press. Copyright © 1977 by University of Chicago Press.

cated information and images thus becomes "just another industry." Historically, it has grown with and prospered from the large-scale urbanization of America over the last century. As a result of this process, about 80 percent of all retail goods are purchased in 300 metropolitan areas, primarily by adults between 18 and 49. With few exceptions (such as the selection of Saturday mornings by each network to schedule programs directed at children, or the appearance of advertisements directed to viewers over 50 on the nightly news programs), this is where the audience sought by the television industry and its advertisers is located. It is defined in terms of each viewer's demographic characteristics (age, sex, income) rather than place of residence. Signals from transmitters located in 235 metropolitan areas reach the entire U.S. population, with the "coverage" area of each television market basically coterminous with the large retail zone in which it operates. Programs and advertisements carried in the 10 largest television markets reach one-third of the population; and in the top 50, three-quarters. By and large, the remaining majority of cities and towns, and the minority of the people in rural areas, or the "wrong" age, education, and income categories, are excluded from the target audience to which the advertisements and (therefore) programs are designed to appeal. Of course, they are all welcomed as additional members of the national viewing audience, of which these groups certainly are a part; up to a point, in fact, the "standard English" used in program dialogues has been found to raise the English proficiency levels of the poorly educated and of children in largely rural areas. However, the programs and world view presented by American television are tailored almost exclusively to appeal to and reinforce the value structure of urban residents. Symbolically, this clearly skews the images presented of people and society, of what is funny, and of what is important. While the economic rationale behind these programming decisions is clear, the sociological functions served are seldom considered or investigated. This is a rare instance, for example, in which makers of economic and marketing decisions may distinguish only minimally between their "have" and "have-not" consumers; for, because of the retail zones in which they reside, programs whose appeal includes the urban poor may be more financially attractive to produce and sponsor than programs whose appeal includes the wealthy, but rural (hence, scattered) farmer.

This economic basis for the provision of television programs is not a recent development. Rather, it follows arrangements pioneered during the heyday of radio, whose owners, in turn, had borrowed some of their own organizational strategies from mass-circulation newspapers and magazines. . . . During the 1800s, the American newspaper was transformed from an elite to a mass medium. Rising literary rates, the growth of cities, and an absence of political controls all contributed to the rise of privately produced and inexpensive newspapers written for a mass, heterogenous audience. The new "penny press" prominently featured stories on crime, sex, and violence, in addition to political news, and, within four years of its appearance on

New York City street corners, sold more copies per issue than all of its "elite" competitors (which featured more partisan political news written at higher levels of sophistication) combined (DeFleur and Ball-Rokeach 1975). This formula for success, immensely attractive to advertisers for its ability to increase the number of readers exposed to their messages, set the pattern for each subsequent mass medium, all of which have adopted its techniques for appealing to and creating a mass audience. Metropolitan dailies developed by providing information and entertainment to local residents, selling advertising space to area retailers, and stressing local news while also forming cooperative syndicates to lower the cost of reporting stories originating in faraway places. While national newspapers developed in many other industrial nations, this medium has retained a predominantly local orientation in the United States, partly because there are so many autonomous governmental units to report on, as well as so many local merchants to place advertising (Bagdikian 1971).

As industrial expansion and railroad links were completed, the first national magazines made their appearance. Initially produced for increasingly literate housewives, these featured in-depth biographies of public figures, short fiction, and information about fashions in clothes, cooking, and home furnishings. They also could be merchandised at low subscription rates by selling advertising space to emergent national manufacturers of brand-name household products and remedies who found magazines with this editorial format an attractive "vehicle" for reaching their consumers. Some of these magazines, which helped to create new standards of taste among the growing middle class, soon broadened their appeal to include a wider cross section of Americans and grew into such widely read paragons of popular culture as *Colliers, Life, Look,* and the *Saturday Evening Post.* While each of these, at the time of their later demise, had millions of subscribers, their economic function— to gather together large numbers of "average" Americans for national (rather than local) advertisers—was made obsolete by the rise of television, a far more "efficient" medium with the same audience profile.

Whereas newspapers, with local readerships and advertisers, did not compete with national magazines, the emergence of radio initially posed numerous questions concerning its most likely audience, content, and sources of financial support. Unlike the print media, its progenitors were neither journalists nor particularly interested in competing for the now-established mass audience for the news of the day. Primarily, the corporations which developed this new invention were concerned with promoting the sale of radio sets; the programs needed to attract buyers were conceived largely as an adjunct to this marketing effort. By 1925, with all available airwaves hopelessly flooded by amateur operators, the industry repeatedly requested the federal government to step in and impose order through licensing and regulation. At first, both Congress and the Executive, in accordance with American political tradition, refused, insisting instead on self-regulation by the new industry.

The Federal Radio Act was passed finally in 1927, only after the industry proved incapable of agreeing on which operators could broadcast on specific frequencies at designated hours. By this time, the Radio Corporation of America, formed by General Electric, Westinghouse, and American Telephone and Telegraph, had established two radio networks (to become NBC and ABC), whose immediate success prompted the formation of CBS in 1928 and a fourth network (Mutual) six years later. Each network contracted with individual stations (affiliates) across the country to simultaneously carry expensively produced programs employing well-known performers and designed to appeal to a large and hitherto nonexistent national audience. Since it also had become clear by this time that listeners would not willingly pay to receive radio programs, their cost would be borne by national advertisers, who learned, to the surprise of all, that radio listeners did not protest their commercial interruptions. In return for "clearing time" to broadcast network programs, local stations would receive a portion of the advertising revenues obtained but, more important, could also sell commercial "time" to local and regional advertisers who wished to take advantage of the opportunity to reach the large audiences attracted by the network programs broadcast in their retail territory.

These arrangements almost instantly resolved the initial set of questions concerning the content and financial base for the new medium. The government's reluctance to interfere in the new "industry" would rule out for many years federal support for educational uses of either radio or television. Instead, programs produced and sponsored by private industry would seek out the largest possible audiences, providing those entertainment formats with the widest appeal. Once cost sharing through network affiliation, or "the interconnection of a number of local stations to produce standardized programming with central control," became the dominant organizational pattern, the economic burden of producing their own programs was thus largely lifted from locally licensed stations. As described by William Henry, a former chairman of the Federal Communications Commission, local stations are thereby able "to throw the network switch, or open a syndicated film package as they would a can of beans" (Bagdikian 1971, pp. 166, 171–72). Local affiliates, however, have long tended to reject low-rated network programs, such as documentaries or symphonic broadcasts, when they are not contractually obliged to carry them. An interesting unanticipated consequence of these types of arrangements is that when (unsponsored) congressional hearings— such as Senate and House committee hearings on the Watergate break-in and impeachment of President Nixon—are broadcast live by the major TV networks, local affiliates often find they must reluctantly "clear" these, if only because they have no alternative programs (or sponsors) to put on the air in their place. Ironically, radio stations, with locally produced programs, seldom if ever "interrupt" or "break in" to provide such coverage of public affairs. In short, while local stations are licensed to serve the communities in which they are located, networking arrangements, first in radio and now in television, facilitate a vast reduction in the number of hours devoted to programs geared to the metropolitan areas in which stations are licensed. That the "national" programs received in their place might be preferred by viewers to the "local" alternatives, and precisely what types of local television programs would fill the broadcast day, are questions that have seldom arisen or been investigated only recently. We do know, however, that local news programs (that is, reports of major events within each station's large coverage area) are widely viewed, and some of the smaller "independent" and educational radio and television stations have long provided coverage of local athletic events and public affairs.

Radio, followed by movies, newspapers, and magazines, has been transformed radically by the public's enthusiastic acceptance of television. First tested in 1927, television set ownership grew at an astonishing rate shortly after the end of World War II. Television networks, formed at this time and following the same audience-building strategies enunciated first by the mass newspaper and further developed by radio, "stole" many of radio's most popular programs and performers, and added the visual dimension. Its impact on the radio industry has been to force upon it new round-the-clock formats directed at individual listeners rather than families, with each one designed to appeal to a specific component of the formerly composite mass audience; hence, the "all-news" or the all-"country and western," "easy listening," "top 40," and "soul music" formats. Each of these is "targeted" to specific segments of the population and "sold" to advertisers seeking to match up with their respective demographic profiles. "All-news" listeners, for example, tend to be high income and well educated, while the profile of listeners to country and western formats is just the opposite. The impact of television on radio has thereby, indirectly, provided these listener aggregates, or subcultures, with far more access to cultural fare which each finds attractive than may have been the case when radio was a less diverse medium, with dominant networks seeking to appeal to "everybody" (Hirsch 1969). At the same time (excepting some talk shows), these radio formats, while locally produced, remain national in orientation, still serving to bring news of the outside world to their listeners—for example, the latest stories from Washington, or a new record by the Rolling Stones—rather than (perhaps improbably) suggesting that events in the listener's life are of equal importance. One of the most important functions of the mass media in urban societies, in addition to helping citizens relate to the outside world, may be that they so effectively transport people "outside" of themselves and thereby continually reinforce the power of our national culture.

The impact of television on radio also has had an indirect though substantial effect on which records are produced by the recording industry and made available to its consumers. When, as part of radio's adaptation to a new environment, some radio stations began featuring "top 40" formats, then rock'n roll records, and later "progressive rock," the diffusion of the new music and its associated life-styles contributed substantially to fostering new forms of "youth culture" by providing what was effectively a private communications medium for teenagers and college students. The lucrative prospect of radio air play for rock music has served to substantially influence decisions taken by record companies concerning which types of styles and performers to record and promote. More generally, American radio now serves to facilitate cultural solidarity within specific subgroups and subcultures (whose members remain tuned to one format, ignoring its available competitors), while television functions as a major communications link *between* groups, collecting together the members of different cultural subgroups for common exposure to the larger, dominant popular culture (Hirsch 1971).

Television's success also significantly altered the movie industry, which suffered a substantial drop in theater attendance as television viewers chose to be entertained at home. Over time, what used to be the "second feature," or "B" movie was dropped from exhibition in movie houses, only to be revived as television networks contracted their production for exclusive showings during the prime-time evening hours. With what were once stock movie plots now the staple of popular television series, today's films (with notable exceptions) are produced for new audiences: those who are least likely to stay home and watch television. The age of the average moviegoer has declined and, like radio formats, movies are now produced with narrower target audience subgroups (rather than "everybody") in mind. Consequently, they are frequently far more violent than previously and feature more explicit sexual sequences than would appeal to the "average" television viewer (who may, however, see a severely edited-for-television version subsequently). Newspapers, once able to deliver primarily just the news of the day and a few features, have adapted to the superior capacity of television to provide the same superficial service at the national level by presenting more in-depth features, local coverage, analysis, and commentary. And magazines, like radio, have sought more limited segments of the population. On the demise of *Life*, for example, Time, Inc., brought out two new publications—*Money* and *People*—geared to different audiences, with higher and lower income and education profiles, respectively, than characterized *Life* magazine, whose more heterogeneous readership was deemed too similar to television's audience by advertisers.

In sum, each of the mass media in America, privately operated and encountering minimal government regulation, has consistently sought to build and attract the largest possible audience and provide it with the types of entertainment and news that are most popular. Presently, television performs best at fulfilling this task, and its success has forced other mass media to adapt by attracting new audiences and offering greater diversity. An increasingly national audience for this created popular culture has been built, carefully nurtured, and maintained for nearly a century by forces basic to the political and commercial tenets of American society. What is known and believed to be some of the outcomes and effects of these organizational arrangements and their production and such widespread dissemination of cultural symbols?

Television's impact on American society consists partly in its spectacularly successful continuation of a trend started by other media, of developing content designed to create and attract massive audiences composed of people from all regions, classes, and backgrounds. Analytically, one of its most potent effects on American society—the provision of a centrally produced, standardized, and homogeneous common culture—is as much an artifact of how this medium's technological capacity has been organized as it is the inevitable result of the technology itself. This distinction is of great importance, for it suggests that some of the "effects" commonly attributed to the television medium should be conceived instead as following from its present organizational form, in which nearly 900 separate channels are effectively reduced to being mere conduits for four centralized TV networks. It is for this reason, and the consequent lack of variation or diversity in program content to which the nation is exposed, that television now serves so well as a proxy for all of the mass media whenever questions arise over mass media effects. Many of the controversial effects often attributed to television and presumed to be unique to this medium were earlier attributed to the predecessor media it has displaced. These include concern over the impact of its reliance on action-adventure formats featuring stories about crime, sex, and violence to attract and maintain its present audience. For example, when (AM) radio stations were divided into affiliation patterns with a few dominant networks, similar fare, or what is better thought of as the same "network effect," was mistakenly conceived by many observers as an effect of radio as a medium, rather than seen as a product of temporary organizational arrangements developed around the technology and largely supplanted by greater audience and regional diversity soon after television's arrival. Similarly, efforts by movie producers and magazine publishers to attract large, heterogeneous audiences were misinterpreted as inevitable characteristics of these media, rather than of what proved to be equally temporary organizational arrangements, also made obsolete by television's appearance as a competing medium.

Over and above television's refinement of formats and organizational arrangements pioneered by others, however, its technical ability to present an unending montage of moving visual images—of fictional characters, aspiring political leaders, comedians, wars, and disasters, in living color and in the privacy of one's home—is a wholly new development. Its political and cultural power lie in this combination of a technical capacity superior to other media, with the organizational arrangements which permit and encourage the absorption by so many millions of viewers of images produced and controlled by so few networks, and made so easily accessible to people throughout the United States and abroad. The resultant "global village" unquestionably plays a significant role in the political and cultural life of contemporary America.

In the short 25-year history of television, its effects have been considered and examined from numerous viewpoints. That some of these may seem to conflict with each other follows partly from observers considering entirely different aspects of television's role in society and then offering broad generalizations about it, based on whichever specific aspects of the topic they see as most important. Each view is then disputed by others as perhaps following logically and directly from an important perspective, but nevertheless unrelated to still other aspects of the question which they consider highly significant. For example, historian Daniel Boorstin (1973), noting statistics on Americans' pervasive exposure to TV and on changes in our use of time following its introduction, concludes that its effects on society have been nothing short of "cataclysmic." Sociologist Joseph Klapper (1960), on the other hand, reviewing studies of whether individuals' attitudes are measurably affected by short-term exposure to single programs, concludes that the medium typically works to reinforce already-existing viewpoints and predispositions, resulting in minimal change on the part of the average viewer. Note that neither perspective summarized in these examples actually contradicts the other, for essentially each is addressing entirely different aspects of television's impact on society. . . .

Television's coverage of national public affairs represents only about 3 percent of the programs it presents, usually at a financial loss and to fulfill part of its legal obligation to operate "in the public interest." It is far more widely and accurately perceived as a medium of mass entertainment. As a business, television network profits derive from presenting entertainment shows which attract a nationwide audience for "delivery" to commercial advertisers. The term, popular or "mass" culture, has come to refer to such mass media content, packaged and designed to appeal to this massive audience. As an enterprise, it has been enormously successful at meeting its goal: the appeal of popular culture on television is pervasive, and its presence insistent and continuous. To remain isolated from its content for an extended period is almost tantamount to being removed from the mainstream of American life (Wilensky 1964); when a writer for *TV Guide* locates someone who has not seen "The Johnny Carson (Tonight) Show," the discovery is grounds for a feature article patterned after Ripley's "Believe It or Not." Inherent in the concept of such national programming is an implicit rejection of cultural differences between viewers in different regions of the country, income and education categories, or with different backgrounds and interests. The logic of reaching "everybody" encourages a leveling of differences, a minimum of sequences which might offend any significant viewer segment, and a standardization of content and expectations. If television programs "teach" viewers anything about American values, norms, and fashions, this aspect—which has been called both debilitating and democratizing, depending on the critic's own values—is an essential component of the curriculum offered. While there is little doubt concerning the validity of these observations, the cultural *mean-*

*ing* and effects of such a successful system have long been a topic of widespread discussion and debate among humanists, social scientists, educators, and professional critics—all of whom offer provocative interpretations and raise important issues, most of which remain unresolved (McQuail 1969; Blumler and Katz 1974). . . .

Television program content has been analyzed from a variety of standpoints and along many dimensions. In the view of producers and literary critics, a key distinction lies in the type of program *genre* being discussed, for each type is written and paced differently, according to implicit or explicit rules (Newcomb 1974). Thus, situation comedies often are found difficult to compare to variety shows, sports broadcasts, action-adventure westerns and detective series, talk shows, or soap operas; and program content shown in the late evening hours (such as "Mary Hartman, Mary Hartman") may bring forth protests if scheduled in prime time—either from too many viewers who would find it offensive, or from network executives if its ratings were unsatisfactory. From this standpoint, it is interesting to examine the *form* of each genre, and learn how its plot lines and characterizations have changed over time. Lowenthal (1944) and W. Wright (1975) have performed this type of analysis for magazine biographies and movie westerns. It is a strategy too seldom applied to the television medium.

Television content is also very amenable to more sweeping and ambitious efforts to develop insights into its formulas, patterned images, and thematic content. One observation along these lines is that its main characters, both fictional (excepting selected villains) and "real" are nearly always intelligent, well-educated, successful, affluent, and from the middle class (Novak 1975). Note that this type of analysis can be performed *across* genres, as can a "census" of the race and sex of the individuals on screen, and a coding of whether they are presented as competent, sympathetic, in positions of authority or subordination, and so on. (Teachers and scientists frequently are presented as either unsympathetic or incompetent in their roles on television, according to a study by Gerbner [1973].) Also, in television dramas, problems usually must be solved by certified experts and heroes, and through ingenuity rather than mere luck. Upward mobility is a desirable goal in life. In action-adventure, and in children's cartoon programs, on-screen violence is ubiquitous, though there remains some ambivalence over coding procedures, as to whether analysts should consider all violent acts categorically or take into account by whom they are committed, under what circumstances, and to what end. Perhaps the most consistent and significant theme, across all genres, is also the simplest: the "latest" fashions in consumer goods are highly desirable and should be purchased. This is the unambiguous message of the commercial advertisements which appear before, during, and after every program and, more subtly, in the stage sets, clothes, and general appearance of most television actors and personalities. The cumulative effect of this brief inventory of common images and themes, viewed by so many millions each day, raises a host of questions about, and interpretations of, the impact of televised entertainment and commercials on American culture and on the perceptions of individual viewers. These divide roughly into three types: (1) those who view it as a public menace and essentially call for its abolition; (2) those who view its homogeneity of content, but not the medium itself, with dismay and advocate more diversity through decentralization of program production and distribution; and (3) those who either approve its present state or seek to alter minor aspects of program content without significantly affecting the organizational arrangements around which television is now structured. In terms of their implications for public policy and practical application, the first of these views is strongest on rhetoric and ideology; in effect, it seeks to argue with what is already a fait accompli. A more real choice is posed by the alternatives of more channels ("more diversity") versus a continuation of the present structure of a few centralized networks whose programs receive maximal exposure. While there are impressive arguments for each, few articulate spokesmen for the present structure (rather than its reform) have come forward. Here, I shall stress and point out a number of its advantages, benefits, and latent functions, as well as review the more well-known catalog of its presumed cultural costs and deficiencies.

The first and most radical school(s) of thought about television, in terms of its implied solution to the "problem," conceive popular culture as immensely harmful: to the vitality of both "high" and "folk" culture, as the handmaiden of a totalitarian state, or as simply an inexcusable waste of the viewer's time, which ought to be channeled into more rewarding and productive areas of social life. Educators have long been sensitive and sympathetic to these concerns for several reasons. First, mass media compete with school for students' time and interest, and often appear victorious; second, the types of values and images of the good life which television presents are largely proconsumption, whereas schools, as socializing institutions, are charged with inculcating norms of production and achievement (Gans 1974). Taken together, mass media partly compete with schools for both students' time and attitudes, particularly where their programs are not utilized by educators to their own advantage, or their techniques co-opted for the production of educational programs, such as "Sesame Street," which compete very successfully as children's shows providing television "entertainment."

During the late 1950s, the extent of the threat posed by mass culture to high culture and American society was debated extensively within the intellectual community (Rosenberg and White 1957; Bauer and Bauer 1962). Although Wilensky's (1964) finding that if high culture is losing vitality it is because so many of its own proponents enthusiastically embrace television entertainment fare defused part of this argument, an important part of the original indictment remains. This concerns the combined facts that the time people spend viewing television is time spent away from other activities, and that the act of watching television is essentially a passive one, encouraging people to vicariously share the experiences of nonexistent others rather than join more organizations and otherwise lead more active lives of their own. The policy implications of both observations, as phrased, however, do not encourage efforts toward "better" or more diverse program content. Rather, as Colman McCarthy (1974, p. 17) has recommended, they lead to "ousting the stranger from the house"; after "kicking" a habit of over 30 hours a week of basically unredeemable programming, he proposed that television cease operation with the following announcement to all viewers: "Come forward and turn off your set. . . . Get up and take a walk to the library and get a book. Or turn to your husband and wife and surprise them with a conversation. Or call a neighbor you haven't spoken with in months. Write a letter to a friend who has lost track of you. . . . Meanwhile, you'll be missing almost nothing."

Related to the alleged consequences of the amount of time Americans spend passively viewing television are two further concerns about the vitality of distinctive local and regional cultures, and the preservation of a democratic political order. Local and regional cultures may be affected adversely by more than the mechanical reproduction of live performances made possible by sound, movie, and videotape technologies. When combined with the nationwide dependence on a small number of technically proficient Los Angeles and New York–based production companies contracted by the major television networks, these factors encourage members of the national audience to look far beyond their own geographical territory for standards of entertainment, talent, and aesthetic enjoyment. Locally gifted performers, if acknowledged, are then more likely to move away to the few "real" centers of popular culture, while those remaining will be regarded by their public (and themselves) as second rate. (Of course, this has long been the case for writers and performers engaged in the production of "high culture" as well; and Hollywood and New York also attracted aspiring popular artists well before the advent of television.) Local taste cultures also will be seen by outsiders, and possibly by their own defensive participants, as holdovers from times past. And finally, the automation of cultural production and its transference to the small screen accelerates the disbanding of many life-performance troupes (circuses, rodeos, vaudeville, fiddlers), which find it increasingly difficult to compete for former patrons' time, money, and interest. The cultural consequences of centrally produced, standardized, slick, and nationally televised entertainment, therefore, diminish the number and quality of local productions and performers, lowering the amount of pride and interest taken in local and regional cultures, and narrowing their range. This further increases the prestige and influence of the more homogeneous national popular culture. A further implication, drawn by critics of mass culture and mass society, is that the *political* correlates of once-distinctive local and regional cultural patterns will similarly decline in strength. That is, a nation whose population stays at home imbibing identical information, symbols, and images will also become more homogeneous in cultural experiences and political knowledge, and less amenable to mediating influences between the passive, possibly atomized individual and the state (Kornhauser 1959; Wilensky 1964). Here, television, as the most national of the mass media, is seen to act as an effective inhibitor of political mobilization by interest groups independent of the state, thus serving as a primary agent of social control. As in the instances of time use and the presumed threat to education and high culture, the simplest and perhaps sole "solution" left available to the problems posed by the abolitionist position is to "oust the stranger from the house" and shut down the medium.

A more realistic alternative is suggested by a second group of concerned observers, who accept the continuing presence of television but wish to see its organization structure decentralized, the number of channels increased, and a greater degree of diversity in program content. Cable television technology is admirably suited to this purpose, though many of the same goals could be accomplished if existing stations relied less on the dominant networks and syndicators for their programming, and if more UHF channels were put into operation. Under these conditions, a variety of possible consequences can be anticipated. If, for example, the amount of time invested by viewers in watching television remained constant, they probably would see more entertainment programs featuring local or regional culture and performers; public affairs coverage of particular interest to members of each channel's viewing audience would very likely rise also. (Exactly how much would depend on policies adopted by the Federal Communications Commission, local performers' and craft unions, and the cost of producing programs—which should decline with the advent of cheaper video production equipment.) If, as industry members predict, viewer interest (and ratings) for such "local" programs is low, and people choose to watch fewer hours rather than old reruns, then more direct patronage of local talent and culture might well follow. Either way, local and regional cultures would receive a boost from a decreased availability of the nationally dominant popular programs now so well entrenched on the medium. An alternative version of more diversified, "subcultural" programming has been proposed by Gans (1975). This would be directed, like radio formats, to particular segments of the now-heterogeneous national audience. Instead of focusing on issues and cultures of possible interest to specific geographic localities, it would develop entertainment and public affairs programs geared to particular demographic segments, including children, the elderly, the poor, women, minorities, and the other groups presently neglected. Gans's proposition, unlike the others reviewed so far, is that the impact of televised programs on individuals and society is *minimal,* and therefore it would be more equitable (at little social cost) to provide each component segment of the mass audience with programs it might prefer, if only the choice were available.

The final interpretation of the cultural impact of television asserts that present networking arrangements serve a variety of socially useful functions, agrees the cultural influence of popular culture is substantial, and argues largely for a continuation of the present system. Following Durkheim (1964), it proposes that in contemporary America we already have a great diversity of economic, ethnic, cultural, and regional divisions, which, further separated by a complex division of labor and pattern of occupational specialization, rely on a national, common popular culture to reintegrate and symbolically unify these many diverse elements. Television, more than any other mass medium, performs this important function by ensuring that virtually the entire population is exposed to the same jokes, sports events, presidential addresses, and dramatic fare. Consequently, if particular program genres are felt to be excessively violent or in poor taste, the solution is to insist on enriching or changing the content presented by existing networks, rather than to encourage further cultural divisions by providing new channels and numerous programs directed at each of the segments which now comprise the heterogeneous mass audience. In large part, this has been the strategy followed by the Public Broadcasting System, with nationally distributed programs like "Sesame Street," and by groups seeking specific changes in the content offered by commercial networks, such as Action for Children's Television and organizations seeking a more positive portrayal of minority groups on popular television programs and commercials.

This position also sees network television as a cultural "melting pot," in which intergroup communication is facilitated when popular entertainment programs, such as "M*A*S*H*" and "All in the Family" present characters which embody different views on public issues, providing the mass audience with information about how conflicting groups in society perceive the questions involved. Social psychologists often label such programs ineffective or harmful on the ground that they fail to convert viewers who agree with one ("bad") character's position to the side of the others (Vidmar and Rokeach 1974). However, this criterion misses a larger point, which is that the key function served is likely to be the viewer's exposure and increased awareness of the tastes and views of the different sides, all presented within a single broadcast. This type of intergroup communication, as characteristic of the old "Ed Sullivan Show" as of "All in the Family," is measured in terms of whether viewers' *information and awareness* levels have risen, rather than whether they were "converted" to a new value position. Finally, the "cultural integration" position argues that even broad educational purposes are best served through the utilization of network facilities, rather than by seeking to reach select target groups through separate programs on a less widely viewed channel. For example, a single episode of "All in the Family," in which Edith Bunker feared she had breast cancer, powerfully and effectively conveyed information to more (rich and poor) people about a major health problem than did practically all of the episodes combined of "Feeling Good," an ill-fated series on public television devoted to health problems, which failed to reach those (poorly educated) viewers it most sought to inform.

It is important to note that each of the interpretations and policy positions just outlined are based on the same body of facts and knowledge from social science. They differ in the conclusions reached because each seeks to relate what is known about television to different *models of society.* The "abolitionist" position conceives of American society as becoming too regimented, bureaucratic, and standardized. Television is seen as contributing to this problem, aggravating an already undesirable situation by providing a homogeneous mass culture for a mass society. The "channel diversity" position presents a less pessimistic model of recent social trends, suggesting the problems faced are more a matter of degree. Television's role is seen as a problem residing in organizational arrangements, rather than as endemic to the medium itself. A decentralization of network dominance would restore public attention to local culture and political affairs or to diverse national subcultures, and thereby help deter nationwide trends toward cultural, and particularly televised, homogeneity. Finally, the "cultural integration" position conceives society as *already fragmented* into stratified groups, and in need of reintegration through shared symbols and a common culture. Here, the precise content of that culture is less important than the fact that it be shared by all. Consequently, network television is seen as contributing to the social good by providing for greater cultural cohesion. Each position agrees on the facts, so far as the organization of the industry and the content of its programs are concerned. To a lesser extent, each also shares a common set of assumptions regarding the importance of television in America's popular culture and political processes, and about how audiences respond to the viewing experience.

# References

BAGDIKIAN, B. *The Information Machines.* New York: Harper & Row, 1971.

BAUER, R., and BAUER, A. "American Mass Society and Mass Media." *Journal of Social Issues* 16 (1962): 3–66.

BLUMLER, J., and KATZ, E. eds. *The Uses of Mass Communication.* Beverly Hills, Calif.: Sage Publications, 1974.

BOORSTIN, D. *The Americans: The Democratic Experience.* New York: Random House, 1973.

DeFLEUR, M., and BALL-ROKEACH, S. *Theories of Mass Communication.* 3d ed. New York: David McKay Co., 1975.

DURKHEIM, E. *The Division of Labor.* New York: Free Press of Glencoe, 1964.

GANS, H. "Mass Communications as an Educational Institution." In *American Education in the Electric Age,* edited by P. Kling. New York: Educational Technology Publications, 1974.

GANS, H. *Popular Culture and High Culture.* New York: Basic Books, 1975.

GERBNER, G. "Teacher Image in Mass Culture: Symbolic Functions of the 'Hidden Curriculum.' " In *Communications Technology and Social Policy,* edited by G. Gerbner, L. Gross, and W. Melody. New York: John Wiley & Sons, 1973.

HIRSCH, P. *The Structure of the Popular Music Industry.* Ann Arbor: University of Michigan Institute for Social Research, 1969.

HIRSCH, P. "Sociological Approaches to the Pop Music Phenomenon." *American Behavioral Scientist* 14 (1971): 371–88.

KORNHAUSER, W. *The Politics of Mass Society.* Glencoe, Ill.: Free Press, 1959.

LOWENTHAL, L. "Biographies in Popular Magazines." In *Radio Research 1942–43,* edited by P. Lazersfeld and F. Stanton. New York: Bureau of Applied Social Research, 1944. Reprinted in *American Social Patterns,* edited by W. Peterson. New York: Doubleday & Co., 1956.

MCCARTHY, C. "Ousting the Stranger from the House." *Newsweek* (March 25, 1974), p. 17.

MCQUAIL, D. *Towards a Sociology of Mass Communications.* London: Collier-Macmillan Publishers, 1969.

NEWCOMB, H. *TV: The Most Popular Art.* New York: Anchor Books, Doubleday & Co., 1974.

NOVAK, M. "Television Shapes the Soul." In *Television as a Social Force: New Approaches to TV Criticism,* edited by D. Cater and R. Adler. New York: Praeger Publishers, 1975.

ROSENBERG, B., and WHITE, D., eds. *Mass Culture.* Glencoe, Ill.: Free Press, 1957.

WILENSKY, H. "Mass Society and Mass Culture: Interdependence or Independence?" *American Sociological Review* 29 (1964): 173–96.

WRIGHT, W. *Sixguns and Society.* Berkeley: University of California Press, 1975.

# 5

# Communication Content

Many research problems in communications require detailed description of the contents of mass media. For this purpose students in the field have developed several methods of content analysis. Content analysis aims at systematically monitoring and summarizing the messages contained in the mass media, and may be contrasted with research on media effects. Content analysis simply tells us how much of which messages are present and makes no attempt to assess their impact on audiences. It has a distinguished record as a research tool in the social sciences, its earliest "classics" including Lasswell's work on propaganda,[1] Lowenthal's famous analysis of biographies in popular magazines,[2] Berelson and Salter's profiles of magazine fiction[3] and Wolfstein and Leites' treatment of movie themes.[4]

The rubric "content analysis" actually encompasses a variety of distinct techniques, but most common in the social sciences has been the quantitative approach. This involves the selection of content categories the analyst finds theoretically relevant and the development of operational measures. Systematic counting using these measures enables the researcher to determine the frequencies with which various content categories appear in the media. Statistical profiles are then drawn up, and the prevalence of a message in one medium may be compared with other media, or a single medium may be compared over different time periods. Lowenthal, for example, found a preponderance of "idols of consumption" among the subjects of popular magazine biographies in the late 1930s, whereas "idols of production" had predominated at the turn of the century in the same magazines. This approach to content analysis represents an attempt to introduce a rigorous scientific method into communications research because it involves the use of operational techniques that are codified in advance and are therefore independent of the subjective penchants of individual researchers.

This method has generally been deemed appropriate for social scientists studying news coverage or public affairs journals. When popular entertainment has been the object of study, however, the appropriate methodology for content analysis has produced an interesting debate between humanists and social scientists. Humanists, who often prefer a kind of "generic" analysis akin to literary criticism, accuse quantitative social scientists of lifting message components out of their various dramatic and symbolic contexts, thereby statistically combining fragments of content that are essentially not comparable. Many segments of popular entertainment, they claim, derive their full meaning only from the narrative flow in which they are embedded. This meaning is lost if the contents are treated as self-contained messages to be counted with others (across television programs or magazine stories) which are only superficially similar.

Holsti discusses some of these issues from the "social science" point of view. His selection provides an overview of the methods of content analysis and includes a discussion of some of the main controversies involved. Holsti describes those principles of content analysis with which most social scientists agree—*objectivity, system,* and *generality.* He also examines the state of unresolved debates over whether or not content analysis must be quantitative and whether it must confine itself to the analysis of manifest or surface content.

Homans's analysis of screen-image Westerns exemplifies the humanist's more generic approach to the study of popular culture. Here, the analysis of popular entertainment treats its object as a serious work of art, an approach that has gained adherents in recent years, due largely to the work of John Cawelti and others.[5] While noting the formulaic character of Westerns, Homans criticizes the kind of "reductionism" that would classify under one rubric all popular works possessing certain thematic similarities (for example, equating the violence in Westerns with violence in horror movies). His emphasis is on the *details* that give the screen-image Western its uniqueness.

Gerbner and Gross's "message system analysis" places them squarely within the social science tradition of content analysis. Their "Violence Profile" systematically monitors the "prevalence, rate, and characterizations involved in violence" found in television drama. In an effort to determine the *effects* of television violence on its audience, Gerbner and Gross move beyond the violence index to what they term "cultivation analysis." (Only their content analysis is included in this volume.) Here they compare the responses of "light" and "heavy" television viewers to survey questions on topics like fear and alienation, on the premise that significant differences, where found, may be attributed to exposure to television violence.

This is a rather unusual step for the content analyst, and a positive step from the social science perspective. It also, however, becomes the focal point for Newcomb's humanistic critique. While crediting Gerbner and Gross for their contribution to a synthesis of humanistic and social science paradigms, Newcomb insists that "A strain on this synthesis . . . begins to develop, however, when it becomes necessary to interpret this environment of symbols." The shortcomings of cultivation analysis forces attention back to the content analysis on which the former is based and here Newcomb contends that the categories used in Gerbner and Gross's "message system analysis" were wanting to begin with. In the humanist tradition, he argues that the violence categories employed, by their very use, highlight the *prevalance* of violence everywhere—whether it occurs in a Western or in a police story—rather than the *differences* between shows, and does not go far enough in drawing out the varoius dramatic functions which violence serves in different contexts. Moreover, Newcomb suggests, the fact that violence occurs with greater statistical frequency on television than in the real world does not yield the conclusion that television projects a world "ruled by violence." Violence is rather a technique used for dramatization and, like other dramatic techniques, can occur regularly on television without necessarily instilling in audiences the misconception that it is ubiquitous outside its dramatic setting.[6] These issues are discussed in greater detail by Dorr, in the section on "Mass Media Effects."

Such debates over the appropriate categories and methods for content analysis will undoubtedly continue. Tangible signs of increased cooperation between the social sciences and the humanities are already visible,[7] and if such controversies contribute to the relaxation of formerly rigid disciplinary boundaries, then we must consider them fruitful debates indeed.

## Notes

1. Harold D. Lasswell, *Propaganda Technique in the World War* (New York: Knopf, 1927), and *idem, Language of Politics* (Policy Sciences Foundation, 1949).

2. Leo Lowenthal, "Biographies in Popular Magazines," in Paul F. Lazarsfeld and Frank Stanton, eds., *Radio Research, 1942–43* (New York: Duell, Sloan and Pearce, 1944).

3. Bernard Berelson and P. Salter, "An Analysis of Magazine Fiction," *Public Opinion Quarterly*, X: 168–197.

4. Martha Wolfstein and Nathan Leites, *The Good-Bad Girl in Movies: A Psychological Study* (New York: The Free Press, 1950).

5. John Cawelti, *The Six-Gun Mystique* (Bowling Green, Ohio: Bowling Green Uni-

versity Popular Press, 1970), and *idem, Adventure, Mystery and Romance* (Chicago: University of Chicago Press, 1976). Also Horace Newcomb, *TV: The Most Popular Art* (New York: Anchor, 1974), and John Fiske and John Hartley, *Reading Television* (London: Methuen, 1978).

6. For a methodological critique of cultivation analysis, see Paul Hirsch, "The 'Scary World' of the Nonviewer and Other Anomalies: A Reanalysis of Gerbner et al.'s Findings on Cultivation Analysis," Parts 1 and 2, *Communication Research 7* (October 1980) and 8 (January 1981).

7. See, for example, the special issue of *Communication Research* devoted to humanistic models in communication research, edited by Paul Hirsch and James W. Carey, Vol. 5, No. 3, July 1978.

# Content Analysis:
# An Introduction

OLE HOLSTI

COMMUNICATION, THE MOST BASIC form of human interaction, is necessary for any enduring human relationship, from interpersonal to international. Groups, institutions, organizations, and nations exist by virtue of communication and cease to exist once communication becomes totally disrupted. Indeed, it is no exaggeration to assert that "communication is at the heart of civilization" (Kuhn, 1963, p. 151). It therefore follows that the study of the processes and products of communication is basic to the student of man's history, behavior, thought, art, and institutions. Often the only surviving artifacts that may be used to study human activity are to be found in documents. . . .[1]

The study of communication content has been approached from a variety of different starting points and undertaken with the tools and conceptual frameworks of several disciplines. Content analysis is a multipurpose research method developed specifically for investigating any problem in which the content of communication serves as the basis of inference. In this article we shall develop this point further from several perspectives: What are the defining characteristics of content analysis? For what types of research problems is it most likely to prove useful? What are the major trends in the nature of the method, and what are the purposes for which it has been used:

Nearly all research in the social sciences and humanities depends in one way or another on careful reading of written materials. Given the ubiquity of this process in research, what characteristics distinguish content analysis

Extract from O. Holsti, *Content Analysis for the Social Sciences and Humanities,* © 1969, Addison–Wesley Publishing Company, Inc., pages 1–23, "Content Analysis: An Introduction." Reprinted with permission.

from any careful reading of documents? Definitions of content analysis have tended to change over time with developments in technique and with application of the tool itself to new problems and types of materials. . . . Despite their diversity, definitions of content analysis reveal broad agreement on the requirements of *objectivity, system,* and *generality.* We shall consider the meanings of these requirements, as well as two others—that it must be quantitative and limited to the analysis of manifest content—which are somewhat more controversial.

*Objectivity* stipulates that each step in the research process must be carried out on the basis of explicitly formulated rules and procedures. Even the simplest and most mechanical forms of content analysis require the investigator to use his judgment in making decisions about his data. What categories are to be used? How is category A to be distinguished from category B? What criteria are to be used to decide that a content unit (word, theme, story, and the like) should be placed in one category rather than another? Once the document has been coded and the findings are summarized, what was the reasoning that led to one inference rather than alternative ones? Objectivity implies that these and other decisions are guided by an explicit set of rules that minimize—although probably never quite eliminate—the possibility that the findings reflect the analyst's subjective predispositions rather than the content of the documents under analysis. Thus, one test of objectivity is: can other analysts, following identical procedures with the same data, arrive at similar conclusions? The investigator who cannot communicate to others his procedures and criteria for selecting data, for determining what in the data is relevant and what is not, and for interpreting the findings will have failed to fulfill the requirement of objectivity.

*Systematic* means that the inclusion and exclusion of content or categories is done according to consistently applied rules. This requirement clearly eliminates analyses in which only materials supporting the investigator's hypotheses are admitted as evidence. It also implies that categories are defined in a manner which permits them to be used according to consistently applied rules. . . . The requirement that research be "systematic" can also be illustrated by a negative example. In a book purporting to demonstrate the intellectual inferiority of certain racial groups, the authors culled from both reputable and highly suspect sources all materials supporting the thesis of inequality, while virtually disregarding the quantitatively and qualitatively superior evidence in support of the contrary thesis (Weyl and Possony, 1963). Although these findings were presented as a "content analysis" of the literature relating race to intelligence, a "study" of this type clearly fails to satisfy even the loosest definition of systematic research.

Important and necessary as these two criteria are, they are not sufficient to define content analysis or to distinguish it from related endeavors. This may be illustrated by several simple examples. Indexes, bibliographies, or concordances are concerned with the content of certain types of documents.

All three can be prepared objectively and systematically, indeed, usually more objectively and systematically than most content analyses. They may also serve as a source of data for subsequent content analyses. . . .

*Generality,* then, requires that the findings must have theoretical relevance. Purely descriptive information about content, unrelated to other attributes of documents or to the characteristics of the sender or recipient of the message, is of little value. The findings that Alexander Hamilton tended to use the word *upon,* that 0.7% of Richard Nixon's statements in the third television debate with John F. Kennedy included evidence (Ellsworth, 1965, p. 800), or that a Greek funeral oration of the eighth century B.C. contained "achievement imagery" are, by themselves, of little importance or interest. Such results take on meaning when we compare them with other attributes of the documents, with documents produced by other sources, with characteristics of the persons who produced the documents, or the times in which they lived, or the audience for which they were intended. Stated somewhat differently, a datum about communication content is meaningless until it is related to at least one other datum. The link between these is represented by some form of theory. Thus all content analysis is concerned with comparison, the type of comparison being dictated by the investigator's theory.

The requirements of objectivity, system, and generality are not unique to content analysis, being necessary conditions for all scientific inquiry. Thus in general terms, content analysis is the application of scientific methods to documentary evidence. At this point some readers may become aware that, like the person who suddenly discovers that he has been "writing prose all his life," they have been engaged in content analysis without knowing it.

## The Quantity-Quality Issue

Along with general consensus that objectivity, system, and generality are defining characteristics of content analysis, two other proposed requirements have generated considerable debate in the recent literature. First, must content analysis be *quantitative?* Second, must it be limited to the *manifest* content, or may it be used also to probe for more latent aspects of communication?

The quantitative requirement has often been cited as essential to content analysis, both by those who praise the technique as more scientific than other methods of documentary analysis and by those who are most critical of content analysis.

The former viewpoint is summarized by the assertion that, "There is clearly no reason for content analysis unless the question one wants answered is quantitative" (Lasswell, Lerner, and Pool, 1952, p. 45). There is, however, considerable disagreement about the meaning of "quantitative" as applied to content analysis. The most restrictive definitions are those which require that content analysis measure the *frequency* with which symbols or other units appear in each category. Other definitions equate it with *numerical:* "Content analysis aims at a classification of content in more precise, *numerical terms* than is provided by impressionistic 'more or less' judgments of 'either-or' " (Kaplan and Goldsen, 1949, p. 83). Others are still less restrictive and include studies in which findings are reported in such terms as "more," "less," or "increasing" (Berelson, 1952, p. 17). Finally, there is a group which accepts the distinction between "quantitative" and "qualitative," but which insists that systematic documentary studies of the latter type constitute an important, and perhaps more significant, form of content analysis. We can illustrate these viewpoints in more detail by examining a hypothetical study of campaign speeches on the Vietnam issue by congressional candidates.

Some of the earlier definitions of content analysis required that inferences from content data be derived strictly from the *frequency* with which symbols or themes appear in the text (e.g., Leites and Pool, 1942, pp. 1–2; Janis, 1943, p. 429). Using frequency counts we might, for example, tabulate how many times certain themes relating to American policy in Vietnam appear in each candidate's speeches. Reporting the number of statements in each category by all candidates (as in Table 1) would satisfy the requirements of many research designs.

**TABLE 1.    Frequency of Themes**

| | FREQUENCY OF REFERENCE | |
| THEME | CANDIDATE A ($N = 10$ SPEECHES) | CANDIDATE B ($N = 12$ SPEECHES) |
| --- | --- | --- |
| U.S. must honor commitment to allies | 15 (56%) | 3 (13%) |
| Appeasement of aggressors leads to war | 9 (33%) | 1 ( 4%) |
| Peace in Vietnam must be based on compromise | 3 (11%) | 14 (58%) |
| U.S. is upholding a corrupt government in South Vietnam | 0 ( 0%) | 6 (25%) |

Restricting content analysis to this single system of enumeration, however, presents a theoretical and a practical problem. Underlying this definition is the assumption that frequency is the only valid index of concern, preoccupation, intensity, and the like. Often this may in fact be a valid premise, but there is also ample evidence that measures other than frequency may in some instances prove more useful. The related practical problem is that this view places a number of standard content analysis methods on the borderline of acceptability, and it removes some of the most imaginative content analysis studies from our consideration. A pioneering application of content analysis, the RADIR (Revolution and the Development of International Relations) studies, combined frequency and nonfrequency techniques. Each editorial in the sample taken from a series of "prestige newspapers" during a 60-year period was coded according to the appearance or nonappearance of certain key symbols (Lasswell, Lerner, and Pool, 1952). Thus at the coding stage an editorial received the same score ("present") whether a symbol occurred once or a dozen times. The findings were then summarized by tabulating the number of editorials in which each symbol was present. Similarly, we might score each category relating to American policy in Vietnam as "present" or "absent" in a speech, and then tally the number of speeches in which any theme occurred, rather than the frequency with which any content unit appeared. The results might then be reported as they are in Table 2.

**TABLE 2.   Presence of Themes**

| | NUMBER OF SPEECHES IN WHICH THEME OCCURS | |
| --- | --- | --- |
| TEME | CANDIDATE A ($N = 10$ SPEECHES) | CANDIDATE B ($N = 12$ SPEECHES) |
| U.S. must honor commitments to allies | 10 (100%) | 3 (25%) |
| Appeasement of aggressors leads to war | 8 ( 80%) | 1 ( 8%) |
| Peace in Vietnam must be based on compromise | 1 ( 10%) | 9 (75%) |
| U.S. is upholding a corrupt government in South Vietnam | 0 ( 0%) | 4 (33%) |

The technique of "contingency analysis," in which the coding of material depends on the absence or presence of the attribute within the document or section of the document, rather than on the frequency of its presence, provides another method of scoring (Osgood, 1959, p. 63). Inferences are then based on the proximity of two or more content attributes within the text. In our study of campaign speeches we might be concerned with discovering what terms occurred in conjunction with references to Vietnam, rather than in the frequency with which these symbols occurred. The results might then resemble Table 3.

Finally, each speech might be given a single score which most closely characterizes its major theme. In this case we make a single qualitative judgment about the entire document without tabulating the frequency with which any content attribute appears. But we may still report our findings quantitatively, as in Table 4.

**TABLE 3.** Contingency Analysis of Terms

| Other Symbols | Number of Sentences in Which Other Symbols Occur | |
|---|---|---|
| | Candidate A (N = 49 Sentences Referring to Vietnam War) | Candidate B (N = 62 Sentences Referring to Vietnam War |
| Commitment | 32 (65%) | 7 (11%) |
| Allies | 29 (59%) | 5 ( 8%) |
| Appeasement | 14 (28%) | 4 ( 6%) |
| Peace | 8 (16%) | 39 (63%) |
| Compromise | 4 ( 8%) | 20 (32%) |
| Corrupt | 0 ( 0%) | 18 (29%) |

**TABLE 4.** Major Theme of Speeches

| Major Theme of Speech | Candidate A (N = 10 Speeches) | Candidate B (N = 12 Speeches) |
|---|---|---|
| U.S. must honor commitments to allies | 5 (50%) | 0 ( 0%) |
| Appeasement of aggressors leads to war | 1 (10%) | 0 ( 0%) |
| Peace in Vietnam must be based on compromise | 0 ( 0%) | 7 (58%) |
| U.S. is upholding a corrupt government in South Vietnam | 0 ( 0%) | 0 ( 0%) |
| None of the above | 4 (40%) | 5 (42%) |

These four examples, all using hypothetical data for illustrative purposes only, by no means exhaust the ways in which content data may be presented. They should, however, indicate that the term "quantitative" may take on many meanings, no one of which will be most suitable for every type of research. Each of the four methods used to present our findings yielded somewhat different results, although the differences are not as dramatic as they sometimes are. On occasion, two systems of enumeration will lead to diametrically opposite conclusions. Therefore, the important question for the analyst to ask himself is not: "Am I being quantitative?" but rather: "What is the theoretical relevance of the measures I am using?"

The case for designing content analysis to yield numerical data—although not necessarily solely in terms of frequency—is a powerful one. Foremost among the arguments is the degree of precision with which one's conclusions may be stated. . . .

A further advantage of quantification is that statistical methods provide a powerful set of tools not only for precise and parsimonious summary of findings, but also for improving the quality of interpretation and inference. In our hypothetical study of the Vietnam issue we might want to know if there is any relationship—and if so, how strong it is—between electoral success and a candidate's position toward American policy in Vietnam. Or, further, is the relationship maintained when we hold age, party, socio-economic, or other attributes of congressional candidates constant? Statistical techniques include a number of methods by which such questions can be answered with precision. In such a study it is also likely that we would not want to analyze all speeches for every candidate in the 435 congressional districts. But if we code only a sample of them, how much confidence can we have that the results are representative of the entire group of speeches? Statistical procedures may be used to indicate how likely we are to be correct—or conversely, what is the probability that we are wrong—when we make generalizations on the basis of a sample. In short, statistics are useful tools at many stages of research, but use of statistical methods is *not* dependent on recording the frequency with which content attributes appear, or on any other single method of enumeration.

Despite the advantages of employing quantitative methods, the tendency to equate content analysis with numerical procedures has come under criticism on a number of grounds. The most general of these is the charge that such a restriction leads to bias in the selection of problems to be investigated, undue emphasis being placed on precision at the cost of problem significance (Smythe, 1952; Barcus, 1959).

Related to this general criticism is the view that one can draw more meaningful inferences by nonquantitative methods (Kracauer, 1952). Qualitative content analysis, which has sometimes been defined as the drawing of inferences on the basis of appearance or nonappearance of attributes in messages, has been defended most often, though not solely, for its superior performance in problems of applied social science. When, for example, content from propaganda sources is used to predict enemy behavior, pressure of time, inability to control variables, and the possibility that nonrecurring phenomena may provide major clues to policy often render exhaustive quantitative analyses uneconomical and difficult to design and carry out. Citing instances in which qualitative analysts were able to draw more accurate inferences from studies of Nazi propaganda during World War II than those using quantitative techniques, A. L. George (1959, p. 7) concluded that, "Qualitative analysis of a limited number of crucial communications may often yield better clues to the particular intentions of a particular speaker at one moment in time than more standardized techniques."

In line with this reasoning, proponents of qualitative techniques also question the assumption that for purposes of inference, the frequency of an assertion is necessarily related to its importance. These critics suggest that the single appearance—or omission—of an attribute in a document may be of more significance than the relative frequency of other characteristics (George, 1959). An example of this point is found in a study of Chinese documents prior to China's active entry into the Korean war in October 1950. The change from the passive term *fan tui* to the word *k'ang yi*, previously used as an exhortation to action against Japan and against the Chinese Nationalists, provided the first clue that Chinese leaders had decided upon overt intervention in the war (Whiting, 1960, p. 99). But even studies which identify and draw inferences from the unique aspects of each document are not simply qualitative; rather than counting frequencies the analysts have chosen to formulate nominal categories into which one of two scores are recorded— present or absent. The results may then be reported quantitatively as, for example, in Table 2. . . .

Thus the content analyst should use qualitative and quantitative methods to supplement each other. It is by moving back and forth between these approaches that the investigator is most likely to gain insight into the meaning of his data. Pool (1959, p. 192) summarizes this point: "It should not be assumed that qualitative methods are insightful, and quantitative ones merely mechanical methods for checking hypotheses. The relationship is a circular one; each provides new insights on which the other can feed.". . .

## The Manifest-Latent Issue

A second major source of disagreement among those defining content analysis is whether it must be limited to *manifest* content (the surface meaning of the text) or whether it may be used to analyze the deeper layers of meaning embedded in the document. Do the requirements of objective and systematic methods restrict the analyst merely to reporting characteristics of the document, and if not, at what point in the research process may he extend his analysis to the latent meaning of the text?

The manifest-latent issue can be considered at two levels. The requirement of objectivity stipulates that only those symbols and combinations of symbols actually appearing in the message be recorded. In other words, at the *coding* stage of research, the stage at which specified words, themes, and the like are located in the text and placed into categories, one is limited to recording only those items which actually appear in the document. "Reading between the lines," so to speak, must be reserved to the interpretation stage, at which time the investigator is free to use all of his powers of imagination and intuition to draw meaningful conclusions from the data. This is vividly illustrated by the example of a mental patient who announced: "I am Switzerland" (cited in Shneidman, 1961). The inference that the patient is stating his desire for release from hospital confinement—by equating Switzerland with freedom—clearly depends on more than the lexical attributes of the sentence. But if we restrict our attention to coding operations, content analysis is limited to manifest attributes of text.

The second aspect of the manifest-latent issue concerns the *interpretation* of results. This debate is essentially one concerning the dimensions of communication which may properly be analyzed (Morris, 1946). Earlier definitions tended to limit content analysis to questions of semantics, the relationship of signs to referents, and to questions of syntactics, the relationship of signs to signs (Kaplan, 1943; Janis, 1949; Berelson, 1952). The restriction against analysis of the pragmatical dimension of language, the relationship of signs to those that produce or receive them, was usually based on the difficulty of drawing valid inferences about the causes or effects of communication directly from content data.

As has been the case in the quantitative-qualitative debate, the recent trend has been in the direction of a broader definition (Cartwright, 1953, p. 424; Barcus, 1959, p. 19). . . . The differences between the broader and more restrictive views are actually not as great as suggested at first glance. Both Kaplan (1943, p. 223) and Janis (1943, p. 437) excluded pragmatical content analysis because inferences about sources from the content of documents they write or receive can rarely be validated solely by analysis of the messages themselves. That is, inferences were limited to describing attributes of documents; inferences from content data to attributes of those who produced them or effects upon those who received them were excluded.[2] On the other hand, proponents of a broader definition generally aware of the dangers of inferring personality traits, intentions, values, motives and other characteristics of communicators without some independent sources of corroborating evidence; hence they usually assume that content analysis data will be compared, directly or indirectly, with independent (i.e., noncontent) indices of the attributes or behavior which are inferred from documents.

I propose a broad definition of the method: *Content analysis is any technique for making inferences by objectively and systematically identifying specified characteristics of messages.*[3] In somewhat more succinct form this definition incorporates the three criteria discussed earlier: content analysis must be objective and systematic, and, if it is to be distinguished from information retrieval, indexing, or similar enterprises, it must be undertaken for some theoretical reason. Our definition does not include any reference to quantification because a rigid qualitative-quantitative distinction seems unwarranted for the purposes of defining the technique, for excluding certain studies from consideration as examples of systematic analysis of documentary data, or, by itself, for praise or condemnation of content analysis. Nor do we include the stipulation that content analysis must be limited to describing the manifest characteristics of messages. It is true that only the manifest attributes of text may be coded, but this limitation is already implied by the requirement of objectivity. Inferences about the latent meanings of messages are therefore permitted, but . . . they require corroboration by independent evidence.

## Notes

1. The term "document" is used here and elsewhere in this book in the broad sense of any communication (novel, newspaper, love song, diary, diplomatic note, poem, transcribed psychiatric interview, and the like), rather than in the restricted sense (official paper) of the historian or political scientist.

2. While definitions restricting inferences from content data were widely accepted until the 1950's, many earlier studies did in fact draw conclusions, often implicitly, about the causes or effects of communication.

3. This definition was developed jointly with Philip J. Stone in conjunction with his book on computer content analysis (Stone *et al.,* 1966).

## References

BARCUS, F. E. (1959). Communications content: analysis of the research, 1900–1958. Unpublished doctor's dissertation, University of Illinois.

BERELSON, B. (1952). *Content analysis in communication research.* Glencoe, Ill.: Free Press.

CARTWRIGHT, D. P. (1953). Analysis of qualitative material. In L. Festinger and D. Katz (Eds.), *Research methods in the behavioral sciences.* New York: Holt, Rinehart, and Winston. Pp. 421–470.

ELLSWORTH, J. W. (1965). Rationality and campaigning: a content analysis of the 1960 presidential campaign debates. *Western Political Quart.,* 18, 794–802.

GEORGE, A. L. (1959). Quantitative and qualitative approaches to content analysis. In I. de S. Pool (Ed.), *Trends in content analysis.* Urbana: University of Illinois Press. Pp. 7–32.

JANIS, I. L. (1943). Meaning and the study of symbolic behavior. *Psychiatry,* 6, 425–439.

———— (1949). The problem of validating content analysis. In H. D. Lasswell, N. Leites, R. Fadner, J. M. Goldsen, A. Gray, I. L. Janis, A. Kaplan, D. Kaplan, A. Mintz, I. De Sola Pool, and S. Yakobson, *The language of politics: studies in quantitative semantics.* New York: George Stewart. Pp. 55–82.

KAPLAN, A. (1943). Content analysis and the theory of signs. *Philos. Sci.,* 10, 230–247.

KAPLAN, A., and J. M. GOLDSEN (1949). The reliability of content analysis categories. In H. D. Lasswell, N. Leites, R. Fadner, J. M. Goldsen, A. Gray, I. L. Janis, A. Kaplan, D. Kaplan, A. Mintz, I. De Sola Pool, and S. Yakobson, *The language of politics: studies in quantitative semantics.* New York: George Stewart. Pp. 83–112.

KRACAUER, S. (1952). The challenge of qualitative content analysis. *Publ. Opin. Quart.,* 16, 631–642.

KUHN, A. (1963). *The study of society: a unified approach.* Homewood, Ill.: Dorsey.

LASSWELL, H. D., D. LERNER, and I. DE S. POOL (1952). *The comparative study of symbols.* Stanford: Stanford University Press.

LEITES, N.C., and I. DE S. POOL (1942). *On content analysis.* Washington, D.C.: Library of Congress, Experimental Division for Study of War-Time Communications, Document No. 26.

MORRIS, C. W. (1946). *Signs, language, and behavior.* Englewood Cliffs, N.J.: Prentice-Hall.

OSGOOD, C. E. (1959). The representational model and relevant research methods. In I. de S. Pool (Ed.), *Trends in content analysis.* Urbana: University of Illinois Press. Pp. 33–88.

POOL, I. DE S. Ed. (1959). *Trends in content analysis.* Urbana: University of Illinois Press.

———— (1961). A psychological analysis of political thinking: the Kennedy-Nixon 'Great Debates' and the Kennedy-Khrushchev 'Grim Debates.' Cambridge: Harvard University. (Mimeo).

SMYTHE, D. W. (1952). Some observations on communication theory. *Audio-Visual Communic. Rev.,* 2, 24–37.

STONE, P. J., D. C. DUNPHY, M. S. SMITH, and D. M. OGILVIE (1966). *The General Inquirer: a computer approach to content analysis in the behavioral sciences.* Cambridge: M.I.T. Press.

WEYL, N., and S. T. POSSONY (1963), *The geography of intellect.* Chicago: Regnery.

WHITING, A. S. (1960), *China crosses the Yalu.* New York: Macmillan.

# Puritanism Revisited: An Analysis of the Contemporary Screen-Image Western

PETER HOMANS

ONE OF THE MOST NOTICEABLE characteristics of popular culture is the rapidity with which new forms are initiated and older, more familiar ones revitalized. While narrative forms of popular culture, such as the detective story, the romance, and the soap opera, have generally been less subject to sudden losses or gains in popularity, the western has within the last few years undergone a very abrupt change in this respect. Formerly associated with a dwindling audience of adolescents, who were trading in their hats and six-guns for space helmets and disintegrators, the western has quite suddenly engaged an enormous number of people, very few of whom could be called adolescent.

This new and far-reaching popularity is easily established. Whereas before, the western story was told from four to six in the afternoon, on Saturday mornings, in comic books and in some pulp fiction, now it is to be seen during the choicest television viewing hours, in a steady stream of motion pictures, and in every drug store pulp rack. At present, on television alone, more than thirty western stories are told weekly, with an estimated budget of sixty million dollars. Four of the five top nighttime shows are westerns, and of the top twenty shows, eleven are westerns. In addition to this, it is estimated that women now compose one-third of the western's heretofore male audience.

Such evidence invariably leads to attempts to explain the phenomenon. Here there has been little restraint in trying to analyse the unique status

Extract from *Studies in Public Communication* (1962), pp. 73–85. Reprinted by permission.

which the western has gained. Some have suggested that it is the modern story version of the Oedipal classic; others find it a parallel of the medieval legends of courtly love and adventure; while those enamoured of psychiatric theory see it as a form of wish-fulfillment, and "escape" from the realities of life into an over-simplified world of good and evil.

Such theories, I suppose, could be described at greater length—but not much. They not only betray a mindless, off-the-top-of-the-head superficiality; they also suffer from a deeper fault characteristic of so many of the opinions handed down today about popular culture—a two-fold reductionism which tends to rob the story of its concrete uniqueness.

This two-fold reductionism first appears as the failure to attend fully and with care the historical roots of any form. For example, to say that the western is a re-telling of chivalric tales is partly true. There is some similarity between the quest of the knight and the quest of the western hero—they both seek to destroy an evil being by force. However, the tales of chivalry grew out of medieval culture, and any effort to account for them must consider their relationship to their culture. Similarly, the western must be seen in relation to its culture—eastern American life at the turn of the century. To relate the two forms without first considering their historical contexts is what may be called historical reductionism.

The second form of reductionism is the failure of most theories to attend the unique details of the story which set it apart from prior forms. This can also be seen in the idea of chivalric tales retold. Holders of this theory notice that both heroes are engaged in a quest, the destruction of evil, and that they both earn some kind of special status in the eyes of the communities they have served. But what is not noticed is that the modern tale betrays an intense preoccupation with asceticism and colorlessness, while the medieval one dwells upon color, sensuousness, and luxury; or, that the medieval hero exemplifies tact, manners, elaborate ceremony and custom, while his modern counterpart seeks to avoid these. Again, the western rules out women; the older story would not be a story of chivalry did not women play an important part. The refusal to attend with care specific and possibly inconsequential details is a form of reductionism which may be called textual reductionism.

Both types of reductionism rob a particular form of possible uniqueness and independence. They force it to be merely a dependent function of some prior form, whatever that form may be. Together, they have become the two main errors which have obscured analysis of many present-day forms of popular culture.

However, these two foci are more than pitfalls to be avoided. The textual and historical aspects of any popular art form are the very points which should be scrutinized most carefully and elaborately. If these points are properly attended, they will yield the greatest insight into the meaning and significance of the story.

## Textual Analysis

Any effort to analyse a particular form of popular culture must begin with the problem of text. Each of us, in thinking and talking about the western, has in mind an overall understanding of it—an ordered vision of character, event, and detail shaped by all the hundreds of different versions which he has seen. Therefore, one must first set forth and defend precisely what it is he thinks the western is, before indicating what it means. Indeed, disagreements as to meaning can often be traced to disagreements as to text.

But we cannot simply lump together everything that has ever happened in every western, fearful of omitting something important. Nor can we refuse to include anything which does not appear in each and every version. For there are westerns which omit details which all critics would agree are characteristic of the story, just as there are others which include details which all would agree are of no consequence. The task consists in selecting, from the endless number of westerns we have all seen, a basic construct of narrative, character, and detail which will set forth clearly the datum for subsequent analysis. This critic's basic construct can be set forth as follows:

## Background

The western takes place in a stark, desolate, abandoned land. The desert, as a place deprived of vitality and life as we know it, is indispensable. The story would not be credible were it set in an equatorial jungle, a fertile lowland, or an arctic tundra. As the classical versions have told us again and again, the hero emerges from the desert, bearing its marks, and returns to it. Already we are instructed that our story deals with a form of existence deprived of color and vitality.

This desert effect is contradicted by the presence of a town. Jerry-built, slapped-together buildings, with falsefronts lined awkwardly along a road which is forever thick with dust or mud, tell us that the builders themselves did not expect them to endure. And of these few buildings, only three stand out as recognizable and important—the saloon, the bank, and the marshal's office (hero's dwelling). Recent westerns have added stores, court houses, homes, and even churches. But for the classical versions such contrived togetherness has never really been necessary.

The saloon is by far the most important building in the western. First of all, it is the only place in the entire story where people can be seen together time after time. It thereby performs the function of a meeting-house, social center, church, etc. More important, however, is its function as locus for the climax of the story, the gun-fight. Even in today's more fashionable westerns, which prefer main street at high noon, the gun-fight often begins in the saloon, and takes place just outside it. . . .

The town as a whole has no business or industry. People have money, but we rarely see them make it. And we are not concerned as to how they got their money—unless they stole it. This town and its citizens lead a derivative, dependent existence, serving activities which originate and will continue outside the town. It is expendable, and will disappear as soon as the activities it serves no longer exist.

Home life, like economic life, is conspicuous by its absence. There simply are no homes, families, domestic animals, or children. The closest thing to a home is a hotel, and this is rarely separated from the saloon. Recent westerns have included homes, along with cozy vignettes of hearth, wife, kitchen, etc. Such innovations do little more than indicate how harassed script writers have become, for these scenes do not contribute to the basic action and imagery of the story. Classically, home life in the western simply isn't.

## Supporting People

As in any good form of popular culture, the number of important people is small. Such people I prefer to call "types." A type is an important figure recurring again and again, whose basic actions and patterns of relationship are relatively enduring from one version of the story to another. The particular vocation, clothing, mannerisms, personal plans, names, are all conventions— concessions to plausibility—which seemingly identify as new someone we know we've seen before. Such conventions I would like to call "role." When we refer to a particular person in a story with the preface "the"—e.g., "the" hero, or "the" good girl—we have penetrated beyond the role and identified a type.

One of the most interesting types is the "derelict-professional." He is one who was originally trained in one of the traditional eastern professions (Law, Medicine, Letters, Ministry), but who has, since his arrival in the west, become corrupted by such activities as drink, gambling, sex, or violence. Most celebrated is Doc Holliday, who trained in the east as a dentist, then came west to practice medicine whenever he was sober enough to do so. The derelict-professional sometimes appears as a judge or lawyer; sometimes as an ex-writer; in other instances he is a gun-toting preacher. The point is the same: the traditional resources of society (healer, teacher, shepherd, counselor) cannot exist in a uncorrupted state under the pressures of western life.[1] Other types include: the "non-violent easterner," the "good girl," the "bad girl," the "attendant" and "the boys.". . .

## Principals and Action

The action of the screen-image western takes place in three phases: the opening, the action, and closing phases; or, everything before the fight, the fight, and everything after the fight.

The opening phase first of all introduces us to the story's setting, to the supporting types (through their roles) and principals. In doing so, however, it not only supplies us with information, but also provides the very important illusion that we are to see for the first time something which we know, in the back of our heads, we have seen many times before. It is important to believe that we are not idiots, watching the same story night after night.

Secondly, the opening phase prepares us for the action by delineating the hero. He is, first of all, a transcendent figure, originating beyond the town. Classically, he rides into town from nowhere; even if he is the marshal, his identity is in some way dissociated from the people he must save. We know nothing of any past activities, relationships, future plans, or ambitions. Indeed, the hero is himself often quite ambiguous about these. There are no friends, relatives, family, mistresses—not even a dog or cat—with the exception of the horse, and this too is a strangely formal relationship.

His appearance further supports this image. In the pre-action phase the hero sets forth a contrived indolence, barely distinguishable from sloth. Lax to the point of laziness, there appears to be nothing directional or purposeful about him. Take that hat, for instance: it sits exactly where it was placed— no effort has been made to align it. His horse is tied to whatever happens to protrude from the ground—and remains tied, although little more than a lazy nod would free it. Clothes and gunbelt also betray the absence of any effort towards arrangement and order. With feet propped up on the hitching rail, frame balanced on a chair or stool tilted back on its two rear legs, hat pushed slightly over the eyes, hands clasped over the buckle of his gunbelt, the hero is a study in contrived indolence.

I have used the word "contrived" to indicate another quality—that of discipline and control—which remains latent, being obscured by apparent laxity. His indolence is merely superficial, and serves to protect and undergird the deeper elements of control which will appear in the action phase. Now he has time on his hands; but he knows his time is coming, and so do we.

The hero's coupling of laxity and control is seen in those recurrent primary images which are ordinarily referred to simply as "typical scenes." With women there is no desire or attraction. He appears somewhat bored with the whole business, as if it were in the line of duty. He never blushes, or betrays any enthusiasm; he never rages or raves over a woman. His monosyllabic stammer and brevity of speech clearly indicate an intended indifference. In the drinking scenes we are likely to see him equipped with the traditional shot-glass and bottle. The latter becomes his personal property, and therefore he is never questioned as to how many drinks he has taken. We rarely see him pay for more than one. While drinking he usually stares gloomily at the floor, or at all the other gloomy people who are staring gloomily at each other. He gulps his drink, rarely enjoys it, and is impatient to be off, on his way, hurrying to a place we are never told about. In the gambling scenes his poker face is to cards what his gloomy stare was to drink—a mask serving to veil any inner feelings of greed, enthusiasm, fear, or apprehension. We note, however, that he always wins, or else refuses to play. Similarly, he is utterly unimpressed and indifferent to money, regardless of its quantity or source, although the unguarded bank is always just around the corner.

The action phase opens with the threat of evil, and extends up to its destruction at the hands of the hero. Although evil is most often referred to as the "villain" or "bad guy" or "heavy," I prefer the terms "evil one" or "adversary."

Of the many hundreds of seemingly different versions, each is unshaven, darkly clothed, and from the west. Little is known about him. We are not told of his origins, his relationships, habits, or customs. Like the hero, he is from beyond the town, rather than identified with the interests, problems, and resources which characterize it. All details of his personal life are withheld. We can only be sure that the evil one unhesitatingly involves himself in the following activities: gambling, drink, the accumulation of money, lust and violence. They are his vocation; with respect to these, he is a professional man. It should be noted, however, that he is inclined to cheat at cards, get drunk, lust after women who do not return the compliment, rob banks, and finally, to shooting people he does not care for, especially heroes.

The impact of this evil one on the town is electric, as though a switch had been thrown, suddenly animating it with vitality, purpose, and direction. Indeed, it is evil, rather than good, which actually gives meaning to the lives of these people—his presence elicits commitment to a cause. The townsfolk now share a new identity: they are "those who are threatened by the evil one." Unified by a common threat, the town loses its desolate, aimless quality. It becomes busy. Some hasten to protect others; some to protect themselves; some run for help; some comment fearfully. Nevertheless, they all know (as do we) that they are of themselves ultimately powerless to meet this evil. What is required is the hero—a transcendent power originating from beyond the town.

Notice what has happened to this power. Gone are the indolence, laxity, and lack of intention. Now he is infused with vitality, direction, and seriousness. Before, the most trivial item might have caught his attention; now, every prior loyalty and concern are thoroughly excluded—he drops everything—in order that the may confront with passion and single-mindedness this ultimate threat. Once this radical shift has been accomplished, the hero (and audience) are ready for the final conflict—the central part of the action phase, the climax of the story.

While the fight can take many forms (fist-fight, fight with knives, whips, etc.—even a scowling match in which the hero successfully glares down the evil one), the classical and most popular form is the encounter with six-guns. It is a built-up and drawn-out affair, always allowing enough time for an audience to gather. The two men must adhere to an elaborate and well-defined casuistry as to who draws first, when it is proper to draw, when it is not, etc. The climax also reflects much of the craft of gunplay, of which both hero and evil one are the skilled artisans (cross-draw versus side-draw, fanning versus thumbing, whether two guns are really better than one, etc.). While these issues are certainly not the main concern of the action, the prominence given them by the story as a whole tends to prolong the climax.

Although the hero's presence usually makes the fight possible—i.e., he insists on obstructing the evil one in some way—it is the latter who invariably attacks first. Were the hero ever to draw first, the story would no longer be a western. Regardless of the issues involved, or of the moral responsibility for what is to follow, the hero's final, victorious shot is always provoked by the evil one. With the destruction of the evil one, the action phase is completed.

In the closing phase the town and its hero return to their pre-action ways. The electric quality of alarm and the sense of purpose and direction recede. People come out of hiding to acclaim their hero and enjoy his victory. He too returns to his pre-action mode of indolence and laxity. At such a moment he is likely to become immediately absorbed in some unimportant detail (like blowing the smoke from his gun), indicating for all to see that he has survived the crisis and is once again his old self.

One more event must take place, however, before the story can conclude. The hero must renounce any further involvement with the town which his victory may have suggested. In some way the town offers him the opportunity to identify with it, to settle down. Traditionally, this means marrying the schoolmarm and settling down. The hero always refuses. He cannot identify himself with the situation he has saved. He forfeits any opportunity to renounce his "beyond the town" origin and destiny. When this forfeiture has been made clear, when both savior and saved realize that it cannot be abrogated, then the story is over.

## Analysis

The western is, as most people by this time are willing to acknowledge, a popular myth. And by myth I mean three things. First of all, it is a story whose basic patterns of character, plot, and detail are repeated again and again, and can be so recognized. Secondly, the story embodies and sets forth certain meanings about what is good and bad, right and wrong—meanings regarded as important by those who view and participate in the myth. And thirdly, some of these meanings are veiled by the story,[2] so that one can affirm them without overtly acknowledging them. Some part of the story (or all of it, perhaps) serves to conceal something from the participant— i.e., there is an unacknowledged aspect to the story. There is, therefore, an

embarassing question which never occurs to those in the sway of the myth—
the posing of which is precisely the critic's most important task.

The meanings which the western sets forth center upon the problem of
good and evil. Evil, according to the myth, is the failure to resist temptation.
It is loss of control. Goodness lies in the power and willingness to resist
temptation. It is the ability to remain in the presence of temptation and
yet remain in control of one's desire. Five activities make up the well-known
content of temptation: drinking, gambling, money, sex, and violence.

Whenever any one of these activities appears it should be seen as a self-
contained temptation episode.[3] Such an episode first of all presents an object
of temptation which can be indulged, should the hero so choose; and secondly,
it sets forth the hero in such a way that he can indulge the temptation in
a preliminary way without becoming absorbed in it—i.e., without losing control. And, of course, it sets forth the evil one in precisely the opposite way.

In the drinking scenes the hero possesses not one drink, but a whole
bottle—i.e., he has at his disposal the opportunity for unlimited indulgence
and its consequent loss of self-control. Gambling is a situation over which
one has rather limited control—you can lose; but the hero does not lose.
He wins, thereby remaining in control (cheating simply signifies the failure
to acknowledge loss of control). Wealth is not seized although it is available
to him through the unguarded bank; and both good and bad girl seek out
the hero in their various ways, but to no avail—he remains a hero. However,
each temptation is presented in its peculiar way in order to set forth hero
and evil one in their respective functions.

The temptation to do violence is more problematic, so much more so
that the climax is given over to its solution. Furthermore, in the climax we
find the key to the meaning of the myth as a whole—i.e., it can tell us
why each type appears as he does, why the temptation episodes have their
unique shape, and why certain fundamental images recur as they do.

We perceive in the evil one a terrible power, one which cannot be overcome
by the ordinary resources of the town. However, he has acquired this power
at great price: he has forfeited that very control and resistance which sustains
and makes the hero what he is. The evil one represents, therefore, not temptation, so much as "temptation-unhesitatingly-given-into." He is the embodiment of the failure to resist temptation; he is the failure of denial. This is
the real meaning of evil in the myth of the western, and it is this which
makes the evil one truly evil. Because of this he threatens the hero's resistance
(and that of the townsfolk, as well, although indirectly): each taunt and
baiting gesture is a lure to the forfeiture of control. This temptation the
hero cannot handle with the usual methods of restraint, control, and the
refusal to become absorbed; and it leads to a temptation which the hero
cannot afford to resist: the temptation to destroy temptation.

The evil one's dark appearance is related to this threat. It tells us two
things. First, that to lose control and forfeit resistance is (according to the

story) a kind of living death, for black signifies death. In terms of the moral instruction of the story, and speaking metaphorically, we know that the evil one has "lost his life." But his black appearance also tells us that, speaking quite literally, this man will die—because of what he is, he must and will be executed. We are therefore both instructed and reassured.

The embarrassing question can now be posed: why must the hero wait to be attacked, why must he refrain from drawing first? Why does he not take his opponent from behind, while he is carousing, or while he is asleep? Anyone in the power of the myth would reply that the gunfight takes place the way it does because this is the way westerns are; it's natural; this is the way it's always done—or, in the language of the myth itself, it was self-defense. But if one moves beyond the grasp of the myth, if one is no longer loyal to its rules and values, the gunfight is never inevitable. The circumstances which force the hero into this situation are contrived in order to make the violent destruction of the evil one appear just and virtuous. These circumstances have their origin in the inner, veiled need to which the story is addressed. This process, whereby desire is at once indulged and veiled I call the "inner dynamic." It is the key to the western, explaining not only the climax of the story, but everything else uniquely characteristic of it. What is required is that temptation be indulged while providing the appearance of having been resisted.

Each of the minor temptation episodes—the typical scenes setting forth hero and evil one as each encounters drink, cards, money, and sex—takes its unique shape from this need. Each is a climax-less western in itself, a play within a play in which temptation is faced and defeated, not by violent destruction, as in the climax, but by inner, willed control. Or, reversing the relationship, we may say that in the gunfight we have writ large something which takes place again and again throughout the story. It is precisely for this reason that no western has or needs to have all these episodes. Therefore westerns can and do depart radically from the composite picture described earlier. We are so familiar with each kind of temptation, and each so re-enforces the others that extraordinary deletions and variations can occur without our losing touch with the central meanings.

The inner dynamic affects the supporting types as well. The derelict-professional is derelict, and the non-violent easterner is weak, precisely because they have failed to resist temptation in the manner characteristic of the hero. Their moderate, controlled indulgence of the various temptations does not conform to the total resistance of the hero. Consequently they must be portrayed as derelict, weak and deficient men, contrasting unfavorably with the hero's virtue. In this sense they have more in common with the evil one.

Because these two types both originate in the east, they have something in common with the good girl. We note that everything eastern in the western is considered weak, emotional, and feminine (family life, intellectual life, domestic life, professional life). Only by becoming western-ized can the east be redeemed. The western, therefore, is more a myth about the east than it is about the west: it is a secret and bitter parody of eastern ways. This is all the more interesting, since it was originally written in the east, by easterners, for eastern reading. It really has very little to do with the west.

Woman is split in the western to correspond to the splitting of man into hero and evil one. Primarily, however, the double feminine image permits the hero some gratification of desire while making a stalemate ultimately necessary. To get the good girl, the story instructs us, our hero would have to become like those despicable easterners; to get the bad girl, he would have to emulate the evil one. In such a dilemma a ride into the sunset is not such a bad solution after all.

The attendant sets forth the inner dynamic by being infinitely close to the action (temptations) while never becoming at all involved in it. It is his task to provide the instruments of temptation (drink, money, cards, guns) while never indulging them himself. He is at once closer to temptation than any other type, and yet more removed than any other type.

The boys function to facilitate the action without becoming involved in it. Without them hero and adversary might find other ways to settle their differences. The boys serve to remind them of their obligations to each other and the story as a whole, thereby structuring the myth more firmly. While they are around nothing less than the traditional gunfight will do. On the other hand, because they never participate in the action, but only coerce and re-enforce it, they are thoroughly resistant to this temptation as well.

In summary, then: the western is a myth in which evil appears as a series of temptations to be resisted by the hero—most of which he succeeds in avoiding through inner control. When faced with the embodiment of these temptations, his mode of control changes, and he destroys the threat. But the story is so structured that the responsibility for this act falls upon the adversary, permitting the hero to destroy while appearing to save. Types and details, as well as narrative, take their shape from the inner dynamic, which must therefore be understood as the basic organizing and interpretive principle for the myth as a whole.

# Notes

1. Such TV versions as *Frontier Doctor* (Medicine), *Jefferson Drum* (Letters) and *Black Saddle* (Law) do not contradict this thesis, although they set forth professional men from the east who are hardly derelict. Close attention, however, reveals a "past" of questionable nature which these men are trying to conceal, but which is always being threatened by exposure. Such figures might best be called "covert" derelict-professionals.

2. This point is drawn from DeRougemont's analysis of the myth of Tristan and Isolde. See Denis DeRougemont, *Love in the Western World*, New York: Pantheon Press, 1956.

3. I am not suggesting that every western has all of these temptations, or that they appear in any given order. The subject of analysis is the representative version—not any particular version or set of versions. Thus any particular western might deal with any one, or a number of such temptations.

# Living with Television: The Violence Profile

GEORGE GERBNER
LARRY GROSS

THE ENVIRONMENT THAT SUSTAINS the most distinctive aspects of human existence is the environment of symbols. We learn, share, and act upon meanings derived from that environment. The first and longest lasting organization of the symbolic world was what we now call religion. Within its sacred scope, in earlier times, were the most essential processes of culture: art, science, technology, statecraft, and public story-telling.

Common rituals and mythologies are agencies of symbolic socialization and control. They demonstrate how society works by dramatizing its norms and values. They are essential parts of the general system of messages that cultivates prevailing outlooks (which is why we call it culture) and regulates social relationships. This system of messages, with its story-telling functions, makes people perceive as real and normal and right that which fits the established social order.

The institutional processes producing these message systems have become increasingly professionalized, industrialized, centralized, and specialized. Their principal locus shifted from handicraft to mass production and from traditional religion and formal education to the mass media of communications—particularly television. New technologies on the horizon may enrich the choices of the choosy but cannot replace the simultaneous public experience of a common symbolic environment that now binds diverse communities,

Extract from George Gerbner and Larry Gross, "Living with Television: The Violence Profile," *Journal of Communication,* Spring 1976, Vol. 26:2, pp. 173–199. Later findings and figures are taken from George Gerbner, Larry Gross, Michael Morgan, and Nancy Signorielli, "The 'Mainstreaming' of America: Violence Profile No. 11," *Journal of Communication,* Summer 1980, Vol. 30:3. Reprinted by permission.

including large groups of young and old and isolated people who have never before joined any mass public. Television is likely to remain for a long time the chief source of repetitive and ritualized symbol systems cultivating the common consciousness of the most far-flung and heterogenous mass publics in history.

Our long-range study of this new symbolic environment developed from, and still includes, the annual Violence Index and Profile of TV content and its correlates in viewers' conceptions of relevant aspects of social reality. . . . The pattern of findings that is beginning to emerge confirms our belief that television is essentially different from other media and that research on television requires a new approach. In this article we shall sketch the outlines of a critique of modes of research derived from experience with other media and advance an approach we find more appropriate to the special characteristics, features, and functions of television. . . .

We begin with the assertion that television is the central cultural arm of American society. It is an agency of the established order and as such serves primarily to extend and maintain rather than to alter, threaten, or weaken conventional conceptions, beliefs, and behaviors. Its chief cultural function is to spread and stabilize social patterns, to cultivate not change but resistance to change. Television is a medium of the socialization of most people into standardized roles and behaviors. Its function is, in a word, enculturation.

The substance of the consciousness cultivated by TV is not so much specific attitudes and opinions as more basic assumptions about the "facts" of life and standards of judgment on which conclusions are based. The purpose of the Cultural Indicators project is to identify and track these premises and the conclusions they might cultivate across TV's diverse publics. . . .

Never before have all classes and groups (as well as ages) shared so much of the same culture and the same perspectives while having so little to do with their creation. Representation in the world of television gives an idea, a cause, a group its sense of public identity, importance, and relevance. No movement can get going without some visibility in that world or long withstand television's power to discredit, insulate, or undercut. Other media, used selectively and by special interests or cultural elites, cultivate partial and parochial outlooks. Television spreads the same images and messages to all from penthouse to tenement. TV is the new (and only) culture of those who expose themselves to information only when it comes as "entertainment." Entertainment is the most broadly effective educational fare in any culture.

All major networks serving the same social system depend on the same markets and programming formulas. That may be one reason why, unlike other media, television is used non-selectively: it just doesn't matter that much. With the exception of national events and some "specials," the total viewing audience is fairly stable regardless of what is on. Individual tastes and program preferences are less important in determining viewing patterns than is the time a program is on. The nearly universal, non-selective, and habitual use of television fits the ritualistic pattern of its programming. You watch television as you might attend a church service, except that most people watch television more religiously. . . .

These considerations led us to question many of the more common arguments raised in discussions of television's effects. An important example is the concern over the consequences of violence on television. The invention and development of technologies which permit the production and dissemination of mass mediated fictional images across class lines seems invariably to raise in the minds of the established classes the specter of subversion, corruption and unrest being encouraged among the various lower orders— poor people, ethnic and racial minorities, children and women. The specter arises when it seems that the lower orders may presume to imitate—if not to replace—their betters. Whether the suspect and controversial media are newspapers, novels, and theater, as in the nineteenth century, or movies, radio, comic books, and television as in the twentieth, concern tends to focus on the possibilities of disruption that threaten the established norms of belief, behavior, and morality.

In our view, however, that concern has become anachronistic. Once the industrial order has legitimized its rule, the primary function of its cultural arm becomes the reiteration of that legitimacy and the maintenance of established power and authority. The rules of the games and the morality of its goals can best be demonstrated by dramatic stories of their symbolic violations. The intended lessons are generally effective and the social order is only rarely and peripherally threatened. The *system* is the message and, as our politicans like to say, the system works. Our question is, in fact, whether it may not work too well in cultivating uniform assumptions, exploitable fears, acquiescence to power, and resistance to meaningful change.

Therefore, in contrast to the more usual statement of the problem, we do not believe that the only critical correlate of television violence is to be found in the stimulation of occasional individual aggression. The consequences of living in a symbolic world ruled largely by violence may be much more far-reaching. . . . TV violence is a dramatic demonstration of power which communicates much about social norms and relationships, about goals and means, about winners and losers, about the risks of life and the price for transgressions of society's rules. Violence laden drama shows who gets away with what, when, why, how and against whom. "Real world" *victims* as well as violents may have to learn their roles. Fear—that historic instrument of social control—may be an even more critical residue of a show of violence than aggression. Expectation of violence or passivity in the face of injustice may be consequences of even greater social concern. We shall return to this theme with data from our studies.

The realism of TV fiction hides its synthetic and functionally selective nature. The dominant stylistic convention of Western narrative art—novels, plays, films, TV dramas—is that of representational realism. However contrived television plots are, viewers assume that they take place against a backdrop of the real world. Nothing impeaches the basic "reality" of the world of television drama. It is also highly informative. That is, it offers to the unsuspecting viewer a continuous stream of "facts" and impressions about the way of the world, about the constancies and vagaries of human nature, and about the consequences of actions. The premise of realism is a Trojan horse which carries within it a highly selective, synthetic, and purposeful image of the facts of life.

A normal adult viewer is not unaware of the fictiveness of television drama. No one calls the police or an ambulance when a character in a television program is shot. "War of the Worlds"-type scares are rare, if they occur at all. Granting this basic awareness on the part of the viewers, one may still wonder how often and to what degree all viewers suspend their disbelief in the reality of the symbolic world.

Surely we all know that Robert Young is not a doctor and that Marcus Welby is an M.D. by only poetic license. Yet according to the Philadelphia Bulletin (July 10, 1974) in the first five years of the program "Dr. Welby" received over a quarter of a million letters from viewers, most containing requests for medical advice. . . .

Anecdotes and examples should not trivialize the real point, which is that even the most sophisticated can find many important components of their knowledge of the real world derived wholly or in part from fictional representation. How often do we make a sharp distinction between the action which we know is not "real" and the accumulation of background information (which is, after all, "realistic")? Are we keenly aware that in the total population of the television world men outnumber women four to one? Or that, with all the violence, the leading causes of real life injury and death—industrial and traffic accidents—are hardly ever depicted?

How many of us have ever been in an operating room, a criminal courtroom, a police station or jail, a corporate board room, or a movie studio? How much of what we know about such diverse spheres of activity, about how various kinds of people work and what they do—how much of our real world has been learned from fictional worlds? To the extent that viewers see television drama—the foreground of plot or the background of the television world—as naturalistic, they may derive a wealth of incidental "knowledge." This incidental learning may be effected by bald "facts" and by the subtle interplay of occurrence, co-occurrence, and non-occurrence of actors and actions.

In addition to the subtle patterns against whose influence we may all be somewhat defenseless, television provides another seductively persuasive sort of imagery. In real life much is hidden from our eyes. Often, motives are obscure, outcomes ambiguous, personalities complex, people unpredictable. The truth is never pure and rarely simple. The world of television, in contrast, offers us cogency, clarity, and resolution. Unlike life, television is an open book. Problems are never left hanging, rewards and punishments are present and accounted for. The rules of the game are known and rarely change. Not only does television "show" us the normally hidden workings of many important and fascinating institutions—medicine, law enforcement and justice, big business, the glamorous world of entertainment, etc.—but we "see" the people who fill important and exciting roles. We see who they are in terms of sex, age, race, and class and we also see them as personalities— dedicated and selfless, ruthless and ambitious, good-hearted but ineffectual, lazy and shiftless, corrupt and corrupting. Television provides the broadest common background of assumptions not only about what things are but also about how they work, or should work, and why. . . .

The implications for research are far-reaching and call into question essential aspects of the research paradigm stemming from historic pressures for behavior manipulation and marketing efficacy. They suggest a model based on the concept of broad enculturation rather than of narrow changes in opinion or behavior. Instead of asking what communication "variables" might propagate what kinds of individual behavior changes, we want to know what types of common consciousness whole systems of messages might cultivate. This is less like asking about preconceived fears and hopes and more like asking about the "effects" of Christianity on one's view of the world or— as the Chinese *had* asked—of Confucianism on public morality. . . .

How should, then, the effects of television be conceptualized and studied? We believe that the key to the answer rests in a search for those assumptions about the "facts" of life and society that television cultivates in its more faithful viewers. That search requires two different methods of research. The relationship between the two is one of the special characteristics of the Cultural Indicators approach.

The first method of research is the periodic analysis of large and representative aggregates of television output (rather than individual segments) as the system of messages to which total communities are exposed. The purpose of message system analysis is to establish to composition and structure of the symbolic world. We have begun that analysis with the most ubiquitous, translucent, and instructive part of television (or any cultural) fare, the dramatic programs (series, cartoons, movies on television) that populate and animate for most viewers the heartland of the symbolic world. Instead of guessing or assuming the contours and dynamics of that world, message system analysis maps its geography, demography, thematic and action structure, time and space dimensions, personality profiles, occupations, and fates. Message system analysis yields the gross but clear terms of location, action, and characterization discharged into the mainstream of community consciousness. Aggregate viewer interpretation and response starts with these common terms of basic exposure.

The second step of the research is to determine what, if anything, viewers absorb from living in the world of television. Cultivation analysis, as we call that method, inquires into the assumptions television cultivates about the facts, norms, and values of society. Here we turn the findings of message system analysis about the fantasy land of television into questions about social reality. To each of these questions there is a "television answer," which is like the way things appear in the world of television, and another and different answer which is biased in the opposite direction, closer to the way things are in the observable world. We ask these questions of samples of adults and children. All responses are related to television exposure, other media habits, and demographic characteristics. We then compare the response of light and heavy viewers controlling for sex, age, education, and other characteristics. The margin of heavy viewers over light viewers giving the "television answers" within and across groups is the "cultivation differential" indicating conceptions about social reality that viewing tends to cultivate.

Our analysis looks at the contribution of TV drama to viewer conceptions in conjunction with such other sources of knowledge as education and news. The analysis is intended to illuminate the complementary as well as the divergent roles of these sources of facts, images, beliefs, and values in the cultivation of assumptions about reality.

We shall now sketch some general features of the world of network television drama. . . . As any mythical world, television presents a selective and functional system of messages. Its time, space, and motion—even its "accidents"—follow laws of dramatic convention and social utility. Its people are not born but are created to depict social types, causes, powers, and fates. The economics of the assembly line and the requirement of wide acceptability assure general adherence to common notions of justice and fair play, clear-cut characterizations, tested plot lines, and proven formulas for resolving all issues.

Representation in the fictional world signifies social existence: absence means symbolic annihilation. Being buffeted by events and victimized by people denotes social impotence; ability to wrest events about, to act freely, boldly, and effectively is a mark of dramatic importance and social power. Values and forces come into play through characterizations; good is a certain type of attractiveness, evil is a personality defect, and right is the might that wins. Plots weave a thread of causality into the fabric of dramatic ritual, as stock characters act out familiar parts and confirm preferred notions of what's what, who's who, and who counts for what. The issue is rarely in doubt; the action is typically a game of social typing, group identification, skill, and power.

Many times a day, seven days a week, the dramatic pattern defines situations and cultivates premises about society, people, and issues. Casting the symbolic world thus has a meaning of its own: the lion's share of representation goes to the types that dominate the social order. About three-quarters of all leading characters are male, American, middle- and upper-class, and in the prime of life. Symbolic independence requires freedom relatively uninhabited by real-life constraints. Less fully represented are those lower in the domestic and global power hierarchy and characters involved in familiar social contexts, human dependencies, and other situations that impose the real-life burdens of human relationships and obligations upon freewheeling activity.

Women typically represent romantic or family interest, close human contact, love. Males can act in nearly any role, but rare is the female part that does not involve at least the suggestion of sex. While only one in three male leads is shown as intending to or ever having been married, two of every three females are married or expect to marry in the story. Female "specialties" limit the proportion of TV's women to about one-fourth of the total population.

Nearly half of all females are concentrated in the most sexually eligible young adult population, to which only one-fifth of males are assigned; women are also disproportionately represented among the very young and old. Children, adolescents, and old people together account for less than 15 percent of the total fictional population.

Approximately five in ten characters can be unambiguously identifed as gainfully employed. Of these, three are proprietors, managers, and professionals. The fourth comes from the ranks of labor—including all those employed in factories, farms, offices, shops, stores, mining, transportation, service stations, restaurants, and households, and working in unskilled, skilled, clerical, sales, and domestic service capacities. The fifth serves to enforce the law or preserve the peace on behalf of public or private clients.

Types of activity—paid and unpaid—also reflect dramatic and social purposes. Six in ten characters are engaged in discernible occupational activity and can be roughly divided into three groups of two each. The first group represents the world of legitimate private business, industry, agriculture, finance, etc. The second group is engaged in activity related to art, science, religion, health, education, and welfare, as professionals, amateurs, patients, students, or clients. The third makes up the forces of official or semiofficial authority and the army of criminals, outlaws, spies, and other enemies arrayed against them. One in every four leading characters acts out a drama of some sort of transgression and its suppression at home and abroad.

Violence plays a key role in such a world. It is the simplest and cheapest dramatic means available to demonstrate the rules of the game of power. In real life much violence is subtle, slow, circumstantial, invisible, even impersonal. Encounters with physical violence in real life are rare, more sickening than thrilling. But in the symbolic world, overt physical motion makes dramatically visible that which in the real world is usually hidden. Symbolic violence, as any show of force, typically does the job of real violence more cheaply and, of course, entertainingly.

Geared for independent action in loosely-knit and often remote social contexts, half of all characters are free to engage in violence. One-fifth "specialize" in violence as law breakers or law enforcers. Violence on television, unlike in real-life, rarely stems from close personal relationships. Most of it is between strangers, set up to drive home lessons of social typing. Violence is often just a specialty—a skill, a craft, an efficient means to test the norms of and settle any challenge to the existing structure of power.

The Violence Profile is a set of indicators tracing aspects of the television world and of conceptions of social reality they tend to cultivate in the minds of viewers. Four specific types of indicators have been developed. Three come from message system analysis: (1) the context of programming trends against which any aspect of the world of television can be seen; (2) several specific measures of violence given separately and also combined in the Violence Index; and (3) structural characteristics of the dramatic world indicating social relationships depicted in it (in the present report, "risk ratios"). The fourth type of indicator comes from cultivation analysis and shows conceptions of reality related to television viewing. Although the Violence Profile is the most developed, the Cultural Indicators project is constructing similar profiles of other aspects and relationships of the media world. . . .

Message system analysis has been performed on annual sample-weeks of prime time and weekend daytime network dramatic programming since 1967 by trained analysts who observe and code many aspects of TV content. The definition of violence employed in this analysis is "the overt expression of physical force against self or other compelling action against one's will on pain of being hurt or killed, or actually hurting or killing." The research focuses on a clear-cut and commonly understood definition of violence, and yields indicators of trends in the programming context in which violence

**FIGURE 1.  Violence Index in Children's and Prime Time Programming, 1967–1979**

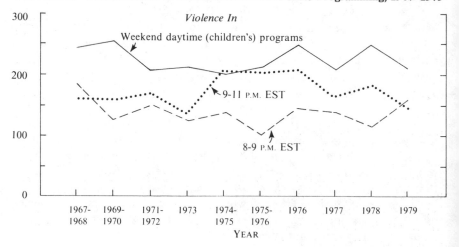

**FIGURE 2.  Violence Index by Network 1967–1979**

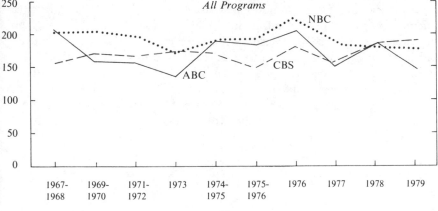

YEAR

occurs; in the prevalence, rate, and characterizations involved in violence; and in the power relationships expressed by the differential risks found in the world of television drama. . . .

The Violence Index combines three sets of observations, measuring the extent to which violence occurs in the programs, its frequency and rate per program and per hour, and the number of roles calling for characterization as violents, victims, or both. The most noteworthy characteristic of trends shown in Figure 1 is their stability. Network differences, shown in Figure 2, are negligible. . . .

The indicators reflected in the Violence Index are clear manifestations of what network programmers actually do as compared to what they say or intend to do. Network executives and their censorship ("Standards and Practices") offices maintain close control over the assembly line production process that results in the particular program mix of a season. While our data permit many specific qualifications to any generalization that might be made, it is safe to say that network policy seems to have responded in narrow terms, when at all, to very specific pressure, and only while the heat was on. After many years of investigations, hearings, and commissions (or since we have been tracking violence on television), seven out of every ten programs (nine out of every ten weekend children's hour programs) still contain some violence. The prime time rate of violent episodes is 6 per hour and the weekend daytime rate is 17 per hour. . . . Overall, about two thirds of the men and half of the women characters (but a much higher percentage in children's programs) have been involved in violence each year since 1969. When involved, women are more likely than men to be the victims of violence. Those cast in minority roles are especially more likely to be shown suffering rather than inflicting violence. . . .

It is clear, at least to us, that deeply rooted sociocultural forces, rather than just obstinacy or profit-seeking, are at work. We have suggested earlier in this article, and have also developed elsewhere, that symbolic violence is a demonstration of power and an instrument of social control serving, on the whole, to reinforce and preserve the existing social order, even if at an ever increasing price in terms of pervasive fear and mistrust and of selective aggressiveness. That maintenance mechanism seems to work through cultivating a sense of danger, a differential calculus of the risks of life in different groups in the population. The Violence Profile is beginning to yield indicators of such a mechanism, and thereby also a theory of basic structural and cultivation characteristics of television. . . .

# Assessing the Violence Profile Studies of Gerbner and Gross: A Humanistic Critique and Suggestion

HORACE NEWCOMB

MORE THAN ANY OTHER research effort in the area of television studies the work of Gerbner and Gross and their associates sits squarely at the juncture of the social sciences and the humanities. Nowhere is this better illustrated than in their article, "Living With Television: The Violence Profile" (1976). . . . There it is clear that the broad concern with violence might be defined in social scientific terms as a "social problem." But the definitions of what television is, how it works in American culture, and how culture itself works, are humanistic in nature. One might wish to quarrel with the inclusion of a view that is essentially anthropological in the domain of the humanities, but the particular approach to culture outlined by Gerbner and Gross places them in the humanistic camp among various anthropological positions. . . .

The intention of this essay is to analyze from a humanistic point of view some of the basic assumptions, definitions, assertions, and arguments in the Violence Profile studies. I should say here that I focus on the Gerbner–Gross studies not only because of their prominence, but because they have been open and forthright in their use of mixed methods of analysis and in their call for the development of new techniques of study appropriate for a

"Assessing the Violence Profile Studies of Gerbner and Gross: A Humanistic Critique and Suggestion," by Horace Newcomb, is reprinted from *Communication Research* Vol. 5, No. 3 (July 1978), pp. 264–282, by permission of the Publisher, Sage Publications, Inc.

new medium. Almost all social scientific studies are at times involved in complex interpretive issues, and many are far more veiled in these steps, or are unwilling to admit to the complexities involved. But the question, "What does it all *mean*?" is, essentially, a humanistic question. Gerbner and Gross have taught us that we shall have to be open to many methodologies in answering that question for television. Indeed, what their work often demonstrates is that rigid distinctions between humanistic and social scientific questions may be useless in this area. . . .

That Gerbner and Gross have a strong basis on which to converse with the humanistic disciplines is clear from their definition of television as an object of study (p. 241). . . .

From that humanistic perspective, from that part of it that has been involved with the study of television formulas rather than with the significance of individual programs, the most significant contribution of the Gerbner-Gross projects has been the careful mapping of television's social world. It is crucial to know the details of, rather than intuit patterns in, that world. For instance, our "sense" that there is a television "type" is made far more definite when we can point to the fact that "while only one in three male leads is shown as intending to or ever having been married, two of every three females are married or expect to marry in the story," or that "nearly half of all females are concentrated in the most sexually eligible young adult population, to which only one-fifth of males are assigned." We feel familiar with, and much more sure of generalizations based upon the observation that "children, adolescents, and old people together account for less than 15 percent of the total fictional populations" (p. 247). Similar statistical definition regarding employment patterns, types of activity, racial demography, and social class add up to a fictional world that is not in any sense a reflection of the statistical patterns of American society as television viewers experience it. Because of this work the specific content of that "environment of symbols" is made far more precise. Such careful work is rarely offered by humanists. Too often we have assumed that significant patterns observed and subjectively marked by trained analysts are equally obvious to viewers. We have asserted our own responses as generalizations. The Annenberg studies offer far more precise indications of the relationship of the "world" of TV fictions to the world of experience.

A strain on this synthesis of the humanities and the social sciences begins to develop, however, when it becomes necessary to interpret this environment of symbols. That strain can be illustrated by focusing on a series of assumptions and assertions about how television works, how viewers perceive it, and what, finally, the symbols mean. Ultimately the strain is sufficient to cause us to return to the initial definition of "symbol" and "environment of symbols" and demand clarification in the use of these terms.

An early difficulty arises when we are told that "The substance of the consciousness cultivated by TV is not so much specific attitudes and opinions as more basic assumptions about the 'facts' of life and standards of judgment on which conclusions are based" (p. 242). I take this to mean that distinctions among programs are far less significant than similarities. On one level this could refer to the plots of individual television dramas in which we notice varying motivation for actions, individual responses to events, speeches or lines or small bits of reaction on the part of actors. On a different level the same judgment could be held against formulaic structures rather than pieces of content. Put concretely this distinction would suggest that it is far more significant that violent actions in westerns and detective formulas are seen as (for example) the actions of certain social types—white, middle-aged, males—than that one is a cowboy and the other a detective, or that one shoots a man in a ritualistic gun duel and the other in a dodging street battle. The implications are that all viewers are "getting" similar messages and that they get certain messages rather than others.

No evidence is offered for this most basic assumption, other than the observation that television viewing is nonselective. That is to say, "Individual tastes and program preferences are less important in determining viewing patterns than is the time a program is on. The nearly universal, nonselective, and habitual use of television fits the ritualistic pattern of its programming. You watch television as you might attend a church service, except that most people watch television more religiously" (pp. 242–3). Without commenting on the possibility that this view of television and religion reflect an essentially Catholic as opposed to Protestant view, I would suggest that the leap from nonselective to nonperceptive is unwarranted. There is, so far as I know, no evidence to support the assumption that "specific attitudes and opinions" are less strongly cultivated by television than " 'facts' of life."

A similar problem emerges in a discussion of the aesthetic composition of television drama. Gerbner and Gross assert that

> The realism of TV fiction hides its synthetic and functionally selective nature. The dominant stylistic convention of Western narrative art—novels, plays, films, TV dramas—is that of representational realism. However contrived television plots are, viewers assume that they take place against a backdrop of the world of television drama. It is also highly informative. That is, it offers to the unsuspecting viewer a continuous stream of "facts" and impressions about the way of the world, about the constancies and vagaries of human nature, and about the consequences of actions. The premise of realism is a Trojan horse which carries within it a highly selective, synthetic, and purposeful image of the facts of life [pp. 243–4].

Many of the terms of this definition are exceptionally congenial to humanistic discussion. But the question again is, on what grounds do the authors assert that "Nothing impeaches the basic 'reality' of television drama." The very quoted nature of "reality" and "facts" indicates that in the totality of the television world the *authors* do not consider these things as factual or real. They are significant, symbolic distortions whose meanings must be interpreted.

Much hinges here on the assertion that the viewer is "unsuspecting." The Trojan horse metaphor implies deceit and subversion. The additional suggestion is made that there may be in television "subtle patterns against whose influence we may all be somewhat defenseless" (p. 244) and that there are other "seductively persuasive" sorts of imagery there. These negative definitions, so crucial to the argument, rest on the unsupported assumptions that viewers are unsuspecting and do not perceive TV constructs as essentially fictional, that nothing impeaches the realistic base of television, and that perception is selective in this, rather than other, directions. Consequently, it is broad facts rather than specific meanings that are assumed to be getting through to the viewer.

Questions of televised violence must now enter our analysis for it is not merely any or all "basic assumptions about the 'facts' of life" that are most often raised about TV. The effects of violence have been the primary concern. Measurement of content has focused on violence portrayed on TV. In part, perhaps, that choice is historical, reflecting our society's generalized concern with the topic and its willingness to fund studies in this area. The Annenberg projects have, of course, been expanded, and it may be that some of the findings with regard to sex role stereotyping and other, broader social areas, will modify findings in this initial area of study. But procedures for discussing violence on television are beset with certain basic problems that go beyond the assumptions I have discussed so far. If the same or similar procedures are applied in other areas it is important that these problems be clearly identified.

The first, from the perspective of the humanist, is that of definition. In measuring violence on television Gerbner and Gross use "a clear cut and commonly understood definition,"

> the overt expression of physical force against self or other, compelling action against one's will on pain of being hurt or killed, or actually hurting or killing [p. 248].

While this definition may be commonly understood by researchers and other citizens in the world of experience, the application of any stipulated, a priori, definition to a world of fiction is highly questionable. From the humanistic perspective it would be both more cautious and useful to try to determine a meaning of violence as it is understood by the characters themselves in the fictional world of television. One could then compare that definition with others, "commonly understood," in order to take the first interpretive step toward understanding the *meaning* of the symbolic distortion. Instead, Gerbner and Gross measure the incidence of violence as they have defined it, impute aesthetic and behavioral effects to the incidence so measured, and then interpret the world of television in light of that effect.

Let me be more specific by using figures averaged over the years 1967–1975. Nine hundred twenty-four programs, 630.2 hours, and 2649 leading characters were analyzed. 79.8% of the programs and 83.6% of the hours contained some violence as defined for the study. Measuring all hours there was an average of 7.4 violent episodes per hour. Of all leading characters 62.9% were involved in some violence, 10.2% were involved in some killing. Presumably it is on this basis, for I can determine no other that does not rest purely on interpretation (and if that is the case the substance of the interpretive process should be presented rather than merely the conclusion), that Gerbner and Gross assert that television provides a "symbolic world *ruled largely by violence*" (p. 243; my emphasis). This is the effect of the incidence of violence as found in fictional television. Yet, it is a long and clearly unwarranted leap from the measured incidence of violence (or any other dramatic element for that matter) to the assertion that that dramatic world is "ruled" by the single, particular dramatic factor in which the researcher is most interested. What Gerbner and Gross seem to be saying, and I emphasize seem because it is not clear, is that we all see violence as more prominent than other aspects of television. The incidence of violence, it is implied, is the most important dramatically in that it governs all sorts of other fictional interactions. It is suggested that violence is more easily understood than attitudes toward it or the context in which it occurs. Such conclusions are obviously dependent upon the earlier assertion that we perceive facts rather than attitudes and opinions. As a consequence of this chain of reasoning, the implication goes, much of what we learn from television is learned in terms of this dominant symbol.

It is crucial that we understood here that violence, for Gerbner and Gross, is a symbol. Perhaps it would be better to say that violence is a metaphor that must be interpreted, for having demonstrated that violence is widely present in television fiction, the authors go on to tell us that fictional violence does not mean violence, in the sense that its primary effect is the stimulation of similar actions. Rather, "TV violence is a dramatic demonstration of power which communicates much about social norms and relationships, about goals and means, about winners and losers, about the risks of life and the price for transgressions of society's rules" (p. 243). Violence structures a world that places, types, and directs viewers. . . .

It is at this point in their analysis that Gerbner and Gross offer their specific demographic outline of the television world and then go on to say that "Violence plays a key role in such a world. It is the simplest and cheapest dramatic means available to demonstrate the rules of the game of power" (p. 247). *That violence, on a statistical basis, plays a key role in the world of television fiction is self-evident. But the meaning of that world as presented by Gerbner and Gross in the interpretation offered above is highly debatable.* The generalization that violence is the "simplest and cheapest dramatic means available to demonstrate the rules of the game of power," is, equally, an interpretation and would hold only in terms of the prior interpretation of the meaning of the television world. Other interpretations of that world have been offered, and in those interpretations the meaning of violence, even in its documented incidence, is very different.[1] In those interpretations it is often impossible to assert that the world of fictional television is "ruled" by violence. This prior interpretation of the meaning of fictional structures in television seriously weakens the interpretation put forward by Gerbner and Gross with regard to the meaning of television content. . . .

I do not wish to be misunderstood here. I am not attacking the "negative" findings of Gerbner and Gross. I am not asserting that . . . television is the pure and gleaming center of a wholesome mass American culture. Societies can formulate rituals celebrating evil symbols and ideas; their fictional worlds can be constituted around both negative and positive meanings; they can maintain themselves around repression as well as liberation. But I think it more likely that most societies are radical mixtures of both. Symbol systems speak of both simultaneously. Surely, in religious systems the fear of hell and the joy of salvation can operate together, perhaps in creative tension. Television is no less complex. . . . Television is fully as complex as the American "mind," the cultural force out of which it is created. It may be that all the messages of television speak with a single intent and are ruled by a single dominant symbol whose meaning is clear to a mass audience, or to that part of the audience heavily involved with those messages. But I have yet to see evidence sufficient to warrant such a reductive view of human experience in America.

## Note

1. Newcomb (1974, 1976); Cater and Adler (1975, 1976); Alley (1977); Real (1977).

## References

ALLEY, R. (1977). Television: Ethics for Hire? Nashville: Abingdon.

CAREY, J. W. (1975). "Communication and culture." Communication Research 2: 173–191.

CATER, D. and R. ADLER [eds.] (1976). Television as a Cultural Force. New York: Praeger.

——— [eds.] (1975). Television as a Social Force. New York: Praeger.

GERBNER, G. and L. GROSS (1976). "Living with television: the violence profile." J. of Communication 26: 173–199.

NEWCOMB, H. [ed.] (1976). Television: The Critical View. New York: Oxford Univ. Press.

——— (1974). TV: The Most Popular Art. Garden City, NY: Doubleday/Anchor.

REAL, M. (1977). Mass Mediated Culture. New York: Prentice-Hall.

# 6

# Theories of Mass Media Impact

The role of the mass media in contemporary society is obviously an important one. Mass communication plays a major part in shaping and articulating the cultural and political world in which we live. Beyond such a general statement, however, very little else is obvious. For once we begin trying to specify precisely *how* influential the media are, we confront a host of intractable questions about conceptualization and measurement. Certainly the media *affect* society, but don't they also *reflect* its values and the status quo? And if so, under what conditions do the media promote change or stability?

The answers to these and other related questions hinge on how we *conceptualize* mass media impact. If we limit our view of mass media effects to include only short-run changes in the behavior or attitudes of individuals, as much of the early research in mass communications did, the problems are simplified by the fact that these types of effects are easily isolated and measured. But these studies by no means exhaust the topic if one asks questions about mass media's long-run effects on society and their impact on culture, politics, and the shaping of social institutions. These issues are less easily resolved by measuring short-run effects. For these problems we need more comprehensive, flexible, and sensitive analytic tools. Issues of conceptualization and theoretical modeling have long been an arena of

257

intense debate among communications researchers. As with any other area of social research, theoretical constructs serve as paradigms for empirical research which ultimately affect findings, and their importance can hardly be overestimated.

Denis McQuail's paper is an appropriate selection to start off this section, since he reviews the history of research on mass media effects and discusses the major issues that pertain to their conceptualization. He emphasizes that scholarly interest in mass media effects has not always been guided by "scientific criteria," but has reflected societal concerns with problems such as crime and violence. The article provides a good overview of the most important explanatory models in the area of mass media effects and a summary of some of the major findings.

Knowledge and information are differentially distributed in society. Part of the mass media's implicit promise is that they hold the technological potential to expose larger numbers of people to high levels of information and therefore, perhaps, to reduce these differentials. Do the media actually do this? Tichenor, Donohue, and Olien's article was the first to formalize the concept of a "knowledge gap" for research purposes. They find that initially, the introduction of new information on a topic actually exacerbates the existing information gap, because the most educated people typically seek out and obtain more information than others. They also find, however, that this gap may be substantially reduced if publicity on a topic continues at a high level past this initial phase, as information will gradually reach less active members of the media's audience.

V. O. Key's essay also concerns itself with elite members of society. His primary interest is their disproportionate impact on public policy. With notable detachment from romanticized notions about the stabilizing power of the public and its sovereign will, he observes that even in the most democratic societies, elites and "activist subcultures" manage to influence political decision-making in excess of their numbers, though democratic societies impose some limits.

Key's observation raises an important issue which more students of public opinion need to take into account. The conventional method of gauging public opinion is by means of the poll or sample survey. This method usually provides each respondent's answers with equal weight, based on the tacit assumption that it is the aggregate of public opinions that exerts restraint on political decision-makers. If Key's observations are valid, we must recall that the opinions of some members of the public clearly carry more weight than those of others.

Janowitz provides a review of trends in the media themselves as well as an assessment of the major research traditions. The contradictory findings that communication researchers ponder today reflect our failure to appreciate the fundamental observation that "the mass media are both independent and dependent variables." While this observation may be disconcerting to

258

the researcher hoping to simplify the design of his or her inquiry, here is an inescapable fact for students of mass communication: The relationship of society and the media is one of reciprocal influence. Janowitz describes this process for the past several decades of United States history from a social control perspective.

# The Influence and Effects of Mass Media

DENIS MCQUAIL

## Introduction

The questions most insistently asked of social research on mass communication, and perhaps least clearly answered, have to do with the effects of social influence of the different mass media. The reasons for asking are understandable enough, given the amount of time spent attending to the mass media in many countries and the amount of resources invested in mass media production and distribution. Although much has been written by way of answer and a good deal of research carried out, it has to be admitted that the issue remains a disputed one—both in general about the significance of mass media and in particular about the likely effect of given instances of mass communication. Inevitably, this discussion has to begin with some clarification of terms, since one of the perennial difficulties in the case has been the lack of communication between those who have investigated the question of media influence on the one hand and, on the other, the public, media producers and those concerned with public policy for the media.

Perhaps it should first be claimed that the question of effects is a somewhat unfair one, one rarely asked of comparable institutions like religion, education or the law which all in their way communicate to the public or to particular publics and where questions about effects as well as aims could well be asked. The mass media are highly diverse in content and in forms of organization and include a very wide range of activities which could have effects on society.

To make the question not only more fair, but also more meaningful, we need to introduce a number of qualifications and specifications. First, we can distinguish between effects and effectiveness, the former referring to any of the consequences of mass media operation, whether intended or not, the latter to the capacity to achieve given objectives, whether this be attracting large audiences or influencing opinions and behavior. Both matters are important, but a different set of considerations relates to each. A second, though perhaps minor, point on which to be clear concerns the reference in time. Are we concerned with the past, or with predictions about the future? If the former, we need to be precise. If the latter, and often it is a prediction about what is going on now and its results which is a main concern, then some uncertainty is inevitable.

Third, we need to be clear about the level on which effects occur, whether this is at the level of the individual, the group, the institution, the whole society or the culture. Each or all may be affected in some way by mass communication. To specify the level meaningfully also requires us to name the kinds of phenomena on which influence may be exerted. We can investigate some phenomena at several levels—especially opinion and belief which can be a matter of individual opinion as well as the collective expression of institutions and societies. On the other hand to study the effect of the media on the way institutions operate requires us to look at the relationships between people occupying different roles and at the structure and content of these roles. Politics provides a good example, where the mass media have probably affected not only individual political opinions but also the way politics is conducted and its main activities organized. Political roles may have been changed, as well as our expectations of politicians, the relationships of followers to leaders, and even perhaps some of the values of political life. All this is a matter of historical change, much slower and less reversible than any influence on opinion, attitude or voting behavior. Again it is clear that difference of level of effect is also related to different time spans. Changes in culture and in society are slowest to occur, least easy to know of with certainty, least easy to trace to their origins, most likely to persist. Changes affecting individuals are quick to occur, relatively easy to demonstrate and to attribute to a source, less easy to assess in terms of significance and performance. Hence we tend to find a situation in which the larger and more significant questions of media effect are most subject to conflicting interpretation and the most certain knowledge we have is most open to the charge of triviality and least useful as a basis for generalization. Perhaps one could usefully add a further set of distinctions which have to be made early on, whatever the level of analysis. This relates to the direction of effect. Are the media changing something, preventing something, facilitating something or reinforcing and reaffirming something? The importance of the question is obvious, but it is worth stressing early in the discussion that a "no change" effect can be as significant as its reverse and there is little doubt that in some respects the media do inhibit as well as promote change.

# The History of Research into the Effects of Mass Communication

Research into mass communication has its own "natural history" and the study of media effects is of so much interest to the public and the phenomenon of mass media so "visible" that it has been strongly influenced by currents which have little to do with scientific criteria of relevance. On the one hand there are staple matters of anxiety like crime, or violence, the state of culture and morals or the power of the media to brainwash or educate. Each of these is subject to historical influences of increasing or decreasing importance. On the other hand, there are the facts of changing technology and social behaviour which introduce changes of media provision and use. The popular newspaper or comic, the cinema, radio and television have been successively objects of research interest, as they have attracted public attention. Of course what we know of the effects of mass media is not only the result of research oriented to social science or public concern. It also stems from the needs of the media industry and, especially, a concern with the effectiveness of advertising. Scientific investigations have thus been carried out typically in a context shaped by the practical interests of media producers to achieve their specific aims or by the anxiety in society to prevent "harmful" effects. The "effects" of the media which relate to neither of these have not always been examined with the same zeal. When we come to assess the state of knowledge about the question as a whole we will have to acknowledge a rather large gap on matters which may be most central to understanding the contribution of mass media in modern society.

There has, nevertheless, been some progress and we can characterize the 50 years or more of interest in media effects in terms of three main stages. In the first phase, which lasts from the turn of the century to the late nineteen thirties the media, where they were developed in Europe and North America, were attributed considerable power to shape opinion and belief, change habits of life, actively mould behaviour and impose political systems even against resistance. Such views were not based on scientific investigation but were based on empirical observation of the sudden extension of the audience to large majorities and on the great attraction of the popular press, cinema and radio. The assumption of media power was also acted upon, as it were, by advertisers, government propagandists in the First World War, newspaper proprietors, the rulers of totalitarian states, and accepted defensively by nearly all as the best guess in the circumstances. It is not irrelevant that this stage of thinking coincided with a very early stage of social science when the methods and concepts for investigating these phenomena were only developing. The second stage extends from about 1940 to the early 1960s and it is strongly shaped by growth of mass communication research in the United States and the application of empirical method to specific questions about the effects and effectiveness of mass communication. The influence of this phase of research is surprisingly great, given the rather narrow range of the questions tackled and relatively small quantity of substantial studies. Most influential, perhaps, were the studies of Presidential elections in 1940 and 1948 by Lazarsfeld (1944), Berelson and others (1954) and the programme of research into the use of films for training and indoctrination of American servicemen undertaken by Hovland et al. (1950). An earlier and longer tradition of social-psychological inquiry into the effects of film and other media on crime, aggression and racial and other attitudes should also be mentioned (e.g. Blumer, 1933). In practice, a small number of much cited studies provided the substance for the general view of media effects and effectiveness which was generally being disseminated in social and political science by the end of the 1960s. Where there was research outside the United States (e.g. Trenaman and McQuail, 1961), it was in the same mould and tended to confirm rather than challenge the agreed version of media effects. Basically, this version affirmed the ineffectiveness and impotency of mass media and their subservience to other more fundamental components in any potential situation of influence. The mass media—primarily radio, film or print at the time most research was conducted—emerged as unlikely to be major contributors to direct change of individual opinions, attitudes or behaviour or to be a direct cause of crime, aggression or other disapproved social phenomena. Too many separate investigations reached similar negative conclusions for this to be doubted. The comment by Klapper (1960) in an influential review of research, that "mass communication does not ordinarily serve as a necessary and sufficient cause of audience effects, but rather functions through a nexus of mediating factors" well sums up the outcome of the second phase. Of course, research has not shown the different media to be without effects, but it had established the primacy of other social facts and showed the power of the media to be located within the existing structures of social relationships and systems of culture and belief. The reversal of a prior assumption by scientific investigation was striking and seemed the more complete because the myth of media power was so strong and occasionally uncritical and naive. At the same time, it should be admitted that neither public anxiety about the new medium of television nor professional opinion in the field of advertising and mass communication was much changed by the verdict of science. In fact, hardly had the "no effect" conclusion become generally accepted than it became subject to re-examination by social scientists who doubted that the whole story had yet been written. The third phase, which still persists, is one where new thinking and new evidence is accumulating on the influence of mass communication, especially television, and the long neglected newspaper press. As early signs of doubts we could cite Lang and Lang (1959) or Key (1961) or Blumler (1964) or Halloran (1964). The case for re-opening the question of mass media effects rests on several bases. First of all, the lesson of "no-effects" has been learned and accepted and more modest expectations have taken the place of early belief. Where small effects are expected, methods have to be more precise. In addition, the intervening variables of social position and prior audience disposition, once identified as important, could now be more adequately measured. A second basis for revision however, rested on a critique of the methods and research models which had been used. These were mainly experiments or surveys designed to measure short-term changes occurring in individuals, and concentrating especially on the key concept of attitude. Alternative research approaches might take a longer time span, pay more attention to people in their social context, look at what people know (in the widest sense) rather than at their attitudes and opinions, take account of the uses and motives of the audience member as mediating any effect, look at structures of belief and opinion and social behavior rather than individual cases, take more notice of the *content* whose effects are being studied. In brief, it can be argued that we are only at the start of the task and have as yet examined very few of the questions about the effects of mass media, especially those which reveal themselves in *collective* phenomena. Some of these matters are returned to later, and at this point it is sufficient to conclude that we are now in a phase where the social power of the media is once more at the centre of attention for some social scientists, a circumstance which is not the result of a mere change of fashion but of a genuine advance of knowledge based on secure foundations. This advance has been uneven and buffeted by external pressure, but it is real enough.

## Processes and Models of Mass Media Effects

One of the spheres in which some progress has been made is in our understanding of how and why effects do or do not take place as expected. One of the reasons why questions about the influence of mass communication are so difficult to answer lies in the uncertainty about the "mechanisms" by which effects are produced. This uncertainty applies even to the relatively simple case of effects at the level of individuals and in practice, both empirical research and speculative comment have tended to be imprecise about the question of *why* any demonstrated or postulated effect should occur at all. Obviously, there is much diversity of explanations, but without some attempt to order the possibilities, the study of media "effects" is likely to be incomplete and possibly sterile.

Some guidance is available from early social psychological investigations of influence, but the lessons have not been generally applied to mass communication research. For instance, Janis and Hovland (1959) discussed various factors associated with "persuasibility" and suggested that "persuasive" effects might depend, amongst other things, on the prestige of the source, or on the significance of the message for the receiver, or on the attitudes of the receiver to the source. Implicitly, such work offers the framework for a more general account of models of the influence process, but no general framework emerges. Kelman (1961) comes closer to this in his analysis of social influence, suggesting that three main processes might be involved in opinion change. One of these, "compliance," refers to the acceptance of influence in the expectations of some reward or to avoid punishment. Another, "identification," occurs when an individual wishes to be more like the source and hence imitates or adopts behaviour accordingly. A third, "internalization," is intended to describe influence guided by the receiver's own pre-existing needs and values. This latter process may be described as a "functional" explanation of influence (or effects), since change is mainly explicable in terms of the receiver's own motives, needs and wishes. Katz (1960) recommends this approach to explaining the influence of mass communication in preference to what he considers to have been the two dominant modes of explanation in the past. One of those he describes as based on an "irrational model of man" which represents people as a prey to any form of powerful suggestion. Another is based on a "rational" model in which people are viewed as using a calculative and logical approach to new information. Both he regards as unrealistic and less likely to account for any change of attitude than his suggested functional approach.

A further example of social-psychological thinking deserves mention, since it does offer a fairly comprehensive framework for studying social influence and social power, even if it is not directly concerned with mass communication. This is the work of French and Raven (1953) which offers five main possibilities of a communicative relationship in which social power may be exercised and influence accepted. Power based on "reward" or on "coercion" are the first two categories and largely self-explanatory, although we need to translate them into concepts appropriate to mass communication. Both imply some interaction between the intentions of the sender and the needs of the receiver. "Referent" power is similar to Kelman's "identification." Fourth, "legitimate" power is based on the assumption of a *right* to expect compliance—present only where such a relationship is institutionally defined, as it may be in a number of different circumstances. Finally, there is "expert" power, based on the attribution of superior knowledge of the sender. While the conceptual framework needs careful adaption to the circumstances of mass communication, it does at least help to supply the missing element in the discussion of effects (McQuail, 1975). An anlaysis which is more specifically concerned with mass communication and which tells us succinctly how thinking has tended to develop is offered by De Fleur (1970). He outlines five types of theory or models of the effects process which have been developed successively as knowledge has advanced. First, there is the model of simple conditioning, stimulus—response, a model which fits with the early views about the power of the media as direct, and dependent on the source rather than the recipient. An early refinement was the "individual differences of theory" of mass communication which sought to take account of the diversity of the audience, acknowledging that the media message contains "particular stimulus attributes that have differential interactions with personality characteristics of members of the audience." In brief, different people are likely to respond differently to what must be complex stimuli. The third phase of thinking is referred to as a "social categories" theory, since it takes account of the fact that the audience is stratified according to such variables of social position as life-cycle, occupation or class, region, sex and so on. De Fleur notes that "members of a particular category will select more or less the same content and will respond to it in roughly equal ways." Here we have the notion of selective exposure and response according to broad social position. A fourth refinement of theory builds in the findings of social group and personal influence studies of the 1940s and 1950s (e.g. Katz and Lazarsfeld, 1956) and is labelled a "social relationships" theory. The basic thought is that inter-relationships between people as well as their individual attributes have to be taken into account, perhaps even more so: "informal social relationships play a significant role in modifying the manner in which a given individual will act upon a message which comes to his attention via the mass media." Finally, De Fleur describes the cultural norms theory which "postulates that the mass media, through selective presentations and the emphasis of certain themes, create impressions among their audiences that common cultural norms concerning the emphasized topics are structured and defined in some specific ways. Since individual behaviour is usually guided by cultural norms or the actors' impressions of what the norms are with respect to a given topic or situation, the media would then serve indirectly to influence conduct." This is an important statement of one of the basic processes which helps to keep alive a concern with the effects and power of the mass media, since it contains the thought that the media work most directly on consciousness, by providing the constructed images of the world and of social life and the definitions of social reality. In effect, the audience member learns about his or her social world and about himself from the media presentation of society (given that most of the time, most of this is not directly accessible). The media provide the materials for responding to experience and these accumulate over time in a long-term process of socialization. The effects of the media on the individual are not only indirect, they may have happened long ago, certainly in the past. The difficulty of investigating such a process need hardly be emphasized, but our attention is at least directed to the content of the media and its consistency or otherwise over time and across different media sources.

These attempts to clarify the effects process in the main deal only with the level of individual effect. In addition, De Fleur's analysis is oriented very much to the persuasion process and to understanding how the media might be used for persuasive objectives. In this, it still deploys a limited version of the general part played by mass media in society. A framework which helps to escape from this early tradition, formulated specifically for the study of politics but generalizable to other cases, is suggested by Seymour-Ure (1974). He asks about the effects of mass media on "political relationships" rather than on individuals. Thus the relationship is not simply an intervening variable in this question, but becomes the dependent variable. The first sort of relationship which he discusses is that between individual and political system. The mass media will affect the individual's knowledge about, and attachment to, the political system as a whole and this can happen over a long period of time as the structure of the media change (for instance, the emergence of a mass press) or it can happen more quickly by coverage of particular issues and people (for instance, immigration and Enoch Powell). Second, the relationship between the political system as a whole and its constituent institutions may be affected. The instances cited include: the institution of the British Monarchy, which receives so much support from the mass media; Parliament itself, whose place in the system could be affected by broadcasting of its proceedings; or the political parties, whose role is open to modification. A third level of media effect is in the relationship between institutions, for instance the relative strength of different political parties or the relationship between the American President and Congress. Fourth, we can look at relations between individuals and institutions, as in the case of support for a particular party or the attraction of individuals to leaders. Finally, the relationship between one individual and another, especially prominent political actors, can be affected by mass media and the case of the Kennedy/Nixon debates comes to mind as well as those other occasions where internal leadership contests are conducted on the public stage of the media.

The particular examples are less important than the general lesson to be learnt from this framework, that in many areas of social life the content and structure of mass media and the lines of activity which are chosen can have profound effects, not through the scale of effects on mass audiences, but through their consequences for particular individuals especially those with power, or the adaptive responses of other institutions when the media provide new ways of meeting old needs or begin to encroach on the territory of other institutions. Some specific cases of institutional effects are mentioned below. Here it should be emphasized that the media are themselves separate institutions with their own place in society, their own objectives to pursue, their own power and institutional dynamics. They are not merely neutral "message-carrying" networks nor is the only or most fundamental relationship involved that between the "mass communicator" and the audience. Our questions about the effects of mass media have to include those which concern the effects of the media *institution* as well as the effect of the media *message*. This matter has been neglected, in part because it requires the skills of rather different sorts of people—historians and political scientists especially. Gradually, the two kinds of knowledge of effects are being brought together, but we are in a phase of speculation rather than demonstrated fact. The connection that needs to be established is between (1) the political, social and economic forces which shape media institutions, (2) the effect of media institutions on other institutions, (3) the effect of media institutions on messages they disseminate, (4) the effect of these messages on people and on institutions.

## The Evidence of Effects

In order to discuss the results of research into mass media effects in a meaningful way, it may be helpful to divide up the problem under a set of headings which in a composite way reflects the various distinctions which have already been mentioned: of level; of kind of effect and of process; of research strategy and method. Although the headings which follow do not divide up the field in a mutually exclusive way, they do separate out the main topics which have been discussed and provide a basis for evaluating research evidence. Basically what is being indicated is a set of media situations or processes which have distinctive features and require separate evaluation. The most important media situations are: (1) the campaign; (2) the definition of social reality and social norms; (3) the immediate response or reaction; (4) institutional change; (5) changes in culture and society.

### The Campaign

Much of what has been written about the effects or effectiveness of the media either derives from research on campaigns or involves predictions about hypothetical campaign situations. In fact, the campaign is not the most common form of media provision nor its reception the most usual audience experience. Nevertheless, because the campaign is often treated as the paradigm case it is useful to pick it out, try and define what it means and what kinds of media experience are illustrated by campaign-based evidence. The kinds of media provision which might fall under this heading include: political and election campaigns, attempts at public information; commercial and public service advertising, some forms of education; the use of mass media in developing countries or generally for the diffusion of innovations. We recognize the similarity of these different activities. The campaign shares, in varying degrees, the following characteristics: it has specific aims and is planned to achieve these; it has a definite time-span, usually short; it is intensive and aims at wide coverage; it's effectiveness is, in principle, open to assessment; it usually has authoritative sponsorship; it is not necessarily popular with its audience and has to be "sold" to them; it is usually based on a framework of shared values. The campaign generally works to achieve objectives which in themselves are not controversial—voting, giving to charity, buying goods, education, health, safety, and so on. We can recall many variants and daily examples and readily see the distinctive features of this form of media content. There are fringe areas where the relevance of the campaign concept is unclear, for instance the case of news which has presumably an informative intention and may be given the features of a campaign by a particular newspaper or regarded in this light by part of an audience.

The main aim in singling out this special kind of media situation is to bring together, in summary form, the accumulated evidence bearing on campaign effects and in doing so to reduce the risk of transferring these conclusions to situations where they may not be appropriate. We can also say more with certainty about the conditions affecting the success of campaigns than about any other kind of media situation. Rather than discuss evidence in detail, which space would not allow, a brief assertion of a general condition of effect is made, with some reference to a source or summarizing work which justifies the assertion. One set of relevant factors has to do with the audience, another with the message and a third with the source or the system of distribution. Amongst audience factors, an obvious primary condition is that a large audience should be reached. Second, the appropriate members of the audience should be reached, since size alone does not guarantee the inclusion of those for whom the campaign is relevant. The classic example of an information and orientation campaign reaching an already informed and well oriented public is described by Star and Hughes (1951). Third, the dispositions of the audience should at least be not antipathetic or resistant. Political campaigning is most subject to this constraint and there is evidence that the lack of strong disposition either way and a condition of casual attention may be most favourable to the success of mass propaganda. (Blumler and McQuail, 1968.) A part of this condition relates to the need for consistency with the norms of locality and sub-culture as well as the presence of broad societal consensus. Fourth, success is likely to be greater when, within the audience, the flow of personal communication and structure of relevant interpersonal status is supportive of the mass media campaign and its aim (Lazarsfeld, 1944; Katz and Lazarsfeld, 1956; Rogers and Shoemaker, 1971). Fifth, it is important that the audience understands or perceives the message as intended by its originators (Cooper and Jahoda, 1947; Belson, 1967) and does not selectively distort it.

Factors to do with the message or content are also important. First, the message should be unambiguous and relevant to its audience. The factor of relevance and a parallel self-selection by the audience makes it likely that campaigns are most successful at reinforcing existing tendencies or channelling them into only slightly different pathways. Second, the informative campaign seems more likely to be successful than the campaign to change attitudes or opinions (Hovland et al., 1951; Trenaman and McQuail, 1961). Third, in general, subject matter which is more distant and more novel, least subject to prior definitions and outside immediate experience responds best to treatment by the campaign. The essential point is that the receiver has no competing sources of information and no personal stake in resisting an appeal or disbelieving information. It is easier to form opinions and attitudes about events abroad than events at home, about unfamiliar than about familiar matters. Fourth, the campaign which allows some immediate response in action is most likely to be effective, since behaviour generally confirms intention and attitude, whether in voting or buying, or donating to a charity. Fifth, repetition can be mentioned as a probable contributor to effect, although this is a common-sense assumption rather than well demonstrated. As far as the source is concerned, we should mention first the condition of monopoly. The more channels carrying the same campaign messages, the greater the probability of acceptance. This is not easy to demonstrate and there are circumstances where an imposed monopoly invites distrust and disbelief (e.g. Inkeles and Bauer, 1959). But, in general, this condition is presupposed in several of the conditions already stated. Second, there is evidence that the status or authority of the source contributes to successful campaigning and the principle is applied in most campaigns whether commercial or not. The source of attributed status can of course vary, including the strongly institutionalized prestige of the political or legal system or the personal attractiveness of a star or other "hero" of society or the claim to expert knowledge. Endorsement by an individual or institution embodying strong claims to trust and attachment can be crucial in a campaign. Third, there is a variable condition of affective attachment to a media source. There is evidence that loyalty and affective ties exist in relation to some media rather than others which may affect their ability to influence (Butler and Stokes, 1969; Blumler *et al.,* 1975).

These factors are all important in the process of intentional influence. While our knowledge of them is variable and incomplete they provide, even in this summarily listed form, some guide to the complex matter of determining or predicting the short-term effects of the media. We need to be careful in translating their lessons to other non-campaign circumstances, but, as we will see, they often do have a wide range of application even in adapted forms. If we accept the validity of these points we are already very far from thinking the mass media to be ineffective, or can it be said that we have no certain knowledge of the effects of mass media.

## The Definition of Social Reality and the Formation of Social Norms

The topics we should look at under this heading are diverse and the processes involved equally so. Here we mainly consider the process of learning through the media, a process which is often incidental, unplanned and unconscious for the receiver and almost always unintentional on the part of the sender. Hence the concept of "effectiveness" is usually inappropriate, except in societies where the media take a planned and deliberate role in social development. This may be true of some aspects of socialist media (see Hopkins, 1970) or of some media in applications in developing countries (Pye, 1963;

Frey, 1973). There are two main aspects to what occurs. On the one hand, there is the provision of a consistent picture of the social world which may lead the audience to adopt this version of reality, a reality of "facts" and of norms values and expectations. On the other hand, there is a continuing and selective interaction between self and the media which plays a part in shaping the individual's own behaviour and self-concept. We learn what our social environment is and respond to the knowledge that we acquire. In more detail, we can expect the mass media to tell us about different kinds of social role and the accompanying expectations, in the sphere of work, family life, political behaviour and so on. We can expect certain values to be selectively reinforced in these and other areas of social experience. We can expect a form of dialogue between persons and fictional characters or real media personalities and also in some cases an identification with the values and perspectives of these "significant others." We can also expect the mass media to give an order of importance and structure to the world they portray, whether fictionally or as actuality. There are several reasons for these expectations. One is the fact that there is a good deal of patterning and consistency in the media version of the world. Another is the wide range of experience which is open to view and to vicarious involvement compared to the narrow range of real experience available to most people at most points in their lives. Third there is the trust with which media are often held as a source of impressions about the world outside direct experience. Inevitably, the evidence for this process of learning from the media is thin and what there is does little more than reaffirm the plausibility of these theoretical propositions. The shortage of evidence stems in part from a failure to look for it, until quite recently, and in part from the long-term nature of the processes which make them less amenable to investigations by conventional techniques of social research than are the effects of campaigns. That the media tend to be both consistent amongst themselves over time and also rather given to patterning and sterotyping has been demonstrated often enough in studies of content. We can cite Galtung and Ruge (1965) on foreign countries, Berelson and Steiner (1950) on American ethnic minorities, Baker and Ball (1969) on the portrayal of violence, De Fleur (1964) on occupations, Franzwa (1974) on the representation of women's roles, Hartmann and Husband (1974) on immigrants in Britain, Halloran et al. (1970) on the newspaper portrayal of a militant demonstration, Hartmann (1976) on reporting of industrial relations. A long list of studies can be cited showing the media to have certain inbuilt tendencies to present a limited and recurring range of images and ideas which form rather special versions of reality. In some areas, as with news reporting, the pattern is fairly inescapable, in others the diversity of media allows some choice and some healthy contradiction. What we lack is much evidence of the impact of these selective versions of the world. In many cases discount by the audience or the availability of alternative information must make acceptance of media portrayals at face value extremely unlikely or unusual. We should certainly not take evidence of content as evidence of effect. There is no close correspondence between the two and some studies show this. For example Roshier (1973) found public views about crime to be closer to the "true" statistical picture than the somewhat distorted version one might extract from the content of local newspapers. Similarly Halloran's study of audience reaction to television reports of the 1968 demonstration shows this to have been rather little affected by the "one-sided" version presented on the screen. Even so, there is enough evidence as well as good theory for taking the proposition as a whole quite seriously. The case of the portrayal of an immigrant, especially coloured, minority provides a good test, since we may expect the media to be a prominent source of impressions for those in Britain who have little or very limited personal contact with "immigrants." Hartmann and Husband (1974), in an investigation of school children, show that, while degree of media exposure and degree of "prejudice" are not directly correlated, the media are a more important source of knowledge and ideas than are personal contacts in areas where immigrant populations are small. They also show that the media are associated with a veiw of immigrants as likely to be a cause of trouble or be associated with conflict. It also seems that impressions attributed to the media as source show a rather higher degree of internal similarity and to be in general less evaluative than those derived from personal contact. The main contribution of the mass media is not, according to this study, to encourage prejudice (often the reverse) but in defining the presence of immigrants as an "objective" problem for the society.

Another case of a somewhat different kind can be found in the portrayal of certain out-groups and in defining the degree and nature of their deviance. Again the media stand in for experience. Cohen's (1973) study of the media portrayal of Mods and Rockers has no evidence of effect, but here the direction of public response, guided by a near-fictional media presentation of events seems predictable. The view taken by Cohen is that "the mass media provide a major source of knowledge in a segregated society of what the consensus actually is and what the nature of deviation is." In his view the media are responsible for promoting "moral panics," identifying scapegoats, and acting as a guide to social control. The terms "amplification" and "sensitization" and "polarization" have been used to describe the tendency of the media to exaggerate the incidence of a phenomenon, to increase the likelihood of it being noticed and to mobilize society against a supposed threat. In recent times, it has been argued that this treatment has been allotted to drug-taking (by Young, 1973), to mugging and to left-wing militants. It is notable that the groups receiving this form of polarizing treatment tend to be small, rather powerless and already subject to broad social disapproval. They are relatively "safe" targets, but the process of hitting them tends to reaffirm the boundaries around what is acceptable in a free society.

When the question of media effects on violence is discussed, a rather opposite conclusion is often drawn. It seems as if general public opinion still holds the media responsible for a good deal of the increasing lawlessness in society (Halloran, 1970), a view based probably on the frequency with which crime and violence is portrayed, even if it rarely seems to be "rewarded." It is relevant to this section of the discussion to explore this view. American evidence obtained for the Kerner Commission on Violence and reported by Baker and Ball (1969) shows there certainly to be much violence portrayed on the most used medium, television. It also shows that most people have rather little contact with real violence in personal experience. The authors chart the public expression of norms in relation to violence and also television norms as they appear in content and find a gap between the two. Thus, while public norms cannot yet have been much affected directly, the gap suggests that the direction of effects is to extend the boundaries of acceptable violence beyond current norms. In brief then, the authors of this study lend support to one of the more plausible hypotheses connecting crime and violence with the media—that the tolerance of aggression is increased by its frequent portrayal and it becomes a more acceptable means of solving problems whether for the "goodies" or the criminals. It should not be lost sight of, even so, that most dependable research so far available has not supported the thesis of a general association between any form of media use and crime, delinquency or violence (Halloran, 1970). The discussion linking social norms with violence takes place on the level of belief systems, opinions, social myths. It would require a long-term historical and cultural analysis to establish the propositions which are involved. Nor should we forget that there are counter-propositions, pointing for instance to the selectivity of public norms about violence and aggression. It is not disapproved of in general in many societies, only in its uncontrolled and non-institutionalized forms. Violence, aggression and competition are often held up for admiration when used with "correct" aims. Whatever the strength and direction of effects, it seems justifiable to conclude that the mass media remain, for most of us, our most persuasive source of representations of violence, crime and socially disapproved behaviour and provide the materials for shaping personal and collective impressions. There is also a strong pattern in the representations put before us, shaped in the one hand by the "demands" of the audience, and on the other by forces of social control seeking to make rules and draw boundaries (Gerbner and Gross, 1976).

Under this heading we can shift ground somewhat to return to a clearer and perhaps better established example of the process of defining reality and influencing norms. It has already been suggested that the media help to establish an order of priorities in a society about its problems and objectives. They do this, not by initiating or determining, but by publicizing according to an agreed scale of values what is determined elsewhere, usually in the political system. Political scientists have been most alert to the process and the term "agenda-setting" has been given to it by McCombs and Shaw (1972). They found the mass media to present a very uniform set of issues before the American public in the 1968 Presidential election and found public opinion to accord in content and order rather closely to this pattern. The phenomenon had been noted earlier in election campaign studies, where order of space given to issues in media content was found to be predictive of changes in order of importance attributed to issues over the course of the campaign (Trenaman and McQuail, 1961; Blumler and McQuail, 1968). In one sense the media only record the past and reflect a version of the present but, in doing so, they can affect the future, hence the significance of the "agenda" analogy. A rather more specific case of this kind of influence from the media is indicated by Seymour-Ure (1974) who correlates exceptional publicity given to Enoch Powell in the media with a marked increase in public importance attaching to the issue of immigration and a polarization of views on the question. The likelihood of this occurring is accentuated by the tendency for agreement on news values between different newspapers and different mass media (Halloran, 1970).

Given the sparseness of evidence, it is not surprising that we cannot so adequately state the conditions for the occurrence or otherwise of effects from the media in the sphere of forming impressions of reality and defining social norms. In particular, we are dealing with society-wide and historically located phenomena which are subject to forces not captured by normal data-collecting techniques in the social sciences. However, if we re-inspect the list of conditions associated with media campaign success or failure, a number will again seem relevant. In particular, we should look first at the monopoly condition. Here what matters is less the monopoly of ownership and control than the monopoly of attention and the homogeneity of content. Uniformity and repetition establish the important result of monopoly without the necessity for the structural causes to be present. The more consistent the picture presented and the more exclusively this picture gains wide attention then the more likely is the predicted effect to occur (cf. Noelle-Newmann, 1972). We can suppose, too, that matters outside immediate experience and on which there are not strongly formed alternative views will also be most susceptible to the level of influence spoken of. Further, we can think that here, as with media campaigns, a trust in the source and an attribution of authority will be an important factor in the greater extension of media derived opinions and values. Other conditions of social organization must also be taken into account. It is arguable, but untestable, that circumstances of greater individuation and lower ties of attachment to intermediary groups and associations will favour an influence from the media. Finally, we might hypothesize that conditions of social crisis or danger might also be associated with strong short-term effects from the media on the definition of problems and solutions.

## Immediate Response and Reaction Effects

To discuss this, we return to questions relating largely to individuals and to direct and immediate effects. We are concerned exclusively with unintended, generally "undesirable," effects which fall into two main categories.

One relates again to the problem of crime and violence, another to cases of panic response to news or information, where collective responses develop out of individual reception of the media. Basically, this field of effects derives from the circumstances of immediacy of reception and from the speed (approximating sometimes to simultaneity) with which information can be transmitted by electronic means. A related factor is the possibility (often realized) of unmediated contact between source and recipient and the relative absence of institutional control over response. It is the possibility enshrined in the ideal type of mass communication proposed by theorists of mass society and students of collective behaviour. While sociologists have generally stressed the dominance of normative controls by the society and group, it is certainly possible for direct uncontrolled responses to take place. There are numerous individual cases of imitation of acts of suicide or crime which have in themselves fed the belief that the media in general must contribute to lawlessness or disorder.

A considerable amount of research attention has been paid to direct response to the media since at least the time of the Payne Fund studies (Peterson, 1933), mainly by social and clinical psychologists, normally using experimental methods. The results remain confusing and contradictory. One school of thought is now convinced that media portrayals of aggression can provoke aggression in child audiences (e.g., Berkovitz, 1964). Another favours the view that the effect of fictional evidence is more likely to be a cathartic or aggression-releasing tendency (Feshbach, 1971). Many experiments have been inconclusive and majority opinion seems inclined to the cautious conclusion that direct effects involving disapproved behaviour are rare or likely to occur only where there is a strong disposition in that direction amongst a small minority of the already disturbed. The problem of interpretation and prediction is exacerbated by the familiar vice of experimentation that its findings cannot easily be transferred to a real-life situation and it can rarely do more than simulate both the stimulus and the response (Noble, 1975). Since the evidence in these matters is so inconclusive, the conditions favouring direct responses in behaviour of a criminal or aggressive kind cannot be stated. At best we can say that solitary use of the media and other conditions of conflict and maladjustment are likely to increase the tendency for the media to stimulate or create fear and anxiety.

There is no shortage of evidence that mass media of all kinds do frequently invoke immediate responses of an affective kind, if any evidence were needed. The responses include fear, excitement, identification, laughter, tears and these are, of course, often the intended and appropriate results of many "performances," to use Chaney's (1972) term. The concern of many investigators has been to trace the longer-term behavioural consequences of these immediate responses and it is this which has presented most difficulties. It might also be suggested that this search has been misconceived, however justifiable the aim. Too little research has been directed at understanding the nature of the immediate response in a real-life setting. To pursue the question of long term consequences without a basis in knowledge of the experience itself is unlikely to succeed.

The possibility that information received from the mass media will "trigger" widespread and collective panic responses has often been canvassed, but rarely demonstrated. The 1938 radio broadcast of Wells' *War of the Worlds* which involved simulated news bulletins reporting an invasion from Mars is the case most often cited in this connection mainly because of Cantril's (1940) research after the event. An event with some similarities in Sweden in 1973 was investigated by Rosengren *et al.* (1975) and the results cast doubt on the thesis as a whole. It seems that in neither case was there much behavioural response, and what there was was later exaggerated by other media. Investigations of news transmission in times of crisis, for instance the studies by Greenberg of the dissemination of news of the assassination of Kennedy (Greenberg, 1965) tells us a good deal more of the processes which begin to operate in such circumstances. Essentially, what happens is that people take over as transmitters of information and those who receive news seek independent confirmation from other media or trusted personal sources. The circumstance of solitary, unmediated, reception and response is unusual and short-lived. Shibutani (1966) reminds us that rumour and panic response are the outcome of situations of ambiguity and lack of information and, on the whole the mass media operate to modify rather than magnify these conditions.

In dealing with this aspect of potential media effects, more attention should perhaps be paid to various kinds of "contagion" or spontaneous diffusion of activities. The situations most often mentioned relate to the spreading of unrest or violence. For instance at times during the late 1960s when urban violence and rioting was not uncommon in American cities it was suggested that television coverage of one event might lead to occurrences elsewhere. Research into the possibility (e.g. Palatz and Dunn, 1967) does not settle the matter and it remains a reasonable expectation that given the right preconditions, media coverage could spread collective disturbance by publicity alone. Political authorities which have the power to do so certainly act on the supposition that unrest can be transmitted in this way and seek to delay or conceal news which might encourage imitators. The imitation of acts of terrorism or criminality, such as hijacking, seems also likely to have occurred, although the proof is lacking and the phenomenon is different because of its individual rather than collective character. In many areas where there is no institutionalized prohibition there is little doubt that spontaneous imitation and transmission do occur on a large scale by way of the mass media. In the sphere of music, dress, and other stylistic forms, the phenomenon is occurring all the time. It is this which has led to the expectation that the media on their own are a powerful force for change in developing countries (Lerner, 1958), through their stimulation of the desire first to consume and then to change the ways of life which stand in the way of earning and buying. Research evidence (e.g. Rogers and Shoemaker, 1971) and more considered thought (e.g. Golding, 1974) have led to the realization, however, that facts of social structure and of social institutions intervene powerfully in the process of imitation and diffussion. Even so, we should beware of dismissing the process as a misconception or, where it occurs, always as trivial. It is at least plausible that the movement for greater female emancipation owes a good deal to widely disseminated publicity by way of mass media.

## Consequences for Other Social Institutions

It was emphasized at the outset that the "effects" of mass media have to be considered at a level beyond that of the individual audience member and the aggregate of individual behaviours. The path by which collective effects are produced is, in general, simple enough to grasp, but the extent to which effects have occurred resists simple or certain assessment and has rarely been the subject of sustained investigation or thought. As the mass media have developed they have, incontrovertibly, achieved two things. They have, between them, diverted time and attention from other activities and they have become a channel for reaching more people with more information than was available under "pre-mass media" conditions. These facts have implications for any other institution which requires allocation of time, attention and the communication of information, especially to large numbers and in large quantities. The media compete with other institutions and they offer ways of reaching continuing institutional objectives. It is this which underlies the process of institutional effect. Other social institutions are under pressure to adapt or respond in some way, or to make their own use of the mass media. In doing so, they are likely to alter. Because this is a slow process, occurring along with other kinds of social change, the specific contribution of the media cannot be accounted for with any certainty.

If this argument is accepted, it seems unlikely that any institution will be unaffected, but most open to change will be those concerned with "knowledge" in the broadest sense and which are most universal and unselective in their reach. In most societies, this will suggest politics and education as the most likely candidates, religion in some cases and to a lesser degree, legal institution. In general we would expect work, social services, science, the military to be only tangentially affected by the availability of mass media. Insofar as we can regard leisure and sport as an institution in modern society this should perhaps be added to politics and education as the most directly interrelated with the mass media. The case of education is an interesting one where we can see at first sight a set of circumstances favourable to the application of mass media, or the technologies of mass media, to existing purposes, yet in practice rather little use made of them. Developed educational institutions have resisted any extensive change of customary ways or adaptation of content to take advantage of new ways of communicating to large numbers (McQuail, 1970). The mass media have often been regarded as a threat to the values of the institution, but also accepted in those spheres where innovation is taking place, for instance for the extension of education to adults or for more general educational purposes in developing countries. This conflict and correlated resistance is partly a consequence of the early definition of mass media as belonging to the sphere of entertainment and leisure and partly due to normal institutional conservatism.

The case of politics, as conducted in those societies with a broadly liberal-democratic basis, provides more evidence of adaptation and change to the circumstances of a society where the mass media are the main source of public information. In this case, the modern mass media inherited from the press, and retained, an established political function as the voice of the public and of interest groups and as the source of information on which choices and decisions could be made by a mass electorate and by politicians. The case presented for analysis involves an interaction between a profound change in the media institution as a result of broadcasting and a response by political systems which were not generally subject to profound changes. In these circumstances, it is easier to trace a plausible line of connection, although even here the process is interactive. The challenge to politics from media institutions has taken several forms, but has been particularly strong just because the press was already involved in political processes and because the introduction of broadcasting was a political act. The diversion of time from political activity was less important than the diversion of attention from partisan sources of information and ideology to sources which were more accessible and efficient, often more attractive as well as authoritative, and which embodied the rather novel political values of objectivity and independent "expert" adjudication. As we have seen, it has increasingly seemed as if it is the mass media which set the "agenda" and define the problems on a continuous, day to day, basis while political parties and politicians increasingly respond to a consensus view of what should be done. The communication network controlled by the modern mass party cannot easily compete with the mass media network and access to the national platform has to be competed for on terms which are partly determined by the media institutions themselves. In Britain, for instance, the last twenty-five years have seen several tendencies which seem related to these circumstances, with particular reference to television: relaxation of controls on coverage of parliament and political events; the use of advertising for political ends; a decline in importance of the face-to-face political campaign; more attention to the personality of the leader; a de-localizing of politics; a form of competition between parties which stresses performance rather than ideology; a convergence of policy aims; some de-politicizing of local government; a greater attention to opinion polls. The connection with television can only be an assertion, but the fact of some important institutional adaptation is unlikely to be denied and recognition of the mass media by politicians as a highly significant factor is easy to demonstrate. Some parts of the story are well-told by Seymour-Ure (1974) or Blumler (1970).


## Changes of Culture and Society

If we follow a similar line of analysis for other institutions, it is not difficult to appreciate that we can arrive at one or more versions of ways in which culture and social structure can be influenced by the path of development of media institutions. If the content of what we know, our way of doing things and spending time and the organization of central activities for the society are in part dependent on the media, then the fact of interdependence is evident. Again, the problem is to prove connections and quantify the links. The "facts" are so scarce, open to dispute and often puny in stature that the question is often answered by reference to alternative theories. For some, the answer may still be provided by a theory of mass society of the kind advanced by Mills (1956) or Kornhauser (1959) and criticized by Shils (1975). Such a theory suggests that the mass media encourage and make viable a rootless, alienated, form of social organization in which we are increasingly within the control of powerful and distant institutions. For others, a Marxist account of the mass media as a powerful ideological weapon for holding the mass of people in voluntary submission to capitalism (Marcuse, 1964; Miliband, 1969) provides the answer to the most important effects of the rise of the mass media. A more complex answer is offered by Carey (1969), in his suggestion that the mass media are both a force for integration and for dispersion and individuation in society. Gerbner (1967) sees the key to the effects of mass media in their capacity to take over the "cultivation" of images ideas and consciousness in an industrial society. He refers to the main process of mass media as that of "publication" in the literal sense of making public: "The truly revolutionary significance of modern mass communication is . . . the ability to form historically new bases for collective thought and action quickly, continuously and pervasively across the previous boundaries of time, space and status." The ideas of McLuhan (1962 and 1964), despite a loss of vogue, remain plausible for some (e.g. Noble, 1975), especially in their particular reference to the establishment of a 'global village' which will be established through direct and common experience from television. The various theories are not all so far apart. A common theme is the observation that experience, or what we take for experience, is increasingly indirect and "mediated" and that, whether by chance or design, more people receive a similar "version" of the world. The consequences for culture and society depend, however, on factors about which the theories are not agreed, especially on the character and likely tendency of this version of reality. Similarly, the available theories are not agreed on the basis of the extraordinary appeal of the mass media, taken in general. Do they meet some underlying human needs? If so, what is the nature of these needs? Alternatively, is the apparent "necessity" of the media merely the result of some imposed and artificial want? Certainly, the question of what most wide-ranging consequences follow from the media must also raise the question of motivation and use.

## The Social Power of Mass Media—
## A Concluding Note

It has been the intention of this whole discussion to make very clear that the mass media do have important consequences for individuals, for institutions and for society and culture. That we cannot trace very precise causal connections or make reliable predictions about the future does not nullify this conclusion. The question of the power of the mass media is a different one. In essence, it involves asking how effectively the mass media can and do achieve objectives over others at the will of those who direct, own or control them or who use them as channels for messages. The history of mass media shows clearly enough that such control is regarded as a valued form of property for those seeking political or economic power. The basis for such a view has already been made clear in the evidence which has been discussed. Control over the mass media offers several important possibilities. First, the media can attract and direct attention to problems, solutions or people in ways which can favour those with power and correlatively divert attention from rival individuals or groups. Second, the mass media can confer status and confirm legitimacy. Third, in some circumstances, the media can be a channel for persuasion and mobilization. Fourth, the mass media can help to bring certain kinds of public into being and maintain them. Fifth, the media are a vehicle for offering psychic rewards and gratifications. They can divert and amuse and they can flatter. In general, mass media are very cost-effective as a means of communication in society; they are also fast, flexible and relatively easy to plan and control. If we accept Etzioni's (1967) view that "to some degree power and communication may be substituted for each other," then mass communication is particularly well suited to the "stretching" of power in a society.

The general case which can be made out along these lines for treating the mass media as an instrument of social power is sufficiently strong for many commentators to regard it as settled. In this view, all that remains is to discover not *whether* the media have power and how it works, but *who* has access to the use of this power. Generally this means asking questions about ownership and other forms of control, whether political, legal or economic. It is arguable, however, that we need to take the case somewhat further and to probe rather more carefully the initial general assumption. That is, we cannot assume that ownership and control of the means of mass communication does necessarily confer power over others in any straightforward or predictable way. The question of how power works may be the critical one. There are likely to be important structural variations in the power relationship established between "sender" and "receiver" in mass communication, which need also to be clarified. Compared to other forms of compliance, the case of mass communication is somewhat unusual, since it is generally entered into voluntarily and on paparently equal terms. Given such a situation, it is not so obvious how a position of dominance can usefully be attained by the "communicators." To analyse the process of influence in either structural or social-psychological terms is beyond the scope of this paper, but it is important to place the matter on the agenda for further study. In particular, more attention should be given to the various structures of legitimation which attract and retain audiences and which also govern their attitudes to different media sources. There are critical differences between alternative forms of control from above and between alternative types of orientation to the media, both within and between societies. This is, as yet, a relatively unexplored area but meanwhile we should be as wary of trying to answer questions of power solely in terms of ownership as we should be of doing so in terms of "effects."

# References

BAKER, R. K. and BALL, S. J. 1969. *Mass Media and Violence.* Report to the National Commission on the Causes and Prevention of Violence.

BELSON, W. 1967. *The Impact of Television.* Crosby Lockwood.

BERELSON, B., LAZARSFELD, P. F. and McPHEE, W. 1954. *Voting.* University of Chicago Press.

BERELSON, B. and STEINER, G. 1963. *Human Behaviour.* Harcourt Brace.

BERKOVITZ, S. 1964. "The effects of observing violence." *Scientific American* vol. 210.

BLUMLER, H. 1933. *Movies and Conduct.* Macmillan.

BLUMLER, J. G. 1964. "British Television: the Outlines of a Research Strategy," *British Journal of Sociology* 15(3).

BLUMLER, J. G. 1970. "Television and Politics." In Halloran, J. D. (Ed.) *The Effects of Television,* Paladin.

BLUMLER, J. G. and McQUAIL, D. 1968. *Television in Politics: Its uses and Influence.* Faber.

BLUMLER, J. G., NOSSITER, T. and McQUAIL, D. 1975. *Political Communication and Young Voters.* Report to SSRC.

BLUMLER, J. G. And KATZ, E. (Eds.). 1975. "The Uses and Gratifications approach to Communications Research." *Sage Annual Review of Communication,* vol. 3.

BUTLER, D. and STOKES, D. 1969. *Political Change in Britain.* Macmillan.

CANTRIL, H., GANDET, H. and HERZOG, H. 1940. *The Invasion from Mars.* Princeton University Press.

CAREY, J. W. 1969. "The Communications Revolution and the Professional Communicator." In Halmos, P. (Ed.), *The Sociology of Mass Media Communicators.* Sociological Review Monograph 13. University of Keele.

CHANEY, D. C. 1972. *Processes of Mass Communication.* Macmillan.

COHEN, S., 1973: *Folk Devils and Moral Panics.* Paladin.

COOPER, E. and JAHODA, M. 1947. "The evasion of propaganda." *Journal of Psychology* 15, pp. 25–35.

DEFLEUR, M. 1964. "Occupational roles as portrayed on television." *Public Opinion Quarterly* 28, pp. 57–74.

———. 1970. *Theories of Mass Communication.* McKay.

ETZIONI, A. 1967. *The Active Society.* Free Press.

FESHBACH, S. and SINGER, R. 1971. *Television Aggression.* Jossey-Bass.

FRANZWA, H. 1974. "Working women in fact and fiction." *Journal of Communication,* 24 (2), pp. 104–9.

FRENCH, J. R. P. and RAVEN, B. H. 1953. "The bases of social power." In Cartwright, D. and Zander, A. *Group Dynamics,* Free Press.

FREY, F. W. 1973. "Communication and Development." In de Sola Pool, I. and Schramm, W. (Eds.) *Handbook of Communication,* Rand McNally.

GALTUNG, J., and RUGE, M. 1965. "The structure of foreign news." *Journal of Peace Research* vol. 1.

GERBNER, G. and GROSS, L. 1976. "The scary world of TV's heavy viewer." *Psychology Today,* April.

GOLDING, P. 1974. "Mass communication and theories of development." *Journal of Communication,* Summer.

GREENBERG, B. and PARKER, E. B. (Eds.). 1965. *The Kennedy Assassination and the American Public.* Stanford University Press.

HALLORAN, J. D. 1964. *The Effects of Mass Communication.* Leicester University Press.

HALLORAN, J. D., BROWN R. and CHANEY, D. C. 1970. *Television and Delinquency.* Leicester University Press.

HALLORAN, J. D., ELLIOTT, P. and MURDOCK, G. 1970. *Demonstrations and Communication.* Penguin.

HARTMANN, P. 1976. "Industrial relations in the news media." *Journal of Industrial Relations.* 6(4) pp. 4–18.

HARTMANN, P. and HUSBAND, C. 1974. *Racism and the Mass Media.* Davis-Poynter.

HOPKINS, M. W. 1970. *Mass Media in the Soviet Union.* Pegasus.

HOVLAND, C. I., LUMSDAINE, A. and SHEFFIELD, F. 1950. *Experiments in Mass Communication.* Princeton University Press.

INKELES, A. and BAUER, R. 1959. *The Soviet Citizen.* Harvard University Press.

JANIS, I. and HOVLAND, C. 1959. "An overview of persuability research." In *Personality and Persuability,* Yale University Press.

KATZ, D. 1960. "The functional approach to the study of attitudes." *Public Opinion Quarterly* 24, pp. 163–204.

KATZ, E. and LAZARSFELD, P. F. 1956. *Personal Influence.* Free Press.

KELMAN, H. 1961. "Processes of opinion change." *Public Opinion Quarterly* 25, pp. 57–78.

KEY, V. O. 1961. *Public Opinion and American Democracy.* Knopf.

KORNHAUSER, F. W. 1959. *The Politics of Mass Society.* Routledge.

LANG, K. and LANG, G. 1959. "The Mass Media and Voting." In Burdick, E. J. and Brodbeck, A. J., (Eds.), *American Voting Behaviour,* Free Press.

LAZARSFELD, P. F., BERELSON, B. and GAUDET, H. 1944. *The People's Choice.* Columbia University Press.

LERNER, D. 1958. *The Passing of Traditional Society.* Free Press.

McCOMBS, M. and SHAW, D. L. 1972. "The agenda-setting function of mass media." *Public Opinion Quarterly* 36.

McLUHAN, M. 1962. *The Gutenberg Galaxy.* Routledge.

———. 1964. *Understanding Media.* Routledge.

McQUAIL, D. 1975. *Communication.* Longman.

———. 1970. "Television and Education." In Halloran, J. D. (Ed.), *The Effects of Television,* Panther.

MARCUSE, H. 1964. *One Dimensional Man.* Routledge.

MILLS, C. W. 1956. *The Power Elite.* Free Press.

MILIBAND, R. 1969. *The State in Capitalist Society.* Weidenfeld and Nicolson.

NOELLE-NEUMANN, E. 1974. "The spiral of silence." *Journal of Communication,* Spring.

NOBLE, G. 1975. *Children in Front of the Small Screen.* Constable.

PALETZ, D. H. and DUNN, R. 1967. "Press coverage of civil disorders." *Public Opinion Quarterly* 33, pp. 328–45.

PETERSON, R. C. and THURSTONE, L. L. 1933. *Motion Pictures and Social Attitudes.* Macmillan.

ROBERTS, D. F. 1971. "The nature of communication effects." In Schramm W. and Roberts, D. F., *Process and Effects of Mass Communication,* University of Illinois Press, pp. 347–87.

ROGERS, E. and SHOEMAKER, F. 1971. *Communication and Innovations.* Free Press.

ROSENGREN, K. E. 1976. *The Bäxby Incident.* Lund University.

ROSHIER, B. 1973. "The selection of crime news by the press." In Cohen, S. and Young, J. (Eds.), *The Manufacture of News,* Constable.

SEYMOUR-URE, C. 1973. *The Political Impact of Mass Media.* Constable.

SHIBUTANI, T. 1966. *Improvised News.* Bobbs-Merril.

SHILS, E. 1975. "The Theory of Mass Society." In *Centre and Periphery,* Chicago University Press.

STAR, S. A. and HUGHES, H. M. 1951. "Report on an educational campaign." *American Journal of Sociology* 55 (4), pp. 389–400.

TRENAMAN, J. and McQUAIL, D. 1961. *Television and the Political Image.* Methuen.

WEISS, W. 1969. "Effects of the Mass Media of Communication." In Lindzey, G. and Aronson, E. (Eds.), *Handbook of Social Psychology,* 2d ed. vol. v.

YOUNG, J. 1973. "The amplification of drug use." In Cohen, S. and Young, J. (Eds.), *The Manufacture of News,* Constable.

# Mass Media Flow and Differential Growth in Knowledge

P. J. TICHENOR
G. A. DONOHUE
C. N. OLIEN

ACQUISITION OF KNOWLEDGE about science and other public affairs issues may be viewed as a component of social change consistent with a cumulative change model. According to this perspective, a given increment of change may lead to a chain reaction appearing as an increased rate of acceptance of a pattern of behavior, a belief, a value, or an element of technology in a social system.[1,2] Because certain subsystems within any total social system have patterns of behavior and values conducive to change, gaps tend to appear between subgroups already experiencing change and those that are stagnant or slower in initiating change.

The intent of this paper is to examine evidence from prior studies and from a recent field experiment in Minneapolis and St. Paul bearing on the following general hypothesis:

> As the infusion of mass media information into a social system increases, segments of the population with higher socioeconomic status tend to acquire this information at a faster rate than the lower status segments, so that the gap in knowledge between these segments tends to increase rather than decrease.

This "knowledge gap" hypothesis does not hold that lower status population segments remain completely uninformed (or that the poor in knowledge

Reprinted by permission of the publisher from "Mass Media Flow and Differential Growth in Knowledge," by P. Tichenor, G. Donohue and C. Olien, in *Public Opinion Quarterly*, Vol. 34 (Summer 1970), pp. 159–70 get poorer in an absolute sense). Instead, the proposition is that growth of knowledge is *relatively* greater among the higher status segments. For this paper, education is assumed to be a valid indicator of socioeconomic status.[3]

Two other assumptions are important for this analysis. One is that growth of human knowledge may be characterized by either linear or curvilinear trends, but that such growth is irreversible within the timespan under study.[4,5] A second assumption is that, for a given topic being studied, a point of diminishing returns from mass media infusion has not been reached, or, if it has been reached, it is possible that it occurs at different levels for different socioeconomic groups. Furthermore, this hypothesis applies primarily to public affairs and science news having more or less general appeal. It would not necessarily apply to more audience-specific topics, such as stock market quotations, society news, sports and lawn and garden care.

## Previous Findings

Although not stated specifically, this knowledge gap hypothesis has been implicit throughout the literature on mass communication effects. Underlying this view is the general finding that education is a powerful correlate of acquisition of knowledge about public affairs and science from mass media.[6]

Increased formal education indicates an expanded and more differentiated life space, including a greater number of reference groups, more interest in and awareness of science and other public issues, more accumulated knowledge of these topics, and more extensive exposure to mass media content in these areas.[7]

The "knowledge gap" hypothesis thus seems to suggest itself as a fundamental explanation for the apparent failure of mass publicity to inform the public at large. In analyzing efforts to inform Cincinnati adults about the United Nations, Star and Hughes point out that persons reached by the campaign tended to be the better educated, the younger, and the men, while less educated and older persons virtually ignored the whole thing.[8] Robinson offers the Newtonian explanation that those who are uninformed remain so unless acted upon by an outside force, while those already informed stay in motion.[9] Robinson's mechanistic perspective seems to say that people may develop trained capacities or incapacities to react to stimuli from both internal and external sources. Hyman and Sheatsley also appear to accept the notion of trained capacities to learn about public affairs: "as people learn more, their interest increases, and as their interest increases, they are impelled to learn more."[10]

Star and Hughes go a step further in specifying the interdependence among education, interest, and exposure, pointing out that highly educated persons reached by the campaign were more likely to be interested and therefore better informed. They concluded that persons reached by the campaign were least in need of it, and the persons missed were the ones the plan tried to reach.[11] Key's analysis of the powerful relationship between audience stratification and political news exposure suggests that one principal function of a presidential campaign would be to increase the difference in level of information between persons at educational extremes, since those at the top have higher rates of exposure.[12] In a more general sense, a widening knowledge gap may be occurring in developing nations as a result of the systems for delivering information to people. As Beers states, the pattern of education improvement in modernizing nations may be such that the relative ignorance of a literate villager today is greater than that of his illiterate father.[13]

There are several contributory reasons why the predicted knowledge gap should appear and widen with increasing levels of media input. One factor is *communication skills*. Persons with more formal education would be expected to have the higher reading and comprehension abilities necessary to acquire public affairs or science knowledge.

A second factor is amount of *stored information*, or existing knowledge resulting from prior exposure to the topic through mass media or from formal education itself. Persons who are already better informed are more likely to be aware of a topic when it appears in the mass media and are better prepared to understand it.

A third factor is *relevant social contact*. Education generally indicates a broader sphere of everyday activity, a greater number of reference groups, and more interpersonal contacts, which increase the likelihood of discussing public affairs topics with others. Studies of diffusion among such groups as doctors and farmers tend to show steeper, more accelerated acceptance rates for more active, socially integrated individuals.[14]

A fourth factor includes *selective exposure, acceptance,* and *retention* of information. As Sears and Freedman have pointed out, voluntary exposure is often more closely related to education than to any other set of variables. They contend that what appears to be selective exposure according to attitudes might often more appropriately be called "de facto" selectivity resulting from educational differences.[15] Selective acceptance and retention, however, might be a joint result of attitude and educational differences. A persistent theme in mass media research is the apparent tendency to interpret and recall information in ways congruent with existing beliefs and values.[16]

A final factor is the nature of the mass media system that delivers information. Thus far, most science and public affairs news (with the possible recent exceptions of crisis events and space spectaculars) is carried in print media which, traditionally, have been more heavily used by higher-status persons. Print media are geared to the interests and tastes of this higher-status segment and may taper off on reporting many topics when they begin to lose the novel characteristic of "news." Unlike a great deal of contemporary advertising, science and public affairs news ordinarily lacks the constant repetition which facilitates learning and familiarity among lower-status persons.

The knowledge gap hypothesis might be expressed, operationally, in at least two different ways:

1. *Over time,* acquisition of knowledge of a heavily publicized topic will proceed at a faster rate among better educated persons than among those with less education; and

2. *At a given point in time,* there should be a higher correlation between acquisition of knowledge and education for topics highly publicized in the media than for topics less highly publicized.

One would expect the knowledge gap to be especially prominent when one or more of the contributory factors is operative. Thus, to the extent that communication skills, prior knowledge, social contact, or attitudinal selectivity is engaged, the gap should widen as heavy mass media flow continues.

## Time Trend Data

Evidence may be taken from both short-term and longer-term studies. Budd, MacLean, and Barnes studied the diffusion over a two-day period of two major news events, the resignation of Nikita Khrushchev and the Walter Jenkins case of 1964. The studies covered the period starting when the events were first announced and continuing for the next day or longer.[17] Although the authors expected socioeconomic differences in knowledge to be *diminished* in such events of major impact, the results were generally consistent with the knowledge gap hypothesis. Respondents with more education learned of the events more rapidly than did those with less education, and a larger proportion of persons with more education were aware of the events two days after they had occurred. Within this timespan, the gap in awareness between socioeconomic groups actually widened.

Another test of the knowledge gap hypothesis would involve data from studies conducted over time, with the same question asked at various intervals. Data on three such topics were gathered by the American Institute of Public Opinion between 1949 and 1965.[18] The topics include earth satellites, man's attempt to reach the moon, and the cigarette-cancer controversy. Each topic received considerable mass media attention during the period under study, and the entire period was one when U.S. mass media in general gave science increasingly heavy coverage.[19] In 1958, managing editors of 240 daily newspapers were asked whether news space given to science, engineering, and medicine had changed in recent years. More than 90 percent said there had been an increase and nearly two-fifths said the increase amounted to at least a doubling of science news space. In a similar study in 1965, nearly half of the editors reported a doubling of science news.[20] Furthermore, each specific topic had received heavy media treatment as the result of specific events.

The principal event in space research was the 1958 launching of the Sputnik I, followed by the several satellite launchings by both the U.S. and Soviet Russia. The possible link between smoking and cancer first received widespread coverage after the 1954 AMA report on the problem.

For each topic, there was general growth in knowledge or acceptance of the stated belief over time. . . . More impressive are results from the four polls asking respondents whether they believed man would reach the moon in the foreseeable future.[21] Again, as general acceptance of this belief increased, the correlation with education showed a statistically significant increase over each 5- or 6-year period. The increasing gap between educational levels is directly visible in Figure 1.[22] Among college-educated persons, belief that man would reach the moon rose from under 20 percent in 1949 to over 80 percent 16 years later; among the grade-school educated, this belief grew to only 38 percent during the same period.

None of these studies measured mass media coverage or exposure directly, and the impact of media information on these patterns must be inferred. It seems quite clear that media publicity is a principal factor here, but it is also possible that far more is involved. The 16-year timespan covers a period of changes in the educational system. The population also changed, with the top educational category including a greater proportion of young persons in 1965 than in 1949. The important point, however, is that the gap does not close in the period studied.

Belief in the cigarette-cancer link also follows the predicted pattern, al-

FIGURE 1.    Percent of Respondents in National Surveys Stating Belief That Man Will Reach Moon, by Education and Year

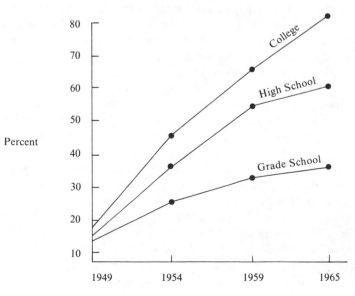

though the correlation in the later year remains low. In the 1954–57 period, however, the smoking and cancer issue was held in far more doubt than is true today. Although more recent studies have been conducted on this issue, they involve different samples and measurement techniques and therefore cannot be compared directly with the AIPO data.

## A Newspaper Strike Study

Another possible way to test the knowledge gap hypothesis is to view the effects of withdrawing mass media publicity. In accordance with the hypothesis, we would expect that removing mass media coverage of a topic would reduce the difference in knowledge between educational groups. While such an experiment is difficult to manage, it might be approximated in a newspaper strike situation. Samuelson in 1959 studied knowledge of current public events in a community where the newspapers were on strike, and in a nearby community where the daily newspaper continued to publish as usual. . . .[23] As hypothesized, the knowledge difference between educational levels is greater in the non-strike community than in the community where the newspaper had been on strike for the previous week (Table 1, difference of 1.08 vs. .44). This interaction, or contrast effect, is statistically significant beyond the .001 level.[24] Again, these data do not rule out alternative explanations, such as the possibility that the strike community may have been characterized by a low correlation between education and public affairs knowledge before the strike. Although the two communities are near each other geographically, the nonstrike community was smaller, less industrialized, and characterized by a generally higher socioeconomic level. In the absence of data before or after the strike, the interpretation of these data must remain tentative.

## The Minneapolis–St. Paul Experiment

Although most of the data above are consistent with the knowledge gap hypothesis, the underlying factors are inferred rather than observed. If the

TABLE 1. Levels of Public Affairs Knowledge for Persons with Different Educational Backgrounds, in a Newspaper Strike Community and a Non-strike Community, 1959*

| COMMUNITY | HIGH SCHOOL EDUCATION | COLLEGE EDUCATION | DIFFERENCE |
|---|---|---|---|
| Newspaper strike | 4.07 ($N = 153$) | 4.51 ($N = 142$) | .44 |
| No newspaper strike | 4.38 ($N = 40$) | 5.46 ($N = 56$) | 1.08 |

* Number of items correct in an 11-item test on current events.

general hypothesis is correct, education should be more closely correlated with knowledge gained from a *specific* article dealing with a topic that has been subjected to heavy previous publicity, compared with articles on less publicized topics. Highly educated persons are more likely to have been exposed to a heavily publicized topic in the past; they are already "in motion" on this topic and are easier to move still farther than less educated persons.[25]

A recent field experiment in the Minneapolis–St. Paul metropolitan area provided for a more direct test of this aspect of the hypothesis. Reader understanding was measured for 22 medical and biological research articles and 21 social science articles, all taken from upper midwest metropolitan papers in the summer of 1967 and the winter of 1967–68. These subject areas were analyzed separately, since for medical news, the relationship between education and understanding is frequently curvilinear.[26,27] Also, it was essential to use articles in areas varying in amount of previous publicity.[28]

An area probability sample of 600 persons was selected in the Minneapolis–St. Paul metropolitan area and interviews were conducted in April, 1968. Each respondent was asked to read two different science news articles.[29] Each article was presented with the question, "Would you please read through this, as you would any news article?" After the respondent had finished reading, the interviewer took the article back and asked: "What, as you best recall, does this article say?" Interviewers were instructed to use two probes for recall. Slightly more than 94 percent of the respondents read at least one of the two articles. Each article was read by a maximum of 20 persons. Pairing was arranged so that a given article was administered first in 10 interviews and second in the other 10. . . .

## Findings

Since responses to a second article read by a person might differ from the first, results were analyzed separately (Table 2). Also, the news article

TABLE 2.  Correlations between Education and Understanding of Science Articles for High and Low Publicity Topics in Two General Areas

| AREA | FIRST ARTICLE READ | | SECOND ARTICLE READ | |
|---|---|---|---|---|
| | *More Publicized Topics* | *Less Publicized Topics* | *More Publicized Topics* | *Less Publicized Topics* |
| Medicine-biology | $r = .109$ ($N = 84$) n. s. | $r = .032$ ($N = 111$) n. s. | $r = .264$ ($N = 90$) $p < .02$ | $r = .165$ ($N = 108$) n. s. |
| Social sciences | $r = .278$ ($N = 104$) $p < .01$ | $r = .228$ ($N = 93$) $p < .05$ | $r = .282$ ($N = 91$) $p < .01$ | $r = .117$ ($N = 97$) n. s. |

assignment led to some overlap in subsamples for first and second articles. However, the data for "first article read" in Table 2 represent four independent subsamples, and the same is true for "second article read."

The general pattern of correlations between education and understanding in Table 3 is consistent with the hypothesis; in each of the four comparisons, the "more publicized" articles tend to show a higher correlation. For the first article read, the correlations do not differ significantly according to previous publicity. However, for the second article read, the coefficient is significantly greater than zero for subsamples reading about more heavily publicized topics and nonsignificant for the less publicized topics. This pattern holds for both medical-biological and social science articles.

As expected, the observed relationship between education and understanding for more heavily publicized medical-biological topics tended to be curvilinear. That is, the sharpest difference in understanding of more and less publicized topics in this area is at the middle, rather than the highest, educational level. This pattern again illustrates the extremely high interest in medicine and health information among moderately educated persons.

## Publicity and Familiarity

Most of the data, then, tend to be consistent with the "increasing knowledge gap" hypothesis. To the extent that this hypothesis is tenable, it provides some sobering reflections on the "mass" impact of the media. At least for the subjects investigated here, the mass media seem to have a function similar to that of other social institutions: that of reinforcing or increasing existing inequities.

If media widen these gaps, under what conditions do the gaps close? Surely, some ideas eventually are universally shared. While data are not yet available, there is little doubt that the "moon walk" of July, 1969, produced widespread acceptance of the fact that man can reach the lunar surface. But media have limited resources, and the 1969 space spectacular may be an outstanding exception that illustrates a more general rule: media coverage tends to wane before the knowledge gap closes, and this tendency may be especially apparent in science, where a new development or finding renders yesterday's news topics obsolete. Once man went into orbit, earth satellites were virtually ignored by the media. If this is generally the case, the prospects for closing knowledge gaps in broad areas of science and public affairs through the mass media appear dismal. Other mass information delivery systems may be required if lower-status segments of the populations are to avoid falling further behind in relative familiarity with events and discoveries of the day.

This analysis has concentrated to a great extent on *print* aspects of mass publicity and may not apply to learning from television—at least, perhaps, not to the same extent. Since television use tends to be less correlated with education, there is a possibility that television may be a "knowledge leveler" in some areas. Whether TV does in fact have such a leveling function seems to be an urgent matter for further research.

Even as the results of this analysis stand, however, they do not necessarily point to a "failure" of information campaigns, as suggested by Hyman and Sheatsley or Star and Hughes. Creation of greater differentials in knowledge across society is itself a profound social effect, and may be a central factor in future social change. To the extent that more highly educated persons are at the vanguard of social and technological change, their accelerated acquisition of mediated knowledge may be socially functional. At the same time, however, differentials in knowledge may lead to increased tension in the social system; one of the recognized disparities between black and white people, for example, is the relative difference in gaining awareness of new information. A knowledge gap by definition implies a communication gap and a special challenge in resolving social problems.

## Notes

1. Wilbert E. Moore, *Social Change*, Englewood Cliffs, N.J., Prentice-Hall, Inc., 1963, pp. 37–38.

2. Charles P. and Zena K. Loomis, *Modern Social Theories*, Princeton, N.J., D. Van Nostrand, 1961, p. 589.

3. Albert J. Reiss, Jr., *Occupations and Social Status*, New York, Free Press, 1961, pp. 115–116.

4. James S. Coleman, *Introduction to Mathematical Sociology*, New York, Free Press, 1964, p. 492ff.

5. Gosta Carlsson, "Change, Growth and Irreversibility," *American Journal of Sociology*, Vol. 73, 1968, pp. 706–714.

6. See, for example, Robert C. Davis, *The Public Impact of Science in the Mass Media*, Survey Research Center, University of Michigan, 1958; Wilbur Schramm and Serena Wade, *Knowledge and the Public Mind*, Institute for Communication Research, Stanford University, 1967; and Serena Wade and Wilbur Schramm, "The Mass Media as Sources of Public Affairs, Science, and Health Knowledge," *Public Opinion Quarterly*, Vol. 33, 1969, pp. 197–209.

7. Merrill E. Samuelson, R. F. Carter, and Lee Ruggels, "Education, Available Time, and Mass Media Use," *Journalism Quarterly*, Vol. 40, 1963, pp. 491–496.

8. Shirley Star and Helen M. Hughes, "Report of an Educational Campaign: The Cincinnati Plan for the United Nations," *American Journal of Sociology*, Vol. 55, 1950, pp. 389–397.

9. John P. Robinson, "World Affairs and Media Exposure," *Journalism Quarterly*, Vol. 44, Spring 1967, pp. 23–31.

10. Herbert H. Hyman and Paul B. Sheatsley, "Some Reasons Why Information Campaigns Fall," *Public Opinion Quarterly*, Vol. 11, 1947, pp. 413–423.

11. Star and Hughes, *op. cit.*

12. V. O. Key, *Public Opinion and American Democracy,* New York, Knopf, 1961, pp. 348–357.

13. Howard W. Beers, *Application of Sociology in Development Programs,* New York, Agricultural Development Council, 1963.

14. Elihu Katz, "The Social Itinerary of Technical Change: Two Studies on the Diffusion of Innovation," *Human Organization,* Vol. 20, No. 2, Summer 1961.

15. David O. Sears and Jonathan Freedman, "Selective Exposure to Information: A Critical Review," *Public Opinion Quarterly,* Vol. 31, 1967, pp. 194–214.

16. Joseph Klapper, *The Effects of Mass Communication,* New York, Free Press, 1960, pp. 15–26.

17. Richard W. Budd, Malcolm S. MacLean Jr., and Arthur M. Barnes, "Regularities in the Diffusion of Two Major News Events," *Journalism Quarterly,* Vol. 43, 1966, pp. 221–230.

18. Data from AIPO surveys were obtained through the Roper Public Opinion Research Center, Williamstown, Mass.

19. Hillier Krieghbaum, *Science and the Mass Media,* New York University Press, 1968, p. 65ff.

20. Krieghbaum, *op. cit.*

21. Specific questions varied slightly. In 1949, 1959, and 1965, respondents were asked whether they expected man to reach the moon within 20 years. In 1954, the question was whether man would reach the moon in the next 50 years. In both these items and those on smoking, "belief" is assumed to reflect increased knowledge.

22. Trend analysis of the data in Figure 1 shows that both linear and quadratic effects are statistically significant beyond the .001 level for all three educational levels. However, the quadratic effect for the college group, for example, accounts for less than .005 additional variance. Thus, it is reasonable to regard these trends as basically linear.

23. Data from a study conducted by Merrill Samuelson for "Some News Seeking Behavior in a Newspaper Strike," unpublished Ph.D. dissertation, Stanford University, 1960.

24. The analysis of variance used in making this test is based upon an approximation procedure in which mean squares are adjusted for unequal numbers of cases in the subcells. See Hubert M. Blalock, *Social Statistics,* New York, McGraw-Hill, 1960, p. 264.

25. Robinson, *op. cit.*

26. P. J. Tichenor, "Communication and Knowledge of Science in the Adult Population of the U.S.," unpublished Ph.D. dissertation, Stanford University, 1965.

27. Hillier Krieghbaum, *Science, the News and the Public: A Report of the National Association of Science Writers, Inc.,* New York University Press, 1958, p. 5.

28. The study involved a total of 60 articles. However, those dealing with subjects other than medicine, biology, or social science varied so greatly in topic and so little in level of previous publicity that they were inappropriate for this analysis.

29. Interviews were conducted as part of a Metro-Poll survey conducted by the Minneapolis Star and Tribune Research Division.

# Public Opinion and Democratic Politics

## V. O. KEY, JR.

THE EXPLORATION OF PUBLIC ATTITUDES is a pursuit of endless fascination—and frustration. Depiction of the distribution of opinions within the public, identification of the qualities of opinion, isolation of the odd and of the obvious correlates of opinion, and ascertainment of the modes of opinion formation are pursuits that excite human curiosity. Yet these endeavors are bootless unless the findings about the preferences, aspirations, and prejudices of the public can be connected with the workings of the governmental system. . . . Consideration of the role of public opinion drives the observer to the more fundamental question of how it is that democratic governments manage to operate at all. Despite endless speculation on that problem, perplexities still exist about what critical circumstances, beliefs, outlooks, faiths, and conditions are conducive to the maintenance of regimes under which public opinion is controlling, at least in principle, and is, in fact, highly influential.

## A Missing Piece of the Puzzle

In an earlier day public opinion seemed to be pictured as a mysterious vapor that emanated from the undifferentiated citizenry and in some way or another enveloped the apparatus of government to bring it into conformity with the public will. These weird conceptions passed out of style as the technique of the sample survey permitted the determination, with some accuracy, of the distribution of opinions within the population. Vast areas of ignorance remain in our information about people's opinions and aspirations;

Extract from *Public Opinion and American Democracy* (Knopf, 1961), pp. 535–43. Copyright 1961 by V. O. Key, Jr. Reprinted by permission.

nevertheless, a far more revealing map of the gross topography of public opinion can now be drawn than could have been a quarter of a century ago.

Despite their power as instruments for the observation of mass opinion, sampling procedures do not bring within their range elements of the political system basic for the understanding of the role of mass opinion within the system. Repeatedly, as we have sought to explain particular distributions, movements, and qualities of mass opinion, we have had to go beyond the survey data and make assumptions and estimates about the role and behavior of that thin stratum of persons referred to variously as the political elite, the political activists, the leadership echelons, or the influentials. In the normal operation of surveys designed to obtain tests of mass sentiment, so few persons from this activist stratum fall into the sample that they cannot well be differentiated, even in a static description, from those persons less involved politically. The data tell us almost nothing about the dynamic relations between the upper layer of activists and mass opinion. The missing piece of our puzzle is this elite element of the opinion system. That these political influentials both affect mass opinion and are conditioned in their behavior by it is obvious. Yet systematic knowledge of the composition, distribution in the social structure, and patterns of behavior of this sector of the political system remains far from satisfactory.

The longer one frets with the puzzle of how democratic regimes manage to function, the more plausible it appears that a substantial part of the explanation is to be found in the motives that actuate the leadership echelon, the values that it holds, in the rules of the political game to which it adheres, in the expectations which it entertains about its own status in society, and perhaps in some of the objective circumstances, both material and institutional, in which it functions. Focus of attention on this sector of the opinion system contrasts with the more usual quest for the qualities of the people that may be thought to make democratic practices feasible. That focus does not deny the importance of mass attitudes. It rather emphasizes that the pieces of the puzzle are different in form and function, and that for the existence of a democratic opinion-oriented system each piece must possess the characteristics necessary for it to fit together with the others in a working whole. The superimposition over a people habituated to tyranny of a leadership imbued with democratic ideals probably would not create a viable democratic order.

## Values and Motives of the Activist Subculture

The traits and characteristics of political activists assume importance in the light of a theory about why the leadership and governing levels in any society behave as they do. That theory amounts to the proposition that these political actors constitute in effect a subculture with its own peculiar set of norms of behavior, motives, and approved standards. Processes of indoctrination internalize such norms among those who are born to or climb to positions of power and leadership; they serve as standards of action, which are reinforced by a social discipline among the political activists. In some regimes the standards of the ruling groups prescribe practices of firmness toward the governed who are regarded as menials with no rights; they deserve no more than the rough and arbitrary treatment they receive. The rules of the game may prescribe that the proper practice for rulers is to maximize their own advantage as well as the correlative deprivations of the ruled. The ignorant, the poor, and the incompetent may be seen as entitled to what they get, which is very little. Or the rules of the game of a regime may mitigate the harshness of these outlooks by a compassionate attitude toward the wretched masses who cannot help themselves. Hence, we may have little fathers of the people. The point is that the politically active classes may develop characteristic norms and practices that tend to guide their behavior. In a loose sense these may be the norms of a subculture, that of the specialists in politics and government. Beliefs generally accepted among these persons tend to establish habits and patterns of behavior with considerable power of self-maintenance or persistence through time.

While the ruling classes of a democratic order are in a way invisible because of the vagueness of the lines defining the influentials and the relative ease of entry to their ranks, it is plain that the modal norms and standards of a democratic elite have their peculiarities. Not all persons in leadership echelons have precisely the same basic beliefs; some may even regard the people as a beast. Yet a fairly high concentration prevails around the modal beliefs, even though the definition of those beliefs must be imprecise. Fundamental is a regard for public opinion, a belief that in some way or another it should prevail. Even those who cynically humbug the people make a great show of deference to the populace. The basic doctrine goes further to include a sense of trusteeship for the people generally and an adherence to the basic doctrine that collective efforts should be dedicated to the promotion of mass gains rather than of narrow class advantage; elite elements tethered to narrow group interest have no slack for maneuver to accommodate themselves to mass aspirations. Ultimate expression of these faiths comes in the willingness to abide by the outcome of popular elections. The growth of leadership structures with beliefs including these broad articles of faith is probably accomplished only over a considerable period of time, and then only under auspicious circumstances.

If an elite is not to monopolize power and thereby to bring an end to democratic practices, its rules of the game must include restraints in the exploitation of public opinion. Dimly perceptible are rules of etiquette that limit the kinds of appeals to public opinion that may be properly made. If it is assumed that the public is manipulable at the hands of unscrupulous leadership (as it is under some conditions), the maintenance of a democratic order requires the inculcation in leadership elements of a taboo against appeals that would endanger the existence of democratic practices. Inflammation of the sentiments of a sector of the public disposed to exert the tyranny of an intolerant majority (or minority) would be a means of destruction of a democratic order. Or by the exploitation of latent differences and conflicts within the citizenry it may at times be possible to paralyze a regime as intense hatreds among classes of people come to dominate public affairs. Or by encouraging unrealistic expectations among the people a clique of politicians may rise to power, a position to be kept by repression as disillusionment sets in.[1] In an experienced democracy such tactics may be "unfair" competition among members of the politically active class. In short, certain restraints on political competition help keep competition within tolerable limits. The observation of a few American political campaigns might lead one to the conclusion that there are no restraints on politicians as they attempt to humbug the people. Even so, admonitions ever recur against arousing class against class, against stirring the animosities of religious groups, and against demagoguery in its more extreme forms. American politicians manifest considerable restraint in this regard when they are tested against the standards of behavior of politicians of most of those regimes that have failed in the attempt to establish or maintain democratic practices.

The norms of the practice of politics in an order that has regard for public opinion include broad rules of etiquette governing the relations among the activists, as well as rules governing the relations of activists with the public. Those rules, in their fundamental effect, assure the existence of a minority among the political activists; if those who control government can suppress opposition activists, an instrument essential for the formation and expression of public opinion is destroyed. A body of customs that amounts to a policy of "live and let live" must prevail. In constitutional democracies some of these rules are crystallized into fundamental law in guarantees such as those of freedom of speech, freedom of press, and the right to appeal to the electorate for power. Relevant also are procedures for the protection of property rights; a political opposition may be destroyed by expropriation as well as by execution.[2] While such rules extend in their application to the entire population, one of their major functions is to prevent politicians from putting each other into jail or from destroying each other in the ordinary course of their competitive endeavors. All these elements of the rules of the game gain strength, not from their statements in the statutes and codes, but from their incorporation into the norms that guide the behavior of the political activists.[3]

## Form and Structure

Certain broad structural or organizational characteristics may need to be maintained among the activists of a democratic order if they are to perform their functions in the system. Fundamental is the absence of sufficient cohesion among the activists to unite them into a single group dedicated to the management of public affairs and public opinion. Solidification of the elite by definition forecloses opportunity for public choice among alternative governing groups and also destroys the mechanism for the unfettered expression of public opinion or of the opinions of the many subpublics. Maintenance of division and competition among political activists requires the kinds of etiquette that have been mentioned to govern their relations among themselves. Those rules, though, do not create the cleavages among the activists. Competitive segments of the leadership echelons normally have their roots in interests or opinion blocs within society. A degree of social diversity thus may be, if not a prerequisite, at least helpful in the construction of a leadership appropriate for a democratic regime. A series of independent social bases provide the foundations for a political elite difficult to bring to the state of unification that either prevents the rise of democratic processes or converts them into sham rituals.

At a more earthy level, maintenance of a multiplicity of centers of leadership and political activism requires arrangements by which men may gain a livelihood despite the fact that they are out of power. Consider the consequences for the structure of opinion leadership of a socio-economic system in which those skilled in the arts of governance have open to them no way of obtaining a livelihood save by the exercise of those skills. In the United States the high incidence of lawyers among the politically influential provides a base of economic independence; the defeated politician can always find a few clients. Extensive reliance on part-time, amateur politicians in representative bodies and in many governing commissions has assured an economic cushion for many political activists. The custom of making many such offices economically unattractive has, in effect, required that they be filled by persons with an economic base independent of the public treasury. Opinion leaders and managers often find economic independence in posts with business associations and other voluntary societies. Communications enterprises, important in the operation of democracies, gain independence from government by their commercial position. The structure of government itself, through its many independent units and agencies, assures havens of some security for spokesmen for a variety of viewpoints. All this may boil down to the contention that development and maintenance of the type of leadership essential for the operation of a democratic political order is facilitated by the existence of a social system of some complexity with many centers that have some autonomy and economic independence. Perhaps a safer formulation would be that societies that do not meet these requisites may encounter difficult problems in the support of a fractionalized stratum of political activists; they need to construct functional equivalents of the means we have been describing to assure the maintenance of competing centers of leadership.[4]

When viewed from another angle, these comments about the utility of independent foundations for competing sectors of the political elite relate to the more general proposition that regimes deferential to public opinion may best flourish when the deprivations contingent upon the loss of an election are limited. The structure of government itself may also contribute to that loss limitation. In federal regimes and in regimes with extensive devolution to elective local governmental authorities the prospect of loss of a national election may be faced with some equanimity, for the national minority may retain its position in many subordinate units of the nation and remain in a measure undisturbed by the alternations of control within the nation as a whole. The same function of loss limitation may be served by constitutional and customary expectations that limit the permissible range of governmental action.

Another characteristic may be mentioned as one that, if not a prerequisite to government by public opinion, may profoundly affect the nature of a democratic order. This is the distribution through the social structure of those persons highly active in politics. By various analyses, none founded on completely satisfactory data, we have shown that in the United States the political activists—if we define the term broadly—are scattered through the socio-economic hierarchy. The upper-income and occupational groups, to be sure, contribute disproportionately; nevertheless, individuals of high political participation are sprinkled throughout the lesser occupational strata. Contrast the circumstances when the highly active political stratum coincides with the high socio-economic stratum. Conceivably the winning of consent and the creation of a sense of political participation and of sharing in public affairs may be far simpler when political activists of some degree are spread through all social strata. The alternative circumstance may induce an insensitivity to mass opinion, a special reliance on mass communications, and a sharpened sense of cleavage and separatism within the political order. The contention made here amounts to more than the axiom that democracies can exist only in societies that possess a well-developed middle class. In a modern industrial society with universal suffrage the chances are that a considerable sprinkling of political activists need to exist in groups below the "middle class," however that term of vague referent may be defined. The correct general proposition may be that the operation of democratic processes may be facilitated by the distribution of persons participating in the order through all strata of the electorate. When the belief that democracy depended upon the middle class flourished, a comparatively narrow suffrage prevailed.

Allied with these questions is the matter of access to the wider circles of political leadership and of the recruitment and indoctrination of these political activists. Relative ease of access to the arena of active politics may be a preventive of the rise of intransigent blocs of opinion managed by those denied participation in the regularized processes of politics. In a sense, ease of access is a necessary consequence of the existence of a somewhat fragmented stratum of political activists. Systems built on rigid class lines or on the dominance of clusters of families may be especially prone to the exclusion of those not to the proper status born—or married. Yet ease of access does not alone suffice. It must be accompanied by means, either deliberate or informal, for the indoctrination of those admitted in the special mores and customs of the activist elements of the polity. Otherwise, ease of access may only facilitate the depredations of those alienated from the values of the political order. By their nature democratic political systems have large opportunity—if there is the necessary will—to extend widely opportunities for political participation in lesser capacities and thereby to sift out those capable of achieving access to the more restricted circles of influentials. Whether the builders of political orders ever set about deliberately and systematically to tackle such problems of recruitment and indoctrination may be doubtful. Those problems may be solved, when they are solved, by the unconscious and unwilled processes of evolutionary adaptation of social systems.

This discussion in terms of leadership echelons, political activists, or elites falls painfully on the ears of democratic romantics. The mystique of democracy has in it no place for ruling classes. As perhaps with all powerful systems of faith, it is vague on the operating details. Yet by their nature governing systems, be they democratic or not, involve a division of social labor. Once that axiom is accepted, the comprehension of democratic practices requires a search for the peculiar characteristics of the political influentials in such an order, for the special conditions under which they work, and for the means by which the people keep them in check. The vagueness of the mystique of democracy is matched by the intricacy of its operating practices. If it is true that those who rule tend sooner or later to prove themselves enemies of the rights of man—and there is something to be said for the validity of this proposition—then any system that restrains that tendency however slightly can excite only awe.

# Notes

1. The politicians of some of the new democracies have installed new regimes as they took the unfortunate step of arousing popular expectations beyond hope of early fulfillment.

2. Rules against the use of public authority for the private advantage of officials also have their political bearing. Officials who build huge fortunes or enterprises by the abuse of official position can yield power only at enormous cost.

3. Probably a critical stage in the evolution toward democracy occurs at the moment when those in authority conclude that their acceptance of the unfavorable outcome of an election would not result in grievous harm to them. Genetic analyses of democracies with a focus of attention on this point would be instructive.

4. Consider the problem of a regime that seeks to carry out economic development in large measure through governmental enterprise.

# Mass Media: Institutional Trends and Their Consequences

MORRIS JANOWITZ

THE INTELLECTUAL HISTORY of the study of the mass media needs to be taken into account in assessing their actual consequences on personal and social control. There have been two perspectives in this intellectual history.[1]

The first, which has been associated with the work of Paul F. Lazarsfeld, asserts that social research has refuted popular views, as well as those of journalists and public relations personnel, that the mass media are powerful and pervasive in industrial society. Instead, the mass media have limited, very specific influences which can best be identified by quantitative social research which focuses on the individual person and his response. This perspective led Lazarsfeld and his collaborators to formulate the concept of the "two-step flow" of communications, that is, mass communications have influence only when the contents are accepted by opinion leaders who in turn influence the mass of the public.[2] The research developed to document this perspective was launched in the 1940s and 1950s mainly by means of sample survey techniques. The stream of research convinced only social-science researchers, so that in 1959 Bernard Berelson, a disciple of Paul F. Lazarsfeld, published a statement anticipating the end of communications research because of the limited influence of the mass media.[3] Within a decade there had arisen within this "school" of research a second "look" which sought to correct the downgrading of the consequences of the mass media.

Reprinted from Morris Janowitz, "Mass Media and Societal Socialization," from *The Last Half Century,* 1978, pp. 330–363, by permission of The University of Chicago Press. Copyright © University of Chicago Press, 1978.

The alternative perspective developed after World War I and is associated with Harold D. Lasswell; it attributed ongoing and more pervasive roles to the mass media. Lasswell emphasized that modern society was dependent on mass communications and that the elite management of the systems of communication had a delimited but decisive consequence on social and political behavior. Harold D. Lasswell analyzed and highlighted the importance of mass communications during a crisis.[4] Lasswell was aware of the powerful resistances to communication appeals and the individual's capacity to select the contents of the mass media on the basis of one's predispositions. However, his outlook concentrated on the systemic consequence of the mass media and their long-term influence rather than on specific responses of individual persons. He implied that the mass media had influence both through opinion leaders—the two-step flow—and directly on mass audiences.

Lasswell's seminal writings have been applied continuously since and have been accompanied by increasingly sophisticated research clarifying the strategic role of mass communications. For example, in the 1930s, a comprehensive series of studies on the importance of the movies in molding youth behavior were completed.[5] During World War II, massive research observed the narrower limits of international political propaganda when directed against totalitarian states, as compared with the settings of World War I.[6] After 1945, extensive research was conducted on the effect of television. That research which emphasized the marginal influence of television has been displaced by a growing body of findings which clarified the strategic role of this medium. In short, the perspective originally formulated by Harold D. Lasswell has come to be accepted and to have central importance for our objective of exploring the mass media as instrumentalities of societal socialization.

As a result, the study of the mass media has been freed from methodological constraints. Much of the Lazarsfeld approach is a reflection of his empirical strategy, namely, the exclusive use of sample surveys. Carl I. Hovland has demonstrated that investigators who use experiments—laboratory or real life—are more likely to be impressed with the influence of the mass media; some of the most trenchant experimental work has been done on the effect of television on children.[7] On the other hand, many survey specialists have collected data which tend to emphasize the limited effectiveness of the mass media for producing specific changes in attitudes and behavior. The survey approach deals with a person's response to specific messages or campaigns rather than the cumulative effect and fails to deal with the role of the mass media in "defining the situation" and posing alternatives. . . .[8] The sophistication of survey research has, however, increased, especially by the use of more refined statistical procedures than were applied by the Lazarsfeld group, so that survey research since 1965 has produced results which support the Lasswell perspective.

Moreover, the systemic investigation of the influence of the mass media is a very complex task because of the inescapable reality that the contents of the mass media both influence the processes of sociopolitical change in society and at the same time reflect the organization and values of society.[9] In the language of social research, the mass media are both independent and dependent variables. Contradictory conclusions—analytic and empirical—about the influence of the mass media in part reflect relative emphasis on either assumption. . . .

My approach shall include a systematic analysis of the institutional structures of mass media. An urban and industrial society—and in turn an advanced industrial society—supplies the institutional basis of the mass media, technological, economic, and organizational. By means of press, radio, TV, films, books, magazines, etc., small specialized groups are able to create and disseminate symbolic content to a large, heterogeneous, and widely dispersed audience. But at the same time the institutions of the mass media are indispensable mechanisms for overcoming the disarticulation of an advanced industrial society.[10] Without the mass media, an industrial society is "unthinkable." In this view, the mass media function as devices for *(a)* the surveillance of the environment, *(b)* the posing of personal, social and political alternatives— that is, defining the situation, and *(c)* the inculcation of standards of behavior—that is elements of morality and relations to authority—and the creation of a basis for citizen participation essential for democratic decision making.[11]

The management of the mass media rests in the hands of various elite groups, and is subject to the pressures and conflicts between elite groups. By their nature, the mass media enable select elite and counterelite groups to appeal to large and "massive audiences." The political goals of these elite groups—and the professionals who actually operate the mass media—and the standards of performance they use are "real" independent variables in analyzing the influence of the mass media. The content which is excluded is as important as that which is emphasized.

There is a direct analogy between the analysis of the mass media and the classic essay by John Dewey criticizing the stimulus-response arc.[12] The mass media produce a continuous flow of communications, and the audience can be thought of as responding to this continuous flow. But a broader perspective is essential. The elites and the professional mass media experts are in effect being influenced by their audiences and audiences' responses. Rather than a stimulus-response arc, it is truly an interacting situation in which the stimulus itself is molded by the antecedent audience response and the larger societal context. (Moreover, the managers of the mass media are not apart from the process but are in fact influenced by their own communication; the person is both the subject and object of communication.)[13] There is a profound imbalance in influence and power—the initiative and power of the elites and the professional specialists overwhelmingly outweigh the contributions of the audience. However, in theory, under a parliamentary system, there are powerful self-correcting mechanisms because of the competition and diversity of content in the mass media. Competition in the mass media, within particular media, and among media, plus the notion that the mass media serve as a "common carrier" of diverse content and viewpoints, have persisted and been enhanced. Despite the growth of interlocking corporate controls, the number of distinct outlets still remains substantial. Thus, the basic question is to describe the balance between uniformity and diversity in the contents of the mass media. . . .

The balance between uniformity and diversity of content is grounded in the technological base of the mass media. The end product is that of a massive national audience which attends to highly standardized content; at the same time the ordered social segments of an advanced industrial society have access to an almost bewildering range of specialized and diverse media content.[14] The uniformity of content is a result of the mechanics of television which enables three national networks to fashion the massive exposure of the U.S. audience to night television. On the other hand, the diversity (and dissenting content) is the result of extensive specialization of the other channels of the mass media, namely, those which operate in radio and print. . . .

In varying degrees the other mass media supply diversified and specialized content. Radio is predominately local and diversified as to audience and content. The press is midway, with considerable variation. Local newspapers reflect territorial diversification. Magazines and books contribute extensively to the variation in media content. Magazines, in particular, are specialized by occupation and interest grouping.

In terms of time, television is the dominant medium. It is compelling in its attractiveness and instant reality. Long-term trend data underscore the expansion of the television audience, and the capacity of the citizenry to consume mass media at the expense of other pastimes. National surveys covering the period from 1960 to 1974 report the person's favorite pastime. From zero in 1938 the television figure rose to 46% of the population in 1974. Television expanded its audience at the expense of reading, which dropped from 21% to 14%, of movies, from 19% to 9%; and of radio, from 9% to 5%. Even dancing suffered; from 9% to 5%. Only playing cards held its own. There were limited increases in staying home with family and visiting with friends, pastimes which can be combined with television viewing. The ability of television to claim leisure time, and in fact to increase its hold on mass audiences, has been precisely documented by the trend survey conducted since 1961 by the Roper Organization.[15] The question posed was simple and direct: "On an average day, about how many hours do you personally spend watching TV? The results indicate that the trend in media exposure has been from two hours and seventeen minutes in 1961 to three hours and two minutes by 1974. While better educated persons spend less time than less educated, the college educated and upper economic levels have demonstrated a parallel upward trend in exposure as follows: One hour and forty-eight minutes in 1961 to two hours and twenty-three minutes in 1974.

# Trends in Media Content

A considerably larger portion of the contents of the mass media is designed to entertain than to inform. More content distracts and diverts attention and less stimulates consideration of the social, economic, and political problems of the period. In other words, there is an extensive difference between the contents of the mass media and the contents of human existence—daily existence and "historical" existence. But the distinction between entertainment and information content is neither definitive nor necessarily appropriate. The entertainment content presents a flow of materials which fashion normative standards and which implant a picture of social reality. Instead our propositions about the content of the mass media deal with "popular culture," on the one hand, or with "public affairs," on the other. As a first step, if one leaves aside the limited but significant core of high culture, it is possible to characterize the long-term trends in popular culture content. For 1920 to 1976, obviously we are encompassing the changing technological spectrum from the dominance of print—in the case of popular culture, mass magazines to radio and movies and in turn to television.

Two observations about trends in popular culture emerge. First, Leo Lowenthal's observation of the shift in popular culture from "idols" of production to "idols" of consumption can be extended.[16] The idols in the mass media up until 1924 were men and women of economic, industrial, and technological achievement. They created goods and machinery. The change in emphasis came rapidly and decisively by the end of the 1920s. The development of an advanced industrialism, in the context of a consumer-oriented society, meant that the idols of consumption became more dominant and more central. There is, of course, no reason to assume that this was an inevitable process or "universal" outcome of industrialism. It is doubtful whether this shift in mass media content and underlying values has, for example, been as extensive in Japan as in the United States.

However, the Lowenthal observation can be extended for the period since the middle of the 1960s. In essence, the shift from mass media themes of production to consumption has been augmented by a third phase, namely, an emphasis on the details involved in the management of interpersonal relations. The economic tensions associated with stagflagtion have not led popular culture to reemphasize production. Themes of consumption still exceeded those of production; the concern is to include excluded groups in the culture of consumption. The new element deals with the strategies human beings use to handle the personal and emotional problems which are rooted in religion, ethnicity, geography, and family status. Occupation is at most a background dimension of tangential significance.

The popular culture content has come to focus on the moral problems of how one behaves in face-to-face situations as the result of the "big" and "little" issues of contemporary society, the appropriate interactions with close acquaintenances or with strangers. If the themes of production concentrated on heroes and men and women of importance and prominence, the shift to consumption broadened the range of idols to include "ordinary" people. The concern with the management of interpersonal behavior means also that ordinary people become the idols and become more important. Progressively, the range of "encounters" has been broadened to include race relations, mental health, and familial arrangements. The presentation of interpersonal management involves moral assumptions and moral implications. Superficially, the morality is relative; no overriding norms guide a person with certainty. The presentations offer a morality which borders on existential morality—the moral need to confront and master the immediate reality. The content trends, as documented by various empirical studies, have shifted the locus of responsibility of behavior and especially of defects in behavior from the individual person to the "social environment.". . .[17]

The second trend in popular culture content is the rise and persistence of violent themes. The expansion of the mass media—movies and television in particular, as well as the comic books—increased vastly the availability of violent content. The amount of "symbolic" violence before 1920 was of a more limited order of magnitude and it appears less realistic and less immediate in content. Description of violence in books and newspapers, and even fairy tales was, on a cumulative basis, at best a fraction of the actual exposure of youngsters in 1976. . . .

The trends in the mass media in thematic content dealing with violence cannot be accounted for in terms of the realities of modern society. Violent themes in the mass media are to be found primarily in the extensive popular culture content and not in the public affairs content. While one expects the public affairs content to reflect sociopolitical reality and thereby present reportage about actual violence, the emphasis on violence in the popular culture is a "market" decision by media specialists and media elites. The pervasive violence in the mass media is not the result of coverage of public affairs. During the Vietnam War, television coverage of the battlefield was extensive and greatly increased the violence content on the public affairs portion of the mass media. But since 1972 this topic has disappeared. Coverage of crime including the seizing of hostages and local natural disaster serves an equivalent "war" news, but the bulk of the violence is not in the public affairs coverage but in the popular culture and entertainment content.

Television epitomizes the extensive focus on violence in the mass media, although movies are by no means far behind. If the "average" adult attends to two to three hours of television daily, it is my estimate that as much as one-half of the context is violence-oriented. For youngsters the exposure to television and to violence is correspondingly greater. Starting in 1967, George Gerbner and his associates have prepared a detailed and continuous audit of violence in television.[18] Covering the period 1967 to 1973, they concluded that the "thematic structure of the world of television drama has not changed much." This was a period of concentrated agitation against the saturation of television with violence. . . . It appears that the limited effort to decrease the amount of violence content by the major networks has the result of shifting the setting from "exotic, historical and distant" to the more immediate.

It is no simple matter to characterize the normative context of violence in the mass media. The volume and extensive diversity dominate and obscure the details of the moral message presented. Commentators and critics have emphasized the pronounced tendency to present violent themes without reference to any moral code. Specifically, in the area of crime and law enforcement, the difference between the criminals and the police in motivation and tactics has been eroded in the name of realism. Even in the absence of careful and reliable content analysis studies, it does appear that the broadcast media have increasingly presented violent behavior, especially criminal violence, with less and less concern with normative evaluations and implications.

However, it may well be that another trend in the presentation of violence may be of more importance in terms of personal and social control. The thrust, has been to present and characterize violence and violent behavior as diffuse, pervasive, and undifferentiated from other types of social behavior. (There is an analogy with the presentation of the management of interpersonal relations, where there is a crude admixture of humor and tragedy almost at random and in an unpredictable fashion.) In part, we are dealing with the changed character of violence. For example, it has been pointed out that the character of warfare after 1945 has undergone an important change.[19] Classic national wars had an episodic nature; periods of violence were followed by periods of peace. There were boundaries to the scope and participants in the military operations. Progressively, the boundaries have become diffuse, and warfare or the threat of warfare has become an ongoing process in which violence and diplomatic persuasion are closely and simultaneously intertwined. It would be unreal if the mass media did not devote considerable attention to the actual patterns of violence in the real world. However, the diffuse, unpredictable, and unbounded character of violence, and its lack of differentiation from other forms of behavior, have become the essential nature of violence in the popular culture of the mass media.

The third trend in content analysis deals with the public affairs presentation in the mass media. The treatment of public affairs is a revealing indicator of modern society. This view was neatly formulated by Walter Lippmann, "on the whole, the quality of the news about modern society is an index of its social organization."[20] The almost endless array of topics and treatments of public affairs presented in mass media can be handled for our purposes by the overarching hypothesis that during the period under study there has been a shift in emphasis in the format for presenting public affairs from the "gatekeeper" style to that of the advocate journalist.[21] The gatekeeper format emphasizes the search for objectivity and the sharp separation of reporting fact from disseminating opinion, commentary, and editorials. . . .

In contrast, the advocate journalist seeks to replace the search for objectivity with a conception of the journalist as critic and interpreter. In this view, the task of the journalist is to present the viewpoints and interest of competing groups, especially those of excluded and underprivileged groups. The role of the journalist is to ensure that all perspectives are adequately represented in the media, for the resolution of social conflict depends on effective representation of alternative definitions of reality. The journalist must "participate" in the advocacy process.

The gatekeeper model was based on a particular conception of professionalism. From the turn of the century, and especially after 1920, efforts were directed to fashioning journalism into a field similar to medicine, where the journalist would develop his technical expertise and also create a sense of professional responsibility. The journalist sought to apply the canons of the scientific method in order to increase his objectivity and enhance his effective performance. Through the application of intellectually based techniques, objective and valid results could be obtained. Those who pressed for the gatekeeper model were aware of the difficulties and inherent limitations, but the ideals supplied guidelines in their view.

In the middle of the 1960s, this gatekeeper model of journalist was called into question. Sociopolitical tensions led to a desire among some journalists for a more activist role. They came to believe that meaningful objectivity was impossible. One sociological investigator sympathetic to this viewpoint drew the conclusion from her field research into the practice of journalists that objectivity was a "strategic ritual" by news personnel to defend themselves from the "risks of their trade" and from "critical onslaught."[22] The model of the advocate journalist was the lawyer, in particular, the adversary lawyer. . . .

The Kerner Commission, established to investigate the causes of the race riots of the 1960s, gave explicit support to the trend.[23] The Kerner Commission criticized the media for failing to cover adequately the plight of minorities and for their ineffective editorial support for necessary social and political change. The recommendations of the Kerner Commission included the employment of additional minority-group members in the mass media, in order to guarantee that the minority point of view would be adequately represented. These recommendations epitomized the advocate orientation. . . .

John Johnstone's sample survey of over 1,300 journalists interviewed in 1971 has presented an overview of the concentration of gatekeeper versus advocate self-conceptions among journalists.[24] He used the more loaded terms "neutral versus participant" as the equivalent of the "gatekeeper versus the advocate." Of his sample, 8.5% were predominately participants in outlook, and 21.4% moderately participant. In addition, 35.4% held balanced views, 25.1% were moderately neutral, and 9.7% were predominately neutral. While these findings indicate that only a limited minority were polarized at each end of the continuum, more than 60% accept some aspect of the advocacy journalism. The result has been an extensive shift in the standards and style of public affairs presentation, especially in the important and pervasive television news broadcast, where the distinction between news and comment has been in effect eliminated. . . .

The emergence of the advocate model in part represents a response to specific practices of political leaders. Political leaders have been more active in seeking to fashion "the news" through either subtle or more outright managements of information. In particular, those responsible for decision making in the Vietnam conflict at times engaged in such practices. In turn, mass media staff members came to believe that it was their obligation to "expose" relentlessly such practices and to inform the electorate of alternative information and opposing points of view. . . .

The fusion of reporting and comment of the advocate journalist has been called the "Europeanization" of the U.S. press, and the contents of the mass media have as a result become more argumentative, contentious, but not necessarily more penetrating or more revealing. With the background of these three trends in the contents of the mass media, it becomes more feasible to assess the influence of the mass media on social personality and social control. While a variety of research data are available, systemic inferences and some reasoned speculation are involved.

## Audience Exposure, Popular Distrust, and Social Control

. . . Our underlying hypothesis is that the major trends in the mass media have not contributed to the growth of those personal controls required for more effective social control in advanced industrial society. More specifically, rather than strengthening those ego controls which contribute to realistic self-interest and stable group attachments required for effective political participation, the long-term effect has been to heighten projective (and accordingly suspicious) personality predispositions and defensive group affiliations. The most adequate research data center on the second content trend, of sustained concern with violent themes, rather than on the first theme, of mass consumption and interpersonal management, or the third one, the rise of advocacy in the presentation of public affairs. But it is the confluence of the three elements that is the essential component in accounting for the mass media contribution to the attenuation of social control.

First, popular culture content, the content dealing with both interpersonal relations and with mass consumption, is augmented by extensive time and space devoted to mass advertising. By and large the audience views the mass advertisements as blending in with the popular culture portion. Raymond A. Bauer and Stephen S. Greyser have summarized the available survey research on attitudes toward advertisements.[25] The audience take advertisements for granted—indeed, they are a positive attraction. The overwhelming, uniform finding is the favorable attitude toward mass advertisements dating from the 1920s when such studies were first executed. Over time there has been no discernible trend. In 1964–1965 considerable debate began about truth in advertising, which led to various legislative and administrative steps. But there is no evidence of any basic change in attitudes toward institutionalized advertising. In fact, the interest of better educated persons in "artistic" advertisements in the "better" magazine has increased and reflects the strong appetite for the symbolic content of consumerism. . . .

In terms of social control, the response to mass advertisements—as well as the consumption content of popular culture—is not to be judged by the sales effectiveness of particular advertisements or campaigns but by the long-term consequences on attitudes and social personality. The most suggestive evidence is contained in the endless series of commercially sponsored research called "motivation research." Social scientists cannot dismiss these findings, although very few of them enter the published literature and most fail to meet minimum research standards. In addition, some of the intensive probing in this type of research may border on violation of privacy.

Such advertising research underlines that an important component of consumer decisions is based on the gratification of primitive impulses—on irrational motivation, if you will—rather than on rational economic choice.[26] Moreover, such research supplies guidelines for mass advertising designed to appeal to the nonrational aspects of social personality, and to give these aspects greater prominence. Of course, the results do not permit quantitative measures of the relative importance of these variables. But the advertising strategy which has been developed can well be described in terms of dynamic personality psychology. The "operational code" of the mass advertiser is, in the simplest language, to reduce conscience (superego) resistance, to appeal directly to primitive pleasure impulses (id), and either to avoid rational objections (ego) or at least to fuse the rational and the pleasure appeals.[27] The long-term results have been to increase impulse buying, as it is called by the experts, which reduces rational considerations and contains personal controls. The availability of credit cards reinforces such consumer behavior. . . .

What can be said about the social implications of the popular culture content of the new style "sophisticated" "soap opera"—the serials concerned with "modern" interpersonal relations and tensions? The soap operas of the 1940s had explicit, simple moral messages. The analysis of housewife reaction to the "traditional" and moralistic "radio daytime serial" prepared by W. Lloyd Warner and William E. Henry showed the symbolic influence of this type of popular culture.[28] They describe these radio—and later television—presentations as "contemporary morality" plays which allowed the housewife vicarious indulgence in other people's adventures and wayward behaviors, but "in the end" her own day-to-day morality was validated. We cannot describe the new sophisticated soap opera as functioning in such a fashion. The comic interludes, even comic definitions of interpersonal strain and trauma, offer considerable catharsis and tension reduction, which no doubt account for the audiences. But the emphasis on the hostile and destructive impulses of the "outsider" and the reliance on humor to deal with hostility is likely to generate suspicious responses. There is little reason to assume that the viewer gains insight into his own motivations or is supplied with enriched understanding of social and psychological reality so as to reinforce or modify moral judgments and enhance self- and personal controls. . . .

The long-term consequence of the strong concentration of violence content on personal and social controls has its crucial test in the impact of television on children and youngsters. Television is the major carrier of violent content. The new generation grow up in a setting of increased access to violent content and they continue to be exposed to varying degrees for a lifetime.

It was not academic interest which produced a comprehensive synthesis of the available analytic thinking and empirical research on televised violence. Rather, Congressional concern with public morality, crime, and aggressive behavior stimulated a cooperative and interdisciplinary review. As a result of the initiative of Senator John O. Pastore of Rhode Island, a government-sponsored panel of social scientists was created. The definition of the problem as a public health issue supplied a basis for the professional detachment of the effort. The Surgeon General's Scientific Advisory Committee on Television and Social Behavior, after two years in 1972 issued a report,[29] by a group of experts who had temporarily abandoned their specialized perspectives and risen above their institutional affiliation and interests.

Aggressive behavior was the focus—the dependent variable. The results of over fifty separate studies, experimental endeavors and sample surveys, indicated that exposure to televised violence increased aggressive behavior as a result of imitation or instigation. The more clear-cut experimental findings were confirmed by sample surveys, although in general surveys produce, for the reason set forth above, less definitive results. The observed relations were low but repeatedly encountered. Given the multiple basis of aggressive behavior, if the encountered influence of televised violence on children and youngsters had been more extensive, the results would have had to be judged as truly devastating. Moreover, if one makes the effort to read the descriptive details of the experimental studies one is struck by the scope and impact of instigated aggressiveness.

Of course, individual studies are only indicators; the essential inferences must be drawn from these findings. If the research methods which sampled social reality at particular moments in time had produced discernible results of increased aggressive behavior, then the long-term cumulative effects on the audience would most likely be stronger and clearer. Moreover, the correct question about televised violence involves a much sharper focus on societal socialization. In the frame of reference of social control, the increased complexity of the occupational sector and the disarticulation of work and communal residence require a higher level of personal controls. Thus, the task of the mass media is to develop a more adequate relation to authority—that is, greater capacity to store and manage aggression. In short, the findings of these researches indicate a tendency toward weaker personal controls, that is, just the opposite. In fact if the mass media exposure to violence had had no effect, the consequences could still be viewed as disruptive, since the societal requirements are for more effective personal control in order for there to be more adequate societal control. In part, this question was argued in 1937 by Mortimer Alder, when he was evaluating the effect of movies on the criminal behavior of youth.[30] Adler's humanistic analysis and the findings of social research converge; if the proportion which has been allocated to violence had been used for civic education, the social personality of the U.S. citizenry would have been discernibly less accepting of illegitimate violence.

In assessing the consequences of the third indicator of mass media content, namely, the shift toward a stronger emphasis on advocacy, our focus must be less on specific subject themes, and more on style and format. Nevertheless, it must be remembered that less than 5% of all of the contents of the mass media, it is estimated, deals with public affairs. This limited amount is given prominent exposure and, because of its political importance and drama, it commands widespread attention. Media competition in the presentation of public affairs makes possible a competitive electoral system with all its inherent and accumulated defects. . . .

It is now necessary to spell out the requirements laid down for the mass media by democratic political theory. Political theorists and sociologists have elaborated these requirements in different language, but there is considerable agreement about the essentials. The mass media must *(a)* contribute to a high level of participation by all ordered segments of society; *(b)* stimulate effective political deliberation on the issues and candidates and contribute a meaningful basis on which citizens make their voting decisions; and *(c)* operate to preclude either side from monopolizing or even exercising pervasive influence by means of them. The mass media must also contribute to a sense of political self-confidence and enlightened self-interest on the part of each citizen. To the extent that these criteria are not met, the election process is not one of consent but degenerates into an exercise in mass pressure. In specific terms, the danger of an advanced industrial society with an elaborate system of mass communication is that the presentation of public affairs will contribute to suspicion and projective distrust and weaken the relevance and legitimacy of the electoral process. . . .

It has been argued by some critics that the mass media inherently contribute to suspicion and projective distrust. In this view, political democracy rests on face-to-face communications and in the real world there is an inherent element of remoteness between the mass communicator and his audience.

In addition, there is an imbalance of influence and in "feedback" which undermines the process of building consent. Such a line of reason is extreme and self-defeating. The interpersonal basis of political democracy is essential, but one can still reject the assertion that the mass media inherently or uniformly undermine the process of political persuasion. In realistic and pragmatic terms, it is sufficient to offer the criterion that democratic debate and elections depend on the extent to which interpersonal influences operate substantially independent of the influence of the mass media. Thus the question is the strategy and tactics in the handling of public affairs content by the mass media. What is the character of the political struggle between the political elites? Is the approach one in which the emphasis is on building realism and insight (appeals to ego), or is it highly personalistic in format, combatative with irrational overtones and appeals to defensive group solidarities (distorted superego appeals)?

Human personality has a great capacity to simplify social reality and to select congenial elements from the mass media. In fact, the immense extent of self-selection is one of the most persistent findings of social psychological research on exposure to the mass media. But the political process of necessity involves simplification of complex issues. The human capacity to simplify the external world makes possible social relations and political decisions. From the point of view of social personality and social control, the basic question is whether these simplifications—stereotypes, in the sense used by Walter Lippmann—are being influenced by a component of personal control and by an appeal to insight, realism, and enlightened self-interest, or by the reverse, including accumulative distrust.

Our hypothesis is that the growing dominance of television, with its stress on a personalistic presentation of public affairs, and the increased emphasis on advocacy journalism make a discernible contribution to the distrustful and projective audience response to public affairs. In essence, the effects of the mass media on public affairs, particularly during election campaigns, conform more to the Lasswell model of systemic significance than to the Lazarsfeld tangential model. . . .

The basis for the "disruptive" contribution of the mass media to the electoral process is a convergence of the dominance of television as the major public affairs medium with its very personalized style plus the growth of the advocacy format. National samples demonstrate the long-term increased reliance on television as the source for "most of your news." The relative standing can be seen in Table 1, where citizen answers are presented. In 1959, 51% reported television, 57 newspapers, and 34 radio; by 1974 television had reached 65%, newspapers had dropped slightly to 47%, and radio had declined to 21%. Perhaps a clearer picture of the dominance of the television is obtained when responses are grouped. By 1974, the largest single group comprised those who relied only on television, 36%; the second, those who relied on television and newspaper, 23%; and the third, those who relied on newspapers only, 19%. By 1972 the reliance on television among the college educated almost equaled that of the less than college educated group. Moreover, television had emerged as the dominant source of news for national, state, and local elections.[31]

**TABLE 1.    Trends in Mass Media Sources for News, 1959–1974
(Based on National Sample Surveys)**

"FIRST, I'D LIKE TO ASK YOU WHERE YOU USUALLY GET MOST OF YOUR NEWS ABOUT WHAT'S GOING ON IN THE WORLD TODAY—FROM THE NEWSPAPERS OR RADIO OR TELEVISION OR MAGAZINES OR TALKING TO PEOPLE OR WHERE?" MOST NEWS:

| SOURCE OF MOST NEWS: | 1959 | 1961 | 1963 | 1964 | 1967 | 1968 | 1971 | 1972 | 1974 |
|---|---|---|---|---|---|---|---|---|---|
| Television | 51% | 52% | 55% | 58% | 64% | 59% | 60% | 64% | 65% |
| Newspapers | 57 | 57 | 53 | 56 | 55 | 49 | 48 | 50 | 47 |
| Radio | 34 | 34 | 29 | 26 | 28 | 25 | 23 | 21 | 21 |
| Magazines | 8 | 9 | 6 | 8 | 7 | 7 | 5 | 6 | 4 |
| People | 4 | 5 | 4 | 5 | 4 | 5 | 4 | 4 | 4 |
| Don't know/ no answer (DK/NA) | 1 | 3 | 3 | 3 | 2 | 3 | 1 | 1 | * |

SOURCE: Adapted for The Roper Organization, "Trends in Public Attitudes toward Television and Other Mass Media, 1959–1974," (New Yok: Television Information Office, 1975), p. 3.

But the most striking aspect is the mass audience's trust and approval of television. The text of the specific question is relevant: "If you get conflicting or different reports of the same news story from radio, television, the magazines and the newspapers, which of the four versions would you be most inclined to believe—the one on radio or television or magazines or newspapers?" From 1959 onward television credibility has grown from 29% to 51%, while newspapers have declined from 32% to 20%. . . .[32]

These findings are noteworthy, in the context of the marked decline in expressed trust in other institutions of U.S. society. The increase in trust in television has been gradual and therefore not linked to particular events. But coverage of the war in Vietnam and of the proceedings of the Watergate investigation has contributed to popular trust in television as a public affairs medium. However, I argue that television and its news commentators are trusted in part because of their consistently suspicious view of public affairs. The commentators help define public affairs as suspect; in effect, they direct suspicion away from themselves to other persons and institutions. They have assisted the audience to project their mistrust and to select targets for their mistrust, almost as if television were a counter "phobic device." The individual must have a focus for his trust, and to trust mainly the devices of the mass media with their exposé orientation is a weak basis for rational appeals and for strengthening ego control. The result is more and more a form of mass media dependency.

The style of the television commentator is to mix news and commentary, to emphasize advocacy posture—often less content and more style.[33] One can point to particular commentators who adhere to a "neutral" style, but the interpretative advocate posture is pronounced. The limitations of time requires more oversimplification than in printed media. If there is to be coverage in depth, one issue is selected—such as the war in Vietnam or Watergate—to the exclusion of others. Television, with its advocacy overtones, is concerned mainly with crises, tensions, and problem formation, not with performance and achievement.[34] Finally, the dissemination of public affairs by personalistic commentators heightens the definition of politics as a struggle between persons, and deemphasizes concern with and debate about underlying issues.[35]

The consequences of public affairs content for the mass media are most directly discernible in the outcome of elections. Such consequences are a function of the relative increase in change in voting intention in the course of the political campaign. . . .

The 1952 election, the intense competition between Dwight D. Eisenhower and Adlai Stevenson, was marked by a more extensive shift in voting patterns than the previous presidential election. The increased amount of voting shifts reflected changes in the social structure and in the strength of the personalities involved. It was also the first election which was studied extensively by national sample surveys.

Of the potential voting population in 1952, 46.5% were regular party voters, that, is they voted for the presidential candidate of the same party—Republican or Democratic—in 1948 and 1952; 16.1% were nonvoters, while all categories of changes amounted to 39.6%. Survey research soon after the 1952 election offered the conclusion that the effect of television on the election campaign was minimal and without real consequences.[36] However, subsequent reanalysis and a more systemic outlook pointed out the role of the mass media in that election, a role which contributed to the emergence of weak political regimes.[37] Three inferences can be drawn from the available analysis of the influence of the media in this campaign. Extensive exposure to the mass media reinforced and mobilized interest in the campaign, increasing final turnout. Increased exposure does not necessarily stimulate participation, although it generally does. . . .[38] Second, in 1952, television assisted the Republican party to mobilize their "stalwarts" to a greater extent than it helped the Democratic "stalwarts." Finally, Eisenhower's appeal, especially on television, had a discernible effect on persons who might be called "indifferent" citizens, those who did not see the election as involving their essential self-interest. In other words, the mass media influenced those persons weakly linked to politics and most disposed to shift from one party to another. . . .

In the 1976 election, available data indicate that the mass media also served to maintain relatively high interest and to stimulate turnout, although the citizenry had reservations about both candidates. The election produced a considerable shift in presidential preference from the previous campaign and changes in preferences in the course of the campaign. Mass media appeals were especially important for those persons with strong political interests, in contrast to the 1952 election. The "independents" have changed their character and include a high concentration of persons with strong political involvements. However, given the complexity of the issues involved and the difficulties of aggegrating one's self-interest, the personality of the candidates was critical, and influenced not only persons with weak political interest but also some of those with strong political interest. This aspect of the campaign symbolism cannot be said to have strengthened rational responses and personal controls. . . .

We are dealing not only with the outcome of specific electoral contests but also with a longer-term trend in media exposure and political response. Our analysis converges with the results of the reanalysis of survey data by Michael J. Robinson for 1960–1968 which emphasized the "counter phobic" or politically suspicious element in the response to television content.[39] He employs the term "political malaise" to describe the loss of political confidence which extensive exposure produces. Of course, an interactive effect is at work. Great reliance on television rather than on the other media for news is found among persons with a low sense of political efficacy. Some self-selection is at work, but this relationship holds for persons with low and high educational backgrounds. Self-selection then is not an adequate explanation of these and other correlates of high exposure to television news. For example, persons who rely more on television news believed more often that Congressmen quickly lose touch with people; and this relationship cuts across education and income groups as well.[40] These results underline the projective influence of television content as it is actually organized and disseminated. Paralleling the consequence of violent content, the effect of television news is cumulative, so that its long-term contribution to political suspicion, which weakens political legitimacy, cannot be denied or overlooked.

In summary, the trends in mass media content and popular response highlight the vulnerabilities of the citizenry to appeals and content which weakened personal control. An advanced industrial society is dependent on the mass media to generate consensus and coordination, but the essential conclusion is that the vast apparatus of the mass media fails to contribute adequately to the articulation of the institutional sectors of society and to contribute to the socialization required for effective social controls. . . .

## Notes

1. Morris Janowitz, "The Study of Mass Communication," *International Encyclopedia of the Social Sciences* 3 (New York: Macmillan and the Free Press, 1968), 41–53.

2. Elihu Katz and Paul Lazarsfeld, *Personal Influence: The Part Played by the People in the Flow of Mass Communication* (Glencoe, Ill.: Free Press, 1955); Joseph T. Klapper, *The Effects of Mass Communication* (New York, Free Press of Glencoe, 1960).

3. Bernard Berelson, "The State of Communication Research," *Public Opinion Quarterly* 23 (1959): 1–7.

4. Harold D. Lasswell, *Propaganda Technique in the World War* (New York: Knopf, 1927).

5. For overall presentation of findings, see W. W. Charters, *Motion Pictures and Youth* (New York: Macmillan, 1933); see especially, for detailed case-study analysis, Herbert Blumer and Phillip M. Hauser, *Movies, Delinquency and Crime* (New York: Macmillan, 1933).

6. Willian E. Daugherty, *A Psychological Warfare Casebook* (Baltimore: The Johns Hopkins University Press, 1958).

7. Carl I. Hovland, "Results from Studies of Attitude Change," *The American Psychologist* 14 (January 1959): 8–17.

8. M. McCombs and D. Shaw, "The Agenda-Setting Function of Mass Media," *Public Opinion Quarterly* 36 (1972): 176–87.

9. W. I. Thomas and Florian Znaniecki, "The Wider Community and the Role of the Press," in *The Polish Peasant in Europe and America,* 4 (Boston: Badger Press, 1920), pp. 241–71.

10. There have been vast historical studies, reports, biographies, autobiographies, and general accounts of journalism and the mass media. These materials are carefully annotated in three bibliographies: Harold D. Lasswell, Ralph D. Casey, and Bruce Lannes Smith, *Propaganda and Promotional Activities: An Annotated Bibliography* (Minneapolis: University of Minnesota Press, 1935); Bruce Lannes Smith, Harold D. Lasswell, and Ralph D. Casey, *Propaganda, Communication and Public Opinion: A Comprehensive Reference Guide* (Princeton: Princeton University Press, 1946); Bruce Lannes Smith and Chitra Smith, *International Communications and Political Opinion: A Guide to the Literature* (Princeton: Princeton University Press, 1956). More recent literature is covered in Donald A. Hansen and J. Herschel Parsons, *Mass Communications: A Research Bibliography* (Santa Barbara: Glendessary Press, 1968).

11. Charles R. Wright, *Mass Communications: A Sociological Perspective* (New York: Random, 1959); Harold D. Lasswell, "The Structure and Function of Communications in Society," in *The Communication of Ideas,* ed. Lyman Bryson (New York: Harper, 1948), pp. 37–52; Caren Siune and F. Gerald Kline, "Communications, Mass Political Behavior, and Mass Society," in *Political Communication Issues and Strategies for Research,* ed. Steven H. Chaffee (Beverly Hills: Sage Publications, 1975), pp. 65–84; Paul M. Hirsch, "Occupational, Organizational and Institutional Models of Mass Media Research: Towards an Integrated Framework," in *Strategies for Mass Communication Reserarch,* ed. Paul M. Hirsch, P. Miller and F. Gerald Kline (Beverly Hills: Sage Publications, 1977), pp. 3–36.

12. John Dewey, "The Reflex Arc Concept in Psychology," *Psychological Review* 3 (July 1896): 357–70; see also Neil Coughlan, *Young John Dewey: An Essay in American Intellectual History* (Chicago: University of Chicago Press, 1975), chap.

8, for a discussion of the intellectual history and context of this formulation.

13. Harold D. Lasswell, "The Person: Subject and Object of Propaganda," *Annals* 179 (May 1935): 187–93.

14. Paul M. Hirsch, "Television as a National Medium: Its Cultural and Political Role in American Society," in *Handbook of Urban Life,* ed. David Street (San Francisco: Jossey Bass, 1978).

15. Annual Reports by the Roper Organization.

16. Leo Lowenthal, "Biographies in Popular Magazines," in *Radio Research, 1942– 1943,* ed. Paul F. Lazarsfeld and Frank Stanton (New York: Duell, Sloan and Pearce, 1944).

17. Arnold S. Linsky, "Theories of Behavior and the Image of the Alcoholic in Popular Magazines," *Public Opinion Quarterly* 34 (1970–1971): 573–81; Charles Y. Glock, "Images of Man and Public Opinion," *Public Opinion Quarterly* 28 (1964): 539–46.

18. George Gerbner and Larry Gross, "Living With Television: The Violence Profile," *Journal of Communication* 26 (1976): 173–99; "Television World of Violence," in *Mass Media and Violence,* ed. D. L. Lange, Robert K. Baker, and Sandra J. Ball (Washington: GPO, 1967), pp. 341–62.

19. Klaus Knorr, *The Power and Wealth: The Political Economy of International Power* (New York: Basic Books, 1973).

20. Walter Lippmann, *Public Opinion* (New York: Macmillan, 1922), p. 274.

21. Morris Janowitz, "The Journalistic Profession and the Mass Media," in *Culture and Its Creators: Essays in Honor of Edward Shils,* ed. Joseph Ben-David and Terry N. Clark (Chicago: University of Chicago Press, 1977), pp. 72–96. See also Barbara Philips, "The Artists of Everyday Life," Ph.D. dissertation, University of Syracuse, 1975.

22. Gaye Tuchman, "Objectivity as a Strategic Ritual: An Examination of Newsmen's Notions of Objectivity," *American Journal of Sociology* 77 (January 1972): 660– 79.

23. U.S. National Advisory Commission on Civil Disorders, *Report* (Washington: GPO, 1968).

24. John Johnstone et al., *The News People: A Sociological Portrait of American Journalists and Their Work* (Urbana: University of Illinois Press, 1976), chap. 7.

25. Raymond A. Bauer and Stephen S. Greyser, *Advertising in America: The Consumer View* (Cambridge: Harvard University Press, 1968), passim; see also Leo Bogart, *Strategy in Advertising* (New York: Harcourt, Brace and World, 1967).

26. Ernest Dichter, *Handbook of Consumer Motivation: The Psychology of the World of Objects* (New York: McGraw-Hill, 1964).

27. For the analytic background of this type of analysis, see Harold D. Lasswell, "The Triple-Appeal Principle," *American Journal of Sociology* (May 1932): 523– 38.

28. W. Lloyd Warner and William E. Henry, "The Radio Day-Time Serial: A Symbolic Analysis," *Genetic Psychology Monographs* 37 (1948): 3–73.

29. U.S. Public Health Service, The Surgeon-General's Scientific Advisory Committee on Television and Social Behavior, *Television and Growing Up: The Impact of*

*Televised Violence* (Washington: GPO, 1972); G. Comstock Rubinstein and J. Murray, *Television and Social Behavior* (Rockville, Md.: National Institute of Mental Health, 1972); for British perspectives, see Hilde T. Himmelweit, A. N. Oppenheim, and Pamela Vince, *Television and the Child: An Empirical Study of the Effects of Television on the Young* (New York: Oxford University Press, 1958); J. D. Halloran, R. L. Brown, and D. C. Chaney, *Television and Delinquency* (Leicester: Leicester University Press), pp. 1–70.

30. Mortimer Adler, *Art and Prudence* (New York: Longmans, Green, 1937).

31. A lower level of reliance on television for news is reported in a survey sponsored by the Newsprint Committee. See H. Bagdikian, *The Information Machines: Their Impact on Men and the Media* (New York: Harper and Row, 1971).

32. The Roper Organization, "Trends in Public Attitudes toward Television and Other Mass Media, 1959–1974" (New York: Television Information Office, 1975), p. 4.

33. Reuven Frank, "An Anatomy of Television News," *Television Quarterly* 9 (1970): 1–23.

34. M. Robinson, "American Political Legitimacy in an Era of Electronic Journalism: Reflections on the Evening News," in *Television as a Social Force: New Approaches to T.V. Criticism,* ed. D. Cater and R. Adler (New York: Praeger, 1975), pp. 97–140. This argument was in the past made about "sensational" newspapers. See H. L. Mencken, "Newspaper Morals," *Atlantic Monthly* 113 (March 1914): 289–97.

35. This analysis of the role of the mass media in creating projective distrust versus insight was stimulated by an essay entitled "Trends in Twentieth Century Propaganda," by Ernest Kris and Nathan Leites, first published in *Psychoanalysis and the Social Sciences* 1 (1947): 393–409. . . .

36. Angus Campbell, Gerald Gurin, and Warren E. Miller, "Television and the Election," *Scientific American* 188 (May 1953): 46–48.

37. Morris Janowitz and Dwaine Marvick, *Competitive Pressure and Democratic Consent* (Chicago: Quadrangle, 1964), pp. 57–71; Kurt Lang and Gladys Lang, *Politics and Television* (Chicago: Quadrangle, 1968); Michael J. Robinson, "Public Affairs Television and the Growth of Political Malaise," *American Political Science Review* 70 (June 1976): 409–32; Michael J. Robinson and Clifford Zukin, "Television and the Wallace Vote," *Journal of Communication* 26 (1976): 79–83.

38. Jay G. Blumler and Dennis McQuail, *Television in Politics* (Chicago: University of Chicago Press, 1969); see especially chap. 13 for discussion of long-term effects.

39. Robinson, "Public Affairs." See also Jarol B. Mannheim, "Can Democracy Survive Television?" *Journal of Communication* 26 (1976): 84–90.

40. As in the election of 1952, the 1968 election, which Robinson analyzes in some detail, television assisted Nixon, the Republican candidate, and Wallace as well, if both income and educational differences are considered.

# 7

# Mass Media Effects

Because of widespread concern over the power of mass media to persuade and control, communications researchers have conducted many empirical studies of media effects since the 1930s. A sizable body of literature is now available on the conditions under which newspapers, radio, film, and television content affect particular audiences and society at large.

The effects of communication are many and diverse. They may be short- or long-range. They may be manifest or latent. They may be strong or weak. They may be considered psychological or political, economic or sociological. Accordingly, researchers have studied such topics as the media's ability to change or determine votes, to stimulate consumption or persuade people which product to buy, to inculcate or change attitudes, and effectively to suggest antisocial forms of behavior. Although short-run measurable effects on individuals have been the most frequently studied question, the media's long run effects on society, and their ability to influence the general shape of culture and politics, are also important topics for research. Because the literature on communication effects is so large, it is impossible to represent fully in one section. The articles to follow, however, present a balanced sampling of important research on mass media impact.[1]

The Langs address the long-standing question of how media coverage affects voter decisions during election campaigns. They suggest that the emphasis of earlier studies on *conversions* to another candidate (which happen infrequently) understated and neglected the power of the media to direct attention to certain issues and away from others. Hence, they elaborate the "agenda-setting function" hypothesis presented by McCombs and Shaw in Section 3. The Langs also call attention to "the continuous, and not only the intermittent aspects of mass media influence" and advocate specific research tasks that reveal a broader perspective than the simple study of vote changes during electoral campaigns.

Shils and Janowitz address an issue that was of particularly grave concern to scholars and political observers during both world wars: the power of exhortative propaganda to influence military behavior. Prior to the pioneering findings which Shils and Janowitz report, many feared that the media were powerful enough to act as a "hypodermic needle" and successfully implant messages in the minds of individuals that could move them to undreamed-of degrees of compliance. This study facilitated a more general "rediscovery" of the primary group as an important influence on individuals' attitudes and behavior, which in turn forced a drastic modification of researchers' faith in (and fears of) the unbridled power of the media. In this article, Shils and Janowitz find that the impact of Nazi propaganda on German soldiers during World War II was minimal when compared with the importance of group solidarity on morale and fighting effectiveness.

Information campaigns are a common practice of both advertisers and public service agencies. Institutions frequently make systematic attempts to inform the public on various matters of concern, but the effectiveness of such efforts is often disappointing. Robinson studies the process by which information from the mass media reaches, or fails to reach, its intended audience. He finds that media information campaigns tend to magnify knowledge differentials that already exist in society, because information tends to reach those who are already the best informed. (For an elaboration of this concept, see Tichenor et al.'s article in Section 6.) Interestingly, while education is the main determinant of media use patterns, it is not necessarily the better educated who become the best informed. Rather, it appears to be "interpersonal social contacts" that account for the largest increases in knowledge and awareness.

On a theoretical level, Robinson argues that the processes of information flow between mass media and their audiences are extremely complex and expresses dissatisfaction with our present inability to specify them more precisely. He points out that even the elegant "two-step flow" model proposed by Katz and Lazarsfeld[2] remains inadequate despite its careful effort to strike a balance between media influence and interpersonal factors.

Dorr's thoughtful article takes us through the various developmental stages of the child's relationship to television. Children do not interpret television as adults do, nor do they interpret it in the same way throughout childhood. Rather, they apply new paradigms as they grow older, each

324

set featuring a more realistic set of constructs. Typically, they make the most "correct" interpretations as they approach adolescence.

## Notes

1. For an excellent historical overview of research and paradigms about mass media effects, see Melvin DeFleur and Sandra Ball-Rokeach, *Theories of Mass Communication,* 3d ed. (New York: David McKay, 1975).
2. Elihu Katz and Paul Lazarsfeld, *Personal Influence.* (Glencoe, Ill.: The Free Press, 1955).

# The Mass Media and Voting

KURT LANG

GLADYS ENGEL LANG

AFTER EACH NATIONAL ELECTION students of political behavior comment on how little effect the mass media appear to have had on the outcome. Franklin D. Roosevelt and Harry S Truman won *in spite of* the press. The personal nature of the Eisenhower victory in 1952 showed that the campaign was so much shouting and tumult; the election was won before the campaign had even begun. Still, all of us politicians, candidates, public servants, symbol manipulators, members of the Great Audience, and even students of political behavior in our private capacities as interested and partisan citizens— much as we may publicly belittle what the mass media do, act most of the time *as if* we believed in their potency. Republican members of the faculty pay for a newspaper ad supporting their candidate; the Democrats must counter with their own publicity. The vagaries of research leads us away from a principal concern with the impact of press, radio, television, and magazines, but nothing would seem to have banished our not yet empirically demonstrated beliefs that the mass media are more influential than we would sometimes wish. Outcries against certain political television shows during and between campaigns, as well as the enduring and enthusiastic acceptance accorded to George Orwell's *1984*, indicate vividly that our research may not tell us what our common sense reveals is there to be told. . . .

None of the three voting studies—Elmira, 1948; Bristol North-East, 1951; the U.S. national survey in 1952[1]—draw any explicit conclusions to the effect that mass communications are *not* an important influence in voting behavior. They all point to their own methodological inadequacies, and in the most

Reprinted with permission of Macmillian Publishing Co., Inc., from Kurt Lang and Gladys Engel Lang, "The Mass Media and Voting," in *American Voting Behavior*, Eugene Burdic and Arthur J. Brodbeck, eds., pp. 217–235. Copyright © 1959 by The Free Press, a Corporation.

recent of the three studies the problem of mass-media impact has actually been avoided.[2] At many points, the importance of the mass media is stressed; nowhere is their role in connection with the vote actually belittled. Yet there may be a difference between the author's own interpretations and more or less popular understandings of what their findings mean.

## Mass Communications During the Campaign

Exactly what do we learn about the influence of mass communication on voting behavior by studying its effect within the scope of a single campaign?

Both the Elmira and the Bristol studies reiterate findings of earlier research. In Elmira the group who changed their voting intentions during the campaign, compared with those who followed through, included fewer people who were interested in the election. They were less "exposed" to the mass media, and they arrived at their decision later. Likewise in Bristol, "floaters [those inconsistent either in their intentions or in their vote], no matter what their final party, listened to fewer broadcasts and read fewer national newspapers than the regular voters."[3] These observations are consistent with the most widely accepted finding on mass-media impact: "Media exposure gets out the vote at the same time that it solidifies preferences. It crystallizes and reinforces more than it converts."[4]

Accordingly, then, the election period serves less as a force for change than as a period for reclarification. There are several concrete circumstances in a campaign which severely circumscribe opportunities for observing the influence of mass-media propaganda.

Most obvious in this connection is the observation, confirmed in different contexts and by different methods, that the minds of most voters are closed even before the campaign officially opens. At various places and at different times, this figure has been set at anywhere from 50 to 84 percent of the voters.[5] But even if a voter arrives at his decision late in the campaign, he is not necessarily in a constant quandary, endlessly pulled in opposite directions by conflicting propaganda. Evidence from panel studies indicates that in most cases where the final decision comes late in the campaign, prior learnings are crystallized into a firm intent. . . . Moreover, during a campaign, people cannot help but be aware, however unhappily, that they are the targets of deliberate propaganda. Neither side enjoys a monopoly of available space or time, and so propaganda is almost always exposed as such. . . . People, being aware of the intent of the messages, tend to avoid views contrary to their own. . . . As long as old loyalties are activated, selective perception will serve as an effective screen. . . .

The campaign period, then, would seem inherently to be less a period of potential change than a period of political entrenchment, a period in which prior attitudes are reaffirmed. This may well be a real paradox of political life: We are accustomed to think of campaign periods as the dynamic times when political passions are aroused and wholesale changeover results, and of periods between as the quiescent years, when people tend to forget about politics and are less attentive to the larger political environment. Yet changes in political opinion and in the general political climate may be less characteristic of the days of arousal than of the "quiescent" times between campaigns.

At any rate, the number of people who have already "made up their minds" before the campaign begins, the overwhelming importance of "filtering" effects resulting from self-selection and selective perception of media content, and the awareness of the intent with which all campaign statements are phrased all work together to make "conversion" through any medium particularly difficult during an election. But, in addition, there is something in the way the problem is approached which may obscure certain ways in which the mass media are effective.

Let us briefly review how the impact of the mass media is detected in the panel studies.[6] The authors of these studies investigate the initial voting intention and how it crystallizes and changes during the course of the campaign. They record individual "exposure" to the campaign—mostly in terms of attention paid to campaign materials, sources relied on, and the operation of self-selection. Then, by relating the voting intention to "exposure" within a framework of contextual factors, they infer the impact of that exposure. But among all the relevant "exposures," specifically what influences a vote cannot be easily inferred. More direct evidence about the content of that "exposure" and what it signifies to the consumer is necessary. . . .

To relate "exposure" to interest and partisanship is not to explain why people vote as they do. For such explanation the authors of the panel studies revert to an examination of people's prior political predispositions, their group identifications, and other variables which, by comparison with mass-media exposure, can be deemed relatively impermeable. These group measures, used in *Voting* and *Straight Fight* to "explain" voting decisions, are analogous to, though less explicit than, the set of "motivational" variables[7] which the more recent Survey Research Center study focuses upon. To be sure these generalized motivational variables—issue orientation, party identification, and candidate orientation—allow for the comparison of elections but still unexamined are the processes by which "weights" come to be assigned to various elements involved in the voting decision.

As long as the loyalties and imagery of the electorate are treated as "givens," as they have been, rather than as themselves in need of explanation, the probability of understanding the nature of mass-media impact is duly minimized. The very emphasis on change *within* the span of a campaign makes it almost inevitable that whatever realignments occur are limited by the more permanent identifications and loyalties existing at the time the study is started. . . . The examination of change within a short span fails altogether to account for the cumulative impact of media exposure which may, over a period of time, lead to such changes in the motivational patterns as differentiate one election from another or to a breaking away of many "primary" groups from older allegiances.

## Political Change

The study of long-range effects leads us to a comparison of elections and especially to a second look at the occasional election in which long-standing habits seem to be upset. . . .

Underlying the "strain toward consistency" observed in election periods is the basic stability of the vote. This stability also extends over longer periods. There is a high correlation between a person's first vote and his subsequent choices. Moreover, geographic, demographic, and social groups often display surprisingly consistent (over time) voting rates and patterns. Such consistent loyalties are fostered, above all, through the linkage of party images which class (and other status) symbols and the reinforcement of these loyalties through the relatively homogeneous political environment in which a majority of voters appear to move.

The study of the Bristol constituency highlights this basic stability. It indicates the importance of party images and the relative insignificance in British politics of "candidate appeal." Only 19 percent of the respondents admitted that, in any of three elections since 1945, they had voted for a party other than the one they were supporting in 1951.[8] Indeed, in 1951 not a single candidate in all of Britain was able to win for Labour a previously Conservative seat and reverse what was a slight (though politically decisive) shift toward the Conservatives. This may be attributed, in part, to the fact that candidates considered valuable to a party may be run in "safe" constituencies. Yet it principally reflects the decisive role of the national party struggle and the importance that must be attached to the efficacy of party images as such. . . .

What seems to matter in British politics is the party image—what the party stands for. As economic and social conditions change, so do the self-images of voters. Inasmuch as party loyalties reflect class loyalties, the successful party must manage to alter its image even if ever so slightly to take account of these shifts. The role of the mass media in disseminating the "appropriate" party image is apparent in *Straight Fight.* It is the national news sources that largely serve to channel to the electorate the party image with the pertinent symbols and clichés. . . .

Such party images are obviously not the product of a single campaign; they are in existence, ready-made, long before the official contest begins. Their reinforcement through local pressures helps to give the vote its fundamental stability and to make much of voting a highly institutionalized and conventionalized activity, especially when, as in Great Britain, the party ties are closely linked with class organizations, trade unions, and the like. But it is not only stability that we have to understand. Also to be explained is how long-standing habits are upset, and upset among many divergent local groups. The mass media would seem to play an indispensable role in producing the cumulative changes that are given expression in a turnover at the polls.

A possible turnover in the United States was forestalled in 1948. A rally back to the Fair Deal "decided" the outcome of the presidential vote in Elmira that year. In particular, the "waverers," strays from the Democratic fold, returned largely because of the salience of class issues, exactly those issues stressed by Truman during his campaign. National surveys confirm this Fair Deal rally as a nationwide phenomenon. Truman's benefits from those who in the early part of the campaign had been "undecided" or did not follow through on their original voting intention were twice as great as Dewey's.[9] These late changers were 1944 Democrats switching back to the administration.

The importance of the mass media for the Fair Deal rally is flatly stated in the Elmira study. (The "salience of class issues was brought home through the mass media.")[10] Though the image of Truman did *not* change, the image of what was important in the campaign did change. As the campaign progressed, socioeconomic issues became dominant. The change was most noticeable among persons high in mass-media exposure. . . .

Legend already has it that Truman, as he whistle-stopped across the nation, took his own case to the people and won despite a hostile press. What Truman actually did, it would seem, was to make "news." The press— or magazines or radio—could editorialize against the administration; their presentation of the news that Truman was making could be more or less subtly biased through headlines, spacing, choice of words, and the like. But since what Mr. Truman said was news, his appeal to class interests commanded attention and helped bring the strays back into the fold.

Nevertheless, the Truman victory in 1948 called attention primarily to what the mass media could *not* do. The results in 1952 surely have led us to reconsider the assumption that people will not, on the whole, cross party lines. The proportion of voters who did cross was undoubtedly small. But there were enough of these, together with previous nonvoters, to produce the Republican landslide. Primary group pressures, local influences, latent dispositions of voters throughout the country failed to reinforce wavering allegiances to the Democratic party. The motivational pattern of the vote was different. If 1948 was largely a party year, in 1952 the "more variable factors of issues and candidates" assumed unusual importance.[11] Some analysts have pointed to the long-term trends underlying these cyclical changes, such as the general prosperity prevailing, the upward mobility of minority groups, the trek to the suburbs, the industrialization of the South, and the general change from "interest" to "status" politics.[12]

That the mass media were a significant force in defining and structuring the decisive issues of the 1952 campaign and in "projecting" the candidates' personalities should be beyond dispute. The extent of this influence can unfortunately only be inferred. The campaign may have reactivated old loyalties, but, if it did, they were not the same old loyalties as in 1948. The issues were drawn differently. Where socioeconomic issues had invoked Democratic loyalties, the issue of national security, especially the Korean war, exercised a new attraction which worked in favor of the GOP. And, along with this, the public personality of General Eisenhower appealed to Democrats and Republicans alike, though not always for the same reasons.

Plausible as it may seem to impute a great impact to advertising techniques employed during the political war, to the novel role played by TV, and especially to the saturation of TV with filmed "spots," there is no evidence that the official campaign propaganda, as such, changed many votes.[13] The "turnover" away from the Democrats had taken place before the official campaign opened. The campaign found the Republicans with a number of issues ready-made. From a postelection perspective, it appears evident that, in order to win, the Republicans had but to bring these vividly before the public. The real influence of the mass media, then, is to be sought in the play given communism and corruption in government and the controversies over Korea. These had been spelled out on front pages and in radio bulletins for some time. . . .

The campaign talk on Korea may not actually have "converted." It nonetheless kept open the psychological wound inflicted by a peacetime war. Straight news and campaign oratory were joined to keep attention on what could, it seemed, only redound to the benefit of Republicans. Only in this sense may the campaign talk have "converted" by preventing the return of Democrats to their party. . . .

## Personal Influence and Mass Influence

The mass media, then, exert some of the influence they do because they are more than a channel through which national party policy is brought before the local electorate. In filtering, structuring, and spotlighting certain public activities, the media content is not confined to conveying what party spokesmen proclaim and what the candidates say. All news that bears on political activity and beliefs—and not only campaign speeches and campaign propaganda—is somehow relevant to the vote. Not only during the campaign but also in the periods between, the mass media provide perspectives, shape images of candidates and parties, help highlight issues around which a campaign will develop, and define the unique atmosphere and areas of sensitivity which mark any particular campaign. Any long-run view, therefore, reveals certain differences among elections which make clear that in each case voters, much as they may respond to traditional allegiances, also respond to a unique historical situation.

The scheme of analysis outlined in *Voting* barely touches upon the role of the mass media in creating a secondhand reality, through which public policy is elaborated and the effects of that policy on the voter clarified and made tangible. The "main concern," we are told, "is with the electorate itself. How many individuals pay *direct* attention to the campaign via the mass media?"[14] In this scheme the mass media act primarily as transmitters of content supplied by the national parties and by their candidates and subsequently consumed, in one way or another, by the electorate. The personal network of communications within the community hooks onto and makes use of the mass media. Opinion leaders usually pay more attention to the mass media than their peers, and they relay relevant information to those less firm in their partisan convictions.

In this transmission system which passes along arguments and information required in voting decisions, personal influence often seems more crucial and persuasive than mass-media content. The reasoning seems to go as follows: The opinion leader can induce compliance not only through *what* he says; he can exert his influence in a flexible fashion and also provide gratifications that go with compliance.[15] The prestige of opinion leaders is often interposed between the mass-media content and those who, on their own, pay no direct attention (or only very little attention) to the content itself. It is in aligning voters with their peers that personal contacts reactivate latent dispositions.

Opinion leaders thus seem often to counter the possible impact of counter-propaganda and to make effective the propaganda favoring their own side. This signal discovery of the ubiquity of opinion leaders has led many to pit the measure of personal influence against that of the mass media. Nothing could obscure the real character of mass-media impact more than to pose the problem in this way. Personal and mass-media influence do not act in the same way. Personal influence may govern a larger segment of any individual's behavior than do the mass media—and it may be easier to demonstrate how a husband influences his wife's voting decision than to demonstrate what the mass media have to do with her voting behavior—but from the viewpoint of the larger society, it is the influence of the mass media which is the most potent.

The persons generally designated by social scientists as "opinion leaders" prepare the ground for mass-media impact. They translate the mass-media reality into the experience of local groups. Some persons may enjoy informal status as opinion leaders precisely because they attend to the relevant mass-media content. Or it may be that in order to wield influence a man may have to be especially knowledgeable about what the mass media do and say. In either case, the opinion leaders exhibit greater responsiveness to the mass media, channeling for their peers—to whose dispositions they are particularly sensitive—that which the mass media have already made significant.

Theirs is essentially a transmission function and through them the views and interests of persons not directly exposed to the content of the mass media are involved. Yet these leaders select what they will transmit, and hence such influentials need not act only as a stabilizing influence. An emergent local leadership at odds with the official party may make use of whatever prestige or credibility the mass-media content has per se to subvert older loyalties.

The short-run frame of reference, with its primary concern with the electorate and how it lines up within the course of a single campaign, has perhaps exaggerated the dominant role of personal influences and the effectiveness of "normal" social pressures. For it puts the accent on the type of changer who is most susceptible—perhaps by a sort of default—to such influences, that is, it draws attention almost exclusively to changers who are converted or whose decision crystallizes only *during the campaign.* In the first place, such persons are, quite logically, those with a relatively low interest in politics and for whom political loyalties are not ordinarily salient; second, they are further characterized by low mass-media exposure.

Moreover, people who do *not* vote with their peers as well as people who do *not* vote in accord with their predispositions appear only as deviant cases among the over-all consistencies found in the panel studies. Deviants somehow get lost in the concern with how A influences B and how both A and B vote in line with their basic predispositions. Yet in order to understand the nature and extent of mass-media influence—and especially their impact on the larger political trends that often mark off one election from another—it is precisely these deviants upon whom we may be forced to concentrate.

By way of brief explication, take the situation described in the Elmira study: Women as a group are less interested in the campaign than men. In their voting decisions, they tend to follow their husbands. Yet at the same time, the "women's vote" is less clearly linked to social class than the male vote. To put it more succinctly, women from the higher socioeconomic levels are less Republican than the men from those classes, whereas women among the working and lower classes are less strongly Democratic.[16] Somehow or other women follow their husbands' leads and yet, by comparison with their husbands, vote less in accord with their class interests. Many plausible explanations commend themselves, but clearly the pattern of the "women's vote" cannot be explained as the simple outcome of personal influence, however helpful this approach is in explaining individual vote changes.

The Bristol study does distinguish the "waverer" from the "changer." And a follow-up of this distinction may serve to sharpen our knowledge of influences upon voting behavior. The "waverer," although consistent in his vote over time, may move into the "undecided" column during any particular campaign or his "intentions" may (judged by what he tells us) appear inconsistent. The "changer" is one whose vote "at present" differs from that of the past, whether or not such a change is recorded within the span of a single campaign. We would contend that there is nothing in the Bristol or other data to indicate that the short-run regularities that mark campaigns reflect accurately the patterns associated with party turnover between elections and over longer periods of time. "Waverers," for instance, may mostly be political indifferents who give way under the pressure of the campaign. But is this true of "changers"? Especially if their conversion occurs during the "quiescent" times between campaigns, when personal pressures are least likely to be deliberately exerted in a politically partisan way, it raises the possibility that such change, or the disposition to change, follows from their private communions with the mass media and the trickle of news reports. During a campaign, women will in all likelihood move toward greater agreement with their husbands. But when the political battle is less obviously joined, the influences weaning women as a group away from the class loyalties of their husbands may well be of a different sort.[17]

The significant question at issue is, then, the pressures that cause people to vote out of accord with their local surroundings and out of accord with their group-anchored attitudes. No speculative answer can be accepted as adequate. Nonetheless, the response of individuals in the mass audience to certain nonlocal influences, however vaguely or indirectly they are perceived, is a problem with which research must contend. Voters, much as they interpret their secondary and symbolic environment in terms of their local milieu, do as individuals acquire certain general political perspectives that shape their responses during campaigns. Notions of politics, of parties, of issues, of candidates, and of their own roles as participating citizens cannot be satisfactorily explained by study of local communication networks. Along these lines, more than along others, ideas are affected by what the mass media present.

## Secondhand Reality and the Mass Audience

Persons in the mass society are, as we all know, members of many more or less formally organized groups. Some of these memberships are, of course, more politically relevant than others. Trade unionists in the United States tend to vote Democratic; in England they most often side with Labour. Some minority groups "stick together" politically, and some organizations formed to defend "majority" interests have their own characteristic voting patterns. We know a considerable amount about the political perspectives that derive from such memberships and about the cross-pressures exerted by multiple allegiances.

We are also aware that most of what people know about political life comes to them secondhand—or even thirdhand—through the mass media. The media do structure a very real political environment but one which, even in these days of TV, we can only know "at a distance." Because of the way people select from the political content of the mass media and interpret what they select, the political communication system serves to transmit materials peculiarly relevant to persons in various milieus. Beyond this, however, the mass media also structure a larger, nonlocal reality from which it is hard to escape. The content filters through, even though people are not directly exposed to it or do not claim to be paying a great deal of attention.[18] There is something obtrusive about what the mass media present, something that makes their influence cumulative.

The mass media have, then, another function. They not only transmit materials that feed into the political perspectives of relevant groups; they leave an impress of their own. There are political perspectives that rise out of an individual's position as a member of a mass, as the object of direct and indirect stimuli coming from the mass media. The relationships between voting behavior and the perspectives developed by virtue of one's position in the mass have as yet been inadequately investigated, perhaps because of the very real methodological difficulties involved, perhaps because we overestimate the difficulties or fear to risk criticism of our results. . . .

The mass media, by the way in which they structure and present political reality, may contribute to a widespread and chronic distrust of political life. Such distrust is not primarily a mark of sophistication, indicating that critical "discount" is at work. It is of a projective character and constitutes a defensive reaction against the periodic political crises known to affect a person's destiny as well as against what are defined as deliberate efforts to mobilize political sentiment. . . .

How does this distrust express itself in voting or nonvoting? After all, people, in order to act politically, must form some credible picture about political questions. If we knew more about who trusts what mass-media sources and how this trust is channeled, this knowledge would be a springboard for assessing how persons who withdraw from political mass-media materials may periodically be stirred out of their apathy.

To study this, we might start with the characteristics of the consumers rather than those of the media. Certainly not all consumers of mass-media materials approach the political content with the same orientations. Persons with above-average political sophistication (and therefore less subject to a "chronic distrust" of politics) are in the habit of checking one source of information against another. While, like all others, dependent on the mass media for information, they have a sort of natural immunity to the news slant of any particular medium. They are a "high" interest group and usually firm in their voting decisions.

But what about those others who feel disbarred from channels of political influence and who would also seem most suspicious of politics in general? Will they distrust all mass-media sources and believe only what their friends tell them? Paradoxically, the withdrawal of "interest" from political mass-media materials may go hand in hand with high reliance on some particular trusted "medium" somehow exempted from the contamination imputed to the mass media as a whole. This would seem to put a high premium on "sincerity" and "honesty" and on a public personality radiating confidence. And, thus, under certain conditions, it would make those most distrustful of politicians most susceptible to mobilization. . . .

The mass media force attention to certain issues. They build up public images of political figures. They are constantly presenting objects suggesting what individuals in the mass should think about, know about, have feelings about. There is implied in the way they address their audience, moreover, an appropriate way of looking at politics. By the materials they choose, the media may give us the semblance of an "acquaintance with" the political world, though most of us have but a most indirect knowledge of what it is all about.

The media can also stifle debate and criticism by defining certain elements in a situation as not *actually* subject to controversy. This is most easily done in relation to public personalities and "moral" issues. For example, during the Truman-MacArthur controversy in 1951, the press reported a striking unanimity of public sentiment. In addition to the official hero's welcome for the ousted General, they reported many minor public demonstrations aimed against the Truman administration and indicating sympathy for MacArthur. In retrospect, the unanimity of this sentiment appears to have been misstated.[19] For some months, however, public discussion took its cues from this assumed sentiment, and only the brave politician dared to raise his voice publicly against MacArthur. Most waited until the storm "blew over" and MacArthur was no longer headline news. In much the same way, Democratic criticism of the Eisenhower administration appears to have foundered on the rocks of the unimpeachable hold of his personality on public imagination. How much, we may inquire, has the assumption of reporters about this unshakable popularity prevented them from featuring less popular images of the Eisenhower personality and thus helped to maintain the popular public image as such? This is one type of impact study which we need.

Such definitions of overwhelming public sentiment—"landslide perceptions"—tend to be cumulative. They influence political strategy; they inject a tone into news reporting; they seem to produce a certain reserve in personal discussion, since much conversation revolves around what is assumed to be held in common (like views on the weather). Politicians themselves believe in the importance of band-wagon effects in victory or defeat, and there have been attempts to assess the impact of election forecasts on election results. But this is not merely a matter of confidence or wanting to be on the winning side. For the communicator, assumptions about the public temper "legitimate" what is communicated to the mass. These assumptions likewise "legitimate" omissions. If the assumption about the unanimity of a public mood is erroneous, omissions of news about dissenting views or dissenting imagery make the unanimity much more marked than it is. For it tends to withdraw from personal discussion the very stuff that can be assumed as common political experience and, conversely, leaves uncriticized what everyone else is believed to approve. By influencing both public and private discussion, the saliency of what is at stake is affected, and where this influence enters campaigns, the election itself may be determined.

Individuals in the mass are likely to imagine what others in the mass are believed to be imagining.[20] Thus not only local influences but the beliefs imputed to nameless others exercise their pressure in the mass. Surely, one of the more interesting approaches to mass-media impact on political participation must be the study of private and public imaginations in relation to each other, and their joint relation to what we consider group-relevant reasons for casting a vote.

## Conclusion

In this article we have set ourselves the task of exorcising the currently prevalent emphasis on *how little* mass media determine votes. We all are constantly exposed and sometimes concerned about mass-media influence, and yet this influence escapes our research endeavor.

Studies in voting behavior have dealt with both long-run trends and short-run changes. In either case, since voting rates and voting decisions can be determined with a high degree of validity, we seek inferences about antecedent conditions influencing these end products of political activity. Such influences as age differences, regional locations, and traditional political affiliations which may affect voting habits can with relative ease be isolated for examination. When we come to deal with mass-media influences, however, these are much more difficult to single out. They operate among a multitude of other factors and their effects do not always take tangible shape. Consequently, the measures of mass-media exposure are usually crude and the effects looked for are relatively specific and short run.

Quite naturally, campaign studies such as we have been considering, have focused on the short-range influences operating during the period of active electioneering and on how these culminate in a final voting decision. It so happens, as we have tried to point out, that this approach to the problem, with its emphasis on individual conversion during the "official" campaign, minimizes the important cumulative influences of the mass media and emphasizes instead how political communications are transmitted through personal networks and how latent tendencies are activated. In this way, attention has been focused on the limits to mass-media influence.

Where the question for study is "What makes the electorate tick?" research is naturally shaped to fit the problem; the mass media become just one among many concerns. On the other hand, experts in mass communications have not in recent years distinguished themselves by probing the long-range influence of mass media on political life—and more particularly on voting behavior. The cumulative and society-wide effects about which we often talk vaguely as shifts in public moods or drifts in political opinion are hard to demonstrate; yet, if we would further our knowledge of political behavior, such effects are much in need of clarification. And they can only be clarified through research specifically designed to get at them.

In turning attention to the continuous, and not only the intermittent, aspects of mass-media influence, we must deal, first, with the role of *mass* communications as such, focusing not only on the communicator's job as a transmitting agent for party propagandists but on the direct impress the communications have on what individuals in the mass society know of the larger political world. We have to get at the political perspectives that rise out of the individual's remote participation in politics as a member of the mass and at the relationships between voting behavior and these perspectives. . . .

A few specific problems for study have been directly outlined or indicated. The imagery made especially relevant by the mass media—the imagery of the "public imagination," of public personalities, of what politics is really like—and the relationship of such imagery to party alignments seem noteworthy. Among other subjects, the specific role of television, its authenticity and the exploitation of that authenticity by public officials and publicity directors, and the impact of such exploitation on voting participation constitute important areas for inquiry.

# Notes

1. B. R. Berelson, P. F. Lazarsfeld, and W. N. McPhee, *Voting* (Chicago: University of Chicago Press, 1954); R. S. Milne and H. C. Mackenzie, *Straight Fight* (London: The Hansard Society, 1954); and Angus Campbell, Gerald Gurin, and W. E. Miller, *The Voter Decides* (Evanston, Ill.: Row, Peterson, 1954).

2. In a separate article, the authors have discussed the role of television but qualify their data in stating that they had "no clear evidence" on how it affected the voting. Cf. Angus Campbell and others, "Television and the Elections," *Scientific American*, 188 (1953), 46–48.

3. Milne and Mackenzie, *op. cit.*, pp. 96 ff.

4. Berelson, Lazarsfeld, and McPhee, *op. cit.*, p. 248.

5. In Erie County, Ohio (1940), roughly one half were precampaign deciders. Cf. P. F. Lazarsfeld, B. R. Berelson, and Hazel Gaudet, *The People's Choice* (2d ed.; New York: Columbia University Press, 1948), p. 53. According to a "Gallup" poll before nomination day, 84 per cent of the British electorate were already decided. Cited by R. B. McCallum and A. Readman, *The British General Election of 1945* (London: Oxford University Press, 1947), p. 201. British figures seem to hover around the 80 per cent mark, with American figures, perhaps because of the more protracted campaign period, on the whole closer to two-thirds.

6. There are important differences between the Elmira and Bristol studies. But our basic interest here is in the logic of their approach, not in a detailed methodological evaluation.

7. Namely, "attitudes, perceptions, and group loyalties which mediate between the external environmental facts and the individual response." Campbell, Gurin, and Miller, *op. cit.*, pp. 7 ff.

8. Milne and Mackenzie, *op. cit.*, p. 26.

9. Campbell, Gurin, and Miller, *op cit.*, p. 12.

10. Berelson, Lazarsfeld, and McPhee, *op. cit.*, p. 264 n.

11. Campbell, Gurin, and Miller, *op. cit.*, p. 184.

12. Cf. S. A. Lubell, *The Future of American Politics* (New York: Harper, 1951); Louis Harris, *Is There a Republican Majority?* (New York: Harper, 1954); and Richard Hofstadter, "The Pseudo-Conservative Revolt," *The American Scholar,* Winter 1955, pp. 9–27.

13. As far as the campaign is concerned, Stevenson, if anyone, gained more in personal appeal than Eisenhower. Cf. Harris, *op. cit.,* pp. 52 ff.; and *The Influence of Television on the 1952 Election by the Oxford Research Associates, Oxford, Ohio, Dec. 1954.*

14. Berelson, Lazarsfeld, and McPhee, *op. cit.*, p. 235. Italics supplied.

15. Elihu Katz and P. F. Lazarsfeld, *Personal Influence* (Glencoe, Ill.: The Free Press, 1955), p. 185. Also J. T. Klapper, *The Effects of Mass Media* (New York: Columbia University, Bureau of Applied Social Research, 1949).

16. Berelson, Lazarsfeld, and McPhee, *op. cit.*, p. 61.

17. Harris, *op. cit.*, Chap. 7, shows that women as a group gave a larger majority to Eisenhower than did men and that, especially, the wives of union members voted contrary to their husbands.

18. Berelson, Lazarsfeld, and McPhee, *op. cit.*, report this "unexpected" finding: "More people showed signs of exposure than claimed to be paying 'attention.'"

19. R. H. Rovere and A. M. Schlesinger, Jr., *The General and the President* (New York: Farrar, Strauss, and Young, 1951), and Kurt and G. E. Lang, "The Unique Perspective of Television and Its Effect," *American Sociological Review,* XVIII (Feb. 1953), 3–12.

20. Gabriel Tarde referred to this phenomenon of contagion in his *L'opinion et la foule* (Paris: F. Alcan, 1901).

# Impact of Allied Propaganda on Wehrmacht Solidarity in World War II

## EDWARD A. SHILS and MORRIS JANOWITZ

AT THE BEGINNING of the second world war, many publicists and specialists in propaganda attributed almost supreme importance to psychological warfare operations. The legendary success of Allied propaganda against the German Army at the end of the first world war and the tremendous expansion of the advertising and mass communications industries in the ensuing two decades had convinced many people that human behavior could be extensively manipulated by mass communications. They tended furthermore to stress that military morale was to a great extent a function of the belief in the rightness of the "larger" cause which was at issue in the war; good soldiers were therefore those who clearly understood the political and moral implications of what was at stake. They explained the striking successes of the German Army in the early phases of the war by the "ideological possession" of the German soldiers, and they accordingly thought that propaganda attacking doctrinal conceptions would be defeating this army.

Studies of the German Army's morale and fighting effectiveness made during the last three years of the war throw considerable doubt on these hypotheses. The solidarity of the German Army was discovered by these studies—which left much to be desired from the standpoint of scientific rigor—to be based only very indirectly and very partially on political convictions or broader ethical beliefs. Where conditions were such as to allow primary

Reprinted by permission of the publisher from "Impact of Allied Propaganda on Wehrmacht Solidarity in World War II," by Edward Shils and Morris Janowitz, adapted from *Public Opinion Quarterly*, Vol. XII (1948), pp. 300–304, 308–315.

group life to function smoothly, and where the primary group developed a high degree of cohesion, morale was high and resistance effective or at least very determined, regardless in the main of the political attitudes of the soldiers. The conditions of primary group life were related to spatial proximity, the capacity for intimate communication, the provision of paternal protectiveness by NCO's and junior officers, and the gratification of certain personality needs, e.g., manliness, by the military organization and its activities. The larger structure of the army served to maintain morale through the provision of the framework in which potentially individuating physical threats were kept at a minimum—through the organization of supplies and through adequate strategic dispositions.

The system of controls which the social structure of the Wehrmacht exercised over its individual members greatly reduced those areas in which symbolic appeals of the Allies could work. But the millions of leaflets which were dropped weekly and the "round-the-clock" broadcasts to the German troops certainly did not fail to produce some reactions.

The very first German Ps/W who were interrogated directly on their reactions to Allied propaganda soon revealed a stereotyped range of answers which could be predicted from their degree of Nazification. The fanatical Nazi claimed, "No German would believe anything the enemy has to say," while an extreme attitude of acceptance was typified by a confirmed anti-Nazi who pleaded with his captors: "Now is the moment to flood the troops with leaflets. You have no idea of the effect sober and effective leaflets have on retreating troops." But these extreme reactions of soldiers were of low frequency; Nazi soldiers might admit the truth of our leaflets but usually would not accept their conclusions and implications.

The fundamentally indifferent reaction to Allied propaganda was most interestingly shown in an intensive study of 150 Ps/W captured in October 1944 of whom 65 percent had seen our leaflets and for the most part professed that they believed their contents. This was a group which had fought very obstinately, and the number of active deserters, if any, was extremely small. Some forty of these Ps/W offered extended comments as to what they meant when they said they believed the contents of Allied leaflets.

> Five stated outright that they believed the messages and that the leaflets assisted them and their comrades to surrender.
> Seven declared they believed the leaflets, but were powerless to do anything about appeals to surrender.
> Eight stated that they believed the contents, but nevertheless as soldiers and decent individuals would never think of deserting.
> Twenty-two declared that events justified belief in the leaflets, but they clearly implied that this had been of little importance in their battle experiences.

In Normandy, where the relatively small front was blanketed with printed material, up to 90 percent of the Ps/W reported that they had read Allied leaflets, yet this period was characterized by very high German morale and stiff resistance.

Throughout the Western campaign, with the exception of periods of extremely bad weather or when the front was fluid, the cumulative percentage of exposure ranged between 60 and 80 percent. (This cumulative percentage of exposure was based on statements by Ps/W that they had seen leaflets sometime while fighting on the Western front after D-Day. A few samples indicated that penetration during any single month covered about 20 percent of the prisoners.) Radio listening among combat troops was confined to a minute fraction due to the lack of equipment; rear troops listened more frequently. In the case of both leaflets and radio it was found that there was widespread but desultory comment on the propaganda, much of which comment distorted the actual contents.

Not only was there wide penetration by Allied leaflets and newssheets, but German soldiers frequently circulated them extensively among their comrades. A readership study of *Nachrichten für die Truppe,* a daily newssheet published by the Allied Psychological Warfare Division, showed that each copy which was picked up had an average readership of between four and five soldiers—a figure which is extremely large in view of the conditions of combat life. Not only were leaflets widely circulated, but it became a widespread practice for soldiers to carry Allied leaflets on their person, especially the "safe conduct pass" leaflets which bore a statement by General Eisenhower guaranteeing the bearer swift and safe conduct through Allied lines and the protection of the Geneva convention. There is evidence that in certain sectors of the front, German soldiers even organized black-market trading in Allied propaganda materials.

It is relevant to discuss here the differences in effectiveness between tactical and strategic propaganda. By tactical propaganda, we refer to propaganda which seeks to promise immediate results in the tactical situation. The clearest example of this type of propaganda is afforded by "cross the lines" loudspeaker broadcasts, which sometimes facilitated immediate capture of the prisoners of war—not by propaganda in the ordinary sense, but by giving instructions on how to surrender safely, once the wish to surrender was present.

No sufficiently accurate estimate is available of the total number of prisoners captured by the use of such techniques, but signal successes involving hundreds of isolated troops in the Normandy campaign have been credited to psychological warfare combat teams. Even more successful were the loudspeaker-carrying tanks employed in the Rhine River offensive, when the first signs of weakening resistance were encountered. For example, the Fourth Armored Division reported that its psychological warfare unit captured over 500 prisoners in a four-day dash from the Kyll River to the Rhine. Firsthand investigation of these loudspeaker missions, and interrogation of prisoners captured under such circumstances, establish that Allied propaganda was effective in describing the tactical situation to totally isolated and helpless soldiers and in arranging an Allied cease fire and thereby presenting an assurance to the German soldier of a safe surrender. The successful targets for such broadcasts were groups where solidarity and ability to function as a unit were largely destroyed. Leaflets especially written for specific sectors and dropped on pin point targets by fighter-bombers were used instead of loudspeakers where larger units were cut off. This method proved less successful, since the units to which they were addressed were usually better integrated and the necessary cease fire conditions could not be arranged.

Less spectacular, but more extensive, was strategic propaganda. Allied directives called for emphasis on four themes in this type of propaganda: *(1)* Ideological attacks on the Nazi Party and Germany's war aims, *(2)* the strategical hopelessness of Germany's military and economic position, *(3)* the justness of the United Nations war aims and their unity and determination to carry them out (unconditional surrender, although made known to the troops, was never stressed), *(4)* promises of good treatment to prisoners of war, with appeals to self-preservation through surrender.

Although it is extremely difficult, especially in view of the lack of essential data, to assess the efficacy of these various themes, some tentative clues might be seen in the answers given to the key attitude questions in the monthly Psychological Warfare opinion poll of captured German soldiers.[1] Thus, there was no significant decline in attachment to Nazi ideology until February and March 1945. In other words, propaganda attacks on Nazi ideology seem to have been of little avail, and attachment to secondary symbols, e.g., Hitler, declined only when the smaller military units began to break up under very heavy pressure.

The . . . effectiveness of considerations of self-preservation, and their vast preponderance over interest in the outcome of the war and the strategic situation, is shown by German prisoner recall of the contents of Allied propaganda leaflets (see Table 1). In the last two months of 1944 and the first two months of 1945, not less than 59 percent of the sample of prisoners taken each month recalled references to the preservation of the individual, and the figure rose to 76 percent in February of 1945. On the other hand, the proportion of prisoners recalling references to the total strategic situation of the war and the prospect of the outcome of the war seldom amounted to more than 20 percent, while references to political subjects seldom amounted to more than 10 percent. . . .

Since the German soldier was quite ignorant of military news on other fronts, it was believed that a great deal of printed material should contain factual reports of the military situation, stressing the strategical hopelessness of the German position. As a result, the third most frequently recalled items of Allied propaganda were the military news reports. It seems reasonable to believe that the emphasis on these subjects did contribute to the development of defeatist sentiment.

Despite the vast amount of space devoted to ideological attacks on German

**TABLE 1. Tabulation of Allied Leaflet Propaganda Themes Remembered by German Ps/W**

| | DEC. 15–31 1944 | JAN. 1–15 1945 | JAN. 15–31 1945 | FEB. 1–15 1945 |
|---|---|---|---|---|
| Number of Ps/W | 60 | 83 | 99 | 135 |
| Themes and appeals remembered: | | | | |
| a. Promise of good treatment as Ps/W and self-preservation through surrender | 53% | 65% | 59% | 76% |
| b. Military news | 15 | 17 | 19 | 30 |
| c. Strategical hopelessness of Germany's position | 13 | 12 | 25 | 26 |
| d. Hopelessness of a local tactical situation | 3 | 1 | 7 | 7 |
| e. Political attacks on German leaders | 7 | 5 | 4 | 8 |
| f. Bombing of German cities | 2 | 8 | 6 | — |
| g. Allied Military Government | 7 | 3 | — | — |
| h. Appeals to civilians | 5 | 4 | 2 | — |

NOTE: The percentages add up to more than 100% since some Ps/W remembered more than one topic. Only Ps/W remembering at least one theme were included in this tabulation.

345

leaders, only about five percent of the Ps/W mentioned this topic—a fact which supported the contention as to the general failure of ideological or secondary appeals. Finally, the presentation of the justness of Allied war aims was carried out in such a way as to avoid stressing the unconditional surrender aspects of our intentions, while emphasizing postwar peace intentions and organizational efforts; much was made of United Nations unity. All this fell on deaf ears, for of this material only a small minority of Ps/W (about 5 percent) recalled specific statements about military government plans for the German occupation. . . .

The single leaflet most effective in communicating the promise of good treatment was the "safe conduct pass." Significantly, it was usually printed on the back of leaflets which contained no elaborate propaganda appeals except those of self-preservation. The rank and file tended to be favorably disposed to its official language and legal, document-like character. In one sector where General Eisenhower's signature was left off the leaflet, doubt was cast on its authenticity. . . .

Belief in the veracity of this appeal was no doubt based on the attitude that the British and the Americans were respectable law-abiding soldiers who would treat their captives according to international law. As a result of this predisposition and the wide use of the safe conduct leaflets, as well as our actual practices in treating prisoners well, the German soldier came to have no fear of capture by British or American troops. The most that can be claimed for this lack of fear was that it may have decreased or undercut any tendency to fight to the death; it produced no active opposition to continued hostilities.

As an extension of the safe-conduct approach, leaflets were prepared instructing noncommissioned officers in detailed procedures by which their men could safely be removed from battle so as to avoid our fire and at the same time avoid evacuation by the German field police. If the Germans could not be induced to withdraw from combat activity, Allied propaganda appealed to them to hide in cellars. This in fact became a favorite technique of surrender, since it avoided the need of facing the conscience-twinging desertion problem.

As a result of psychological warfare research, a series of leaflets was prepared whose attack was aimed at primary group organization in the German Army, without recourse to ideological symbols. Group organization depended on the acceptance of immediate leadership and mutual trust. Therefore this series of leaflets sought to stimulate group discussion among the men and to bring into their focus of attention concerns which would loosen solidarity. One leaflet declared, "Do not take our (the Allies) word for it; ask your comrade; find out how he feels." Thereupon followed a series of questions on personal concerns, family problems, tactical consideration and supply problems. Discussion of these problems was expected to increase anxiety. It was assumed that to the degree that the soldier found that he was not isolated in his opinion, to that degree he would be strengthened in his resolve to end hostilities, for himself at least.

## Conclusion

At moments of primary group disintegration, a particular kind of propaganda less hortatory or analytical, but addressing the intensified desire to survive and describing the precise procedures by which physical survival could be achieved, is likely to facilitate further disintegration. Furthermore, in some cases aspects of the environment towards which the soldier might hitherto have been emotionally indifferent were defined for him by prolonged exposure to propaganda under conditions of disintegration. Some of these wider aspects, e.g., particular strategic consideration, then tended to be taken into account in his motivation and he was more likely to implement his defeatist mood by surrender than he would have been without exposure to propaganda.

It seems necessary, therefore, to reconsider the potentialities of propaganda in the context of all the other variables which influence behavior. The erroneous views concerning the omnipotence of propaganda must be given up and their place must be taken by much more differentiated views as to the possibilities of certain kinds of propaganda under different sets of conditions.

It must be recognized that on the moral plane most men are members of the larger society by virtue of identifications which are mediated through the human beings with whom they are in personal relationships. Many are bound into the larger society only by primary group identifications. Only a small proportion possessing special training or rather particular kinds of personalities are capable of giving a preponderant share of their attention and concern to the symbols of the larger world. The conditions under which these different groups will respond to propaganda will differ, as will also the type of propaganda to which they will respond.

## Note

1. See Gurfein, M. I., and Janowitz, Morris, "Trends in Wehrmacht Morale," *The Public Opinion Quarterly*, Vol. 10, No. 1 (1946), p. 78.

# Mass Communication and Information Diffusion

JOHN P. ROBINSON

SOCIAL COMMENTATORS AND OBSERVERS of the changes in modern society are continually amazed by mounting evidence of an incredible increase in the information that flows through society. The rapid diffusion of the electrical devices of radio, television, and more recently the computer, is usually taken as the most impressive evidence on this score, and incipient innovations such as cable television, home video recorders and computer terminals promise to accelerate this "information explosion" even more rapidly in the not-too-distant future. Moreover other indicators point to much the same conclusion: the tremendous proliferation of magazine and book titles over the last 25 years, the increasing audience for education television, and, for the critics of the "vast wasteland" of commercial television, reports from experienced kindergarten and first grade teachers that their students come to school with far greater verbal skills and wider interests than their predecessors.

Against such an impressive array of evidence, elements of which are well wired into the conventional wisdom, the mass communication researcher usually encounters at best a skeptical audience to his proclamation that research fails to corroborate any such utopian effects of the media. To be sure, the researcher does find that people already well informed can become better informed by attention to the media, but for any particular topic these people do constitute a small, and often insignificant, segment of the total mass audience. Such results are consistent with findings from research into the media's effects on audience propensity to engage in violent behavior, to

"Mass Communication and Information Diffusion" by John Robinson is reprinted from *Current Perspectives in Mass Communication Research* (Sage Annual Reviews of Communication Research, Vol. 1), F. Gerald Kline and Phillip J. Tichenor, eds., copyright 1972, pp. 71 93, by permission of the Publisher, Sage Publications, Inc.

become unduly swayed in their political or electoral decisions, to become less intellectually active as a response to the easier availability of media fare, as summarized in Klapper's (1960) famous summary of the research literature:

> Regardless of the condition in question—be it the vote intentions of audience members, their tendency toward or away from delinquent behavior, or their general orientation toward life and its problems—the media are more likely to reinforce than to change.

But converging evidence of this sort is still likely to be of little consolation to persons conditioned to the argument that modern man's increased exposure to media[1] and other information sources has inevitably resulted in him becoming more informed, occasionally to the point of information overload, than he was in prior eras.

Public opinion researchers have perhaps uncovered the most persuasive evidence of the failure of all segments of the population to share in the information explosion, with their documentation of the shocking ignorance of the American public on matters of basic national concern. In 1964, half of a national sample were unaware of the existence of two Chinas with their opposing political loyalties (Robinson, 1967). In 1969, a CBS survey found only a third of the country had heard of the Kerner Commission Report. In a 1970 national survey, less than a third of the population could provide even rudimentary identification of Ralph Nader, Robert Finch, or Martha Mitchell (Robinson, 1972). Collections of further items on which the public seems ill informed have been provided in Lane and Sears (1964), Erskine (1962, 1963a, 1963b), Schramm and Wade (1967) and Robinson (1967).

Moreover the evidence has been slowly accumulating that more directly links these discouraging information levels to a dearth of information flow from the media to the public, even if one talks only of the actual audience for any given message and excludes the usual majority of the public who are not in the audience at the time of the message. McLeod and Swinehart (1960) found almost no increase in public awareness of the detailed scientific purpose of space satellites six months after extensive media coverage of the implications of the launching of Sputnik I. Robinson and Hirsch (1969) found teenagers unable to describe even the basic themes, much less the subtle meanings, of the lyrics in various popular "message" songs which had received maximum exposure on Top 40 radio stations and which most teenagers indeed claimed to have heard. More disturbing is Stern's (1971) finding that half the audience of a national network news program could not recall even one of the 19 news stories on the program shortly after they were broadcast. . . .

Now to some extent, the above collection of research is an exaggeration to make a point seldom acknowledged in intellectual debates about the power of the media. Mass communication and public opinion researchers do have evidence of apparently successful transmission of information from the media to the public. Some of these will be examined later in the article. Thus, in the McLeod and Swinehart investigation (1960), the proportion of the population able to describe the less detailed purposes for satellites doubled (although only from 8 to 16 percent) and those larger proportions of the population who saw satellites as the basis of a race with the Russians may have been simply reflecting the framework in which the news media interpreted the importance of Sputnik I. It is unlikely that widespread public awareness of the dangers of cigarette smoking, the signs of cancer, or the causes of forest fires would be possible without the torrent of public service announcements through the media. Public opinion researchers find so few people unable to complete the beginnings of commercial slogans and jingles (Ward, 1972) that they can hardly dismiss the power of media advertising. . . .

How has it been possible for researchers to compile such a dismal scorecard on the effectiveness of the media in conveying news information? One researcher, William McPhee (1956) developed the following line of explanation:

> Imagine trying to transmit complex and sophisticated knowledge to students who walk in and out as they please, when some of the most valuable effects might occur to a passerby who wanders in by chance, when most volunteer students already know what is to be learned, while those who do not already know are not available, when motivation is low, and when neither the subjects nor the teacher have any clear idea about the rewards for learning.

To this, one might add the coping and perceptual mechanisms whereby the public protects itself from the bombardment of media information to which it is exposed. It has been estimated that the average American is exposed to hundreds of messages just about advertising on an average day. Add to this all the "bad news" messages propagated by the news media and it is not difficult to imagine why the audience is highly selective about what news it chooses to attend to or seek out in the media.

More fundamental reasons may be involved. News changes daily and hence cannot be packaged as neatly as a classroom lecture. It is not difficult to imagine that news messages and arguments, designed by news personnel who have undergone considerable exposure to the disciplines of advanced education, could be too difficult to comprehend by a mass audience composed of less than 15 percent college graduates. Moreover, few news stories would seem to provide the fuel for as lively interpersonal conversation among peers in the general public as it would among average members of the news profession, and communications research offers ample evidence of interpersonal conversation being a more powerful transmission mechanism than the media (Weiss, 1970), even among the elites in our society (Bauer et al., 1963).

The research evidence in the following section can be conveniently explained by and subsumed under the above type of arguments. However, while most research results are consistent with this formulation, which builds upon a model of a series of segmented media audiences who tend to become increasingly dissimilar from one another, a significant body of research points to quite different processes of information flow that may operate under certain conditions. These divergent research findings and conditions are then reviewed in the subsequent section, before some final implications and conclusions are drawn.

## Media Usage and Information Levels

There are, first of all, strong linkages that are found between media usage and information. Briefly stated, heavier users of print media are better informed than light users or nonusers.[2] It is immediately obvious, however, that there are intervening audience factors that need to be taken into account in such a formulation. Of the several factors in the audience itself, research indicates that the extent of the audience member's exposure to formal education is the most powerful factor intervening between media usage and information level.

For example, Figure 1 breaks the American population down into six groups that were maximally different in terms of their information about the Far East in 1964 (Robinson, 1967). The information index was based on answers to the following four questions:

1. What kind of government does most of China have?
2. Have you heard anything about another Chinese government?
3. Has the U.S. been treating China and Russia the same or differently?
4. Have you heard anything about the fighting in Vietnam?

The average score in the population on this index, which runs between 0 (no correct answers) and 4 (four correct answers), was 2.2, a score not significantly better than what could be achieved by unembarrassed guesswork on the part of a respondent. Group I (that 9 percent of the sample who were nonwhites with less than a high school education, earning under $7,500 per year) averaged just over half of one of the four questions correct compared to that 10 percent of the sample in Group VI (college graduates in white-collar jobs) who achieved a nearly perfect score of 3.6 items correct. While other factors were important in predicting public knowledge of these items,[3] it is obvious from Figure 1 that education was the dominant factor in distinguishing the six groups in terms of their information levels.

Thus, when one finds significant parallel differences in mass media usage among these six groupings of the population, one strongly suspects that education is the major factor at work here as well. The data are presented in Table 1 and show proportions of a 1958 national sample[4] claiming various usage of the media. While only 1 percent of persons in the Group I category reported reading a nonfiction book in the previous year, almost one in four persons in Group VI did. Even readership of *Look* and *Life*, "magazines for people who can't read," was four times higher in Group VI than in

**FIGURE 1. Combinations of Background Factors for Each of the Six Groups Within the United States Population Showing Large Differences in Information Scores About the Far East**

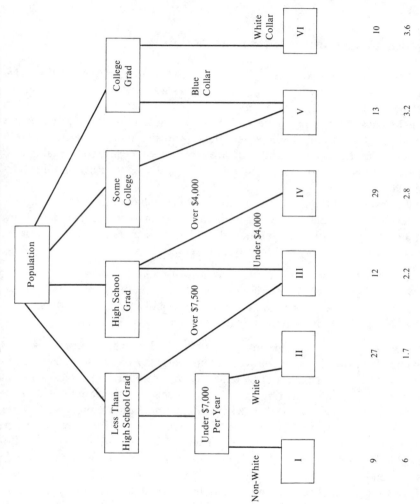

**TABLE 1. Percentage Within Each Social Group in Eight Separate Types of Sophisticated Usage[a]**

| Group | Books (Non-Fiction) | Analytic Commentary Magazine | News and Business Magazine | Pictoral and Interest Magazine | Read All or Most Foreign News in Paper | Read at Least Some Foreign News in Paper | Listen to News on Radio | Watch News on TV |
|---|---|---|---|---|---|---|---|---|
| I | 1 | 0.0 | 3 | 15 | 7 | 27 | 49 | 10 |
| II | 5 | 0.2 | 3 | 21 | 15 | 45 | 58 | 25 |
| III | 8 | 0.4 | 9 | 37 | 20 | 63 | 63 | 28 |
| IV | 8 | 1.1 | 13 | 47 | 25 | 69 | 57 | 33 |
| V | 15 | 0.5 | 24 | 53 | 36 | 80 | 62 | 34 |
| VI | 24 | 10.0 | 44 | 61 | 40 | 83 | 69 | 42 |
| Total Sample | 8 | 1.1 | 11 | 34 | 21 | 57 | 59 | 28 |
| National Opinion Leaders (Rosenau)[b] | 17 | 30 (est.) | 60 (est.) | 12 (est.) | NA | 94 (est.) | 10 (est.) | 10 (est.) |
| National Business Leaders (Bauer et al.) | NA | 20 (est.) | 88 (est.) | 40 (est.) | NA | 98 (est.) | NA | NA |

a. 1957 Survey Research Center data.
b. See Text for explanation of the Rosenau. Bauer et al. data.

Group I. Similar differences are found for readership of foreign affairs news in the newspaperand claiming news to be among one's usually viewed television programs and, to a much lesser extent, claiming news to be among one's usually heard radio programs.

These two sets of data on information and media usage, unfortunately taken six years apart, still strongly point to a strong relation between the two variables mediated by the factor of education. That is, it is the best educated segments of our population who are both well informed and who keep themselves better informed by more serious usage of the mass media for informational content. Nevertheless these data refer to aggregated groupings in the population and cannot be used to imply that such processes hold for individuals in the society. Indeed, one of the well-known methodological caveats of social science research is that relations that hold for aggregates oftentimes do not hold at the individual level (Robinson, 1950).

However, a study of adults in the Detroit, Michigan area in 1964 did collect simultaneous data on media usage, information level (again about foreign affairs) and education. These data not only corroborate the Figure 1 and Table 1 aggregative findings (Robinson, 1967), but also verify that the above interpretation holds at the individual level as well.[5]

Recent data from more appropriately designed national samples have not only extended these results to information areas beyond foreign affairs, but have allowed analyses by sophisticated multivariate methods, more appropriate to verifying the extent to which specific usage of each of the media predicts to information levels once other background factors are taken into account. . . . Data from the Survey Research Center's 1968 national election study do suggest that the various media do not perform the same functions in all segments of the poluation. Heavy usage of any medium seems to do little to raise information levels of college graduates, who are well informed whether they use the media or not. The same generally holds true, although not as strongly, and with some exceptions, for high school graduates. Among that majority of the population who did not graduate from high school, however, there are pronounced increases in information level associated with more regular usage of the media. While there are still significant differences between persons of different education levels, these become minimal among heavier users of the media. The data strongly suggest, therefore, that more extensive attention to the media can act to level the tremendous differences in information that obtain due to education. Somewhat similar conclusions were reached by Campbell (1966) in his analysis of political information data collected in the 1964 political campaign. . . .

A somewhat different tack characterized analysis of the public's ability to identify various people in the news[6] in a small 1970 national survey of television usage (Robinson, 1972). Instead of searching for the complex sort of interactions between variables uncovered in Figure 2, the attempt here was to examine how much of an overall idfference usagc of each medium made in explaining information levels, once other background factors (such as education, sex, age, race) and alternative media usage had been taken into account. All of these variables were subjected to a Multiple Classification Analysis (MCA), a recent computer program developed by Andrews et al. (1967) to examine the effects of single variables once the effects of all other variables are held constant.

The calculations of Table 2 result from applying MCA to these data. The first column of Table 2 refers to the average number of correct identifications for persons reporting various usage of each of the mass media and

**TABLE 2.** Average Number of News Personalities Recognized According to Media Usage (National sample)

| | | DEVIATION FROM OVERALL MEAN | |
| --- | --- | --- | --- |
| | | *Before Correction* | *After Correction*[a] |
| *Hours of TV on an average day* | | | |
| Less than 2 hours (n = 64) | 1.9 | +.4 | +.1 |
| Three hours (n = 172) | 1.8 | +.3 | +.1 |
| Four-five hours (n = 127) | 1.3 | −.2 | −.1 |
| Six or more hours (n = 67) | .6 | −.9 | −.2 |
| *Frequency of national news viewing* | | | |
| At least twice a week (n = 270) | 1.6 | +.1 | +.1 |
| About once a week (n = 81) | 1.8 | +.3 | +.1 |
| Never (n = 82) | .7 | −.8 | −.3 |
| *Reads a news magazine* | | | |
| Yes (n = 60) | 3.0 | +1.5 | +.6 |
| No, but reads other magazines (n = 214) | 1.5 | 0 | 0 |
| Does not read any magazines (n = 159) | 1.6 | −.7 | −.2 |
| *Reads a newspaper* | | | |
| Everyday (n = 293) | 1.8 | +.3 | +.2 |
| At least once a week (n = 99) | 1.1 | +.4 | −.3 |
| Less often (n = 41) | .1 | −1.4 | −.5 |
| *Hours of radio on an average day* | | | |
| Less than 2 hours (n = 235) | 1.5 | 0 | 0 |
| Two-three hours (n = 113) | 1.6 | +.1 | 0 |
| Four-five hours (n = 34) | 1.2 | −.3 | −.3 |
| Six or more hours (n = 51) | 1.5 | 0 | +.1 |
| *Number of movies seen (in previous three months)* | | | |
| None (n = 270) | 1.2 | −.3 | −.1 |
| One-two (n = 116) | 2.2 | +.7 | +.1 |
| Three or more (n = 47) | 1.4 | −.1 | +.1 |

a. After correction for usage of other media, sex, race, and education.

the second column refers to the deviation of these scores around the average score of 1.5 (out of a possible 7) correct identifications. Thus persons who report watching television less than two hours per day average 1.9 correct identifications, which is .4 identifications above the 1.5 general average. Entries in the third column refer to the average scores, once all the above-mentioned factors have been taken into account. Here persons who watch less than two hours of television per day now score only .1 identifications above the average, probably reflecting the lighter TV viewers' already-existing higher information levels and better education.

It can be seen that the figures in the third column indicate *print* media usage to be much more crucial in explaining differentials in information levels than does *broadcast* media usage. Readers of news magazines score .6 above average in information levels and nonreaders .2 below average, while regular newspaper readers score .2 above average and nonreaders .5 below average. In contrast frequent TV news viewers score only .1 above average and non-viewers of news programs only .3 below average. . . . Table 2 does not indicate heavy exposure to TV news leading to greater information accrual than occasional exposure.

Our confidence in the Table 2 results is strengthened when we find virtually the same pattern of results among a cross-section of 1,000 teenagers in a single large suburban county (Robinson, 1972) asked the same information and media usage questions. In fact, almost identical results were obtained when the analysis was performed on these teenagers' ability to answer factual questions about foreign countries.

Even further support for the applicability of these results in other areas of knowledge is provided by Schramm and Wade (1967). These authors conducted analyses parallel to those performed here for public awareness of health and science information. In both areas, print media usage was also found to predict to information levels better than broadcast media usage.[7]

Thus a substantial body of survey research data converges on the findings (a) that it is the best educated segment of society that keeps itself informed about what is happening in the world, and (b) that it is exposure to print media (the favored media mode of the better educated) which is mainly associated with greater likelihood of being informed or becoming better informed. These behaviors have recently been formally described under the hypothesis of an "increasing knowledge gap" by Tichenor et al. (1970). . . . which suggests that the mass media largely function to increase those already-existing gaps in information that separate the college graduate from the rest of society and hence may have been responsible for creating even wider divisions of opinion in our society than might have been the case without the media. Certainly the implications of these results need to be taken more seriously by media practitioners.

Tichenor et al. wisely note that their results largely were found with, and hence may only apply to, the print media and to academic "hard" news, i.e., items of public affairs and science rather than audience-specific topics (such as society news or garden care). It is to some similar exceptions to the above pattern of results, some of which do involve the "hard" news items that we have mainly discussed in this section, that we now turn our attention.

## Exceptions to Restricted Information Flow

The above body of literature clearly suffers from a lack of cumulative research enterprises (in which investigators can build upon and extend findings from previous endeavors), but the following exceptions are gleaned from an even more diverse body of research and speculation. These exceptions mainly concern the *type* of information under consideration. That is, it appears that *some types* of information in the media *can be conveyed* to the broader mass audience—i.e., beyond simply those portions of the audience who are already predisposed to absorb the information. Nevertheless, our discussion will touch on other communication variables as well, particularly the type of medium (learning via print as opposed to broadcast media) under consideration.

There is, first of all, the type of information that media observers, following from Lazarsfeld and Merton (1948), have labeled "status conferral." That is, persons, issues, or objects to which the media pay attention have increased status conferred on them merely by being exposed to media attention. Weiss (1970) reviews several examples of this phenomenon, the most well accepted perhaps being the increased importance or salience in the public of issues discussed by candidates during political campaigns (e.g., Eisenhower's raising of the Korean War as a campaign issue in 1952, the issue of bombing the islands of Quemoy and Matsu in the Kennedy-Nixon debates). To this, one might add the apparent correlation between media coverage and public perception of important national problems in noncampaign periods (a recent example being media discussion of ecology and pollution problems). A similar connection is not unlikely for people in news, which perhaps explains why politicians are so anxious for media coverage.[8] Advertising, particularly brand-name advertising, seems predicted on the notion that the public will attach higher status to products that have been brought to their attention by the media. . . .

While this discussion borders on the highly speculative, it is precisely these more subtle and difficulty measured types of information on which appropriate research is in short supply. Despite Herzog's (1944) well-publicized and intriguing finding that soap-opera fans found in these programs solutions to and philosophies about their own everyday problems, researchers have yet to undertake systematic measurement of what people learn from everyday dramatic media fare. Recent television surveys have demonstrated that the public generally perceives television dramatic programs as reflecting real life, and more viewers claim to learn something from their favorite dramatic programs than do not (Robinson, 1972). . . .

Finally, evidence now exists that information campaigns of the variety studied in Cincinnati need not be doomed to failure. Douglas et al. (1970) have reported a successful six-month media blitz to improve public information about the mentally retarded. Overall information levels on seven of ten information items examined were practically twice as high in the community subjected to the campaign as in a comparable community in which no special campaign was mounted. Moreover, those with least education picked up most campaign information. . . .

## Summary and Conclusions

Like almost every other institution in society, abundant evidence suggests that the mass media tend to reinforce and accentuate existing conditions rather than promote egalitarianism or abrupt change, at least with regard to information diffusion. The evidence is persuasive and pervasive that persons already well informed are more motivated to become better informed through the mass media than persons less well informed. The shocking ignorance of American citizens on issues of vital political and personal concern testifies to the limited fruitfulness of the interaction between the mass media and the public in the governmental process. One suspects that persons who claim to be getting most of their information from television may be euphemistically reporting that they are not receiving much information at all about what is happening.

At the same time, there is precious little evidence that education, the variable which mainly determines the patterns and consequences of media usage examined in this chapter, itself has any effect. One study found college seniors no better informed about public affairs than their freshmen counterparts (Turner and McClintock, 1958). High school students[9] who have had a course in civics are no better informed about government affairs than those who have not (Jennings and Langton, 1968).

How then do we learn anything, if media and education institutions have so little effect? Communication researchers strongly suspect that the key element may lie in the pattern of one's interpersonal social contacts (see Chaffee's chapter on this point). Overwhelming evidence is available to suggest that interpersonal means are more persuasive than mass media appeals (Weiss, 1970); greater credibility and understandability are two of several obvious reasons Robinson (1967) cites for this.

Nevertheless the exact processes whereby information flows through social networks is not well understood. The earlier hypothesis of the two-step flow of information from the media to "opinion leaders" to the rest of the public clearly distorts the nature and complexity of the information diffusion process. To be sure, one could almost define media information which fails to excite interpersonal discussion in the public as having the same impact as the philosophical tree falling in the wilderness. But exactly what information excites discussion, what norms and circumstances allow information transmission in ordinary conversation, how information gets distorted in interpersonal transmissions, or how lengthy or persuasive the claims of information are in these processes have only been vaguely touched in information diffusion research thus far.

The diffusion literature is far more valuable in suggesting an approach whereby media can exploit the powers of interpersonal communication. Rogers and Shoemaker (1971) mention several "media forms" that have worked out well in practice. Relevant individuals in a community are brought together as a group to listen to or watch a salient media presentation. Later, an extension worker leads a group discussion in which arguments in the presentation are debated and discussed in detail, hopefully pointing up irrational or invalid counterarguments. Although life in more modern societies is often too formal for such get-togethers to be practicable in the long run, the more likely the media practitioner successfully approximates interpersonal conditions, the more information will likely be conveyed.

Implicit in both this argument and in our discussion of the exceptions to our main rule-of-thumb is the need for more functional definitions of information so that institutions whose role it is to diffuse information through society should explore more utilitarian methods of reaching people with information they need when they need it. A recent synthesis of what is known about man's selective methods of attending to and processing information to which he is exposed (Sears and Foreman, 1968) concluded by reiterating a point made by researchers on the Cincinnati project, namely that people expose themselves to and absorb information which is useful. Whether one calls it useful or functional, a more rational approach to the business of reaching the public with information vital to a democratic society might begin by taking a thorough inventory of what it is that members of society would like to know more about, what they think they know and do not, and what might be a desirable mixture of the two from utopian conceptions of society. . . .

# Notes

1. Evidence from research on how time is spent does suggest that the arrival of a television set results in about twice as much time spent in contact with all mass media as was spent previously (Robinson, 1969).

2. As we shall see below, heavy viewers of television *news* programs are about as well informed as light or nonusers. It is the heavy users of television *generally* who are less well informed.

3. In addition to income, race, and occupation (variables included in Figure 1), sex, age, region of country, and size of place, were consistent predictors of knowledge. Men scored half a point higher than women, persons aged 55–64 scored half a point higher than persons in other age groups, residents of the South half a point less than average, and residents of rural areas half a point lower than average— holding constant all the Figure 1 factors. These same factors were very much associated with amount of print news usage, a leading predictor of information level as noted below.

4. These 1958 data are used in Table 1 because they represent the only such data available from a national sample at approximately the same point in time. No media usage questions were asked of the 1964 sample.

5. One important difference in the Detroit study is that specific questions on the frequency of viewing news programs were asked about radio and television, rather than types of programs to which the set is *usually* tuned. The two types of questions produce somewhat different types of results because the better educated spend much less time in contact with the broadcast media, especially television (Robinson, 1969). For this reason, the Detroit study finds the better educated attending to radio and television news programs about as often as the rest of the population, rather than the higher frequency implied in Table 1. For more detailed breakdown of the audience for network television news programs, see Robinson (1971).

6. The seven news personalities whom the public was asked to identify were: Robert Finch, Bob Dylan, Calvin Hill, Joseph Tydings, Tom Hayden, Ralph Nader, and Martha Mitchell. Recognition levels for some of the individuals were described in the introductory portions to this chapter.

7. In the area of political information however, television usage was the stronger predictor. We shall review and discuss this datum in the following section.

8. The phenomenon may also account for participation in certain forms of abberrant behavior. On the one hand, the media confer "status" to some individuals who engage in such deviance and in so doing may create some greater acceptance of the behavior than existed before, and on the other, focus attention on the particular individual who has performed it. Other persons in the audience who feel they are not receiving the attention they deserve may thus engage in some form of the behavior to achieve a similar end. The descriptions of motivations of airplane hijackers, for example, seem consistent with such a formulation as does the rash of imitators who follow the methods of novel crime reported in the media. Certain accounts of James Earl Ray's behavior would be consistent with his murder of Martin Luther King for some status-conferral motivations.

9. Few teenagers use the media for informational purposes (Robinson, 1971). Perhaps this is because they seldom learn anything in their high school years about *how* to use the media for such purposes. Educational institutions could profitably incorporate liaisons with mass media (the other educational institution in society) into their curricula so that media could more efficiently continue the education process into and through adulthood. Otherwise we might continue with the competitive model implied in Marshall McLuhan's observation that the child goes to school to interpret his education.

# References

ANDREWS, F., J. MORGAN, and J. SONQUIST (1967). Multiple Classification Analysis. Ann Arbor, Mich.: Survey Research Center.

BAUER, R. I. POOL, and L. DEXTER (1963). American Business and Public Policy, New York: Atherton Press.

CAMPBELL, A. (1966). "Political information through the mass media." Institute for Social Research.

CBS NEWS (1969). "In Black America." New York: Columbia Broadcasting System.

CHAFFEE, S., L. WARD, and L. TIPTON (1970). "Mass communication and political socialization in the 1968 campaign." Journalism Q. 47: 647–659.

DeFLEUR, M. and L. DeFLEUR (1967). "The relative contribution of television as a learning source for children's occupational knowledge." Amer. Soc. Rev. 32: 777–789.

DOUGLAS, D. B. WESTLEY, and S. CHAFFEE (1970). "An information campaign that changed community attitudes." Journalism Q. 47: 479–487.

ERSKINE, H. (1962). "The polls: the informed public." Public Opinion Q. 26.

———— (1963a). "The polls: textbook knowledge." Public Opinion Q. 27.

———— (1963b). "The polls: exposure to international information." Public Opinion Q. 28.

HERZOG, H. (1944). "What do we really know about daytime serial listeners?" pp. 3–31 in P. Lazarsfeld and F. Stanton (eds.) Radio Research 1942–43, New York: Duell, Sloan, & Pearce.

JENNINGS, M. and K. LANGTON (1968). "Political socialization and the high school civics curriculum in the United States." Amer. Pol. Sci. Rev. 62: 163–204.

KATZ, D. (1960). "The functional approach to the study of attitudes." Public Opinion Q. 24: 163–204.

KLAPPER, H. (1969). "Children's perceptions and moral evaluations of television programs." Paper presented at the 1969 meetings of the American Association of Public Opinion Research, Lake George, N.Y. Abstract in Public Opinion Q. 33: 460–461.

KLAPPER, J. (1960). The Effects of Mass Communication. New York: Free Press.

LANE, R. and D. SEARS (1964). Public Opinion. New York: Prentice-Hall.

LAZARSFELD, P. and R. MERTON (1948). "Mass communication, popular taste, and organized social change," in L. Bryson The Communication of Ideas. New York: Institute for Religious and Social Studies.

McCLINTOCK, C. and H. TURNER (1967). "The impact of college upon political knowledge, participation and values." Human Relations 15: 163–176.

McLEOD, J. and J. SWINEHART (1960). Satellites, Science and the Public. Ann Arbor, Mich: Survey Research Center.

McLEOD, J., R. RUSH, and K. FRIEDERICH (1968). "The mass media and political information in Quito, Ecuador." Public Opinion Q. 32: 575–587.

McPHEE, W. (1956). Unpublished memorandum on Mass Dynamics.

ROBINSON, J. (1972). "Toward defining the functions of television," in E. Rubinstein, G. Comstock and J. Murray (eds.) Television and Social Behavior Vol. 4, Television in Day-to-Day Life: Patterns of Use, Washington: Government Printing Office.

—————— (1971). "The audience for national TV news programs." Public Opinion Q. 35: 403–405.

—————— (1969). "Television and leisure time: yesterday, today, and (maybe) tomorrow." Public Opinion Q. 33: 210–222.

—————— (1967). Public Information About World Affairs. Ann Arbor, Mich: Survey Research Center.

ROBINSON, J. and P. HIRSCH (1969). "It's the sound that does it." Psychology Today: 42–95.

ROBINSON, W. (1950). "Ecological correlations and the behavior of individuals." Amer. Soc. Rev. 25.

SCHRAMM, W. and S. WADE (1967). Knowledge and the Public Mind. Palo Alto/ Stanford, Calif.: Institute for Communication Research.

SCHRAMM, W., J. LYLE, and E. PARKER (1962). Television in the Lives of Our Children. Stanford: Stanford University Press.

SEARS, D., and J. FREEDMAN (1967). "Selective exposure to information; a critical review." Public Opinion Q. 31: 194–213.

STAR, S. and H. HUGHES (1950). "Report on an educational campaign: the Cincinnati plan for the United Nations." Amer. J. of Sociology 50: 389–400.

STERN, A. (1971) Article in Time Magazine, October 18.

TICHENOR, P., G. DONOHUE, and C. OLIEN (1970). "Mass media flow and differential growth in knowledge." Public Opinion Q. 34: 159–170.

WEISS, W. (1970). "Effects of the mass media of communication," pp. 77–195 in G. Lindzey and E. Aronson (eds.) Handbook of Social Psychology Vol. 5. Boston: Addison-Wesley.

WARD S. (1972). "Effects of television advertising on children," in E. Rubinstein, G. Comstock, and J. Murray (eds.) Television and Social Behavior Vol. 4, Television in Day-to-Day Life: Patterns of Use. Washington: Government Printing Office.

# How Children Make Sense of Television

AIMEE DORR

CHILDREN, BUSY EXPLORING AND UNDERSTANDING OUR WORLD, seem for years to have constructed their own world out of pieces of ours. Within the changing limits of their information processing capacity, they construct models of the world as they expereience it. These models are then used to decode, encode, recall, and act. They make childhood a unique, but natural, period. The truth of this has been recognized for eons, captured in the biblical statement "When I was a child, I thought as a child . . . ," in Rousseau's admonitions (1762) to "leave childhood to ripen in your children" and to leave the mind "undisturbed till its faculties have developed," in Piaget's more than forty years of work (e.g., Piaget and Inhelder, 1969), and in current child development research (e.g., Kohlbert, 1969a; Shantz, 1975).

Yet an alternative characterization of children as tabulae rasae upon whom we "write" also has some demonstrated accuracy. It too has been endorsed throughout history in philosophical writings, in advice to parents and educators (e.g., Locke 1963; Spock, 1946), and in child development research (e.g., Bijou and Baer, 1961). If we are to progress in our understanding, this view of children as tabulae rasae must somehow be combined with the fact that they are also actively making their own sense of what we try deliberately or inadvertently to "write." Such activity may in significant ways alter the meaning of their experiences.

Much of the research on children and television to date could perhaps best be characterized as concerned with what happens when the black box transmits messages to the tabula rasa (see such recent reviews as Leifer,

Excerpted from "When I Was a Child, I Thought as a Child," in *Television and Social Behavior*, edited by S. Withey and R. Abeles. Hillsdale, N.J.: Lawrence Erlbaum, 1980.

1975; Leifer, Gordon and Graves, 1974; Liebert, Neale and Davidson, 1973; Stein and Friedrich, 1975). We have looked at the straightforward content messages of television and then examined the extent to which they appear in children's learning, attitudes, or behavior. Not many of us have very often undertaken the difficult task of understanding what sense children make of what they see, what constructs they use to interpret television, or what these constructs mean for the role that television plays in their development.[1]

This is not meant to imply that such research on children and television has produced no significant findings. On the contrary, I think it has provided substantial evidence that children will learn attitudes, information, and behaviors from television. Television is almost certainly not the major influence on a child's development that a few researchers imply, but some of its content some of the time does go straight into the child and come back out in almost unadulterated form. Yet once we have demonstrated this for cognitive information and skills (e.g., Ball and Bogatz, 1970, 1973; Ball *et al.*, 1974; Bogatz and Ball, 1971), for aggression (Goranson, 1970; Liebert, Neale and Davidson, 1973; Stein and Friedrich, 1975), for sex-roles (Frueh and McGhee, 1975; Pingree, 1975), for race-roles (Graves, 1975), and for advertising (Adler *et al.*, 1977), what shall we do?[2] The answer seems to be, for research on children and television, as well as for child development research in general, that we should look at how children construct models for what they experience and what this may mean for television's role in their development.

Consider some of the "facts" about television as a medium that children must reconstruct from their experience with the world, with television, and with what people tell them about both. Television is a representational system, not little people behaving in a box. Programs are made and broadcast by other people who have a variety of motives, not the least of which is pecuniary, for doing so. There is an underlying structure of information we consider to be important, and usually deliver, in a plot. Plot lines in American television are generally stereotyped in the dilemmas presented and in the ways in which they are worked out. Finally, programs have a variety of specific production techniques for symbolizing specific content.

In addition to reconstructing these facts about the medium, children interpret the social life they see on the screen, just as they do that in "real life." Children continuously make their own kind of sense of the television programs they see, using the constructions of social life they have derived from their own life experiences as well as from the media. . . . These constructions of television as a medium and of the social life it portrays, and the variations in constructions based on experience, age or stage, cognitive abilities, needs, social class, ethnicity, and unfathomable idiosyncrasies, must surely have implications for the different roles that television plays in the lives of different children. In what follows I will explore six aspects of the medium and its stories as they may be understood by children and suggest some of the implications of these understandings. . . .

## What, Really, Are Those Things in the Box?

Children begin watching television when they are babes in arms. They orient to its light and sound and may even be entertained by it for awhile (Slaby and Hollenbeck, 1977). By the time they are two or three, viewing is a regular pastime for most children (Lyle and Hoffman, 1972b; Schramm, Lyle and Parker, 1961). Much of what they see has commonalities with the "real world." There is form, movement, people, animals, objects, interaction, and linear sequencing in time. Programs with live actors, in all ways except size, dimensionality, and perhaps color, present experiences not at all unlike those children observe in the rest of their lives. What sense does a child make of this? Are these little people? Do they see the child?

Perhaps even the youngest child equates the television image with the real thing. Work in other areas certainly suggests that this is so. Infants as young as five months have been shown to recognize photographs and . . . drawings of people and objects (Cohen, DeLoache, and Pearl, 1977; Dirks and Gibson, 1977; Field, 1976; Strauss, DeLoache, and Maynard, 1977). . . . This is not to say that infants do not distinguish between two- and three-dimensional presentations; they do (Fantz, Fagan and Miranda, 1975; Ruff, Kohler, and Haupt, 1976). It does, however, indicate that they do not need to learn to recognize two-dimensional representations of their three-dimensional world. They can apparently do this in infancy. If young children link the objects and people on television to their equivalents in the concrete world, as the research suggests they would, then perhaps they incorporate the television information into their growing conceptions of them.

It is not at all uncommon for children of two or three or even four to believe that the people they see on television can, in some mysterious way, engage in social interaction with them. Preschoolers talk to the characters of some children's programs they are viewing and many characters talk to them. Mister Rogers says "I like you just the way you are," Bob of *Sesame Street* asks children if they got the right answer in the preceding grouping task, and Captain Kangaroo says "Good" when child viewers "respond affirmatively" to his query about wanting to watch a film about the circus. When the medium of television is understood in this way, some of the programs the child watches may serve as simply another social interaction in which the child participates.[3] If this is true, then the young child may understand and learn from television programs in ways that are quite similar to those in other daily social encounters. We could expect information, requests, emotional displays, and orders to be responded to as they are when a live adult delivers them to a child.

Noble (1975), repeating an idea advanced years ago by Horton (Horton and Wohl, 1956), has argued that television viewing is appealing to children precisely because it provides them with parasocial interactions such as these. Modern children's lives are viewed as impoverished by the lack of a small, stable, multi-aged community within which to come to know one's self and the world (as the world would be defined by one whose life was lived out in the small village). Television, albeit an imperfect substitute for human encounters, makes up for some of these deficits. Accepting for the moment such a view, one could argue—as Noble does—that television should be striving to present even greater congruity between the lives of its people and the lives of ordinary citizens. Yet such congruities may also present problems for children who do not fully understand the nature of the programs they are viewing. Programs present accurate and inaccurate information about our culture to children who have not yet acquired their own stable, family- or community-based conceptions of life. Television's isomorphisms with "real life" may lead young children to greater acceptance of the reality of television life than their families or communities consider appropriate.

The extent of reality ascribed to entertainment programs seems to undergo major changes during the preschool and early elementary school years. Children seem to learn to grant greater credibility to the three-dimensional world, discounting the more fantastic television capabilities of objects, animals, and people. They come to understand that most television representations are fabricated and transmitted into the box and that the realism of these fabrications varies enormously.

By the time children are about five they probably understand that the television host is not big brother watching them. Somewhat later they may begin to understand that television programs are not glimpses into everyday social life. These understandings are, however, still a major issue for the child. In discussing what is real and pretend on television, most of the children in the early elementary grades with whom I have worked[4] focus on the fact that the actors are real people but what they do is pretend. Unlike children around ten years of age, they do not seem to assume this and go on to evaluate how realistic characters and their actions are. Their concern is still with understanding the nature of the representation on television, and their major heuristic seems to be that everything, except the actors themselves, is pretend.[7]

This heuristic—everything is pretend—is adamantly applied by children in the early elementary grades to judgments about the reality of television programming in general, of entertainment programming, and of specific actions and relationships (Dorr and Graves, 1978). Fundamentally, however, children at this age are still uncertain. The concrete, visual presentation of a television program is difficult to override with cognitive controls. This is illustrated in our recent interviews by the second grader who told us that the bullets used to shoot people in entertainment programs were all fake. Later, however, he added "they all wear vests just in case they try putting real bullets in there. That should help some." . . . Thus the child's initial judgment that something was pretend on television is later somewhat modified to give more credence to what was actually seen on television. . . .

The experiences which lead children to these varying constructions of the television medium are at present undocumented. Presumably parents, siblings, peers, teachers, and others in the child's life explain the medium at least occasionally when confusions are apparent. Most television viewing by preschool and elementary school children occurs with other people, usually parents and/or siblings, thereby providing opportunities for these younger children to learn about the medium and its content from parents' and siblings' reactions to it and to them. Television programs are favorite topics among groups of elementary school children and among young adolescents, and such conversations may help them to evaluate the medium and its content more accurately. Perhaps repeated failures by a television character to respond to the child also contribute to a reformulation of explanations for the character's presence in the livingroom. Perhaps the repeated discontinuities in the social reality on television and elsewhere contribute.

All of these suggestions about what may lead to changing constructions of the television medium are purely speculative. If we could determine the experiences which lead to the changing interpretations of television as a medium, we might then know how to help children earlier acquire more accurate conceptions. Failing that we might try to learn more about the sequence of constructions children make of the medium and use this knowledge to anticipate how they will react to the variety of programming they watch. Such undertakings will demand great skill because they require us to understand the cognitive constructs of children who are either preverbal or else verbal but largely inarticulate and unintrospective.

## How Come Those Programs Are There?

Understanding that television programs are usually fabricated does not logically lead to questioning why they are fabricated. Nonetheless understanding why entertainment programs are there to be seen does seem to develop as part of a child's increasingly accurate construction of television as a medium. From work which my colleagues and I did it appears that explanations for why programs are there to be watched develop throughout middle childhood and adolescence (Phelps, 1976). Recognition grows that programs are designed to make money by entertaining, but even adults seem to have very limited understanding of the economic structure of the American television industry. Such conceptions of why programs are produced and broadcast may be important if they mediate the effects that programs can have on the viewer.

For adults, acceptance of information depends at least partially on an evaluation of the credibility of the source of that information. Information is more believable if the source is judged to be knowledgeable in that area, to have good reasons for presenting the truth, or to achieve minimal personal gain from having the information accepted (Insko, 1967; McGuire, 1969). Our knowledge of the extent to which children and adolescents employ similar processes in evaluating information presented to them is quite limited, although there are indications that such processes are not present until middle childhood (Aronson and Golden, 1959; Roberts, 1968). At whatever point they do appear the child's construction of why television programs are there to be seen may become an important predictor of the credibility attached to what is seen.

The earliest explanations that children seem to have for why programs are available are only likely to enhance the perceived veracity of program content—if children at all use these explanations in evaluating content. Consonant with adult beliefs and industry intentions children often told us that entertainment programs are broadcast to amuse them:

> "To entertain people when they have nothing to do." [thirteen-year-old]
> "To entertain people. And to help me think. If they didn't have TV, when you come in and you sit down and you just want to do something, you don't have anything to do." [second grader]
> "For kids to watch them." [kindergartener]

While adults may discount content presented with a primary goal of amusement, the same may not be true for children. In fact, most of the children whom we interviewed believed that those amusing programs were also made to teach, to tell the truth:

> "To be educational things; they try to do it to help people." [sixth grader]
> "To teach children . . . about how to act and all that." [second grader]

It is clear from data that even at the beginning of our adolescence children have only meager understanding of the economics of the television industry, but it should not be assumed that complete understanding develops during adolescence. Our interviews with adolescents and their parents indicated that even the adults had limited understanding of the relationships between audience size (and sometimes characteristics), sale of advertising time, and income, although most understood that television broadcasting was a profit-making enterprise. In fact, the economics of all the mass media are beyond the ken of most of the adult population (Hirsch, personal communication).

## What Can Be Understood in a Story?

Most of what children watch on television is plotted. While the models for plot lines may differ somewhat from writer to writer, at base each contains an initiating event or problem, the internal responses of the protagonists to it, attempts at resolving the problem, the consequences of the attempts, and reactions to them (see Rummelhart, 1974, for a "grammar" of stories, and

Labov, 1972, for a "grammar" of well-formed, extended narratives). If children do, in fact, construct models of aspects of their world and use them to interpret it, we should expect that with time they must develop some construct, like the suggested one, for an ideal plot (which may be congruent with notions of real-life cause-and-effect sequences). Each successive construction of an ideal plot model would then have implications for the sense children make of the television programs they watch.

Child development and cognitive psychologists, using experimentally constructed stories, are currently studying the constructs children have of storybook plots and what these mean for their understanding and recall of stories (Brown and Smiley, 1977; Mandler, 1977; Mandler and Johnson, 1977; Stein, 1976, 1977; Stein and Glenn, 1975). . . . In the early grades of elementary school children need and expect to find in a story an initiating event, an attempt at resolution, and the consequences of that resolution. . . . In studies of children's reports of their own adventures (Kernan, 1977) and of their processing of storybook adventures (see preceding citations) we see a gradual increase during the years of elementary school in the number of elements considered to be important (especially those dealing with motivation and affect) and in the expectation of connected elements of plot rather than simple actions. From both there are indications that children construct grammars for plots. From the studies of story plots these are indications that plots which conform to the ideal grammar are easiest to understand and recall and that the grammar is actively used to understand and recall. All of these findings have potential relevance for children's understanding of plotted television programs.

Television plots are most often like those in storybooks, and we can reasonably expect that children construct ideal plot lines for them too. This has implications for what we can anticipate they might take away from different programs they watch. Prior to the development of the concept of an ideal plot, children's understanding or recall of a program is not as likely to be disturbed by randomly sequenced events, multiple plot lines, flashbacks, and inverted time sequences. One study with television provides evidence in line with this hypothesis. Collins and Westby (1975) found that randomly sequencing events from a crime drama program had little detrimental effect, compared to the correct temporal sequence, on second graders' recall of the plot, while it did affect fifth graders' recall. Such a result might be explained by assuming that the second graders had not yet developed the construct of a temporally ordered ideal plot line and that the fifth graders had developed such a concept but were not yet adept at picking out disordered elements of a program and putting them in the right slot in the ideal format. . . .

In addition to not being affected by temporal arrangements of elements of the plot, we might expect that children who have not yet constructed a model of an ideal plot would not be disturbed by the absence of the motivations for or the consequences of actions nor would they necessarily include them in retelling a plot (with or without them). There are a few studies which give some credence to these expectations. They show that in retelling plots children younger than seven cite only the most active occurrencs—the attempts at resolution of a problem . . . (Collins, Berndt, and Hese, 1974; Leifer *et al.,* 1971).

Perhaps the lack of a concept of a plot line explains why young children have such an appetite for programming with lots of action, changes, and noise. They aren't looking for a plotted story—they don't really understand there should be one—they are looking for stimulation. Once a program meets their requirement of high activity, young children may be the most undiscriminating of viewers. Inane, disordered, partial plots may be just as appealing as are sensible, linear plots with all necessary elements present—and just as understandable.

Later, when children have first constructed the concept of an ideal plot line, what they understand of different programs and what they extract from them should reflect their changed model. Obviously, the programs truly designed for these children will have an initiating event, an attempt to resolve it, and the consequences of that attempt—in that order. Such programs might add the internal responses of the protagonists, but they would not add more in terms of subplots, nor would they diverge from the model order for the plot elements. . . .

While those of us who talk with children about the television they watch know that they understand programs differently at different ages and differently from adults, we have as yet arrived at few paradigms for predicting what their construction of a program will be. Interpreting their understanding as derived from successively more complex—and in our view more correct—models for a plot and from increasing ability to utilize plot information presented in other than ideal form may aid us in arriving at more accurate predictions for what they will understand about a television plot. It may also ultimately aid us in predicting what effects various programs will have on children of different ages if different understandings lead to the drawing of predictably different messages from a program.

## What Does It Mean That Things Are So Much the Same on Television?

In addition to almost consistently employing plots whose "deep structures" conform to an ideal model, American television programs are generally consistent in the portrayals they present of various types of people (e.g., United States Commission on Civil Rights, 1977), in the ways in which people try to resolve the initial conflict situation (e.g., Gerbner and Gross, 1976) and in the final resolutions of the conflict (e.g., Larsen, Gray, and Fortis, 1968).[5] They may therefore present children with another opportunity for constructing a model of television programs. As an illustration, consider the final resolution of a program. Most dramatic programs, and most programs that children watch, are episodes in a series with a limited number of recurring, main characters. . . . The child who watches television with any regularity must come to understand that the hero must prevail. What happens when the child recognizes this necessity? Right now we have no inkling of the consequences of recognizing what some call consistency and others call stereotypy in entertainment programming, but let me suggest a few disparate alternatives all drawn from my conversations with people about television.

One possibility would be that consistency of content would lead one to reject its veracity. We all know, for example, that the flesh-and-blood good guy does not always win. Knowing this and seeing that television heroes violate this reality, one might come to reject these heroes as representative of real life. . . . Many of the older children, adolescents, and adults I have interviewed use just this reasoning:

> "I think a lot of that is fake [portrayals of Puerto Rican women]. Like the way they are all getting beat up and this and that, you know. They are *always* swearing and yelling and having kids and all that. I think a lot, I think *most*, of that is all fake." [sixteen-year-old]
>
> "You know it's going to have a dippy ending, but when you put the facts down, you know this happens, and they get caught. It always happens. They're always caught." "Do you think that that happens in real life?" "No." [sixth grader].

Logical as this possibility seems to me, I have interviewed a good many people who apparently do not reason this way. Some of them seem to use consistency of portrayals as evidence that real-life people must be like those on television. As one white woman said:

> I don't know much about it, but it seems that all the black shows are all the same. It seems that they're showing all black people in one way on almost all the shows, so maybe this is true. . . . I don't know much about them, but all the shows show them and have them act the same way. But as far as white people, I know they try to make them true-to-life so people can sympathize with them.

While at first glance I find this an amazing flight of fancy in adults, it is altogether understandable if one assumes that viewers, like this woman, believe that television producers are generally committed to presenting accurate portrayals of our culture and if one accepts the thesis of this article that people construct models for the world based on the consistencies they find in it. Viewed in this way it is not altogether unreasonable that people would interpret consistency as truth. Such a view receives some support from the finding that children, adolescents, and adults ascribe greater veracity to the portrayals of people with whom they have less real-life contact (Greenberg and Reeves, 1976; Leifer, 1976). Obviously consistency in portrayals for these viewers has entirely different implications from those it has for some other viewers.

A third possibility is that consistency is recognized but dismissed in reasoning about television, because one holds some other more compelling explanation about the veracity of entertainment content. In these instances consistency may be explained in any manner which makes it consistent with the overarching explanation (if the child has come to believe that explanations should be logically consistent) or it may be explained in any "illogical" fashion or left unexplained. The best example I have found of explaining consistency so that it is consonant with another paramount belief comes from a conversation with a thirteen-year-old girl. To understand her interchange with the interviewer, you must realize that she believed that Perry Mason actually was a practicing attorney. When asked what she thought about the fact that he always won his cases (the interviewer obviously endorsed the first alternative effect of consistency); she reasoned that he used the series much like advertising for his services:

"Oh, Perry Mason, he never loses a case."
["What do you think about that?"]
"I enjoy watching it."
["But do you think it is true?"]
Yeah.
["That a man could be so good at his job that he would never lose his case?"]
"Well, not never. He would lose them once in awhile."
["So how come he never loses?"]
"It's his program. It wouldn't be too good for him if he loses."

On a different vein from that of veracity is the possibility that understanding the consistency of plots diminishes the emotional involvement of the viewer. Where is the high drama if you know that Steve, Austin, the bionic hero, must slay the shark and rise to the surface before his air runs out? This fourth possibility was suggested to me by my son, who was seven at the time. As I grew nervous during the suspenseful part of some program and asserted that I couldn't watch any more, he scornfully asked why I was so nervous when I knew the protagonist has to be all right by the end of the program. This realization, that main characters had to be resurrected by the end of each program in a series, was a relatively new one for him. It had clearly diminished his uncertainties during a program and it seemed to have also decreased his own emotional arousal. Of course, diminution of uncertainty and arousal is not a necessary consequence of understanding consistency in series' plots; I, the adult facilitator of his concept, was clearly anxious. Still, I think we might want to explore this possibility of decreased arousal further; it may for awhile play some role in children's reactions to programming.

We are left then with a variety of consequences and nonconsequences as possible outcomes of recognizing the consistency of television fare. Each is based on the assumptions that children construct models of television content from their experiences with it and that these models (or lack of them) may have implications for their understanding of and reactions to television programming. As yet we have no real evidence to support the assumptions or the possible outcomes for consistency in plots and portrayals, but the tantalizing tidbits gleaned from interviews and personal life suggest we may want to follow the trail further. In doing so, we will need to take account of the possibility that consistencies may not generally be recognized by viewers. Or, people may be sufficiently noncritical during viewing that the implications of consistencies over time or across programs may have no impact unless discussion—or interviews like those we conducted—essentially force examination of them.

## Interpreting the Visual Medium

Thus far I have discussed television programming from the vantage point of my literate, print-oriented heritage, neglecting McLuhan's sage reminder that television is not a print medium (McLuhan, 1964). While its plot lines and consistencies draw heavily on our oral and print storytelling traditions, its visual mode presents the opportunity for the development of other traditions. An increasingly sophisticated technology permits us to convey information through slow motion, quick cuts, camera angles, chroma-key, and a host of other visual techniques. Television presents us with a visual quasi-grammar which we must learn, along with the print-based grammar, if we are to understand its messages (Huston-Stein and Wright, 1977; Salomon, 1974). . . .

While I know of no data on children's interpretations of television's visual grammar, indications of the difficulties they have abound in my informal viewing and conversations with them. For some children, slow motion sequences are accepted as the literal truth. When we watch Steve Austin running slowly down the road, I think "He's using his bionics to catch up with the bad guys" and the five- to seven-year-old children with whom I am viewing ask how he can catch them when he's running so slowly. When slow motion is seen so literally, some of the meaning intended by the producer is lost for the child. When slow motion is recognized as a symbolic form, it is probably most often first given only one meaning. For children without much exposure to bionic heroes and heroines, this meaning is most likely to be one of thinking or dreaming, since that is what slow motion is most often used to mean. Similar problems of literal interpretation of visual symbolism and of unitary constructs for techniques which can have multiple meanings must surely arise for all visual forms in television.

## Making Sense of Television's Social World

Television presents interpretative problems for a child which depend both on its characteristics as a medium, which have been discussed in the preceding sections, and on its social content, to which we now turn. The people on television and their interactions present interpretative tasks which are common to all presentations of social life, whatever the medium. They include such tasks as understanding that another person has his or her own perspective, inferring the other's perspective, and judging the morality of another's action. Within the past decade work in child development has indicated that children do indeed develop a series of constructs for interpreting these aspects of social life and that the constructs they employ at any given time have implications for their understanding of social life (e.g., Shantz, 1975).

Successful social interaction demands an awareness of the possibility that the social other may differ in significant ways from the self. Such understanding comes gradually to children—and imperfectly to adults. One formulation of the development of the ability to take the role of another has been suggested by Selman (Selman and Byrne, 1974). Before the age of about four the child is believed to be devoid of understanding that the social other has any perspective. Over the next eight years, approximately, the child progresses through the following stages: understanding that the other has a perspective but assuming it is the same as the child's (4–6 years), understanding that the perspective may be different and inferring what it is (6–8 or 10 years), understanding that the other is inferring the child's perspective just as the child infers the other's (8–10 or 12 years), and being able to see a social interchange in which one is participating as though one were a third-party observer—the fly on the wallpaper (after 10 years of age).

Such a progression in role-taking ability, to the extent that it is pervasive and consistent, has implications for children's understanding of television programming. Take the simplest example, children who do not understand that another has an unique perspective. Such children will certainly miss the humor attendant in some interchanges between characters with different goals, feelings, or knowledge. They also will not understand visual attempts to portray a character's internal perspective. When, during a social interchange, the camera closes in on Joe hardy's head, cuts quickly to another experience he has had, and then cuts back to his head, the child will not understand that we are seeing Joe's thoughts, that those thoughts are not apparent to the other interactant, and that those thoughts are relevant to what Joe does in the social interchange. . . .

Descriptions of role-taking often focus on children's ability to understand the motivations of another or at least on attempts to do so. Several lines of evidence indicate that motivations become an increasingly significant consideration for children during the elementary school years. Selman's formulation, for which there are supportive data (Selman and Byrne, 1974), suggests that it is not until the age of about six that a child will attempt to understand another's motivations (which says nothing about the ability to do so accurately). Traditional studies of moral reasoning have been interpreted as demonstrating that it is not until approximately seven to ten years of age that children begin to take motivations for action into account in reasoning about the moral rectitude of another's action (Kohlberg, 1969b), as has at least one study of children's judgments of kindness (Baldwin and Baldwin, 1970). More recent work in an information integration framework suggests that children from kindergarten on (the youngest age tested) utilize both motivations and consequences in judging behavior, with increasingly more weight being given to motivations as children mature (Surber, 1977). Nonetheless, evidence for the influence of motivations is clearly present in kindergarteners' judgments. Finally, the previous discussion of children's conceptions of plotlines in storybooks and in their own narratives also indicated that the motivations for action do not become an accepted part of the story until the early elementary grades.

Such findings, if replicated for television, present important considerations for those interested in children's understanding of television and its effects on them. From the time children are three or four they primarily watch plotted programs. For many of these programs, though surely not for all, the motivations for action are important elements for understanding the "message." Our condemnations of the rebuffed father and the shark-trainer daughter who destroyed the sub and intimidated its crew in an episode of the *Six Million Dollar Man* are moderated by understanding their motivations to avenge old wrongs and to force due recognition of genius. For anywhere from three to six years children may watch such programs and generally judge action and character by actions themselves, by their consequences, or by the standards they have inculcated from their home. If the effects of a television program on viewers are in any way determined by the messages they drew from it and if motivations are an important part of the message, then young children's failure to use them in interpreting the message may lead to effects we would not otherwise predict.

Such an analysis is not meant to imply that effective messages must always be imbedded in a motivation-action-consequence sequence or that these three elements are the only ones within a program which children may use to evaluate action and characters. Most of the plotted material that children view features one or more main characters—the "good guys"—who appear week after week.[6] Through some process which we do not understand, even very young children soon learn who they are. Once such learning has occurred, it would certainly reduce the need for children to evaluate specific depicted motivations in order to arrive at an adult-like judgment about the morality of a character's actions. What the familiar "good guy" does must be good (his motivations usually are good) and what the usually unfamiliar opponents do must be bad (their motivations usually are bad). Even in those few series which feature the same "bad guys" each week there are numerous cues to status other than motivations—such as relative success of each character, amount of time each is on the screen, and the reactions of other characters. Similar cues, plus the stereotyped white and black hats or their present-day equivalents, probably also operate in programs which appear only once on television rather than in a series. Thus, most television programs provide multiple cues as to the moral judgments one "should" make about characters and their actions, and a complete analysis of such judgments would obviously consider as many of them as possible.

A few studies suggest that young children do, in fact, tend to neglect motives in recalling and understanding television programs. Looking first at children's retelling of the plot of a television program, we find—as we would expect from studies of children's concepts of storybook plots—that kindergarten and second grade, but not fifth and eighth grade, children are likely to omit motives in recounting a popular crime drama (Collins, Berndt, and Hess, 1974). In fact, only one second grader included motives at all! The program itself had been edited down to only eleven minutes, thereby decreasing the likelihood that material intervening between motives, action, and consequences or that incidental information would seriously interfere with children's learning of the motives (see respectively Collins, 1973, and Collins, 1970; Hale, Miller and Stevenson, 1968; and Hawkins, 1973, for evidence for such effects). About half of the fifth graders and two-thirds of the eighth graders included motives in their retelling, but we might expect less even from them when viewing full-length crimes dramas where intervening and incidental material would be greater.

There are also indications that younger children do not understand motives well when directly questioned about them. In the study just described (Collins, Berndt, and Hess, 1974), almost all the subjects (96%) could, when directly questioned, describe the consequences to the characters. There was, however, a strong, linear increase with age in their ability to describe the motivations for aggression. Leifer et al. (1971) and Leifer and Roberts (1972) also have reported a linear increase with age in ability to describe correctly or recognize the motivations for actions when directly questioned about them . . . .

Finally, there are indications—as one would expect from the literature on the development of moral reasoning—that younger children are not as likely to use motives in evaluating television characters as are older children. In the Collins, Berndt, and Hess (1974) study, kindergarten and second grade children were more likely than the two groups of older children to refer to aggressive acts in justifying their evaluations of characters, and the older groups were more likely than the younger to refer to motives. In the Leifer and Roberts (1972) study, kindergarten children tended to view as "bad" all characters who engaged in aggression, while from third grade on children (and adults) separated aggressors into "good guys" and "bad guys" apparently based on the motives for their aggression.

It should be noted in reviewing these studies that the greatest "deficits" in apparent understanding of motivations tend to occur in situations in which children are asked to produce them. Retelling plots and justifying evaluations of characters (Collins, Berndt, and Hess, 1974) both allow children to choose what they would tell the interviewer. The omission of motivations in such cases may indicate that children did not recognize or understand them, that they did not consider them important, that they did not believe the interviewer would consider them important, or that they forgot them because they occurred early in the program. Explaining motivations (Collins, Berndt, and Hess, 1974; Leifer et al., 1971) did require children to discuss motivations with the interviewer. The less adequate explanations of the younger children may, however, be due to the lack of vocabulary or to forgetting motivations, which typically occur earlier than do consequences, just as much as they may be due to children's lack of recognition or understanding. . . . It is, therefore, possible that our estimates of young children's understanding of motivations (especially as opposed to consequences) are biased by our testing procedures. Children may understand motivations earlier than conventional tests suggest yet be unable or unwilling to verbalize them well. . . .

I believe, however, that the evidence that children at different ages recognize, understand, and utilize motivations differently is strong enough and the hints that such differences may modify the effects of the (motivated) behaviors to which they are exposed on television are sufficient that the area is worth further investigation. Such research will have to select carefully the presentations, the motivations, the extent to which motivations are presented or must be inferred, measures of depicted and undestood motivations, the ages of the subjects, and a host of other variables. But its results might help us better to know when and how to use television (as we now try to do) to teach children such concepts involving motivations as crime does not pay, it is wrong to use epithets intentionally to hurt, and handicapped persons must be valued for trying to be fully competent and friendly whether or not they succeed.

# Conclusion

At points in writing this article it has seemed that one could just as well compose a general paragraph and stop. The paragraph would read somewhat as follows. Children, like adults, strive to make sense of television, both as a medium and as a social world. They develop constructs and paradigms and apply them in interpreting their television-based experiences. There may be a relatively regular course of development for these constructs and paradigms. Even if their developmental course is not regular, it is clear that for many years they are not the same as those employed by adults. Different constructs and paradigms, when applied to television, lead to different understandings of the medium and its content. Such differences in understanding naturally mean that television viewing is a different experience for viewers of different ages. They may also mean that the effects of television viewing, where they generally exist, will differ for these viewers and that effects will occur for some viewers and not others. . . .

The six areas in which I have tried to illustrate the general theme are not empty elaboration of it. Making sense of television requires knowledge of many different aspects of the medium and its content. We need to know where its sounds and images come from, why they are broadcast, what structures are used to tell its stories, how to interpret the consistency of its stories, what the various visual techniques signify, and how to make sense of the social world we see on it. . . . I have tried to indicate what there is to learn in each of these areas, the ways in which children of various ages may make sense of them, and some approximate ages at which different constructs are likely. Table 1 summarizes much of the material presented. It is offered with trepidation. The formality of a table with age norms and constructs filled in suggests far more certainty about the concepts and the ages at which they occur than is at all warranted. It also suggests greater uniformity within an age group than I would necessarily expect to find in real life. Nonetheless, it is hoped that the table will help to summarize many of the speculations I have made and provide the reader with some indications of the kinds of changes one might expect as children develop.

There are good reasons to believe that children do progress through a series of constructs for understanding television and its content and that, from an adult's viewpoint, these constructs come increasingly close to being correct—even though we are a long way from being able to specify constructs and ages. Yet it would be foolhardy to assert that "correct constructs" are fully understood and consistently applied by all adults. . . .

Children's constructions of television are, for some, important only because they are interesting, amusing, or strange. Variations in humankind—whether they be among adults grouped by such variables as social class, ethnicity, or experience or among children grouped by age—always intrigue us. I, too, have derived great pleasure from talking with children and glimpsing the various ways in which they can make sense of television. I believe, however, that there is a more practical reason for understanding what sense children are likely to make of it.

Television, intentionally and unintentionally, does teach children. If we know how they are likely to interpret it, we can then use the medium as a more effective, positive aid in socialization. *Sesame Street* can teach cooperation better, *Mister Rogers* can better help children to explore their feelings, *The Jeffersons* may not unduly influence the segregated white child's view of blacks, and young children (unlike some we have talked with) may not be so sanguine about accidents whose damages cannot really be repaired with bionics. This is not meant to imply that a "bad" television experience

**TABLE 1. Very Approximate Age Breakdown**

| AREA | 0–5 | 5–7 | 7–10 | 10–13 | 13 ON |
|---|---|---|---|---|---|
| Reality of TV Images | Images represent real thing | Actors real, but acting pretend; Judgment influenced by visual representation | | Evaluate realism → | |
| Actor–viewer interaction | Actors and viewers truly interact | Actors cannot see viewers or interact with them → | | | |
| Why programs are broadcast | To entertain and inform | | | | To make money → |
| Elements of plot | None | | Initiating event, attempts to resolve, consequences; Sequences meaningfully consequentially connected | Motivations, emotions, internal responses → | |
| Order of plot elements | None | Ideal order preferred and easiest to manage | | Variations in order matter → | |
| Consistency of portrayals and plots | | Insufficient data for even rough age breakdown | | | |
| Visual grammar | | Insufficient data for even rough age breakdown | | | |
| Role taking | Other has: no perspective | same perspective / own perspective | Other infers one's perspective; Watch own interaction as third party would → | | |
| Use of motivation to judge character | Motivation of less importance, consequences matter more | | Motivations of primary importance → | | |

379

is likely to have substantial long-range effects on children. In my view children are remarkably resilient creatures, whose development is influenced by a multitude of people and experiences. We should try to have as many of these as possible—including television—be good for children. Knowing more about the sense they make of the medium and its content can help us to achieve this. . . .

## Notes

1. I am grateful to my fellow members of the Social Science Research Council Committee on Television and Social Behavior and to Barbara Flagg for their helpful comments on an earlier draft of this paper and to Donald Dorr-Bremme and Paul Hirsch, who critiqued an earlier draft with special care and enthusiasm, pointed me to bodies of theory and research other than those in which I usually forage, and asked questions which helped me to clarify my thoughts and the expression of them.

2. While each of the cited studies and literature reviews looked primarily for straightforward stimulus–response effects, many of them explored other issues as well.

3. Adults too engage in social interactions with television characters. I talk back to newscasters and sports announcers, sports fans yell encouragement, advice, and threats to players, coaches, and officials, and characters in situation comedies come in for their share of praise and abuse from viewers. While such activities by adults may be important indicators of involvement in or functions of viewing for them, they probably do not serve as the same kinds of social interaction via television as they do for young children.

4. Except where otherwise noted, the quotations and examples of children's, adolescents', and adults' reasoning about television are all taken from research supported by the Office of Child Development under a grant (Number 90-C-247) originally made to Aimee Dorr Leifer, Sherryl Browne Graves, and Neal J. Gordon.

5. Although these citations do not cover all possible content areas and all content analyses necessarily report data for nothing more recent than the previous season, each successive year of content analysis has indicated at best gradual declines in the consistency of whatever area is measured.

6. Paul Hirsch deserves the credit for pointing this out to me.

## References

ADLER, R. P., et al. Research on the effects of television advertising on children: Review and recommendations. Final report for National Science Foundation Grant Number APR 75–10126, 1977.

ARONSON, E., and GOLDEN, B. The effect of relevant and irrelevant aspects of communicator credibility on opinion change. *Journal of Abnormal and Social Psychology,* 1959, *59,* 177–181.

BALDWIN, C. P., and BALDWIN, A. L. Children's judgments of kindness. *Child Development*, 1970, *41*, 29–47.

BALL, S., and BOGATZ, G. A. *The first year of Sesame Street: An evaluation.* Princeton, N.J.: Educational Testing Service, 1970.

BALL, S., and BOGATZ, G. A. *Reading with television: An evaluation of The Electric Company.* Princeton, N.J.: Educational Testing Service, 1973.

BALL, S., BOGATZ, G. A., KAZAROW, K., and RUBIN, D. B. *Reading with television: A follow-up evaluation of The Electric Company.* Princeton, N.J.: Educational Testing Service, 1974.

BERKOWITZ, L., and RAWLINGS, E. Effects of film violence on inhibitions against subsequent aggression. *Journal of Abnormal and Social Psychology*, 1963, *66*, 405–412.

BIJOU, S. W., and BAER, D. M. *Child development, vol. 1, A systematic and empirical theory.* New York: Appleton-Century-Crofts, 1961.

BOGART, L. News as reality and as dream. In P. Tannenbaum (Ed.), in press.

BOGATZ, G. A., and BALL, S. *The second year of Sesame Street: A continuing evaluation.* Princeton, N.J.: Educational Testing Service, 1971.

BROWN, A., and SMILEY, S. Rating the importance of structural units of prose passages: A problem of metacognitive development: *Child Development*, 1977, *48*, 1–8.

CHANDLER, M., GREENSPAN, S., and BARENBOIM, C. Judgments of intentionality in response to videotaped and verbally presented moral dilemmas: The medium is the message *Child Development*, 1973, *44*, 315–320.

COHEN, L. B., DeLOACHE, J. S., and PEARL, R. A. An examination of interference effects in infants' memory for faces. *Child Development*, 1977, *48*, 88–96.

COLLINS, W. A. Effects of temporal separation between motivation, aggression, and consequences: A developmental study. *Child Development*, 1973, *8*, 215–221.

COLLINS, W. A. Learning of media content: A developmental study. *Child Development*, 1970, *41*, 1133–1142.

COLLINS, W. A., BERNDT, T. J., and HESS, V. L. Observational learning of motives and consequences for television aggression: A developmental study. *Child Development*, 1974, *45*, 799–802.

COLLINS, W. A., and WESTBY, S. D. Children's processing of social information from televised dramatic programs. Paper presented at the biennial meeting of the Society for Research in Child Development, Denver, April 1975.

DIRKS, J., and GIBSON, E. Infants' perception of similarity between live people and their photographs. *Child Development*, 1977, *48*, 124–130.

DORR, A., and GRAVES, S. B. Children's critical evaluation of television content. Final report to the office of Child Development, in preparation. Harvard University, 1978.

EMMERICH, W. Young children's discriminations of parent and child roles. *Child Development*, 1959, *30*, 403–419.

EMMERICH, W., GOLDMAN, K. S., and SHORE, R. E. Differentiation and development of social norms. *Journal of Personality and Social Psychology*, 1971, *18*, 323–353.

FRANTZ, R. L., FAGAN, J. F., and MIRANDE, S. B. Early visual selectivity. In L. B. Cohen and P. H. Salapatek (Eds.), *Infant perception, vol. 1.* New York: Academic Press, 1975.

FELDMAN, J. Children's moral judgments to traditional dilemmas presented with and without pictures and background information. Unpublished class paper, Stanford University, 1968.

FESHBACH, S. Reality and fantasy in filmed violence. In J. P. Murray, E. A. Rubinstein, and G. A. Comstock (Eds.), *Television and social behavior, vol. 2, Television and social learning.* Washington, D.C.: U.S. Government Printing Office, 1972.

FIELD, J. Relation of young infants' reaching behavior to stimulus distance solidity. *Developmental Psychology,* 1976, *12,* 444–448.

FLAPAN, D. *Children's understanding of social interaction.* New York: Teachers College, Columbia University Press, 1968.

FLAVELL, J. H. Concept development. In P. H. Mussen (Ed.), *Carmichael's manual of child psychology, vol. 1,* New York: Wiley, 1970.

FRANCK, G. J. *Über Geschehensgestaltungen in der Auffassung von Filmen durch Kinder.* Leipzig: J. A. Barth, 1955. (As cited in Noble, 1969)

FRUEH, T., and McGHEE, P. E. Traditional sex role development and amount of time spent watching television. *Developmental Psychology,* 1975, *11,* 109.

GERBNER, G., and GROSS, L. P. Living with television: The violence profile. *Journal of Communication,* 1976, *26,* 172–199.

GORANSON, R. E. Media violence and aggressive behavior: A review of experimental research. In L. Berkowitz (Ed.), *Advances in experimental social psychology, vol. 5.* New York: Academic Press, 1970.

GRAVES, S. B. Racial diversity in children's television: Its impact on racial attitudes and stated program preferences in young children. Unpublished Ph.D. dissertation, Harvard University, 1975.

GREENBERG, B. S., and REEVES, B. Children and the perceived reality of television. *Journal of Social Issues,* 1976, *32,* 86–97.

HALE, G. A., MILLER, L. K., and STEVENSON, A. W. Incidental learning of film content: A developmental study. *Child Development,* 1968, *39,* 69–78.

HAWKINS, R. P. Learning of peripheral content in films: A developmental study. *Child Development,* 1973, *44,* 214–217.

HIRSCH, P. Personal communication. December 1977.

HOCHBERG, J. E., and BROOKS, V. Pictorial recognition as an unlearned ability: A study of one child's performance. *American Journal of Psychology,* 1962, *75,* 624–628.

HORTON, D., and WOHL, R. R. Mass communication and parasocial interaction: Observations on intimacy at a distance. *Psychiatry,* 1956, *19,* 215–229.

HUSTON-STEIN, A., and WRIGHT, J. Effects of formal properties of children's TV programs. Paper presented at the biennial meetings of The Society for Research in Child Development, New Orleans, March 1977.

INSKO, C. A. *Theories of attitude change.* New York: Appleton-Century-Crofts, 1967.

KERNAN, K. T. Semantic and expressive elaboration in children's narratives. In S. Ervin-Tripp and C. Mitchell-Kernan (Eds.), *Child discourse.* New York: Academic Press, 1977.

KOHLBERG, L. State and sequence: The cognitive-developmental approach to socialization. In D. A. Goslin (Ed.), *Handbook of socialization theory and research.* Chicago: Rand McNally, 1969(a).

KOHLBERG, L. *Stages in the development of moral thought and action.* New York: Holt, Rinehart and Winston, 1969(b).

LABOV, W. *Language in the inner city: Studies in the black English vernacular.* Philadelphia: University of Philadelphia Press, 1972.

LABOV, W., and WALETZKY, J. Narrative analysis. In J. Helm (Ed.), *Essays on the verbal and visual arts.* Seattle: University of Washington Press, 1967.

LARSEN, O. N., GRAY, L. N., and FORTIS, J. G. Achieving goals through violence on television. In O. N. Larsen (Ed.), *Violence and the mass media.* New York: Harper and Row, 1968.

LEIFER, A. D. Research on the socialization influence of television in the United States. *Fernsehen und Bildung,* 1975, *9,* 26–53.

LEIFER, A. D. Factors which predict credibility ascribed to television. Paper presented at the annual meeting of the American Psychological Association, Washington, D.C., September 1976.

LEIFER, A. D., GORDON, N. J., and GRAVES, S. B. Children's television: More than mere entertainment. *Harvard Educational Review,* 1974, *44,*

LEIFER, A. D., and ROBERTS, D. F. Children's responses to television violence. In J. P. Murray, E. A. Rubinstein, and G. A. Comstock (Eds.), *Television and social behavior, vol. 2, Television and social learning.* Washington, D.C.: U.S. Government Printing Office, 1972.

LEIFER, A. D., et al. Developmental aspects of variables relevant to observational learning. *Child Development,* 1971, *42,* 1509–1516.

LIEBERT, R. M., NEALE, J. M., and DAVIDSON, E. D. *The early window.* New York: Pergamon Press, 1973.

LOCKE, J. *Some thoughts concerning education.* London: A. and J. Churchill, 1699. First published in 1693.

LYLE, J., and HOFFMAN, H. R. Children's use of television and other media. In G. A. Comstock, E. A. Rubinstein, and J. P. Murray (Eds.), *Television and social behavior, vol. 4, Television in day-to-day life: Patterns of use.* Washington, D.C.: U.S. Government Printing Office, 1972. (a)

LYLE, J., and HOFFMAN, H. R. Explorations in patterns of television viewing by preschool-age children. In E. A. Rubinstein, G. A. Comstock and J. P. Murray (Eds.), *Television and social behavior, vol. 4, Television in day-to-day life: Patterns of use.* Washington, D.C.: U.S. Government Printing Office, 1972. (b)

MANDLER, J. M. A code in the node: Developmental differences in the use of a story schema. Paper presented at the biennial meeting of the Society for Research in Child Development, New Orleans, March 1977.

MANDLER, J., and JOHNSON, N. Remembrance of things parsed: Story structure and recall. *Cognitive Psychology,* 1977, *9,* 111–151.

McGuire, W. J. The nature of attitudes and attitude change. In G. Lindzey and E. Aronson (Eds.), *The handbook of social psychology, vol. 3.* Reading, Mass.: Addison-Wesley, 1969.

McLuhan, M. *Understanding media, the extensions of man.* New York: McGraw-Hill, 1964.

Noble, G. *Children in front of the small screen.* Beverly Hills, California: Sage, 1975.

Noble, G. The English report. In J. D. Halloran (Ed.), *Findings and cognition on the television perception of children and young people.* Munich: Internationales Zei tralinstitut für das Jugend- und Bildungsfernsehen, 1969.

Phelps, E. M. Knowledge of the television industry and relevant first-hand experience. Paper presented at the annual meeting of the American Psychological Association, Washington, D.C., September 1976.

Piaget, J., and Inhelder, B. *The psychology of the child.* New York: Basic Books, 1969.

Pingree, S. A developmental study of the attitudinal effects of non-sexist television commercials under varied conditions of perceived reality. Unpublished Ph.D dissertation, Stanford University, 1975.

Reeves, B. Children's perceived reality of television and the effects of pro- and anti-social TV content on social behavior. Unpublished manuscript, Michigan State University, June 1977.

Roberts, D. F. A developmental study of opinion change: source-orientation versus content orientation at three age levels. Unpublished Ph.D. dissertation, Stanford University, 1968.

Rossiter, J. R., and Robertson, T. S. Children's TV commercials: Testing the defenses. *Journal of Communication,* 1974, *24,* 137–144.

Rousseau, J.-J. *Emile, or on education.* London: Dent, 1911. First published in French in 1762.

Ruff, H. A., Kohler, C. J., and Haupt, D. L. Infant recognition of two- and three-dimensional stimuli. *Developmental Psychology,* 1976, *12,* 455–459.

Rummelhart, D. E. Notes on a schema for stories. Paper presented at the Carbonell Memorial Conference, Pajaro Dunes, California, May 1974.

Salomon, G. Annual report of the first year of research on cognitive effects of the media. Submitted to the Spencer Foundation. Hebrew University, Jerusalem, Israel, September 30, 1974.

Schramm, W., Lyle, J., and Parker, E. G. *Television in the lives of our children.* Stanford: Stanford University Press, 1961.

Selman, R. L., and Byrne, D. F. A structural-developmental analysis of levels of role taking in middle childhood. *Child Development,* 1974, *45,* 803–806.

Shantz, C. V. The development of social cognition. In E. M. Hetherington (Ed.), *Review of child development research, vol. 5.* Chicago: University of Chicago Press, 1975.

Slaby, R. G., and Hollenbeck, A. R. Television influences on visual and vocal behavior of infants. Paper presented at the biennial meeting of the Society for Research in Child Development, New Orleans, March 1977.

SPOCK, B. *The pocket book of baby and child care.* New York: Pocket Books, 1946.

STEIN, A. H., and FRIEDRICH, L. K. Impact of television on children and youth. In E. M. Hetherington (Ed.), *Review of child development research, vol. 5.* Chicago: University of Chicago Press, 1975.

STEIN, N. L. The effects of increasing temporal disorganization on children's recall of stories. Paper presented at the meeting of the Psychonomic Society, St. Louis, November 1976.

STEIN, N. L. The role of structural variation in children's recall of simple stories. Paper presented at the biennial meeting of the Society for Research in Child Development, New Orleans, March 1977.

STEIN, N. L., and GLENN, C. A developmental study of children's recall of story material. Paper presented at the biennial meeting of the Society for Research in Child Development, Denver, April 1975.

STRAUSS, M. S., DeLOACHE, J. S., and MAYNARD, J. Infants' recognition of pictorial representations of real objects. Paper presented at the biennial meeting of the Society for Research in Child Development, New Orleans, March 1977.

SURBER, C. F. Developmental processes in social inference: Averaging of intentions and consequences in moral judgment. *Developmental Psychology,* 1977, *13,* 654–665.

UNITED STATES COMMISSION ON CIVIL RIGHTS. *Window dressing on the set: Women and minorities in television.* Washington, D.C.: U.S. Government Printing Office, 1977.

ZAZZO, R. L'influence du cinema sur le developpement de la pensée de l'enfant. *L'Ecole des Parents,* Paris, 1956 (as cited in Noble, 1969).

# 8

# Advertising and Opinion Change over Time

This final section complements the previous one while also returning to some of the broad theoretical questions raised originally in Section 1. In addressing the long-range impact of the mass media we round out our understanding of mass communication effects. In this section there are three important models of the sociocultural process of advertising and two selections outlining changes in public attitudes over extended periods.

The contemporary cultural and economic importance of advertising makes it a field from which students of mass communication and public opinion have much to learn. Most advertising consists of an amalgam of persuasive *techniques* which can be pressed into the service of an almost limitless variety of goals. McClure and Patterson address the controversial question of whether the advent of such instruments represents a positive or negative development for our society. The article, however, is primarily concerned with the effectiveness of paid political advertising. Their study of the Nixon–McGovern presidential campaign of 1972 finds that audiences actually learned more about the candidates from campaign advertisements (by both sides) than from the news coverage of the campaign.

Advertising is no longer the stepchild of academic social science but is today the beneficiary of commercially sponsored research that has yielded important new theories and findings. In this connection, Krugman and Ehrenberg focus on the broader contours of how advertising works. Krugman argues that advertisers must bear in mind that audience involvement in television is low, and so commercials must be designed with the idea that viewers are relatively inattentive to what they see. Ehrenberg's view is similar in many ways. He further elaborates the idea that the consumer's "low involvement" extends to the advertised product as well. Particularly with inexpensive items such as toothpaste, shampoo, or spaghetti, many consumers have little brand-name loyalty and often are susceptible to the suggestion they try another product. But in the absence of dissatisfaction with such products or their price, buyers may stay with the same brands unless invited to switch. Krugman and Ehrenberg both extend the "congitive dissonance" tradition in social psychology by proposing that *behavior* (in this case buying a particular product) *precedes* the favorable attitude posited by many psychologists as necessarily *prior* to taking action. Actions not crucial to the individual's sense of self may be taken without extensive reflection. This view also implicitly contradicts the work of many content analysts (Section 5) whose attention to the details of media content may well assume a higher level of involvement on the part of audience members than is the case empirically, as Marshall McLuhan also has suggested.[1]

We conclude with an essay that exemplifies one of survey research's most felicitous contemporary tools: the repeated administration of the same questions over time. Duncan, Schuman, and Duncan's analysis of long-term changes in family, religious, and social values demonstrates the utility of time series compilations for the study of social change. Its appearance here is ample evidence of the growing sophistication of public opinion research and enables us to conclude that the field has "come of age": The young science of the 1940s is now able to document social change by utilizing its own research history to inform us better about outselves in the 1980s.

# Note

1. McLuhan, Marshall, *Understanding Media*. New York: McGraw-Hill Book Co., 1965.

# Television News and Political Advertising: The Impact of Exposure on Voter Beliefs

ROBERT D. McCLURE
THOMAS E. PATTERSON

IN THE PRETELEVISION ERA of American politics, campaign research indicated the mass media had little direct effect on voters (Lazarsfeld, Berelson, and Gaudet, 1944; Berelson, Lazarsfeld, and McPhee, 1954). Today, in the media environment of television political advertising and network news, some observers believe those findings are obsolete (DeVries and Tarrance, 1972; Mendelsohn and Crespi, 1970; Lang and Lang, 1968; Wyckoff, 1968). They suggest television has a unique and powerful campaign impact because it instantly and vividly reaches the most persuadable voters who ignore, or fail to be exposed to, political information presented in other media.

Supporters of the traditional view of media effectiveness, however, find such speculation unconvincing. They maintain television's uniqueness is exaggerated and its impact mitigated by the same intervening factors that blunt the direct effects of other forms of mass communication. Consequently, the mass media—including television political advertising and network news—continue to play a limited role in presidential election campaigns.

In this paper, by examining the relationship between voter belief change and exposure to both political commercials and weeknight network news, we assess television's impact during the 1972 general election presidential campaign. Specifically, we intend to show that while traditional media effects

These excerpts from "Television News and Political Advertising" by Robert McClure and Thomas Patterson are reprinted from *Communication Research*, Vol. 1, No. 1 (January 1974), pp. 3–26, 30–31, by permission of the Publisher, Sage Publications, Inc.

arguments adequately account for the minimal belief change associated with voter exposure to television news, they cannot account for the direct and dramatic belief change consistently and systematically associated with voter exposure to political advertising.

## Data and Methods

The data in this paper come from a study of the 1972 presidential election. Two types of data are used—voter survey and news and advertising content.

The survey data come from a panel survey of a stratified sample of voters who were selected by standard area probability techniques from the Syracuse, New York, metropolitan area. During the first wave, September 7 through 18, 731 respondents were interviewed. In the second wave, October 7 through 15, 650 respondents were interviewed. In the third wave, October 30 through November 6, 650 of the original respondents were contacted again. Overall, 626—or 86%—of the original panel were interviewed three times prior to the election. In addition to the three preelection personal interviews, each of which lasted about 90 minutes, a short postelection telephone interview was conducted. Of the initial 731 respondents, 676 were contacted for this final interview.

Data on the information contained in television news and political commercials come from content analyses of tape recordings of all weekday evening network newscasts and political spot announcements broadcast during the period September 18 through November 6.

A belief (b) refers to a perceived connection between one object and another object, such as the connection a voter may see between a political candidate and an issue position. For example, a voter may have believed that a presidential candidate was either for or against immediate withdrawal from Vietnam.

Thus, "belief about" a candidate is the probability or improbability, as perceived by a voter, that some specific relationship exists between an object and a candidate. We measured such beliefs by having respondents locate the candidates on seven-point scales with statements like the following:

Richard Nixon favors an immediate pull-out of all U.S. troops
from Vietnam

LIKELY _____ : ___ : _____ : _____ : ____ : ___ : _____ UNLIKELY[1]
extremely  quite  slightly  not sure  slightly  quite  extremely

George McGovern favors an immediate pull-out of all U.S. troops
from Vietnam

LIKELY_____ : _____ : _____ : ____ : ____ : ____ : ____UNLIKELY

This approach also directs attention to campaign effects other than simply attitude change. Most research examining media effects on voters has concentrated on attitude change. But, by adopting such a focus, it has taken a narrow view of the persuasive process. It is seldom that attitudes are the direct target of campaign persuasion. Most campaign messages—be these communicated through news or advertising channels—are directed at voter "beliefs."

*Long-term* changes in public demands and support for various policy alternatives are largely a function of voter attitudes. Acceptance or rejection of policies and policy proposals is basically an attitudinal response. And these attitudes tend to have an enduring quality; attitudinal change is usually a gradual process, particularly if the attitude object is important to the voters. More than being objects of change in political campaigns, attitudes help define the salient issues for debate. . . .

The research question is the extent to which voters received and accepted news and commercial messages. Our data permit a somewhat precise test of the question. Both in early September, *before* their exposure to this television content, and also in early November, *after* their expsoure, we asked our respondents to indicate their "beliefs about" the following by indicating how likely or unlikely the statements were to them.[2]

$b_{cM}$: George McGovern favors wiping out all political corruption and favoritism.

$b_{cN}$: Richard Nixon favors wiping out all political corruption and favoritism.

$b_{vM}$: George McGovern favors an immediate pull-out of all U.S. troops from Vietnam.

$b_{vN_2}$, $b_{vN_3}$: Richard Nixon favors an immediate pull-out of all U.S. troops from Vietnam.

$b_{msM}$: George McGovern favors spending less money on the military.

$b_{msN}$: Richard Nixon favors spending less money on the military.

$b_{csM}$: George McGovern always makes it clear where he stands.

When information on these beliefs is presented subsequently, it will be referred to by letter and subscript—e.g., $b_{msM}$ means McGovern belief on military spending.

If television news and advertising were effective channels of communication, then more voters—during the campaign period—should have been changing on these items in a direction consistent with the information conveyed than were moving in a direction inconsistent with that information. Consider, for example, voter beliefs about McGovern and military spending:

$b_{msM}$: George McGovern favors spending less money on the military.

The commercial informed voters that McGovern would reduce military spending. Consequently, if the ad is to be judged effective, more voters must have changed toward the likely end than changed toward the unlikely end. On the other hand, if more voters changed toward the unlikely end than the likely end, the ad was ineffective.

In reporting the results, we will present three values for each entry in a table, e.g.

$$+10$$
$$(25 - 15).$$

The first value in parentheses (25) will be the percentage of voters who changed in the direction consistent with the media message. The second value in parentheses (15) will be the percentage of voters changing in the other direction. The top value (+10) will be the difference between the two values in parentheses. If the number is positive, as in this example, more voters changed in the direction consistent with the message. If the number is negative, then more voters changed in the opposite direction.

In addition to requiring that more voters change in the message's intended direction, a second criterion for media effect is that voters with high exposure must show greater movement in the direction of the message than voters with low exposure. Our measures of exposure come from television logs filled out by our respondents.[3] The procedure used to obtain the logs is one commonly employed in commercial audience research.

## The Effects of Political Advertising

Exposure to political advertising was consistently related to voter belief change (see Table 1). Beliefs about military spending give the clearest example of effect. Among high television viewers, 29% more voters changed their beliefs about McGovern in the direction of the message than changed in

TABLE 1.   The Relationship Between Voters' Belief Changes and Their Exposure to Prime-Time Television

| EXPOSURE | MILITARY SPENDING McGOVERN $(b_{msM})$ | MILITARY SPENDING NIXON $(b_{msN})$ | CHANGING STANDS McGOVERN $(b_{csM})$ |
|---|---|---|---|
| High TV viewers | +29[a] | +19 | +3 |
| | (44 − 15) | (43 − 24) | (32 − 29) |
| Low TV viewers | +11 | +10 | −8 |
| | (30 − 19) | (34 − 24) | (26 − 34) |

[a] The top figure is the difference between percentage of voters changing in direction of Nixon message (which is first figure in parentheses) and the percentage changing in direction away from message (which is second figure in parentheses). Therefore, a positive (+) number in top figure represents the net Nixon gain and a negative (−) number represents the net Nixon loss.

the other direction. This difference was considerably higher than the 11% difference for low exposure voters. The changes in voters' beliefs about Nixon were not as clear-cut, but they also give an indication of exposure effect. High television viewers moved more disproportionately in the message's direction than low television viewers (19% to 10%).

The changing stands ad had less impact. However, differences between voters with high and low exposure to prime-time television still exist. Among high exposure viewers, the proportion that moved toward the message (32%) exceeded the proportion that moved away (29%), while among low exposure viewers, the pattern was reversed (34% to 26%).

To what extent are these findings explained by the viewer's level of interest? In the pretelevision period of American politics, voter research discovered that low-interest voters ignored most political messages. Today, advocates of television's unique capacity to communicate argue that commercials effectively overcome low-interest voters' avoidance of political information.

The data indicate commercial messages did reach low-interest voters, and, in fact, exposure to these Nixon ads had more impact on low than high interest voters (see Table 2). With the exception of beliefs about Nixon's military spending stand, the net change in the direction of the message was

TABLE 2. The Relationship Between Voters' Belief Changes and Their Exposure to Prime-Time Television Controlling for Level of Political Interest

| LEVEL OF INTEREST | MILITARY SPENDING MCGOVERN ($b_{msM}$) | MILITARY SPENDING NIXON ($b_{msN}$) | CHANGING STANDS MCGOVERN ($b_{csM}$) |
|---|---|---|---|
| High Interest | | | |
| High TV viewers | +23 | +19 | −3 |
| | (38 − 15) | (46 − 27) | (24 − 27) |
| Low TV viewers | +8 | +27 | −8 |
| | (28 − 20) | (47 − 20) | (25 − 33) |
| Moderate Interest | | | |
| High TV viewers | +30 | +26 | +1 |
| | (45 − 15) | (46 − 20) | (35 − 34) |
| Low TV viewers | +14 | −2 | −11 |
| | (31 − 17) | (26 − 28) | (28 − 39) |
| Low Interest | | | |
| High TV viewers | +33 | +12 | +9 |
| | (48 − 15) | (37 − 25) | (35 − 26) |
| Low TV viewers | +12 | +8 | −4 |
| | (30 − 18) | (31 − 23) | (26 − 30) |

Note: See Table 1 for meaning of figures.

greater for low- than high-interest voters. And without exception, high television exposure resulted in greater gain for low-interest voters.

These are surprising findings—to our knowledge, the only research data showing more information gain for low than high interest voters—but they do need qualification.

First, voting studies have established that high-interest voters are considerably more likely than low-interest voters to rely on multiple information channels. Since other sources will provide the same information for high-interest voters, commercial exposure will have less effect on their information gain.

Second, the relative inattention of low-interest voters to other media sources means their beliefs will be more impoverished prior to commercial exposure. Consider, for example, the distribution of beliefs about McGovern's military spending stand in early September (before the military spending ad appeared on television):

George McGovern favors spending less money on the military

High-interest
voters:  LIKELY <u>50%</u> : <u>20%</u> : <u>9%</u> : <u>13%</u> : <u>3%</u> : <u>2%</u> : <u>3%</u> UNLIKELY

Low-interest
voters:  LIKELY <u>21%</u> : <u>24%</u> : <u>12%</u> : <u>33%</u> : <u>5%</u> : <u>3%</u> : <u>2%</u> UNLIKELY

Clearly, low-interest voters were in a position to benefit more from exposure to a commercial about McGovern's stand on military spending; their beliefs were so poorly formed that the potential for commercial impact was much greater.[4]

However, these qualifications should not diminish the importance of our finding about low-interest voters. These voters obviously learned substantially from these two "Democrats for Nixon" commercials.[5]

Moderate-interest voters also were substantially affected by commercial messages, perhaps even more so than low-interest voters. High television exposure resulted in gains for moderate-interest voters that, on the average, exceeded those of low-interest voters. And this gain was registered despite their initial distribution of beliefs being substantially more accurate, for example:

George McGovern favors spending less money on the military

Moderate-interest
voters:  LIKELY <u>42%</u> : <u>21%</u> : <u>9%</u> : <u>18%</u> : <u>3%</u> : <u>5%</u> : <u>2%</u> UNLIKELY

Further, moderate-interest voters were attentive to the most obscure of the belief messages. Television exposure made a great difference to their information gain on Nixon's military spending stand.[6]

In summary, exposure to television political advertising seems to immediately and directly influence voter beliefs about the candidates and to challenge traditional theories about mass media effects.[7]

## The Effects of Television News

Unlike exposure to political advertising, exposure to television network news had almost no direct and independent effect on voters. Overall, the relationship between exposure and voter acceptance of network messages is weak and inconsistent. Even though on all five items voters generally were changing their beliefs in a direction consistent with the information the networks were broadcasting, on only two items do high news viewers exhibit greater net change than low news viewers. And in both of these instances— McGovern's position on corruption and Nixon's position on Vietnam troop withdrawal prior to the October peace overtures—the difference in net change between high and low exposure is almost negligible (see Table 3). This contrasts sharply with the size of the differences between high and low advertising exposure categories found in Table 1.

TABLE 3. The Relationship Between Voters' Belief Changes and Their Exposure to Television Network News

| Exposure to News | $b_{cM}$ | $b_{cN}$ | $b_{vM}$ | $b_{vN_2}$ | $b_{vN_3}$ |
|---|---|---|---|---|---|
| High | +1 | +8 | +10 | +23 | +9 |
| | (28 − 27) | (35 − 27) | (22 − 12) | (41 − 18) | (31 − 22) |
| Low | −4 | +13 | +10 | +18 | +12 |
| | (27 − 31) | (36 − 23) | (24 − 14) | (40 − 22) | (36 − 23) |

Controlling the relationship between news exposure and belief change for the viewer's level of political interest does not modify the initial finding of minimal effects (see Table 4). Among high- and moderate-interest voters, exposure is again unrelated to change. Under this control condition, the contrast between advertising and news effects is clearly apparent (see Table 2). Only among low-interest voters does exposure to network news indicate any consistent relationship with belief change.

But taken as a whole, the data indicate exposure to television news affected voter belief change less directly, less consistently, and less strongly than exposure to television advertising.[8] However, at least three factors limit the scope of this conclusion.

First, our conclusions about political advertising are based on the analysis

TABLE 4. The Relationship Between Voters' Belief Changes and Their Exposure to Television Network News Controlling for Level of Political Interest

| LEVEL OF INTEREST | $b_{cM}$ | $b_{cN}$ | $b_{vM}$ | $b_{vN_2}$ | $b_{vN_3}$ |
|---|---|---|---|---|---|
| **High Interest** | | | | | |
| High news viewers | $-5$ <br> $(33-38)$ | $+4$ <br> $(30-26)$ | $+3$ <br> $(17-14)$ | $+17$ <br> $(34-17)$ | $+15$ <br> $(31-16)$ |
| Low news viewers | $+2$ <br> $(34-32)$ | $+9$ <br> $(33-24)$ | $+8$ <br> $(20-12)$ | $+29$ <br> $(41-12)$ | $+13$ <br> $(33-20)$ |
| **Moderate Interest** | | | | | |
| High news viewers | $-5$ <br> $(20-25)$ | $+14$ <br> $(42-28)$ | $+8$ <br> $(19-11)$ | $+28$ <br> $(47-19)$ | $+3$ <br> $(28-25)$ |
| Low news viewers | $-2$ <br> $(29-31)$ | $+24$ <br> $(45-21)$ | $+11$ <br> $(24-13)$ | $+7$ <br> $(33-26)$ | $+9$ <br> $(35-26)$ |
| **Low Interest** | | | | | |
| High news viewers | $+17$ <br> $(30-13)$ | $+7$ <br> $(32-25)$ | $+23$ <br> $(34-11)$ | $+27$ <br> $(47-20)$ | $+9$ <br> $(36-27)$ |
| Low news viewers | $-9$ <br> $(21-30)$ | $+5$ <br> $(30-25)$ | $+11$ <br> $(28-17)$ | $+23$ <br> $(47-24)$ | $+13$ <br> $(35-22)$ |

of the effects of only two commercials. These ads may or may not be representative of commercial effects in general.[9]

Second, our findings apply only to the impact of television news on voters' beliefs about the candidates' *issue* positions. Our conclusions do not apply to how television news, by allowing the voter to see the candidate, may or may not affect the voter's judgment about the candidate's personal capacities and character, or how exposure to network news affects the level of contextual information necessary for the voter to have a *full understanding* of the candidate's issue positions.

Third, our findings apply only to the question of whether television news had effects independent of and separate from other channels of communication. Our conclusion of minimal effects rests on the absence of a consistent relationship between voter belief change and television news exposure. But it should be emphasized that voter belief change, while largely unrelated to television news exposure, occurred in the hypothesized direction in almost every instance. Voters were getting political information, and they had very accurate perceptions of where the candidates stood on the issues. Television news undoubtedly contributed to the accuracy of these voter judgments. But television shares its influence with other mass communications channels, and all the mass media share their influence with the voter's family, friends, and co-workers. Most voters, on highly publicized issues such as Watergate and Vietnam, are nestled in a network of communications; disentangling the influence of one source, when the same information could have been obtained from any of several sources, presents a difficult problem.

On this point, the data in Table 4 are suggestive. In the high- and moderate-interest categories, which contain voters more likely to expose themselves to alternative information sources, network news exposure was unrelated to belief change. In the low-interest category, which contains voters more likely to rely heavily on television for their political information, news exposure shows some relationship with belief change.

This relationship is particularly strong on the two McGovern items. The belief change of low-interest voters about McGovern's position on political corruption was substantially affected by news exposure. In the high exposure category, 30% moved in a direction consistent with the news message, while 13% moved in the opposite direction. In the low exposure group, the pattern was nearly reversed—21% accepted the news message and 30% rejected it. Similarly related to low-interest voters' network news exposure was the change pattern on McGovern's position on Vietnam troop withdrawal. This pattern may be due, in part, to George McGovern having been a newcomer to national politics and low-interest voters having had little prior information about him. But we also suggest that television news exposure may have some direct effect on voters who rely heavily on it for their political information. Among voters who have multiple information sources, however, television news has no unique, independent power. Among these voters, network news merely supplements and reinforces information gained from other communication channels.[10]

## The Conditions Affecting Television Impact

Both advocates of minimal television effects on voters and advocates of maximal television effects err in their judgments. Television operates under conditions which both advantage and disadvantage it as a source of political information. We will conclude with some observations on the importance of these conditions.

Television is the nation's major entertainment medium. Because political ads are brief and appear during prime entertainment hours, they exploit television's most potent capability—the capacity to reach voters who would not normally be willing to attend to alternative information sources requiring greater effort. Political commercials simply reach out to voters who otherwise give little attention to political messages.

Television news does not have such an advantage. On a day-to-day basis, it not only reaches a smaller, but also a more informed and interested audience. Consequently, television news serves to provide supportive and background information to voters who already possess considerable information. Televised ads, on the other hand, are more likely to carry information to voters who were previously ignorant of the material conveyed.

In addition, unlike product ads and nightly news, political ads supporting presidential candidates are not everyday occurrences. Their uniqueness generates a level of viewer attentiveness that makes them minute-for-minute more efficient message transmitters than the commonplace and often dull television news stories. At the campaign's outset, voters appear to be particularly attentive to these intruders on their daily fare. For example, approximately 75% of all voters who told us, using unaided recall questions, that they could remember seeing a political commercial, could also accurately describe its intended message. This percentage far exceeds the intended message recall for product advertising and, from our analysis of unaided recall of television news stories, far exceeds that for news stories.

There are several reasons why individual news stories during a half-hour nightly newscast do not stand out as well as political commercials broadcast during prime entertainment hours. Each night, the networks give some coverage to a large number of stories rather than in-depth coverage to a smaller number of stories. Our data indicate the average campaign story was some one hundred seconds in length, hardly enough time to provide more than a quick topical sketch. While this time period is marginally longer than the sixty seconds given to many commercials, the surrounding material is not an entertaining program, but other news stories. This news format creates a montage effect that actually reduces the impact of television news. In response to open-ended survey questions, many respondents could not recall what they had seen on the previous evening's news, explaining that the stories had run together in their minds. Most television programming will accommodate considerable viewer inattention and distraction. But the short and rapid presentation of news stories demands rather close viewer attention, a level of attention many viewers are unwilling to provide and, contrary to what many believe, a level of attention that may be little different from what is required to gain information from the other media.

The greater penetration of political commercials, when compared with television news stories, rests on another difference. Completely controlled by the candidates, ads can be used as frequently as the budget permits to hammer away at certain specific and limited themes. As the findings of advertising and mass communication research make clear, sheer repetition plays a key role in learning, and political ads stress again and again the same messages. Television news does not do this. Since the entire audio transmission of a thirty-minute televised newscast can be fitted on the front page of a daily newspaper, television simply cannot provide extensive and repetitive issue coverage. During the 1972 general election campaign, only two issues—Vietnam and corruption—received such continuing coverage. And this coverage was repetitive in only a limited sense—it largely involved the reporting of new developments regarding these issues and, often, the new information conflicted with the old.

Television news' efficiency as a transmitter of straightforward issue information is also inhibited by its preference for visual effects. During the campaign, for example, George McGovern gave a speech in New York City, where he detailed his approach to crime. Although this was the first time McGovern had given a lengthy address on the crime issue, the campaign stories broadcast by two of the networks that evening were devoted, not to McGovern's crime proposals, but to the enthusiasm of the crowds which greeted him at a rally later that day. Presumably, crowds make for more visually interesting stories than issues. In short, the issue content of many political commercials is higher than the issue content of many network news stories.

In fact, if coverage of events like the Watergate incident and the peace talks is eliminated, television news gave more coverage to campaign activity—rallies, polls, strategies—than to issues. Footage of the candidate mixing with a crowd, the actions of hecklers, and general campaign hoopla may make for exciting stories. But it is questionable whether an inefficient news medium like television should devote a full one-third of its campaign coverage to such stories. . . .

Infrequently, television network news can have a unique and powerful impact on its voters. To do so, we believe the networks must be reporting stories that meet all, or at least most, of the following five conditions. First, the coverage must be of "real, live" events from which viewers get the feeling that they are witnessing something important in the making. Second, the visual presentation must be exciting and interesting. Third, the story must seem to be uncomplicated and easily understood. Fourth, the coverage must be regularly repeated over a long period of time, or it must totally saturate shorter time periods. And, finally, the event must take place outside the context of a political campaign. . . .

## Notes

1. All subsequent scales shown in this paper will omit the labels for each category. Labels were used on scales given to the respondent.

2. There are two exceptions to this. The first is $b_{csM}$ which was not measured until early October. However, this was still prior to the showing of the "changing stands" commercial. The second is $b_{cM}$ and $b_{cN}$ which also were first measured in early October. Thus, voters did have prior exposure to information about the corruption issue. However, the bulk of the network news references to corruption occurred *after* our initial measurement of these items.

3. To obtain the measure of advertising exposure, we divided voters into high and low categories on the basis of their viewing of prime-time television programs. The cutoff point between high and low is slightly more than an average of one hour of prime-time viewing per evening. Consequently, many of the voters in the low exposure category still watched considerable television. This should have the effect of *underestimating* the power of exposure. The same logs were used to measure news exposure. Voters in the high exposure category watched the network news at least four nights a week. Exposure to network news was modestly correlated with political interest (.23) and not all with years of formal education (−.02). When exposure was related to the number of items about national politics which our respondents could recall having seen on television news, the gamma for the table was .49. Exposure, however, was not related to recall information from other channels. For example, the gamma between television news exposure and newspaper recall is .09.

4. This example illustrates one of our concerns about the seven-point scales. If there is response instability, individuals in the extreme categories have nowhere to go but toward the center. Thus, the number of cases on the extreme will have a decisive effect on the results.

5. This is not to say, of course, that low-interest voters are indistinguishable from high-interest voters on these belief dimensions. The gain of low-interest voters from commercial exposure does not begin to offset the information gap that existed before the commercials were shown.

6. We are not certain what accounts for the apparent attentiveness of moderate-interest voters to commercials, but we think the play theory of mass communication (Stephenson, 1967) offers a partial explanation. The theory proposes that certain voters will, despite not being highly involved in politics, be interested

enough to find enjoyment in a presidential campaign when it is thrust upon them and when the messages involve play rather than work—e.g., where messages come from televised news or commercials rather than from lengthy, more complicated newspaper articles. While the theory is somewhat imprecise, one could conclude that individuals who fit this description are likely to be moderate-interest voters and that information gain would differ clearly for the high and low exposed categories which it does.

7. A more extended analysis of commercial effects and a more complete discussion of our views on political advertising can be found elsewhere (Patterson and McClure, 1974).

8. A more extended analysis of news effects and a more complete discussion of our views about network news in the 1972 election can be found elsewhere (McClure and Patterson, 1973).

9. An analysis of the effects of all political commercials used in the 1972 presidential campaign is under way currently. To date, we have no reason to believe the two commercials examined in the paper are atypical in their effects on voters.

10. When all our survey and media content data is available for analysis, direct measures of information intake from alternative sources will be available to test directly the argument in this paragraph.

# References

BERELSON, B., P. LAZARSFELD, and W. McPHEE (1954). Voting. Chicago: Univ. of Chicago Press.

CAMPBELL, A., P. CONVERSE, W. MILLER, and D. STOKES (1960). The American Voter. New York: John Wiley.

DEVRIES, W. and V. L. TARRANCE (1972). The Ticket-Splitter: A New Force in American Politics. Grand Rapids, Mich.: Richard Eerdmans.

FISHBEIN, M. (1967). "A consideration of beliefs and their role in attitude measurement," in M. Fishbein (ed.) Readings in Attitude and Measurement. New York: John Wiley.

———— (1965). "A consideration of beliefs, attitudes, and their relationships," in I. Steiner and M. Fishbein (eds.) Current Studies in Social Psychology. New York: John Wiley.

———— (1963). "An investigation of the relationship between beliefs about an object and an attitude toward that object." Human Relations 16 (August): 233–239.

———— and F. COOMBS (1971) "Basis for decision: an attitudinal approach toward an understanding of voting behavior." American Political Science Association. (unpublished)

LANG, K. and G. LANG (1968). Politics and Television. Chicago: Quandrangle.

LAZARSFELD, P., B. BERELSON, and H. GAUDET (1944). The People's Choice. New York: Duell, Sloan & Pearce.

McCLURE, R. and T. PATTERSON (1973). "Television news and voter behavior in the 1972 presidential election." American Political Science Association. (unpublished)

MENDELSOHN, H. and I. CRESPI (1970). Polls, Television, and the New Politics. San Francisco: Chandler.

PATTERSON, T. and R. MCCLURE (1974). Political Advertising: Voter Reaction to Televised Political Commercials. Princeton, N.J.: Citizens' Research Foundation.

STEPHENSON, W. (1967) The Play Theory of Mass Communication. Chicago: Univ. of Chicago Press.

WYCKOFF, G. (1968). The Image Candidates. New York: Macmillan.

*Author's Note: The research presented here was conducted under National Science Foundation grant GS-35408, Robert D. McClure and Thomas E. Patterson, principal investigators. The support of the Foundation is gratefully acknowledged.*

# The Impact of Television Advertising: Learning Without Involvement

HERBERT E. KRUGMAN

AMONG THE WONDERS of the twentieth century has been the ability of the mass media repeatedly to expose audiences numbered in millions to campaigns of coordinated messages. In the post–World War I years it was assumed that exposure equaled persuasion and that media content therefore was the all-important object of study or censure. Now we believe that the powers of the mass media are limited. No one has done more to bring about a counterbalancing perspective than Joseph Klapper, former president of the American Association of Public Opinion Researchers (AAPOR), with his well-known book *The Effects of Mass Media*,[1] and the new AAPOR president Raymond Bauer, with such articles as "The Limits of Persuasion."[2]

It has been acknowledged, however, that this more carefully delimited view of mass media influence is based upon analysis of largely noncommercial cases and data. We have all wondered how many of these limitations apply also to the world of commerce, specifically advertising. These limitations will be discussed here as they apply to television advertising only, since the other media include stimuli and responses of a different psychological nature, which play a perhaps different role in the steps leading to a purchasing decision.

The tendency is to say that the accepted limitations of mass media do apply, that advertising's use of the television medium has limited impact. We tend to feel this way, I think, because (1) we rarely feel converted or

Reprinted by permission of the publisher from "The Impact of Television Advertising," by H. Krugman, in *Public Opinion Quarterly* (Fall 1965), pp. 349–356.

403

greatly persuaded by a particular TV campaign, and (2) so much of TV advertising content is trivial and sometimes even silly. Nevertheless, trivia have their own special qualities, and some of these may be important to our understanding of the commercial *or* the noncommercial use and impact of mass media.

To begin, let us go back to Neil Borden's classic Harvard Business School evaluation of the economic effects of advertising.[3] Published in 1942, it concluded that advertising (1) accelerates growing demand or retards falling demand, i.e. it quickens the pulse of the market, and (2) encourages price rigidity but increases quality and choice of products. The study warned, however, that companies had been led to overlook price strategies and the elasticity of consumer demand. This was borne out after World War II by the rise of the discounters! . . .

What is lacking in the required "evaluation" of TV advertising is any significant body of research specifically relating advertising to attitudes, and these in turn to purchasing behavior or sales. That is, we have had in mind a model of the correct and effective influence process which has not yet been verified. This is the bugaboo that has been the hope and the despair of research people within the industry. . . .

The economic impact of TV advertising is substantial and documented. Its messages have been learned by the public. Only the lack of specific case histories relating advertising to attitudes to sales keeps researchers from concluding that the commecial use of the medium is a success. We are faced then with the odd situation of knowing that advertising works but being unable to say much about why.

Perhaps our model of the influence process is wrong. Perhaps it is incompletely understood. Back in 1959 Herbert Zielske, in "The Remembering and Forgetting of Advertising," demonstrated that advertising will be quickly forgotten if not continuously exposed.[4] Why such need for constant reinforcement? Why so easy-in and easy-out of short-term memory? One answer is that much of advertising content is learned as meaningless nonsense material. Therefore, let us ask about the nature of such learning.

An important distinction between the learning of sense and nonsense was laid down by Ebbinghaus in 1902 when he identified the greater effects of order of presentation of stimuli on the learning of nonsense material. He demonstrated a U curve of recall, with first and last items in a series best remembered, thus giving rise also to the principles of primacy and recency.[5]

In 1957, many years later, Carl Hovland reported that in studying persuasion he found the effects of primacy and recency greater when dealing with material of lesser ego-involvement. He wrote, "Order of presentation is a more significant factor in influencing opinions for subjects with relatively weak desires for understanding, than for those with high 'cognitive needs.' "[6] It seems, therefore, that the nonsensical à la Ebbinghaus and the unimportant à la Hovland work alike. . . .

What is common to the learning of the nonsensical and the unimportant is lack of involvement. We seem to be saying, then, that much of the impact of television advertising is in the form of learning without involvement, or what Hartley calls "unanchored learning."[7] If this is so, is it a source of weakness or of strength to the advertising industry? Is it good or bad for our society? What are the implications for research on advertising effectiveness?

Let us consider some qualities of sensory perception with and without involvement. . . . Maccoby reported some studies conducted with Leon Festinger in which fraternity members learned a TV message better when hearing the audio and watching unrelated video than when they watched the speaker giving them the message directly, i.e. video *and* audio together.[8] Apparently, the distraction of watching something unrelated to the audio message lowered whatever reistance there might have been to the message.

As Maccoby put it, "Comprehension equals persuasion": Any disagreement with any message must come after some real interval, however minute. Bauer proposed a restatement of this point as "Perception precedes perceptual defense," to which Maccoby agreed. The initial development of this view goes back before World War II to the psychologist W. E. Guthrie.[9] It receives more recent support from British research on perception and communication, specifically that of D. E. Broadbent, who has noted the usefulness of defining perception as "immediate memory."[10]

The historical importance of the Maccoby view, however, is that it takes us almost all the way back to our older view of the potent propaganda content of World War I, that exposure to mass media content is persuasive per se! What is implied here is that in cases of involvement with mass media content perceptual defense is very briefly postponed, while in cases of noninvolvement perceptual defense may be absent.

Does this suggest that if television bombards us with enough trivia about a product we may be persuaded to believe it? On the contrary, it suggests that persuasion as such, i.e. overcoming a resistant attitude, is not involved at all and that it is a mistake to look for it in our personal lives as a test of television's advertising impact. Instead, as trivia are repeatedly learned and repeatedly forgotten and then repeatedly learned a little more, it is probable that two things will happen: (1) more simply, that so-called "overlearning" will move some information out of short-term and into long-term memory systems, and (2) more complexly, that we will permit significant alterations in the *structure* of our perception of a brand or product, but in ways which may fall short of persuasion or of attitude change. One way we may do this is by shifting the relative salience of attributes suggested to us by advertising as we organize our perception of brands and products.

Thanks to Sherif we have long used the term "frame of reference," and Osgood in particular has impressed us with the fact that the meaning of an object may be perceived along many separate dimensions. Let us say that a number of frames of reference are available as the primary anchor for the percept in question. We may then alter the psychological salience of these frames or dimensions and shift a product seen primarily as "reliable" to one seen primarily as "modern."[11] The product is still seen as reliable and perhaps no *less* reliable than before, but this quality no longer provides the primary perceptual emphasis. Similarly, the product was perhaps previously seen as modern, and perhaps no *more* modern now—yet exposure to new or repeated messages may give modernity the primary role in the organization of the percept.

There is no reason to believe that such shifts are completely limited to trivia. In fact, when Hartley first introduced the concept of psychological salience, he illustrated it with a suggestion that Hitler did not so much increase anti-Semitic attitudes in Germany as bring already existing anti-Semitic attitudes into more prominent use for defining the everyday world.[12] This, of course, increased the probability of anti-Semitic behavior. While the shift in salience does not tell the whole story, it seems to be one of the dynamics operating in response to massive repetition. Although a rather simple dynamic, it may be a major one when there is no cause for resistance, or when uninvolved consumers do not provide their own perceptual emphases or anchors.

It may be painful to reject as incomplete a model of the influence process of television advertising that requires changes in attitude *prior* to changes in behavior. It may be difficult to see how the viewer of television can go from perceptual impact directly to behavioral impact, unless the *full perceptual impact is delayed.* This would not mean going into unexplored areas. Sociologists have met "sleeper effects" before, and some psychologists have long asserted that the effects of "latent" learning are only or most noticeable at the point of reward. In this case, it would be at the behavioral level involved in product purchases rather than at some intervening point along the way. That is, the purchase situation is the catalyst that reassembles or brings out all the potentials for shifts in salience that have accumulated up to that point. The product or package is then suddenly seen in a new, "somehow different" light although nothing verbalizable may have changed *up to that point.* What we ordinarily call "change of attitude" may then occur after some real interval, however minute. Such change of attitude after product purchase is *not,* as has sometimes been said, in "rationalization" of the purchase but is an emergent response aspect of the previously changed perception. We would perhaps see it more often if products always lived up to expectations and did not sometimes create negative interference with the emerging response.

I have tried to say that the public lets down its guard to the repetitive commercial use of the television medium and that it easily changes its ways of perceiving products and brands and its purchasing behavior without thinking very much about it at the time of TV exposure or at any time prior to purchase, and without up to then changing verbalized attitudes. This adds up, I think, to an understandable success story for advertising's use of the television medium. Furthermore, this success seems to be based on a left-handed kind of public trust that sees no great importance in the matter. . . .

The distinction between the commercial and the noncommercial use of the mass media, as well as the distinction between "commercial" and "academic" research, has blinded us to the existence of two entirely different ways of experiencing and being influenced by mass media. One way is characterized by lack of personal involvement, which, while perhaps more common in response to commercial subject matter, is by no means limited to it. The second is characterized by a high degree of personal involvement. By this we do *not* mean attention, interest, or excitement but the number of conscious "bridging experiences," connections, or personal references per minute that the viewer makes between his own life and the stimulus. This may vary from none to many.

The significance of conditions of low or high involvement is not that one is better than the other, but that the processes of communication impact are different. That is, there is a difference in the change processes that are at work. Thus, with low involvement one might look for gradual shifts in perceptual structure, aided by repetition, activated by behavioral-choice situations, and *followed* at some time by attitude change. With high involvement one would look for the classic, more dramatic, and more familiar conflict of ideas at the level of conscious opinion and attitude that precedes changes in overt behavior.

I think now we can appreciate again why Madison Avenue may be of little use in the Cold War or even in a medium-hot presidential campaign. The more common skills of Madison Avenue concern the change processes associated with low involvement, while the very different skills required for high-involvement campaigns are usually found elsewhere. However, although Madison Avenue generally seems to know its limitations, the advertising researchers tend to be less clear about theirs. . . . What has been left out, unfortunately, is the development of a low-involvement model, and the pretest measures based on such a model. The further development of this model is an important next step, not only for the perhaps trivial world of television advertising but for the better understanding of all those areas of public opinion and education which, socially important as they may be, may simply not be very involving to significant segments of the audience.

In time we may come to understand the effectiveness of mass media primarily in terms of the *consistency* with which a given campaign, commercial or noncommercial, employs talent and research sensitively attuned to the real level of audience involvement. In time, also, we may come to understand that behavior, that is, verbal behavior and overt behavior, is always consistent provided we do not impose premature and narrowly conceived rules as to which must precede, or where, when, and how it must be measured.[13]

# Notes

1. Joseph Klapper, *The Effects of Mass Media,* Glencoe, Ill., Free Press, 1960.
2. Raymond Bauer, "The Limits of Persuasion," *Harvard Business Review,* September-October, 1958, pp. 105–110.
3. Neil Borden, *The Economic Effects of Advertising,* Chicago, Irwin, 1942.
4. H. A. Zielske, "The Remembering and Forgetting of Advertising," *Journal of Marketing,* January 1959, pp. 239–243.
5. H. Ebbinghaus, *Grundzuge der Psychologie,* Leipzig, Germany, Veit. 1902.
6. C. T. Hovland *et al., The Order of Presentation in Persuasion,* New Haven, Yale University Press, 1957, p. 136.
7. This is the title of a working manuscript distributed privately by E. L. Harley in 1964, which concerns his experimentation with new methods of health education in the Philippine Islands.
8. L. Festinger and N. Maccoby, "On Resistance to Persuasive Communications," *Journal of Abnormal and Social Psychology,* Vol. 68, No. 4, 1964, pp. 359–366.
9. E. R. Guthrie, *The Psychology of Learning,* New York, Harper, 1935, p. 26.
10. D. E. Broadbent, *Perception and Communication,* London, Pergamon Press, 1958, Chap. 9.
11. Psychological salience was first discussed in this manner by E. L. Hartley, *Problems in Prejudice,* New York, Kings Crown Press, 1946, pp. 107–115.
12. *Ibid.,* p. 97.
13. The consistency of verbal and overt behavior has also been reasserted by Hovland, who attributes pseudo-differences to those *research designs* which carelessly compare results of laboratory experiments with results of field surveys (C. I. Hovland, "Reconciling Conflicting Results Derived from Experimental and Survey Studies of Attitude Change," *American Psychologist,* Vol. 14, 1959, pp. 8–17); by Campbell, who attributes pseudo-differences to the fact that verbal and overt behaviors have different situational thresholds (D. T. Cambell, "Social Attitudes and Other Acquired Behavioral Dispositions," in S. Koch, ed., *Psychology: A Study of a Science,* Vol. 6, McGraw-Hill, 1963, pp. 94–172); and by Rokeach, who attributes pseudo-differences to the fact that overt behavior is the result of interaction between *two* sets of attitudes, one toward the object and one toward the situation, and that most research leaves one of the two attitudes unstudied (M. Rokeach, "Attitude Change and Behavior Change," paper presented at the annual conference of the World Association for Public Opinion Research, Dublin, Ireland, Sept. 9, 1965).

# Repetitive Advertising and the Consumer

ANDREW S. C. EHRENBERG

ADVERTISING IS IN an odd position. Its extreme protagonists claim it has extraordinary powers and its severest critics believe them. Advertising is often effective. But it is not as powerful as is sometimes thought, nor is there any evidence that it actually works by any strong form of persuasion or manipulation.

Instead, the sequence, awareness/trial/reinforcement, seems to account for the known facts. Under this theory, consumers first gain awareness or interest in a product. Next, they may make a trial purchase. Finally, a repeat buying habit may be developed and reinforced if there is satisfaction after previous usage.

Advertising has a role to play in all three stages. But for frequently bought products, repeat buying is the main determinant of sales volume and here advertising must be reinforcing rather than persuasive.

These conclusions are based largely on studies of consumer behavior and attitudinal response. They are important both to our understanding of advertising's social role and to the execution and evaluation of advertising as a tool of marketing management.

In this paper I first examine advertising and the consumption of goods in general. I then discuss competition among brands and the factors affecting consumers' brand choice, particularly for established brands of frequently bought goods.

Reprinted from the *Journal of Advertising Research* (April 1974). Copyright © 1974 by the Advertising Research Foundation.

## The Demand for Goods

Advertising is widely credited with creating consumer demand. Sol Golden was quoted in 1972 as saying:

Advertising is the lynch-pin by which everything in the system hangs together—the consumer benefits, the economic growth, the corporate profits, the technological advancement. . . .

Many of advertising's critics from Professor Galbraith downwards also believe it has powers—to create demand, to manipulate the consumer, to build our acquisitive society. But let us look at these supposed powers.

Product class advertising as a whole—"Buy more cars," "Drink more tea," etc.—certainly cannot be held responsible for consumer demand. For one thing, there is relatively little of this form of advertising. For another it generally has only minor effects, increasing a market by a few percentage points or slightly slowing a rate of decline. These effects are worthwhile to the producer, but neither can be credited with creating demand or manipulating the consumer on any substantial scale.

The primary target of criticism is repetitive advertising for individual brands—"Buy Fords," "Drink Lipton's Tea," etc. This is where the bulk of mass advertising is concentrated. Such competitive advertising for different brands can lead to a higher level of consumption of the product class as a whole than would exist without it, but there is no evidence that such secondary or even unintended effects are either big or particularly common. There are not even any dramatic claims in the literature (if I have missed one, that is the exception). In many product classes with heavy competitive advertising, total consumption is rising little if at all; in some it is falling. On the other hand, there are many product classes with little if any mass media advertising—like sailboats or marijuana—where consumption is increasing quickly.

Advertising for new products cannot bear the blame for consumer demand either. Undoubtedly advertising can help to speed up the initial adoption of a new product by creating awareness and, indirectly, by gaining retail distribution and display. But advertising works as a lubricant in such cases—to ease and speed things—and not as the prime mover. Getting an initial purchase for a new product is not the point at issue in understanding society's continuing demand for goods. The key question is whether people continue to buy something *after* they or their friends and neighbors have used it. . . .

The usual reason why people buy things is that they want them. Anyone who has washed dishes knows that the demand for nonstick frying pans or dishwashers did not have to be created. Rather, suitable products had to be developed, and then advertising undoubtedly helped to speed their adoption.

There is no need to suppose that the role of advertising here is fundamental. It is a peculiar form of snobbism to suppose that if *other* people want to smoke cigarettes, to smell nice, to have bathrooms, or to drive in motor cars, it is only because they have been manipulated by advertising. Sometimes this view can go as far as John Hobson's statement at his Cantor Lectures (1964): "Almost certainly the increase in motoring has been the result of competitive petrol [gasoline] advertising." The alternative is to suppose that people want to go from A to B, or like driving, or want to get away for week-ends, and that rightly or wrongly they often find cars more convenient or pleasing than walking or other forms of transport. . . .

The effects of paid advertising on consumer demand must not be confused with the effects of the mass media as such or with people's developing education and greater mobility. People increasingly see how other people live and this has led to vastly increased expectations.

People "want" many things once they have become aware of their existence—food, warmth, good looks, money, power, to drive a car, to be a concert pianist, to avoid washing dishes, etc. Some of these things are very difficult to achieve, others are easier. To acquire goods, one only needs some money, someone to produce them, and a precedent of other people owning them in order to overcome cultural habits or inhibitions. . . .

The products he demands are mostly genuinely wanted or even needed by him. Manufacturers seldom create the needs, but they do attempt to fill them. As a result we have competition and competitive advertising among different brands or makes of the same product. This we now examine in more detail.

## Competition and Persuasive Advertising

Most advertising aims to promote a particular brand or make of product in a competitive situation. Because it often takes an emotional instead of an informative tone, such advertising is generally thought to work by persuasion. A typical critic like Boulding (1955), as quoted for instance by Achenbaum (1972) wrote in his economics text:

> Most advertising, unfortunately, is devoted to an attempt to build up in the mind of the consumer *irrational preferences for certain brands or goods.* All the arts of psychology—particularly the art of association—are used to persuade consumers that they should buy Bingo rather than Bango.

It is generally recognized that advertising's effects on sales are not necessarily immediate or direct. Instead, it is thought to work through people's attitudes as an intermediary stage to changing their behavior.

Advertising therefore is often thought of as aiming to attach an image or some special consumer benefits to a brand, in an effort to distinguish it from its competitors in the mind of the consumer. This is attempted especially in situations where there are no physical or quality characteristics to differentiate it. Gasoline advertising that stresses "extra mileage," or "smoothness," or "enjoyment," or "power," is a case in point, and Rosser Reeves' Unique Selling Proposition (USP) was an extreme version of the view that advertising can only work by offering buyers of Brand X something which no other similar brand has.

In the last 50 years, various theories have been put forward to try to explain how advertising works, taking attitudes into account (e.g., Joyce, 1967). One simple version is the well-known AIDA model, which stands for the chain:

$$\text{Awareness} \rightarrow \text{Interest} \rightarrow \text{Desire} \rightarrow \text{Action.}$$

This sequential pattern—or something like it put in different words—is treated as common sense: It only says that people need to be aware of a brand before they can be interested in it, and that they need to desire it before they can take action and buy it. This imputes two roles to advertising: (1) an informational role—making them aware of the product—and (2) a persuasive role—making people desire it before they have bought it.

In its informational role, it might seem that when there are no deeper benefits to guide a consumer's brand choice, he will be influenced by the last advertisement seen or by the general weight of past advertising. This assumption has led to the use of awareness and recall measures in pretesting and monitoring advertisements. But there is little direct evidence that advertising for established brands works like this. The evidence that does exist is either negative (e.g., Achenbaum, 1972) or at best shows effects which are not dramatically large and which still require confirmation (e.g., McDonald, 1970; Barnes, 1971).

In its persuasive role, advertising is thought to create a desire or conviction to buy, or at least to "add value to the brand as far as the consumer is concerned" (e.g., Treasure, 1973). For this reason advertisements take on persuasive methods like creating a brand image, selling a USP, or informing consumers that they need a special product to meet a special need (e.g., a special shampoo for oily hair). But again, there is no empirical evidence that advertising generally succeeds in this aim, when there are no real differences to sell.

In fact, these models of hierarchical or sequential effects have been generally criticized on the grounds of lack of evidence (e.g., Palda, 1966). They also fail to explain many of the known facts.

For example, they do not explain stable markets where shares of advertising and shares of sales are roughly in line for each brand. The small and medium-sized brands survive year-in and year-out, even though their consumers are exposed to vast amounts of advertising for the brand leaders. . . .

More generally, the models do not explain why advertising generally has only a marginal effect on total demand for a product group; nor why it is only rarely capable of shifting people's attitudes and behavior on social issues like smoking, racial discrimination, voting, etc. . . .

In recent years a good deal of attention has been paid to alternative explantions of the advertising process, based on mechanisms like satisfaction after previous usage, reinforcement, reduction of dissonance and selective perception. The argument later in this paper is grounded on these processes. But the most direct advances have been in our understanding of consumers' buying behavior and attitudinal responses in a competitive brand situation.

## Buyer Behavior

Brand choice and repeat buying are regular and predictable aspects of buyer behavior.

The economic viability of any frequently bought product depends on repeat buying. It follows simple patterns. If 10 percent of consumers buy Brand X an average of 1.5 times each in a given time period, then in the next time period 45 percent of that group can be expected to buy the brand again on an average of 1.8 times each (as modeled for example by the "NBD" theory [e.g., Ehrenberg 1972, Table B4]). This is what is normally found under a wide range of conditions, both for food and nonfood products, in the U.S. and the U.K., for leading brands and smaller ones, and so on. The 55 percent who do *not* buy the brand in the second period are however not lost for good. Instead, they are merely relatively infrequent buyers of the brand who buy it regularly but not often. . . .

In general . . . repeat buying and brand switching patterns do not vary materially from one brand or product to another. A particularly simple result is that in a relatively short time period the frequency with which consumers buy a brand varies only marginally within the same product group. The main difference between a leading and a small brand is that the leader has more buyers. With ready-to-eat breakfast cereals, for example, consumers make on average three purchases of a brand over a three-month period. This varies between only 2½ and 3½ for different brands (Charlton, et al, 1972), and this small variation is itself highly predictable from buyer behavior theory, with the larger selling brands being generally bought slightly more frequently by their buyers.

This is what occurs in relatively short time periods. In periods which are very long compared with the product's average purchase cycle (e.g., a year or more), the opposite sort of effect appears to operate because most consumers will have had *some* experience of most brands (even if only a single purchase). This leads to the view that a brand's sales can only increase if people buy it more often (e.g., Treasure, 1973). But in a shorter period, like three months for cereals, higher sales show themselves in terms of having to have more people buy in that period.

These various results are no longer isolated empirical regularities but are becoming increasingly well explained and integrated into coherent theory (e.g., Ehrenberg, 1972; Goodhardt and Chatfield, 1973). The theory applies primarily when a brand's sales are more or less steady. This holds true most of the time—it is a basic characteristic of the market structure of branded frequently bought products that sales levels are *not* in a constant state of flux.

Occasional trends and fluctuations caused by promotions, etc., may be important from a marketing management point of view, perhaps adding up to five percent more sales in a year or 20 percent more in a particular month. But they do not amount to big, dynamic changes in consumer behavior as such. The individual's buying behavior remains broadly characterized as being steady and habitual rather than as dynamic and erratic.

## Attitudes and Attitude Change

Since on the whole there are no large behavioral differences among brands except that more people buy one than another, there are not many things that need to be explained by differing motivations and attitudes. In fact, attitudinal responses to branded products tend to be fairly simple.

The evidence shows that most attitudinal variables are largely of an "evaluative" kind, plus some highly specific "descriptive" differences for certain brands (Bird, et al., 1969; 1970; Collins, 1973; Chakrapani and Ehrenberg, 1974).

An "evaluative" response to a brand is equivalent to saying "I like it" or perhaps even only "I have heard of it." Evaluative attitudes therefore differ between users and nonusers of a brand, but they do not differ between brands. For example, 67 percent of users of Brand A say it has the "right taste" with only six percent of nonusers of A saying so about it, and 69 percent of users of Brand B that B has the "right taste" with only five percent of nonusers of B saying so, and so on, as illustrated in Table 1. Brand A may therefore have more people in all saying it has the "right taste" than Brand B, but only because more people use Brand A, not because its users look at it differently: To give an evaluative response about a brand largely depends on whether or not one is using it.

Certain large exceptions to this pattern occur. These usually reflect some physical "descriptive" characteristics of one particular brand. For example, if a brand is fairly new, consumers tend to be aware of this and dub that brand exceptionally "modern," compared with older brands. If one brnd of indigestion remedies can be taken without water and the others not, people notice this and far more regard it as "convenient," as is illustrated for Brand C in Table 1. Promotional policies can also make a brand appear "descriptively" different: A slim cigarette advertised in women's magazines as being

**TABLE 1.** Typical "Evaluative" and "Descriptive" Attitudinal Responses to Different Brands

| | EVALUATIVE: E.G., "RIGHT TASTE" | | DESCRIPTIVE (FOR BRAND C): E.G., "CONVENIENT" | |
| | Users of the Stated Brand % | Nonusers of the Brand % | Users of the Stated Brand % | Nonusers of the Brand % |
| --- | --- | --- | --- | --- |
| Brand A | 67 | 6 | 19 | 3 |
| Brand B | 69 | 5 | 17 | 2 |
| Brand C | 62 | 4 | 55 | 48 |
| Brand D | 60 | 3 | 17 | 2 |
| etc. | | | | |

smoked by feminine women may be rated more "female" than a standard full-flavored cigarette packaged predominantly in red, with advertisements placed in sporting magazines and featuring cowboys.

A "descriptive" characteristic is usually perceived also by people who do not use the brand. A "female" cigarette will be seen so by people who smoke it and by those who do not. Nonusers of an indigestion remedy which does not require water will *also* regard it as exceptionally "convenient," as for Brand C in Table 1, but they nonetheless do not use it. "Descriptive" differences between one brand and another therefore seldom relate to whether anyone actually *uses* the brand. "Evaluative" responses on the other hand, while distinguishing between users and nonusers, generally do not differentiate one brand from another. Such results are therefore simple but not very helpful in explaining brand choice.

Attitude Change. The conventional results of research into consumers' attitudes show how they feel about products, but not how they *change* their feelings. Very little work has been reported about changes in attitude. What work there is is difficult to interpret (Fothergill, 1968).

It seems to be generally assumed that improving the attitudes of a nonuser towards a brand should make him use the brand, or at least become more predisposed to doing so. But this amounts to assuming that people's attitudes or image of a brand can in fact be readily changed, and that such attitude changes must precede the desired change in behavior. There is little or no evidence to support these assumptions.

The example of a successful change in image that is commonly quoted is for Marlboro cigarettes—few people volunteer another. Marlboro as a brand dates back to the turn of the century. It was considered a "ladies" brand, at one stage holding a major share of the "older society women's market." But in the 1950s, Phillip Morris, the maker, started advertising it very differently, in a male, outdoor manner—Marlboro Country, the Marlboro

Man, and the famous tatoo. Sales rose dramatically and Marlboro became a market leader. There is little doubt that Marlboro's advertising had much to do with its success. But there is no evidence that the advertising created a change in "image" or that a change in consumers' attitudes caused the vast increase in sales. The explanation is much simpler.

The change in Marlboro was a change in *product.* The new Marlboro of the 1950s was a standard tipped cigarette, full-flavored, packed in the new flip-top package, with a strong design, and introduced at the start of the growth of the tipped market (the tipped sector of the U.S. market grew from one percent in 1950 to more than 60 percent by the mid-Sixties). For the first half of the century, Marlboro had been expensive, high quality, and with a pink paper wrapper (so as not to show up lipstick). No wonder people thought of it as different. . . .

Other Factors. Conventional thinking about how advertising works rests on the sequence:

$$\text{Awareness} \rightarrow \text{Attitudes} \rightarrow \text{Behavior.}$$

Although this appears like commonsense, various studies in social psychology have cast doubt on it. There are well-established psychological mechanisms which can act in the opposite direction—with behavior actually affecting attitudes.

For instance, behavior (the act of buying or using a brand) can lead to greater awareness of information to which one is normally exposed (selective perception). Behavior can even lead to the deliberate seeking out of information, and to changes in attitude (notions of congruence and reduction of dissonance). The well known illustration is the study where buyers of Ford cars were found to look at Ford advertisements *after* their purchases. This is common.

Usually a consumer is not convinced that a brand he has not bought before has all the advantages over the alternatives. To reduce the "dissonance" between what he has done and what he knows or feels, he changes his attitudes after the purchase to make his chosen brand appear adequate. He needs to do this even more if the chosen brand in fact differs little from the others, because there is then no tangible reason or "reward" to justify his choice— e.g., "maybe it is not very good but at least it cost less.'"

These processes are consistent with the known facts of consumer attitudes, such as those illustrated in Table 1. We will now see how they also fit into the broader picture.

## Brand Choice and the Consumer

The consumer's choice among different brands or products is widely thought of as irrational and based on ignorance. This is how advertising is supposed to get its effect: "The scope of advertising depends on the ignorance of the people to whom it is addressed. The more ignorant the buyer, the more he relies on advertising" (Scitovsky, 1951).

No one doubts or criticizes advertising's role when it is a question of supplying basic information or creating awareness—e.g., a house for sale, a job vacancy, a play at the theatre, or even for a new consumer product. But where advertising is regarded as persuasive rather than informational, there *is* criticism because of the view that the ignorant consumer's choice is influenced by the last advertisement seen or by the brand image he is being told to believe.

But this is all wrong. Buyers of frequently bought goods are not ignorant of them. They have extensive usage experience of the products—after all, they buy them frequently. As we have seen earlier, they usually have direct experience of more than one brand, plus indirect word of mouth knowledge of others. The average housewife is far more experienced in buying her normal products than the industrial purchaser buying an atomic power station. She is also far less likely to make a mistake.

In regarding the private consumer's brand choice as irrational, the view seems to be that if there is little real difference among the brands, then it is not possible to choose rationally among them. This ignores the fact that the consumer *knows* there is little difference and that he *wants* to buy the product. In choosing between similar brands, it is equally rational to choose the same brand as last time, or to deliberately vary it, or even to toss a coin. Any brand would do because the differences do not matter.

Just because Brand X is advertised as having some specific "consumer benefit," it does not follow that anyone buying that brand must have believed or been influenced by that aspect of the advertising.

In practice, people seem to find it simplest to develop repeat buying habits covering a limited repertoire of brands. Our task is to discover and understand the consumer's reasons for choosing brands, instead of imposing our own preconceptions of how he ought to think and behave and dubbing anything else as irrational. The questions are: How do these habits develop, and what is advertising's role in this?

## ATR: Awareness, Trial, and Reinforcement

Three main steps can account for the known facts of brand choice behavior: (1) gaining awareness of a brand, (2) making a first or trial purchase, and (3) being reinforced into developing and keeping a repeat buying habit.

Some initial awareness of a brand usually has to come first, although occasionally one may find out a brand's name only after buying it. Awareness operates at different levels of attention and interest and can be created in many different ways, of which advertising is clearly one. Awareness may build up into the idea of looking for more information about the brand, asking someone about it, and so on.

A trial purchase, if it comes, will be the next step. This does not require any major degree of conviction that the brand is particularly good or special. Buyers of Brand A do not usually feel very differently about A from how buyers of Brand B feel about B, as was illustrated in Table 1. If that is how one feels afterwards, there is therefore no reason why a consumer should feel strongly about a different brand *before* he has tried it. All that is needed is the idea that one might try it. A trial purchase can arise for a variety of reasons: a cut price offer, an out of stock situation of the usual brand, seeing an advertisement or display, bordeom, etc.

After trying a different brand, people usually return to their habitual brands as if nothing had happened. This is so even when new purchasers have been attracted on a large scale, with free samples or an attractive short term promotion (e.g., Goodhardt and Ehrenberg, 1969; Ehrenberg, 1972).

But sometimes a repeat buying habit develops. This is the crucial determinant of long term sales. The way this habit develops for a particular brand is primarily a matter of reinforcement after use. Any feeling of satisfaction—that the brand is liked at least no less than the previously bought ones—has to be nurtured. Evaluative attitudes have to be brought into line with the product class norms. But no exceptional "liking" need arise, because similar brands are known to be similar and the consumer does not inherently care whether he buys Bingo or Bango (which only matters to the manufacturer).

According to this viewpoint, development of a repeat buying habit remains a fragile process, probably influenced by a variety of almost haphazard factors. The consumer knows there is little to choose between, but he must choose. The critical factor is experience of the brand and no other influences seem to be needed. Thus it has been found that something close to the normal repeat buying habits can develop without any explicit external stimuli such as product differentiation or advertising (Ehrenberg and Charlton, 1973), and preferences for particular price levels can also develop without any external support or manipulation, just by trial and the development of habits (McConnell, 1966; Charlton and Ehrenberg, 1973).

But this process does not in itself determine how *many* people become aware, make a trial purchase, and are reinforced into a repeat buying habit. This—and hence the sales level of a brand—can therefore be influenced by other marketing factors, including advertising.

## The Place of Repetitive Advertising

Advertising can act in the various stages of the ATR process.

Firstly, it can create, reawaken, or strengthen awareness. Secondly, it is one of the factors which can facilitate a trial purchase. For an established brand, the consumer may already have been aware of it and even have tried it, but this would have been in the past. The problem is that now he is ignoring the brand and may even be imperceptive of the general run of its advertising. Typically, a special effort like a new product feature, a new package, a new price or special offer, or a new campaign—anything "new"— is needed to give the advertising an edge for this purpose and be noticed. Obtaining awareness and trial for a brand is nonetheless relatively easy.

The difficulty is at the third stage, of turning new triers into satisfied and lasting customers. This generally has to be achieved in the context of consumers already having a repertoire of one or more other brands which they are buying more or less regularly.

What happens in detail is not yet known—do heavy buyers of X switch to being heavy buyers of Y, or is this a gradual process, or is it the *light* buyers who are most easily affected? What is it in fact that advertising has to try and support or accelerate? The knowledge of buyer behavior outlined earlier puts some constraints on the possibilities, but this is one of the purely descriptive features of consumer behavior which is not yet understood.

The process can, however, seldom amount to manipulating the consumer. Real conversion from virgin ignorance to full-blooded, long term commitment does not happen often. A substantial leap forward in sales occurs only once in a while and sales levels of most brands tend to be fairly steady. Trends and even short term fluctuations tend to be smaller and more exceptional than is often thought.

The role of repetitive advertising of well-established brands is therefore predominantly defensive—to reinforce already developed repeat buying habits. The consumer tends to perceive advertising for the brands he is already buying, and repetitive advertising enables the habit to continue to operate in the face of competition. The consumer does not have to be persuaded to think of his habitual brands as better than others, but has to be reinforced in thinking of them as at least no worse. . . .

According to the ATR model, increasing the amount of advertising would not by itself have much effect on sales, but cutting it is likely to lose sales. This is because some reinforcing action would be withdrawn, allowing competitive brands to gain customers more easily. For an established brand the loss of sales would by definition be quite slow, and no special theory of lagged effects of advertising is needed. Furthermore, reducing an advertising budget *after* a drop in sales to bring the two in line would not necessarily lead to any further substantial drop in sales. The ATR model is consistent with a more or less constant advertising to sales ratio.

The model also explains the survival of a small brand with a small advertising budget. For its users, the large amount of advertising for a larger brand which they do not use performs no function and generally is not even noticed. When a consumer buys two or more brands, some more heavily advertised than the others, each brand's advertising primarily reinforces that brand and the status quo can continue.

High levels of advertising mostly occur in product fields where consumer demand is strong and the product is easy to supply (because of low capital costs, or excess capacity). This leads to active competition and hence the need to defend one's share of the market, either by price cutting or by heavy advertising.

Economists are frequently concerned that high advertising levels act as a barrier to entry for new brands and hence deter competition. This is wrong on two accounts. Firstly, it is the high risk of *failure* with a new brand that acts as the barrier—"four out of five new products fail." The barrier is spending a million and probably having nothing to show for it. Secondly, heavily advertised product fields are in fact characterized by heavy competition and a high incidence of new brands—but generally launched by firms already in the market. Simply having a million to spend on advertising is not enough; general marketing skills and experience of the other factors in the marketing mix (e.g., a suitable sales force) are also needed.

## Remaining Problems

The ATR approach outlined here is no more than a broad verbal statement of how advertising works that seems consistent with the known facts. Detailed quantitative flesh needs to be put on the model, but its differences with the theory of *persuasive* advertising already raise many questions—e.g., about the content of advertising, about the setting of advertising appropriations and the evaluation of advertising, and about product policy.

As regards content for example, use of attitudinal research results to try to improve one's image or to produce persuasive messages of how Brand X is "best" seem mostly to mislead the advertiser and critic rather than the consumer. Advertising research has failed to show that consumers think of their chosen brands as necessarily better than do buyers of *other* brands think of *their*. The consumer needs merely to be told that the brand has all the good properties he expects of the product, and there can be a renewed emphasis on creative advertising telling a good advertising story well.

More generally, since consumers rightly see competitive brands in most product fields as very similar, it seems unnecessary to strive compulsively to differentiate brands artificially from each other. The clutter of marginally different brands, types, and sizes and the corresponding costs of product development and distribution may be unnecessary. This is not a plea for uniformity but for real research into consumers' attitudes and motives to gain a better understanding of their, rather than the advertiser's, needs for product differentiation.

# Conclusion

Most mass media advertising is for competitive brands. It is a defensive tool and a price the producer pays to stay in business.

Consumers' attitudes to similar brands are very similar. Purchasers of frequently bought goods usually have experience of more than one brand and they mostly ignore advertising for brands they are not already using.

It follows that there can be little scope for persuasive advertising. Instead, advertising's main role is to reinforce feelings of satisfaction for brands already being used. At times it can also create new sales by reawakening consumers' awareness and interest in another brand, stimulating them to a trial purchase and then sometimes, through subsequent reinforcement, helping to facilitate the development of a repeat buying habit. This is the main determinant of sales volume.

The Awareness-Trial-Reinforcement model of advertising seems to account for the known facts, but many quantitative details still need elucidation. Such developments could markedly influence the planning, execution, and evaluation of advertising.

With persuasive advertising, the task might be seen as persuading the pliable customer that Brand X is better than other brands. Under the ATR model, advertising's task is to inform the rather experienced consumer that Brand X is as good as others. The language of the advertising copy might sometimes look similar (still "better" or "best"), but the advertiser's aim and expectations would differ.

# References

ACHENBAUM, A. A. Advertising Doesn't Manipulate Consumers. *Journal of Advertising Research*, Vol. 12, No. 2, pp. 3–13.

BARNES, M. *The Relationship Between Purchasing Patterns and Advertising Exposure.* London: J. Walter Thompson Co., 1971.

BIRD, M., C. CHANNON, and A. S. C. EHRENBERG. Brand Image and Brand Usage. *Journal of Marketing Research*, Vol. 7, 1969, pp. 307–314.

BIRD, M. and A. S. C. EHRENBERG. Consumer Attitudes and Brand Usage. *Journal of the Market Research Society*, Vol. 12, 1970, pp. 233–247; Vol. 13, pp. 100–1; 242–3; Vol. 13, pp. 57–8.

BOULDING, K. *Economic Analysis.* New York: Harper and Row, 1955.

CHAKRAPANI, T. K. and A. S. C. EHRENBERG. "The Pattern of Consumer Attitudes." AAPOR Conference, Lake George, May 1974.

CHARLTON, P., A. S. C. EHRENBERG, and B. PYMONT. Buyer Behaviour Under Mini-Test Conditions. *Journal of the Market Research Society*, Vol. 14, 1972, pp. 171–183.

CHARLTON, P. and A. S. C. EHRENBERG. McConnell's Experimental Brand-Choice Data. *Journal of Marketing Research,* Vol. 11, 1973, pp. 302–7.

COLLINS, M. A. Market Segmentation—The Realities of Buyer Behaviour. *Journal of the Market Research Society,* Vol. 13, 1971, pp. 146–157.

COLLINS, M. A. The Analysis and Interpretation of Attitude Data. Market Research Society, Course on Consumer Attitudes, Cambridge, March 1973.

CONNOR, J. T. "Advertising: Absolutely Indispensable." Address before the Cleveland Advertising Club, Cleveland, Ohio. New York: American Association of Advertising Agencies, 1966.

DOYLE, P. Economic Aspects of Advertising: A Survey. *The Economic Journal,* Vol. 78, 1966, pp. 570–602.

EHRENBERG, A. S. C. *Repeat-Buying: Theory and Applications.* Amsterdam: North Holland; New York: American Elsevier, 1972.

EHRENBERG, A. S. C. *Data Reduction.* London and New York: John Wiley, 1974.

EHRENBERG, A. S. C. and P. Charlton.

The Analysis of Simulated Brand-Choice. *Journal of Advertising Research,* Vol. 13, No. 1, 1973, pp. 21–33.

EHRENBERG, A. S. C. and F. G. Pyatt (Eds.). *Consumer Behavior.* London and Baltimore: Penguin Books, 1971.

FOTHERGILL, J. G. Do Attitudes Change Before Behaviour? *Proceedings of ESOMAR Congress, Opitija.* Amsterdam: ESOMAR, 1968.

GOODHARDT, G. J. and C. CHATFIELD. The Gamma-Distribution in Consumer Purchasing. *Nature,* Vol. 244, No. 5414, pp. 316.

GOODHARDT, G. J. and A. S. C. EHRENBERG. Evaluating a Consumer Deal. *Admap,* Vol. 5, 1969, pp. 388–93.

HOBSON, J. The Influence and Techniques of Modern Advertising. *Journal of the Royal Society of Arts,* Vol. 112, 1964, pp. 565–604.

JOYCE, T. *What Do We Know About How Advertising Works?* London: J. Walter Thompson Co., 1967.

MCCONNELL, J. D. The Development of Brand Loyalty: An Experimental Study, and The Price-Quality Relationship in an Experimental Setting. *Journal of Marketing Research,* Vol. 5, 1968, pp. 13–19 and pp. 300–303.

MCDONALD, C. D. P. What Is the Short-Term Effect of Advertising? *Proceedings of the ESOMAR Congress. Barcelona.* Amsterdam: ESOMAR, 1970.

PALDA, K. S. The Hypothesis of a Hierarchy of Effects: A Partial Evaluation. *Journal of Marketing Research,* Vol. 3, 1966, pp. 13–24.

SCITOVSKY, T. *Welfare and Competition.* Chicago: Richard Irwin, 1951.

TREASURE, J. A. P. The Volatile Consumer. *Admap,* Vol. 9, 1973, pp. 172–182.

# Social Change in a Metropolitan Community

OTIS DUDLEY DUNCAN
HOWARD SCHUMAN
BEVERLY DUNCAN

THE SUBJECT OF SOCIAL CHANGE is much discussed these days, both by those who put forward "demands for meaningful change in the system" and those who regret the seeming "erosion of values embodied in the traditions of our national life." There can be no doubt that things really are changing, whatever our individual desires for change may be. Yet, when so much is in flux, it is not easy to be sure exactly what is going on. . . .

This report submits a . . . body of social facts obtained by a well-developed and time-tested method—the sample survey of a human population. . . . In undertaking this study, it was our intention to demonstrate the potential usefulness of the survey method for analyzing social change and at the same time to generate measurements of some important changes occurring in a metropolitan community during the past two decades.

A project of this kind was feasible because of the work of previous investigators. Since 1952, the Detroit Area Study, a facility for training graduate students in social research at the University of Michigan, has carried out an annual study in metropolitan Detroit. By repeating portions of a survey done in 1956, for example, we could secure comparative measurements spanning a 15-year period. . . .

In regard to the topics to be studied—or, aspects of change to be measured—our approach was opportunistic and eclectic. . . . In this report we

From *Social Change in a Metropolitan Community,* by Otis Duncan, Howard Schuman, and Beverly Duncan, pp. 1–3 and 81–88. Copyright © 1973 by The Russell Sage Foundation, Basic Books, Inc., Publishers, New York.

focus on changes in attitudes toward public institutions and have tried to be sure that the changes described are statistically reliable even if their causation and implications may be obscure. Although there is no display of the apparatus of statistical inference, chi-square tests have been carried out in all cases to rule out the possibility that an ostensible change might easily have resulted from mere accidents of random sampling. Unless there is indication to the contrary, differences between years discussed in the text are statistically significant at the nominal .05 level of probability. . . .

We treat the citizen as a passive consumer of the outputs of public institutions or evaluator of their performance. With the well-advertised rise of "consumerism" in recent years, we shall not be surprised if the public seems more critical of the services it receives than it was in the past.

In Table 1 we show the distribution of "good," "fair," and "poor" scores awarded by respondents to the performance of seven kinds of institutions in 1959 and 1971. One uniform result stands out: each of these institutions is seen as doing a good job by fewer respondents in 1971 than in 1959. In every case, there is a significant shift out of the good category and into the fair; in all cases but two—radio and television networks, and scientists— there is also a significant gain for the poor category. This monotonously repeated pattern suggests that something more than the actual performance of the seven institutions may be at stake. It is, to be sure, logically possible

## TABLE 1.  Evaluation of Institutions

| NOW HERE IS A LIST OF ORGANIZA- TIONS AND GROUPS THAT PEOPLE HAVE DIFFERENT OPINIONS ABOUT. AFTER EACH ONE, WOULD YOU TELL ME IF, IN YOUR OPINION, IT IS DOING A GOOD JOB, JUST A FAIR JOB, OR A POOR JOB. HOW ABOUT: | | PERCENT DISTRIBUTION | | | |
|---|---|---|---|---|---|
| | | *Good* | *Fair* | *Poor* | *Total* |
| The radio and TV networks? | 1959 | 55 | 37 | 8 | 100 |
| | 1971 | 46 | 44 | 10 | 100 |
| Most high schools in this country? | 1959 | 45 | 45 | 10 | 100 |
| | 1971 | 29 | 46 | 25 | 100 |
| Most doctors? | 1959 | 76 | 20 | 4 | 100 |
| | 1971 | 62 | 30 | 8 | 100 |
| Most colleges? | 1959 | 75 | 22 | 3 | 100 |
| | 1971 | 42 | 44 | 14 | 100 |
| Most scientists? | 1959 | 83 | 15 | 2 | 100 |
| | 1971 | 78 | 19 | 3 | 100 |
| The Federal Courts? | 1959 | 63 | 30 | 7 | 100 |
| | 1971 | 24 | 46 | 30 | 100 |
| The Boy Scouts? | 1959 | 93 | 6 | 1 | 100 |
| | 1971 | 87 | 10 | 3 | 100 |
| Most Michigan State officials? | 1971 | 22 | 53 | 25 | 100 |

that all seven are actually performing less effectively in 1971 than they did a dozen years earlier. But a simpler explanation would be that the public has escalated its standards across the board; that is, it has simply adopted more demanding criteria for all organizations rendering service to the public.

We do not imply, however, that the only change has been that of taking a dimmer view of every agency. To the contrary, it is the fact that the changes, although all in the same direction, are at quite different rates. The Boy Scouts and scientists, evaluated quite favorably in 1959 by comparison with the other institutions, lost only a little ground and retained their relatively favored positions. But note the contrast between the doctors and the colleges: they were in about the same reasonably high position in 1959, with three-fourths of their ratings good. By 1971, the doctors had declined appreciably to three-fifths good ratings, but colleges had declined precipitously to two-fifths. The Federal Courts in 1959 were seen in a more favorable light than the radio and television networks or the high schools; but in 1971 they received the lowest rating among the seven institutions. The high schools, too, slipped rather badly, though not so seriously as the courts, while the networks lost comparatively little ground.

We are thus led to a second obvious generalization: the institutions suffering the greatest loss in their ratings are the three—the schools, the colleges, and the courts—that have been centers of controversy in recent years. If a causal inference is justified here, then we are warned that the 1959–1971 changes may not necessarily be prognostic of future trends. Other institutions may become the foci of public discontent, and the ones losing public confidence in the 1960s could perhaps regain some of it in future years.

The last group listed in Table 1, most Michigan State officials, was rated in this particular format only in 1971. A fairly similar question appears in Table 2, along with a parallel one on local government. If we add "good" and "very good" together in Table 2 for the 1971 distribution of ratings of state government, we get a distribution roughly the same as the one at the bottom of Table 1. It seems reasonable, therefore, to assume that the change in ratings of state government from 1954 to 1971 shown in Table 2 is representative of what we would have found had there been a base-line measurement for Table 1. We conjecture that the decline in performance rating for state government would be very much like that measured for Federal Courts, were the two on the same scale of measurement and for the same years. That is, the loss in confidence in state officials has been one of the more decided losses of this kind. In any event, using Table 2 alone we can say for sure that the deterioration of performance rating has been more pronounced for the state government than for local government. In 1954, state officials and agencies had somewhat more favorable ratings than did the local ones, whereas the comparison had been reversed by 1971.

Still another series of ratings is offered in Figure 1 here in terms of satisfaction with three major local governmental services. Respondents in 1971 were

**TABLE 2.   Evaluation of State and Local Government**

| DO YOU THINK THE [NAME OF LOCAL COMMUNITY] OFFICIALS AND BUREAUS ARE DOING A POOR, FAIR, GOOD, OR VERY GOOD JOB? | PERCENT DISTRIBUTION | | | | |
|---|---|---|---|---|---|
| | Poor | Fair | Good | V.G. | Total |
| 1954 | 6 | 40 | 42 | 12 | 100 |
| 1971 | 18 | 48 | 29 | 5 | 100 |
| AND THE STATE GOVERNMENT— DO YOU THINK THE STATE OFFICIALS AND BUREAUS ARE DOING A POOR, FAIR, GOOD, OR VERY GOOD JOB? | | | | | |
| 1954 | 4 | 33 | 52 | 11 | 100 |
| 1971 | 19 | 56 | 23 | 2 | 100 |

rather less satisfied than those interviewed in 1959 with the public schools, garbage collection, and police services. Again, we might assume an overall decrease in willingness to express satisfaction with anything, but that would not explain the fact that the schools lost ground rapidly while the drop in ratings of garbage collection was fairly modest.

Instead of asking respondents how well groups and agencies perform, we might have asked them about their confidence in future performance. The one item of this general type relates to science: "Given enough time and money, almost all of man's important problems can be solved by science." (Respondents were asked to choose among strongly agree, agree, disagree, and strongly disagree.) In 1959, 43 percent said agree or strongly agree; by 1971, this had declined to 32 percent. Since about three-fifths of respondents think that scientists are doing a good job, it must be that many respondents realize that "a good job" may not be good enough to solve all our problems. In other words, it seems entirely possible that what we are measuring in these several series of evaluations is partly an increasing sophistication about the difficulties faced by public institutions.

We do not have questions that require the respondent explicitly to take into account the problems that government and other public institutions are attempting to solve, as well as their performance in solving them. Tangentially relevant is the question presented in Table 3, which asks respondents to weigh the costs and benefits of government services in general. In 1954, just over half the population felt that costs and benefits were about equal, and only a third felt that government asks more from the public than it returns in help and services. By 1971, the two proportions had just reversed; now, the most frequent answer is that costs outweigh benefits.

FIGURE 1.   Evaluation of Government Services (percent distribution). In general, would you say that you are well satisfied, more or less satisfied, or not at all satisfied with the job the public schools here are doing? . . . with the city garbage collection here? . . . with the protection provided for your neighborhood by the police?

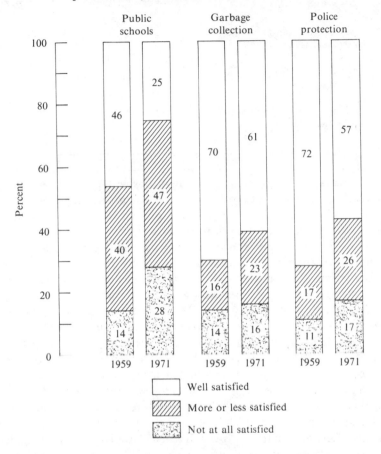

One other means of gaining some insight into the deterioration of performance ratings is to look at public agencies, not from the standpoint of the services they render, but in terms of their desirability as employers. For if local governmental agencies, for example, were seen as doing a worse job primarily because of internal deficiencies which are not shared with private firms, then we might expect their image as employers to deteriorate. In studying the prestige of public employment, we are dealing with a replication of a replication. In the 1954 DAS, Janowitz and Wright sought to measure the trend by duplicating some of the questions which had been used by L. D. White in his Chicago study of 1929. Their comparisons with White's data suggested that there had been a marked improvement in the prestige

**TABLE 3.  Costs and Benefits of Government**

| WHICH ONE OF THESE STATEMENTS COMES CLOSEST TO YOUR OWN OPINION? | PERCENT DISTRIBUTION | |
|---|---|---|
| | *1954* | *1971* |
| The help and services that the public gets from the government is worth what it asks from the public. | 53 | 29 |
| The government asks more from the public than it gives in help and services. | 32 | 53 |
| The public gets more from the government than it gives the government. | 15 | 18 |
| | 100 | 100 |

of jobs in government agencies relative to similar jobs with private employers over the preceding quarter of a century. The conclusion was subject to some uncertainty, owing to the shift in study locale from Chicago to Detroit and the differences in sampling and survey techniques.[1]

We tried to repeat the procedure of Janowitz and Wright exactly, so that any difference between the 1954 and 1971 results would be due solely to changing assessments of prestige and not to variations in technique. There remains some question as to whether we were entirely successful. The most obvious trend in Table 4 is that for each of the four illustrative occupations, the percentage who declared there is "no difference" between the prestige of public and private employment diminished considerably over the seventeen-year period. Now, the alternative, "no difference" was not explicitly offered to the respondent, and his answer was coded in this category only if he declined to make a choice between the two alternatives presented to him. It may be that our interviewers in 1971 were more assiduous in probing for a decision than was true in 1954.

Let us, therefore, eliminate the "no difference" category and recompute the percentages of respondents attributing the higher prestige to the job with a public employer. In regard to the occupation of stenographer, the preference for public employers declined from 66 to 64 percent; and for accountants it declined from 50 to 42 percent. Only the latter difference is large enough to rule out sampling fluctuations as the explanation. For the night watchman, the prestige of public employment increased by virtue of the shift from 46 to 51 percent favoring that alternative, and for doctors, there was also an upward shift, from 32 to 35 percent. Neither of these changes, however, is large enough to be statistically significant in the sense of ruling out chance variation as the source of the apparent change.

Our finding, then, is that the evidence is mixed. The only change we can assert with confidence pertains to a single occupation, accountant. It

TABLE 4.   Prestige of Public Employment

| WE'D LIKE TO KNOW WHAT PEOPLE THINK OF GOVERNMENT JOBS AND GOVERNMENT WORKERS. IF THESE JOBS ARE ABOUT THE SAME IN KIND OF WORK, PAY, AND SO FORTH, WHICH HAS THE MOST PRESTIGE? | | PERCENT DISTRIBUTION | | | |
|---|---|---|---|---|---|
| | | *Private* | *Public* | *No difference* | *Total* |
| Stenographer in a life insurance company | 1954 | 27 | 53 | 20 | 100 |
| . . . in the city tax assessor's office | 1971 | 33 | 59 | 8 | 100 |
| Accountant in a private accounting firm | 1954 | 42 | 42 | 16 | 100 |
| . . . in the Detroit Dept. of Pub. Works | 1971 | 55 | 40 | 5 | 100 |
| Night watchman in a bank | 1954 | 43 | 37 | 20 | 100 |
| . . . in the city hall | 1971 | 45 | 46 | 9 | 100 |
| Doctor on staff of private hospital | 1954 | 58 | 27 | 15 | 100 |
| . . . in the Detroit Receiving Hospital | 1971 | 61 | 33 | 6 | 100 |

should be noted that the ostensible deterioration in the prestige of public employment for this occupation could be due to a worsening of the image of the Detroit Department of Public Works, in particular, rather than a drop in the attractiveness of the public sector in general. We do not, of course, have any definite evidence to this effect. Perhaps the safest conclusion to draw is that the pronounced trend of improvement in the prestige of public employment discerned by Janowitz and Wright in 1954 had about peaked out by that time, so that subsequent changes may largely reflect idiosyncratic features of particular occupations or particular public agencies. In any case, we do not find the decisive deterioration in prestige of public employment that we might have expected from the drastic decline in favorable performance ratings of public agencies.

# Note

1. Morris Janowitz and Deil Wright, "The Prestige of Public Employment: 1929 and 1954," *Public Administration Review,* 16 (Winter 1956): 15–21.

# Index

440     INDEX

Whiting, John, 67$n$.
Wilcocke, S. H., 27$n$.
Wilensky, H., 207, 209, 211
Wilson, M. O., 66$n$.
Wise, D., 90, 95
Wohl, R. R., 365
Wolfstein, M., 215, 217$n$.
Wright, C. R., 319$n$.
Wright, D., 427–429
Wright, J., 373

Wright, W., 208
Wyckoff, G., 389

Zander, A., 66$n$.
Ziegler, H. O., 27$n$.
Zielske, H., 404, 408$n$.
Zimmerman, D. H., 182$n$.
Zimmerman, J. G., 22
Znaniecki, F., 319$n$.
Zukin, C., 321$n$.